Global Capitalism and the Future of Agrarian Society

Global Capitalism and the Future of Agrarian Society

Edited by
ARIF DIRLIK
ROXANN PRAZNIAK
AND ALEXANDER WOODSIDE

Routledge
Taylor & Francis Group
LONDON AND NEW YORK

First published 2012 by Paradigm Publishers

Published 2016 by Routledge
2 Park Square, Milton Park, Abingdon, Oxon OX14 4RN
711 Third Avenue, New York, NY 10017, USA

Routledge is an imprint of the Taylor & Francis Group, an informa business

Library of Congress Cataloging-in-Publication Data
Global capitalism and the future of agrarian society / edited by Arif Dirlik, Roxann Prazniak, and Alexander Woodside.
p. cm.
Includes bibliographical references.
ISBN 978-1-61205-037-9 (hardcover : alk. paper)
1. Capitalism—History—21st century. 2. Land tenure—Case studies. 3. Peasants—History—21st century. 4. Urbanization—Government policy—Case studies. I. Dirlik, Arif. II. Prazniak, Roxann. III. Woodside, Alexander.
HB501.G544 2012
338.1—dc23

2011046771

ISBN 13: 978-1-61205-037-9 (hbk)
ISBN 13: 978-1-61205-038-6 (pbk)

Contents

Acknowledgments

This volume, and the original Wall Summer Institute from which it is derived, would have been impossible without the generous support of the Peter Wall Institute for Advanced Studies of the University of British Columbia. Our deepest gratitude goes to the director of the Institute, Dr. Dianne Newell, who participated personally in the project from its initial conception to its fruition in this volume. In a personal sense, the volume is a product of three decades of friendship between Dianne and the editors, who also served as codirectors of the Summer Institute. Deep thanks are also due to Ms. Jenny MacKay, assistant director of the Institute at the time of the 2008 Summer Institute, for her efficient and graceful handling of the organization of the weeklong event.

The keynote addresses by Jomo Kwame Sundaram and Immanuel Wallerstein played a central part in bringing our concerns to the Vancouver and UBC public. We are especially grateful to Jomo for taking time off from his urgent duties as Assistant Secretary-General for Economic Development at the United Nations, rendered even more urgent at the time of the Summer Institute by the food crisis of that spring. We would also like to thank participants in the Summer Institute who are not represented in this volume but made valuable contributions to the initial discussions: Gregory E. Guldin, Ashok Kotwal, Lu Xingyu, Patricia Marchak, and Xuan Phuc. We would also like to acknowledge the contributions of the participants in the UBC graduate student conference held in conjunction with the Summer Institute. Two of those contributions, by Fabio Cabarcas and Leslie Shieh, are included in this volume.

We are grateful to Ms. Ana Maria Candela, a PhD candidate at the University of California–Santa Cruz, for her conscientious work as "official scribe" for the conference, which has been invaluable in compiling the volume.

Last but not least, the editors would like to thank Dean Birkenkamp, publisher of Paradigm Publishers, for his customary astute handling of the manuscript.

Part I

Introductory

Chapter 1

Introduction

The End of the Peasant? Global Capitalism and the Future of Agrarian Society

Arif Dirlik and Roxann Prazniak

This volume issued from the Wall Summer Institute, "The End of the Peasant? Global Capitalism and the Future of Agrarian Society," held over a week in late June 2008 at the Peter Wall Institute for Advanced Studies of the University of British Columbia. The Institute was followed in June 2009 by a weeklong field trip by selected participants to the People's Republic of China (PRC) to witness cooperative efforts in Henan Province, inspired by the efforts of Professor Wen Tiejun of People's (Renmin) University in Beijing. The conclusions from the field trip were discussed in a daylong workshop at the Advanced Institute for Sustainable Development of the School of Agricultural Economics and Rural Development at that university. The Institute discussions, the field trip, and the workshop presentations confirmed the sense of a major transformation of agrarian societies at work globally, reversing radical hopes of the post-WWII years but quite in keeping with long-term developments under the regime of capital. Whether or not this is a cause for optimism or pessimism is entangled very much in attitudes toward the capability of capitalism to solve the problems of its creation. These conflicting attitudes have a history of their own, as Alexander Woodside's introductory chapter outlines. It remains to be seen whether present uncertainties over the future of agrarian society are merely a replay of the past or products of an unprecedented world situation.

Because of, for the most part, the organizers' interests and areas of expertise, the transformation of agrarian society in the People's Republic of China over the last three decades, and the sense of crisis that has enveloped that nation over the last decade, provided the initial impetus for the undertaking. Developments over the last two decades have catapulted the PRC to the forefront of speculation over the future of capitalism and the world economy. The future of agrarian society is part of this speculation. Since the early 2000s, the Chinese leadership has openly recognized the seriousness of what is described as the "three-nong" problem, referring to *nongye*/agriculture, *nongcun*/village, and *nongmin*/peasant (or cultivator, see below). The regime has made the creation of a "new socialist village" (*shehui zhuyi xincun*) into one of its top priorities, at least in word. What this means remains unclear, as "the new socialist village" is likely to point to something quite different from the conventional understanding of the "village," where the village is not so much a unit of agrarian society as it is an integral part of a nationwide urban network. This also has radical implications not only for the understanding of the "peasant," but for the organization of agriculture.[1]

The coverage of the undertaking was expanded almost immediately, however, to place developments in China in a comparative perspective but also to get at structural problems that are global in scope. The food crisis of spring 2008 confirmed the validity of these concerns. As Jomo Kwame Sundaram observed in his keynote address for the Summer Institute, the food crisis had many long- and short-term causes, among them price manipulation, but a structural transformation of agriculture was one of the fundamental, long-term reasons exacerbated by neoliberal policies. Different societies are placed differently in the global topography of capitalism. But there is also a great deal of commonality in the problems they face in terms of parallel trajectories of development, as well as increased interdependence in the supply of agricultural commodities. Ironically, what distinguishes China may be the willingness of the regime to recognize the problem and plan for the future, as was observed by Joao Pedro Stedile, a prominent leader of the Landless Workers Movement in Brazil who was a participant in the workshop at People's University.[2]

We would like to single out here three issues that emerged in the course of the discussions in the various meetings, which also guide the essays included in this volume: the long-term relationship between capitalism and agrarian society, the city and the countryside in the analysis of agrarian society, and the question of the peasant as a social category.

CAPITALISM AND AGRARIAN SOCIETY

The impact of capitalism on agrarian society does not call for extensive discussion here, because it is masterfully summarized in Chapter 3 by Immanuel Wallerstein. Where agrarian society is concerned, the history of capitalism appears as one long process of "de-ruralization" and "de-peasantization," in the words of Wallerstein, or, "de-agriculturalization," as Gregory Guldin (also at the conference) has put it with reference to contemporary China.[3] Over the last half millennium, agriculture has come progressively under the domination of the capitalist market, transforming productive relations in the countryside. The transformation has changed not only social relationships in the countryside, including labor relations, but also peasant cultural identity as the "peasantry" has been integrated into the production and consumption practices of capitalism and the political demands of the nation-state.

In this perspective, what may be novel presently is the globalization of this process accompanying the globalization of capital: the transformation of the Global South along the trajectory traversed earlier by advanced capitalist societies. The sense of novelty is enhanced by the reversal of the emphasis on agrarian society of Third World national liberation movements of only a generation ago that not only perceived in the peasantry the key to national identity and autonomous development but promised to subject metropolitan areas globally to the rule of the countryside. While memories of national liberation continue to dynamize agrarian-inspired social movements, such as the Via Campesina, what has happened over the last three decades is the opposite: the urbanization of the countryside led by developmentalist states that have internalized a basic premise of global capitalism as the only available path to survival and prosperity. Urbanization has changed the nature of these movements as well, which can hardly be described as "peasant" or even agrarian movements, as much of their activity is conducted in urban centers. We will say more on this below.

THE CITY AND THE COUNTRYSIDE

This discussion of urbanization leads directly to the second issue: the relationship between the city and the countryside in the analysis of agrarian society. If capitalism has had a transformative impact on the countryside, the city has served as the medium and the agent of transformation. Recognition of the fundamental importance of this relationship forces two considerations, one analytical, the other political: Is it possible to understand change in the countryside without reference to the city, and, for the same reason, can the problems of the countryside be resolved without change in urban existence? And if the country and the city are interdependent in many ways, from the economic to the cultural, can the city survive the disappearance of the country?

The primacy of the city over the countryside long has been an assumption of social theory. The city is not just the center of economic, political, and cultural life but also, for the same reasons, a manifestation of civilization and an emblem of progress. Thus Marx and Engels wrote in *The German Ideology* that "the separation of town and country" represented the "the greatest division of material and mental labour," tracing its origins to "the antagonism between town and country [beginning] with the transition from barbarism and civilization."[4] The city is nearly synonymous with civilization and, as such, the civilizer of the countryside as well.

It does not follow, however, that the domination of the countryside by the city is a foregone conclusion, that it has the same form and character at all times, or that the relationship between the two is of necessity an antagonistic one. Marx and Engels followed the statement above with an account that historicized the evolution of the city under different social formations, culminating with the capitalist city. Fernand Braudel would write with reference to the precapitalist city (in different forms) that "town and country never separate like oil and water because the bond uniting them neither breaks nor pulls lone way only. They separate and draw closer at the same time, split up and then regroup."[5] Since Marx and Engels were interested primarily in the emergence of the capitalist city, they projected its characteristics on its genealogy, ignoring that the relationship between town and country historically was marked as much by symbiosis (not just economically but socially and culturally as well) as antagonism. In this account, cities that could not liberate themselves from the countryside suffered from rural inertia, unable to generate the dynamism that, for better or for worse, had created capitalist society in Europe.[6]

From an ecologically sensitive contemporary perspective, the "modern" city appears instead as a betrayal of the premodern city's promise of a more ecologically sound and sociable relationship between the city and the countryside. Making an unconventional distinction between city (or town) and the urban, Eco-Anarchist social theorist Murray Bookchin writes that "born of the city, urbanization has been its parent's most effective assailant, not to speak of the agrarian world that it has almost completely undone."[7] Bookchin, who idealized the classical city, viewed "urbanization" not simply as "citification" but as the defining characteristic of the modern city that distanced the city from the countryside, followed by the urban "engulfing" of "the agrarian and natural worlds," which in turn created the conditions for the city turned in upon itself to "devour . . . city life based on the values, culture, and institutions nourished by civic relationships." A symbiotic relationship between town and country, in other words, was turned into an antagonism between town and country that would result not only in the erasure of the countryside but the end of the city itself as the location for political and cultural sociability. "Even if we think in the old terms of city versus country," he continues, "urbanization threatens to replace both contestants in this seeming historic antagonism. It threatens to absorb them into a faceless urban world in which the words 'city' and 'country' will essentially become social, cultural, and political archaisms."[8]

Bookchin surprisingly left out of his analysis the relationship between democracy and slavery in the classical city he admired, but that is not a pertinent issue here.[9] Two aspects of his analysis are important for historical and critical reasons. His distinction between the urban and the city (or town) has important analytical implications: if capitalism has had a transformative impact on agrarian society, it has done so through urbanization of both town and country, rendering the urban into the indispensable referent (or even, context) in any analysis of agrarian society. Urbanization here becomes a feature of the "modern" (capitalist) city, rather than a referent for all city formation. The transformation of the countryside also requires the transformation of the city, so that the analysis of one is inextricably entangled in the analysis of the other. Within the context of the Global South presently, urbanization would mean, by implication, the transformation of existing cities and towns along trajectories demanded by global capitalism, in the process also bringing the countryside under the hegemony of capitalist relations of production. Conversely, the transformation of the rural areas of the globe has an impact on cities in both the developed and the developing worlds, if only in the form of migrant labor from the "countryside"—hence Bookchin's conclusion that the city/country distinction itself is on its way to becoming "archaic."

The second important aspect of the analysis is its normative but analytically relevant suggestion that the end of the country also means the end of the city. Marxists, and Marxist-inspired analysts such as Braudel, exhibit ambivalence toward the city that has come to pervade most social science analysis: the city as a realm of contradictions, of both freedom and creativity, and alienation and self-destruction. Such contradictions are clearly visible in contemporary analyses of what have been designated "world" or "global" cities, especially as they assume "mega-" sizes, as realms both of transnationalist cosmopolitanism and ethnic segmentation and parochialism.[10] Bookchin's criticism of urbanization as the death of the city forces another mode of thinking. As city-city relationships over long distances come to overshadow the relationship of the city to its hinterland, they distance the one from the other, rendering a symbiotic into an antagonistic relationship in which the countryside is the first casualty. But it is not the only casualty, because the city itself becomes subject to forces beyond its control, and the management of those forces takes priority over modes of governance that are intended to enhance the sociability that is its very reason for existence. The city is transformed into a location in a network of locations through which capital and its auxiliary services move and serves as such as a link in the process of capitalist production. As a recent Marxist analysis observes, cities provide the ideal spaces for the accumulation of capital, which in turn transforms the city on an ongoing basis in the process of its production and reproduction: "Capital accumulation and the production of urbanization go hand in hand."[11]

The logical conclusion here is that the grounding of capital in the city simultaneously off-grounds the city from its ecological setting by yoking it to the motions of capital. Fernand Braudel, explicitly in agreement with Marx, wrote pessimistically that,

> It is the inequalities, the injustice, the contradictions, large or small, which make the world go round and ceaselessly transform its upper structures, the only really mobile ones. For capitalism alone has relative freedom of movement. . . . Faced with inflexible structures . . . it is able to choose the areas where it wants and is able to meddle, and the areas it will leave to their fate, incessantly reconstructing its own structures from these components, and thereby little by little transforming those of others.[12]

The statement successfully captures what may be distinctive about the forces driving the modern capitalist city, confirmed daily in our time by the globalization of urban forms. Neither limitations on the motions of capital nor urban and rural struggles to ground it in accordance with local needs is sufficient to refute that city and country alike have been integrated into its domain. The distancing of the city from the countryside means only that the city is now shaped by forces beyond the local, not that there is a literal separation between the two. On the contrary, as Bookchin suggests, the integration of the country to the city may be more thorough presently than ever before in history. It is also marked by its own peculiar contradictions. Cities continue to consume the countryside. The countryside strives to become citified, to partake of the promises of globality, even as it also resists appropriation by the city. But cities in their expansion bring the countryside into their midst (whether as fields or as people), so that global forces and forces of the immediate hinterland play out their antagonism in the city. At the same time, the emptying out of the countryside into the city raises the questions of what agrarian society might mean under the circumstances and what is to become of all those activities associated with it, most crucially but not just food production. It is impossible to address the dynamics of one without also referring to the dynamics of the other, more so for the country than for the city as it is drawn into the force field of urbanization, but by no means unidirectionally.

Regardless of where they stand on issues of capital and classes, or space and place, most of the outstanding works on contemporary urban formations share one shortcoming: a seeming obliviousness to the relationship of world-cities to the countryside. Whether out of a sense of an academic division of labor, or an ideological fascination with urban networks, there is little discussion in these works of world cities' changing relationship to their hinterlands (including lesser urban configurations), extending to and possibly beyond national boundaries. This omission may be more the case with those who stress the global over the transnational, and spaces over places, but it is difficult to find, in these works, any sustained analysis of urban-rural relations that received far greater attention in approaches based on "central places." Where the countryside comes into analysis, it is in the guise of "transnational villages," rural settlements in some distant location in some other nation that have come to gain a foothold in world-cities. Analyses of migration rarely attempt to account for migrations within nation-states that swell the rapidly growing slums of world-cities, especially in countries of the Global South.[13]

It is as if world-cities are off-grounded from their concrete environment, and their relationship to one another renders invisible any relationship to the countryside. Some analysts, such as the advocate of borderless globalization, Kenichi Ohmae, go so far as to celebrate the distancing of the world-city from its environment as a condition of efficient development.[14] The result, as Riccardo Petrella of the European Union has noted, is a portrayal of world-cities as a "wealthy archipelago of city regions . . . surrounded by an impoverished *lumpenplanet*."[15]

The "disappearance" of the countryside from theorizations of the city may be attributable to actual changes globally. More than half the world's population presently resides in urban areas (not all of them world-cities), and the figure is expected to rise to 60 percent over the next two decades.[16] If the evacuation of the countryside into the city has been underway since the origins of capitalism half a millennium ago, what we are witnessing presently is the latest phase of this development in which problems of urbanization in the Global South have moved to the center of attention.[17] In some instances, such as in the People's Republic of China, the forces of political economy are reinforced by actual state policy that perceives in urbanization in megaurban complexes the resolution of problems of agrarian society as well.[18] The urbanization of the rural population is also expected to contribute to further agricultural development by replacing the family farm with "agricultural production that mimics the agribusiness management techniques of North America."[19]

The case of China is particularly important in illustrating the dramatic shift that has taken place from Maoist policies of self-sufficiency and self-reliance that presupposed the priority of national surfaces over city networks, to an export-oriented transnational economy that has marginalized the countryside and reduced the peasantry to second-class citizenry. It is arguable that while Maoist policies placed a premium on agriculture, they, too, helped "de-peasantize" the countryside through collective organization that mimicked industrial organization (see below). Those policies were also responsible for the *hukou* (household registration) system that divided the city and the country. Megacities, rather than resolve this problem, are more likely to bring the urban-rural bifurcation into the structure of urban complexes, as has happened already in cities like Beijing.[20] The system of hereditary registration in place of birth, moreover, has rendered the urban-rural division into a caste-like system, denying rural migrants to the city full citizenship in their inability to access basic needs like education and health.[21] In this regard, they are not all that different in the difficulties they face from the so-called illegal immigrants that are flowing into cities around the world.[22]

These developments hardly justify the neglect of the countryside. On the contrary, the absorption of the countryside into urban areas presents problems of long-reaching significance: the disappearance of the peasantry as a source of labor power; uncertainty over the future of agricultural production, which already shows signs of crisis in chronic food shortages; the ecological consequences of the redistribution of population from the rural to the urban; and the psychic costs of the concentration of populations in enormous megacities.[23] No less important are the political consequences that include new challenges in urban governance and have led already to increased surveillance of populations, proliferation of instruments of repression in anticipation of possible urban disorder, and, internationally, intensified competition for resources necessary for the sustenance of national populations. Jane Jacobs argued in her influential book *Cities and the Wealth of Nations* that the relationships of cities to their hinterlands have been of great importance in determining the welfare of either and that this also was of consequence in shaping transnational urban relationships. The latter may be quite effective in generating wealth and security for classes and groups that are its beneficiaries, but its distancing from the former raises serious questions of sustenance and sustainability in the long run for the urban populations at large.[24]

The continued insistence in China on "socialist" planning in a market economy makes it especially interesting in offering glimpses into the imagination of the future relationship between the countryside and the city. The incorporation of the countryside into the city, initially through "townization" (village becoming town) due to market pressures from both the city and the countryside, in recent years has become part of planning into the future. "Townization" was, in the early 1990s, restricted mostly to the coastal areas and was a product as much of local initiative as of the forces of global capitalism refracted through the major urban sites of "reform and opening" such as Guangdong and Shanghai.[25] While agricultural change in the 1980s served as the motor force of development, a decade later agriculture was in trouble as the countryside lagged behind the cities in development. The "three-nong" problem was so serious that it led to renewed attention to agrarian society, not to reproduce but to urbanize it. Changing "property regimes," discussed in Chapter 9 by Pitman Potter, are one instrument utilized to this end. Even more significant may be changes envisaged at the macro level of urban planning. These plans include the building of megacities that will serve as magnets in their respective areas and turn villages into towns, as more efficient means of providing jobs to increasingly superfluous rural populations, concentrating the production of resources, and establishing more effective controls over environmental damage. The countryside, in the meantime, will be available for more efficient modes of agricultural production. What is at work is planned obsolescence of the urban/rural division of the past.

PEASANTS INTO URBANITES?

The third issue is the peasant in the conventional sense, which the disappearance of the countryside has made into an endangered species. The conventional image to which we refer is that of a tiller of the land, who lives in a village surrounded by fields, and with the help of family labor, produces mainly for subsistence, marketing the surplus in exchange for the few items beyond the ability of the household to produce. How close this image was to the historical reality of so-called peasant societies has always been an issue of contention. Different societies named "peasants" differently, emphasizing one aspect or another of their existence (countryperson, villager, tiller of the land, farmer, etc.). Be that as it may, modernity in its globalization has called into question the reality of the image and the possibility of what it represented, if only with differences in the depth and pace of change in different locations.

The conversion of the peasant into a producer for the market, and, politically, into the citizen of the nation-state, has followed inexorably the appropriation of the countryside into the urban spaces of capital and the nation-state.[26] This has been as true of socialist as of capitalist modernization. As we noted above, with reference to Maoist policies, socialist collectivization, too, sought to remake the peasantry in the image of the factory worker and to relocate agricultural labor from the family and the village in state-enforced collective organization. The enforcement was made possible by the hukou (household registration) system, which introduced a caste-like *division* between the urban and rural populations that is the legacy of collectivization to the present. While the peasantry was "de-peasantized," the division guaranteed the persistence of agriculture. The present seems set to complete the task by abolishing the distinction altogether as the rural is inexorably drawn into the urban, or is remade in the latter's image. As the essays by Alexander Day and Pitman Potter suggest, present-day conceptions of the peasant seek to transform both the peasant and agriculture. The proletariat as the model for the peasantry has been replaced by an image of the peasant as successful entrepreneur in the marketplace. And agriculture is reconceived as one more aspect of an economy dominated by the productive relations of capitalism. The increased porosity of the nation-state with the globalization of the political economy further permits, if it does not encourage, the transnationalization of the "peasant."[27]

Alexander Day's discussion in Chapter 4 of the post-1978 Chinese discourses on the peasant shows clearly that neither the naming of the "peasantry" nor the evaluation of its consequences is politically innocent. Recognition of the consequences of capitalism or the city for the countryside does not require surrender to its inevitability or to its self-image of progress. The peasant as the symbol of an alternative mode of existence continues to inspire the search for an alternative to the capitalist transformation of the city and the countryside. Potter's discussion of disagreements over "property regimes" indicates that the issue remains to be settled among Chinese leaders. More eloquent is the resistance of the peasantry to forced incorporation in the international division of labor, as discussed for China, Latin America, India, and Africa in the essays by Wen Tiejun and Dong Zhenghua, Alejandro Rojas and Fabio Cabarcas, Utsa Patnaik, and Sam Moyo and Paris Yeros.[28] The issue in these cases is not just a romantic attachment to the image of the peasant, but the association of the figure of the peasant with essential human needs, chief among them food security.[29] Rojas's argument is particularly interesting in its insistence that even if the peasantry disappears, it is important to preserve "peasant knowledge," which may be crucial to overcoming the ecological difficulties the world faces. The "peasant," albeit a very different kind of peasant, continues to stand for an alternative to the surrender of the most basic human needs to corporate agriculture and a new kind of accommodation between the city and the countryside.

FINAL REMARKS

The purpose of a volume such as this one is not just to chronicle and illustrate a historical teleology but also to make some slight contribution to the imagination of alternatives to it—unless we are convinced that the world at hand is the best of all possible worlds and talk of alternatives is merely a form of intellectual mischief. The contemporary preoccupation with alternatives on a wide range of fronts may be taken itself as manifestation of a sense of crisis. The crisis of agriculture is foremost among the many crises that we face. There is no single alternative appropriate to all of the societies discussed here, not to speak of the many more that are beyond the purview of this volume. The same forces may be compelling changes globally, but what effect they have locally is a product of their interactions with the circumstances of concrete localities. As the problems differ, they also demand different solutions. To ignore this is to fall in with the universalist self-images of neoliberal capitalism, or to fall back on the similarly informed universalist prescriptions of an earlier socialism.

But neither should local particularities be allowed to conceal the forces at work globally. Local interactions have been at work all along. We need also to uncover what is novel about the forces that are giving them a new power and direction, for the same tendencies would seem to be at work globally, regardless of local variations due to social, political, and cultural circumstances. The problems of China and Bolivia may be quite different, but they also have a commonality: the disappearance of the countryside under the force of a relentless urbanization, itself empowered by the global motions of capital. The disappearance of the countryside evacuates rural populations into urban areas, while opening up rural areas to more efficient modes of production, which inevitably under the hegemonic corporate paradigm favors size and corporate management over small-scale family farming. The result is more evacuation. Local differences are not inconsistent with parallel trajectories, as the following statement suggests:

> For most peasant farmers in Mexico, Asia has always seemed literally and figuratively a world apart. But when Uthai Sa Artchop of Thailand described how transnational corporations sought to patent and control their varieties of rice seed, Mexican peasants realized that the Thais' rice was their corn. When Indonesian farmer Tejo Pramono spoke of how remittances from sons and daughters working in Hong Kong and the

> Middle East subsidize a dying countryside, Mexican farmers thought of their own relatives forced to migrate to the United States.[30]

Commonalities are not restricted to such parallel developments. As the market dependency that "de-ruralizes" agrarian societies becomes globalized, societies around the world face critical new risks. Rural areas no doubt may flourish with increased access to urban markets, as some economists argue (as one of the participants in the Institute, Ashok Kotwal, did). But the globalization of agrarian products brings with it new uncertainties and risks. Dependency on long-distance urban markets makes rural livelihood subject to fluctuations in demand in faraway places and other unforeseeable contingencies.[31] The commercialization of production most importantly creates uncertainties in access to food, as food production is commercialized and subject to global circulation like any other agricultural commodity. The disappearance of peasant farming in a country like China leaves commercial farming as the most likely outcome (discussed in Chapter 7 by Dong Zhenghua). Urban encroachment on farmland (through communications requirements and real estate development) reduces already meager arable land. On the other hand, agricultural activity is "exported" as China obtains land in Africa and South America to supply food needs, and maybe even to compete on the global food market. The ecological consequences of this activity are highly uncertain. So are the social consequences. Already, the provision of male workers to urban development has depleted villages of adult males, with debilitating consequences for both family and village structure. Such separation, needless to say, also takes place on a global scale. The "de-peasantization" of the countryside is accompanied inevitably by the "peasantization" of the city and the burdens it imposes on urban management and sustainability. For now, as Mike Davis has argued, rural population has no choice but to pour into growing slum populations around the globe. Some countries like China have managed to avoid slum growth through social controls, as well as the legacies of organization that enable self-organization among migrants. That, too, presents new challenges to urban governance.[32] Advocates of globalization cannot have it both ways. The globalization of the economy brings in its wake the globalization of its problems, which have acquired serious dimensions with the urbanization of agrarian societies.

Given these circumstances, efforts to resolve these problems can no longer be restricted to the defense of agrarian society, but need to confront issues across the full spectrum of the urban-rural nexus. This is indeed the case with social movement organizations such as Via Campesina. Responding to critics who view "peasant mobilization" as nostalgic reaction to "modern society," Philip McMichael has written that organizations like Via Campesina seek to transcend "conventional peasant politics, reframing its ontological concerns via a critique of neoliberalism, and reformulating the agrarian question in relation to development exigencies today."[33] The exigencies that have received the greatest attention from contemporary rural social movements include massive destitution in the countryside and its extension into city slums, ecological issues raised by urbanization as well as the commercialization of agriculture, the dangers of genetically modified crops, the plight of women and indigenous peoples, breakdown of social institutions, cultural dissolution, and, as keys to the solution of all of the above, food sovereignty and the right to land.[34] Many of these, it needs to be underlined, are problems not just of the countryside but also of the city—and the global political economy of which it is at once producer and product. The resolution of these problems at their most fundamental will require overhauling the global political economy and the direction it has taken with the globalization of neoliberal technocratic principles.

If decline is reversed and the countryside once again is recognized as the crucial location for the solution of not only rural but also urban problems, it will likely have a spatial organization quite unlike that of the village or the individual family farmer. The peasant, too, is not likely to resemble any social subject associated with that term. To say what the outcome may be in either case would be difficult. The only thing possible to say with some certainty presently is that the subjection of the countryside to the rule of the neoliberal market economy is likely to produce more of the problems that threaten welfare not only in the countryside but also in the city. People's struggles to overcome this threat quite appropriately have brought together urban and rural activists united in a single struggle, which draws its inspiration from long-held beliefs in the countryside as a source of welfare and contentment but promises an alternative future that is very much refracted through the realities of the present. Top-down projects of "the ecological city" or "rubanisation," referred to above, are also most likely to be successful only in alliance with these struggles from the bottom, and not against them in accordance with the dictates of placeless global capital.

NOTES

1. See Dong Zhongtang, *Jianshe shehui zhuyi xin nongcunde lungang* [An Outline of the Construction of the New Socialist Village] (Beijing: People's Daily Press, 2005), for an example of many publications on the issue. The plan offered includes "integration of town and country" (*chengxiang yitihua*, literally, "becoming one body") as well as transformation of the peasant.

2. For more on the part the manipulation of grain indices played in the crisis of spring 2008, see Frederick Kaufman, "The Food Bubble: How Wall Street Starved Millions and Got Away with It," *Harper's Magazine* 321, no. 1922 (July 2010): 27–34.

3. Gregory E. Guldin, *What's a Peasant to Do? Village Becoming Town in Southern China* (Boulder, CO: Westview Press, 2001), passim.

4. Karl Marx and Frederick Engels, *The German Ideology*, edited with an introduction by R. Pascal (New York: International Publishers, 1947).

5. Fernand Braudel, *Capitalism and Material Life, 1400–1800*, trans. Miriam Kochan (New York: Harper Torchbooks, 1967), 376–377.

6. Some Chinese Marxist historians attributed to domination of the city by the countryside the abortiveness of capitalist development in China. For a discussion, see Arif Dirlik, *Revolution and History: Origins of Marxist Historiography in China, 1919–1937* (Berkeley, CA: University of California Press, 1989), Chapter 4. Another explanation was political: domination of the city by the state, which Braudel also has used to explain the different fates of cities in Europe and elsewhere. See Braudel, *Capitalism and Material Life*, 440.

7. Murray Bookchin, *The Rise of Urbanization and the Decline of Citizenship* (San Francisco: Sierra Club Books, 1987), 12.

8. Ibid., 2–3.

9. Braudel, by contrast, perceived in the medieval town in Europe the freedom that created capitalism, not the top-down capitalism of which he was critical, but the democratic small-scale capitalism of the individual entrepreneur.

10. Ash Amin and Nigel Thrift, *Cities: Reimagining the Urban* (Cambridge, UK: Polity Press, 2002).

11. David Harvey, *The Urban Experience* (Baltimore, MD: The Johns Hopkins University Press, 2009), 22.

12. Fernand Braudel, *Capitalism and Material Life, 1400–1800*, trans. Miriam Kochan (NY: Harper Torchbooks, 1967), 445.

13. Mike Davis, *Planet of Slums* (London: Verso, 2006).

14. Kenichi Ohmae, *The End of the Nation State: The Rise of Regional Economies* (New York: The Free Press, 1995).

15. Riccardo Petrella, official forecaster for the European Union, cited in J. V. Beaverstock, R. G. Smith, and P. J. Taylor, "World-City Network: A New Metageography?," *Annals of the Association of American Geographers* 90, no. 1 (March 2000): 123–134.

16. Brian C. O'Neill and others, *Demographic Research: A Guide to Population Projections*, Vol. 4, Article 8 (June 2001): 203–288.

17. See Chapter 3, Immanuel Wallerstein, "The Return of the Peasant: Possible? Desirable?" For a discussion of over- or hyper-urbanization in the megacities of the Global South, see J. D. Kasarda and E. M. Crenshaw, "Third World Urbanization: Dimensions, Theories, and Determinants," *Annual Review of Sociology* 17 (1991): 467–501.

18. See Andrew Moody and Lan Lan, "Focusing on Future Urbanization," *China Daily*, March 22, 2010, 13, for the development of megacities that are expected to resolve questions not only of poverty and urban-rural differences but ecological problems as well. Some Chinese advocates of urbanization may have been influenced by the work of Paul Romer, who has emerged as the most recent prophet of alleviating poverty through urbanization. See Quentin Hardy, "Postcolonialism: An Economist's Plan to Save the World's Poor; New Cities Built Around Profits," *Forbes*, September 21, 2009, 38. If this report is to be believed, Romer's "charter cities" seem to differ from Ohmae's "region-states" mainly in his concern for alleviating poverty and his proposal to internationalize city governance (hence, postcolonialism). One recent study proposes Shanghai during the pre-1949 colonial period as a model for a new Hanseatic League appropriate to the globalized world. See Geoffrey Bracken, "The Shanghai Model," *IIAS (International Institute for Asian Studies) Newsletter* 52 (Winter 2009): 4–5. For a contemporary example of labor export to cities to relieve poverty, see "Work Dries Up in Rural Areas," *China Daily*, April 1, 2010, 4. On occasion, forced urbanization is intended to undercut peasant mobilization for politics, as is argued in Chapter 11 by Abidin Kusno, "Peasants in Indonesia and the Politics of (Peri)Urbanization." The absorption of villages into urban areas is discussed in Chapter 8 by Leslie Shieh, "Awaiting Urbanization: Urban Village Redevelopment in Coastal Urban China." For peasants as "management problem," see Alexander Woodside, "The 'End of the Peasantry' Scenario: Dream and Nightmare," Chapter 2 in this volume.

19. Gregory E. Guldin, "Desakotas and Beyond: Urbanization in Southern China," *Ethnology* 35, no. 4 (Fall 1996): 265–284, 268.

20. For an illuminating and critical study, see Dorothy J. Solinger, *Contesting Citizenship in Urban China: Peasant Migrants, the State, and the Logic of the Market* (Berkeley, CA: University of California Press, 1999). On the other hand, the new category of "peasant-worker" (*nonggong*) also suggests the possibility of some integration, which presently has taken the path of "the urbanization of the countryside," by force if necessary, which is quite often. For a discussion of urban-rural becoming "one body" (*yiti*) in the Chengdu "model," see Ni

Pengfei et al., *Zhongguo xinxing chengshihua daolu chengxiang shuangying: yi Chengdu wei anli* [New Urbanization Path of China: Urban and Rural Win-Win—Take Chengdu as a Case] (Beijing: Social Sciences Academic Press, 2007).

21. Dorothy Solinger has documented this in depth in *Contesting Citizenship in Urban China.* For an up-to-date report, see "Millions of Chinese Rural Migrants Denied Education for Their Children," *The Guardian,* March 15, 2010. A more optimistic assessment is offered in Yu Keping, "The New Migration Movement, Citizenship, and Institutional Change at the Global Age: A Political Understanding of Large-Scale Urban Migration of Rural Workers Since the Reform in China," unpublished paper (2010). Yu believes that marketization, globalization, and efforts to equality of migrant workers themselves have created forces for democratization that will lead to eventual resolution of this problem. We are grateful to Dr. Yu for his willingness to share this unpublished paper with us. For migrant struggles to overcome their status, see "Unlike Parents, Young Migrants Won't Take Their Fate Lying Down," *China Daily,* March 23, 2010.

22. The internal migrant population in Chinese cities is presently estimated at around 160 million. For an interesting discussion of the internal organization of one migrant community that shaped up as an urban enclave beyond the formal city government, the "Zhejiang Village" on the outskirts of Beijing, see Li Zhang, "Migration and the Privatization of Space and Power in Late Socialist China," *American Ethnologist* 28, no. 1 (February 2001): 179–205. Whether or not this kind of organization can achieve permanence against the high-tech visions of the regime is an open question in a society in rapid transformation where governance itself is subject to ongoing experimentation.

23. Richard York and others, "Footprints of the Earth: The Environmental Consequences of Modernity," *American Sociological Review* 68, no. 2 (April 2003): 279–300. For the city as both ecological problem *and* ecological solution (presently more the former than the latter), see Mike Davis, "Who Will Build the Ark?," *New Left Review* 61 (January/February 2010): 29–46. Chinese planners meanwhile are working toward the "ecological city." See Wu Haifeng, *Shengtai chengshi dai jianshe yu quyu bantiao fazhan* [Construction of Ecological Metropolis and Coordinated Development of Regions] (Beijing: Social Sciences Academic Press, 2009). Possible urban food shortages as a result of the destruction of the countryside, with the most serious implications for the urban poor, have become not just a social but security concern. For a recent discussion with reference to ASEAN, see Paul Teng, Mely Caballero-Anthony, Margarita Escaler, and Paul Khan Khup Hangzo, "Ensuring Urban Food Security in ASEAN," Policy Brief, Food Security Expert Group Meeting, Singapore, 4–5 August 2010. The authors offer what they describe as "rubanisation" as a possible solution (and an alternative to the "Western" model of development).

24. Jane Jacobs, *Cities and the Wealth of Nations* (New York: Vintage Books, 1985).

25. Gregory E. Guldin, ed., *Farewell to Peasant China: Rural Urbanization and Social Change in the Late Twentieth Century* (Armonk, NY: ME Sharpe, 1997).

26. For nation-building and peasant resistance to it, see Roxann Prazniak, *Of Camel Kings and Other Things: Rural Rebels Against Modernity in Late Imperial China* (Boulder, CO: Rowman & Littlefield, 1999).

27. See Harry Bernstein, "Farewells to the Peasantry," *Transformation* 52 (2003): 1–19, for the incorporation of the peasantry into an international division of labor through nationalism and colonialism. For a study of "transnationalism," see Peggy Levitt, *The Transnational Villagers* (Berkeley, CA: University of California Press, 2002).

28. While most such resistance has been peaceful, as with Via Campesina, or restricted to localized acts of violence, there are also instances of the resurgence of armed struggle, as in the case of the Maoist-inspired Naxalite uprising in India that draws on tribal populations,

or the recent confrontations in Thailand, that display all the characteristics of class struggle in which urban/rural divisions and inequalities created by globalization play a determinant part. For recent reports on the Naxalite uprising that point to these issues, see Arundhati Roy, *Broken Republic: Three Essays* (Delhi: Penguin Books, 2011), and Robert M. Cutler, "Naxalites Drill Away at India's Wealth," *Asia Times Online*, May 20, 2010. Available: http://www.atimes.com/atimes/South_Asia/LE20Df02.html.

29. See also, Philip McMichael, "Peasants Make Their Own History, But Not Just as They Please . . .," *Journal of Agrarian Change* 8, no. 2–3 (April and July 2008): 205–228.

30. Laura Carlsen, "Via Campesina Sets an International Agenda," ibid. (2007): 221–222.

31. As we write these lines, the Internet is full of stories on the economic impact of the volcanic eruption in Iceland that has brought airline transport to a stop, with problems of food shortage in Europe and producers' problems in faraway places from Kenya to India with products that cannot be shipped out. For one example, see "Flight Ban Could Leave UK Short of Fruit and Veg," *The Guardian*, April 16, 2010. Available: http://www.guardian.co.uk/business/2010/april/16/flight-ban-shortages-uk-supermarkets.

32. Li Zhang, "Migration and Privatization of Space and Power in Late Socialist China," *American Ethnologist* 28, no. 1 (February 2001): 179–205.

33. McMichael, "Peasants Make Their Own History," 207.

34. Via Campesina, "The Tlaxcala Declaration," International Conference on the Via Campesina, Tlaxcala, Mexico, April 18–21, 1996.

Chapter 2

The "End of the Peasantry" Scenario: Dream and Nightmare

Alexander Woodside

In the second half of the twentieth century, global planning elites made an unprecedented effort to reconceptualize the whole nature of farming. This elite reconceptualization of farming, along much more industrial, more purely commercial lines, was never just an empirical recognition of what was actually happening in some, if not all, countrysides. It was also an attack on the past history of human farming, driven by science-worshipping norms and a salvationist gospel of economic efficiency.

Neoclassical economics were usually thought to be the source of this gospel. For example, the Via Campesina, a global movement of farm leaders from around the world, was founded in 1993 in explicit rejection of liberalizing economic policies that were impoverishing far too many farm workers. The Via Campesina leaders demanded that the World Trade Organization itself withdraw from agriculture and that increased liberalization of the international trade in food be halted.[1] But neoclassical economics are only part of the story. The twentieth century, with its two world wars, was a century of managers, not just of neoclassical economists. As Peter F. Drucker, one of the most famous "fathers of modern management," put it in 1988, the Germans were the better strategists in World War II, but the Allies won because of their management prowess.[2] However dubious this sweeping claim might be in whole or in part, the claim itself suggests the uncompromising ambition of the professional ideology behind it and the self-interested nature of the new management experts' disdain for the millions of small family farms all over the world that, until recently, lay outside their reach.

The managerial bias in world development, like the urban bias, deserves more emphasis than it usually gets. A Chinese State Council research office leader said in 2003 that the World Trade Organization and the "internationalization" of Chinese farming were good for China because they would enable the elite to deepen Chinese village reforms, promote the development of a pan-Chinese "agricultural regulation" system, and enhance the "management levels" of Chinese farm businesses through fewer, bigger, more scientific farms.[3] Optimists assumed, until recently, that the world food supply as a whole would benefit from such "internationalized" reforms.

THE GOLDEN AGE OF FARM PRODUCTIVITY

The Chinese commentary on the relationship between industrialization and agriculture has a long genealogy. As early as 1907, the famous Chinese anarchist Liu Shipei alarmed his readers by predicting that industrialization in China would lure debt-ridden peasants out of farming in the Chinese countryside into factories in cities like Shanghai. Urban populations would increase, the price of cereals would soar, and poor people would not be able to afford enough to eat.[4] Yet when rising rice and wheat prices in Asia, Africa, and the Caribbean, caused in part by the conversion of cereals into biofuels and by the increased costs of chemical fertilizers, triggered food riots in the spring of 2008, the establishment news media in the West expressed surprise at the sudden possibility of global food shortages.

If Liu Shipei's grim premonitions were ignored for over a century, the main reason surely lay in the extraordinary rise in the productivity rates of the world's farmland between 1950 and the 1980s. Indeed, most of the twentieth century appeared, at first glance, to be a golden age of agriculture, if not of politics. The world's population more than doubled in size between 1950 (2.5 billion people) and 2000 (6.1 billion people). Yet global food output increases, until the late 1980s at least, exceeded the population increases.

Three technologies, one very old and two fairly new, facilitated the great expansion in farmland productivity. The old technology was irrigation, traceable back several millennia and crucial to the farming connected to Asia's big river systems (the Yellow and Yangzi Rivers, the Mekong and the Irrawaddy, the Brahmaputra and the Ganges). Between 1950 and 1978, global per capita irrigated acreage for farming expanded by almost one-third. The two newer technologies were the application of chemical fertilizers to nutrient-poor soil (the volume of such fertilizers used in world farming increased ninefold between 1950 and 1998) and the use of genetic engineering in plant breeding. Its origins lay in the discovery of the laws of plant genetics in late-nineteenth-century Europe.[5]

The expansion of farming growth rates was accompanied by a sharp decline, in some parts of the world, in the numbers of farming people, thanks to urbanization. This decline reinforced an already strong faith, among global planners, in the universal applicability of the patterns of the world's earlier industrial revolutions, beginning with the British one. As early as 1851, townspeople outnumbered country people in Britain for the first time in British history.[6] Other Western countries followed. As late as 1930, the United States had 2.5 million farms that were less than fifty acres; but it had only 500,000 such small farms by 1992. Close to 40 percent of the French labor force was engaged in agriculture in the 1950s but less than 3 percent by 2004.[7] Even in backward Fascist or communist European states with no interest in democracy, the farming population shrank drastically after 1950. One worker in two was employed on the land in Franco's Spain in 1950, but only one in five Spaniards still remained in agriculture in 1971. In Nicolae Ceausescu's Rumanian police state (which deliberately attacked peasant society and moved peasants into concrete agrotowns), only 28 percent of the labor force worked the land by 1986.[8]

Even the post-1945 eastern Asian experience seemed to confirm the global appropriateness of the decline of farming people in the British industrial revolution. As one Chinese Central Party School economist put it in 2006, the rapid shrinkage of the Japanese and South Korean labor forces engaged in farming after 1945 suggested that the percentage of farming people in labor forces in all industrial revolutions ought to fall from 50 percent to about 10 percent within twenty-five to thirty years, given the right policies of modernization.[9]

Dramatic farm productivity increases, at the same time as a reduction in the number of farming people, inevitably stimulated end-of-history projections of the usual utopian kind. In 1995, E. J. Hobsbawm proposed that the "death of the peasantry" was the single most far-reaching change in the history of the post-1945 world. As recently as the 1930s, "the refusal of the peasantry to fade away" had been used "as an argument against Karl Marx's prediction that they would."[10] Yet even before Marx, for centuries the peasantry had been regarded in stereotyped fashion as enemies of human progress, or at least as symptoms of a lack of progress. In the 1700s, American Jeffersonian democrats flattered themselves that the new U.S. republic's food growers were civilizing, frontier-taming farmers; food growers in the monarchical, despotic Europe, on the other hand, were peasants.[11] Chinese intellectuals before 1949 inherited this partly ideological tendency. If they thought that China had already entered the more progressive capitalist stage of history, they would call Chinese farming people farmers; if they assumed that Chinese society was still feudal or semifeudal, they would call them peasants.[12]

Economic development literature after World War II demonized the peasantry as a "primitive community" whose limited wants as consumers jeopardized economic growth. W. Arthur Lewis, a Nobel prize winner in economics (1979), even went so far as to picture non-Western economies in dualistic terms as having a dynamic "capitalist" sector and a static "subsistence" sector. In the former lived highly Westernized "trousered natives" who gloried "in Beethoven, Mill, Marx, or Einstein." In the latter could be found "the great mass of their countrymen who live in quite other worlds."[13] Anthropologists followed in the wake of such economists in seeing the peasantry as a psychologically antimodern cultural system. In 1966, for example, Oscar Lewis decided that the rural communities he studied in the Caribbean suffered from a "culture of poverty"; they were not poor because of political and economic exploitation but because they chose to be poor, conditioned by their self-isolating negative cultural characteristics.[14]

Not everyone accepted this prejudiced characterization of small food producers with limited educations as "peasants," especially if the purpose of such an act was to stigmatize them as wants-free economic primitives. As a leading anthropologist recently put it, dichotomous conceptions and related evolutionary models that assume that tradition, stasis, subsistence orientations, and general backwardness are natural features of non-Western villagers must be considered "both theoretically moribund and empirically unsupported."[15] Chinese small farm households have been involved in various market economies for centuries; Indonesian upland villagers sold the "New World" crops they grew (maize and tobacco) in lowland markets as early as the 1600s; Balkans mountain shepherds, who had to pay cash taxes to the Ottoman empire, sold their livestock and related products to lowland merchants also by the 1600s, if not before. The term "peasantry" will nonetheless be used here precisely because of the need to illuminate global ideological practices that arbitrarily marginalize large numbers of rural people in order to deny them political and social rights. The peasant-bashing language games of the national and international elites who rule such people may or may not be a threat to our food supply, but they certainly threaten our understanding of what human rationality is in transhistorical and transcultural terms.

THE RETURN OF AGRARIAN CATASTROPHE THEORY

The world's peasantries, of course, have not died. Even Hobsbawm had to admit that, at the time of his writing in 1995, the global "regions of peasant dominance"—Africa, South and Southeast Asia, China—"still represented half the human race."[16] The Chinese debate about this is instructive. For China, the best evidence for the possibility that peasants might someday disappear was the official statistic that their numbers had dropped from 849.9 million people in 1992 (roughly 72 percent of the population) to 745.3 million people in 2005 (57 percent).[17] But as one senior Chinese agrarian economist warned, in terms of household registration status, China's agrarian population was really 949 million people in 2005; another 200 million peasants were living a precarious life in Chinese cities without having evolved into officially urban people. Chen Xiwen went on to assert that the vast scale of China's rural population was historically unprecedented. Chinese elite planners could not find proper precedents for their policy-making anywhere in the past human experience of industrialization. Yet the conviction that they could was damaging the Chinese countryside. Some 20,000 natural villages were vanishing in China every year, as their lands were requisitioned for non-farming purposes, or their inmates were otherwise forced to flee as a result of natural disasters or expropriation for the construction of dams and reservoirs.[18]

China has never been a "typical" non-Western agrarian society. Compared to another big industrializing country like Brazil, for example, China has a worse ratio of people to available cultivable farmland, lower state investment in agriculture, and far weaker permitted mobilization (so far) of the rural poor to defend their own interests. Yet both China and Brazil have witnessed the growth of urban slums that are characterized by poverty, violence, and repression. Masses of slum-dwelling peasants with few citizenship rights live in such slums, into which they have been driven or enticed. In this sense, China may be regarded as a global trendsetter.

Elite planners and the social scientists who study their work accommodate the formation of these "postmodern" slums by referring to it as "quasi-urbanization" (*zhun chengzhenhua* in Chinese) or "peri-urbanization" or "de-peasantization."[19] Such terms often merely disguise a failed economic vision. The planners who employ these terms resemble portrait painters who can no longer bring themselves to paint completely idealized portraits of their ugly subjects but remain reluctant to paint their subjects as they really are, warts and all.

Others have not been so reticent. An historical catastrophe theorist, Mike Davis, published a horrifying book in 2006, *Planet of Slums*, which portrayed the alleged "death of the peasantry" as a nightmare, not as a development ideal. Davis wrote that gigantic increases in urbanization in Africa, Latin America, and Asia were nothing but "over-urbanization" promoted by the reproduction of poverty, not by the supply of jobs. Periurban poverty was simply "the radical new face of inequality." It led to a "grim human world largely cut off from the subsistence solidarities of the countryside" yet decoupled from genuine industrialization.[20] A tour of multiple hells, Davis's book compelled its readers to visit such sufferers as the one million poor people who used the tombs of Cairo's City of the Dead for their "prefabricated housing." Significantly, Davis proposed parallels between nineteenth-century colonialisms and the contemporary neoliberal globalization that turned rural poor people into urban squatters "surrounded by pollution, excrement, and decay."[21]

Davis's book takes its place as an event in the more general advance, in the early twenty-first century, of what has come to be known as agrarian catastrophe theory. Simply put, the catastrophe theorists suggest that, by the year 2050, there will be nine to ten billion people on the planet, and it will be necessary to feed them on the basis of less farmland, less water, less energy (at least of the present kind), and fewer chemicals. Among other things, such population increases mean that the global per capita availability of fresh water is likely, in 2050, to be only about one-quarter of what it was in 1950; numbers of underground water aquifers, from the Americas to North Africa to the Middle East to north China, are declining. And from the late 1980s, the global food output increases that exceeded population growth after 1945 have begun to show signs of lagging behind them.[22]

As Davis suggests, the rates of consumption of resources like grain or rice are affected by changes in class privilege, nationally and globally. The world could support a population of nine or ten billion people in 2050 if those people's grain consumption rates resemble present-day Indian ones, but only two and a half billion people if all of them consume grain at the rate of contemporary Americans. The presumed link between consumption rates and class privilege is hardly new. At the dawn of the industrial age, a thinker of some importance wrote that the society he knew best was endangering itself by food and clothing consumption rates that it could not sustain; what was needed was for the elite of this society to control themselves better, by practicing greater consumer restraint. The thinker in question, who sounds not unlike the contemporary American catastrophist Lester Brown, was actually Hong Liangji (1746–1809), a Chinese scholar official of the Qing dynasty. In the West, catastrophe theory can be traced back to the Bible; but perhaps its time has arrived.

Land-poor countries that can afford to do so are trying to stave off food supply crises by outsourcing their agriculture. Kuwait, Qatar, Abu Dhabi, and the United Arab Emirates, but also South Korea and China, have bought or leased millions of hectares of arable land in such African countries as Madagascar, Zambia, and Mozambique to allow their agribusinesses to escape the consequences of dwindling farmland and real or potential water shortages at home. Outsourcing has an obvious resemblance to an old strategy of European colonialism. As early as the sixteenth and seventeenth centuries, for example, English advocates of the colonization of Ireland or Virginia saw such colonies as places for crop experimentation and for the export of "people poor and seditious." Global modernity, as Arif Dirlik has argued, does not necessarily end colonialism so much as "deepen" and "reconfigure" it.[23]

Agrarian catastrophe thinkers' grim forebodings raise questions about more than just the future security of the human food supply. Also at stake is the future of a particular dream of convergence among the world's peoples, a "positivist theory of modernization," traceable to the eighteenth-century Western Enlightenment. This theory proposed that all civilizations would gradually adopt the same general, rational, scientific, and liberal thought that industrialization required and would see their own future evolution by looking into a Western mirror.[24] Just what would happen to those parts of the non-Western world that failed plausibly to see themselves in a Western mirror was left unclear. Western critics of this convergence doctrine, at least in the 1800s, tended to be racists. One London anthropological review in 1865, calling the Chinese people a "naturally non-progressive race," claimed that they were utterly incapable of rising to Western standards of historical achievement.[25]

After World War II, the economist Alexander Gerschenkron reinforced the convergence dream by arguing that "backward" countries could industrialize more rapidly than their Western prototypes by borrowing the more "advanced" countries' technologies. Gerschenkron conceded that the backward countries would need a powerful "ideology of delayed industrialization" to make the pains of industrialization easier to accept, such as "Saint Simonianism" or Marxism.[26] Ironically, his own theory about the history-accelerating management of borrowed technology came, in many places, to take on aspects of such an encouraging ideology.

Now, however, innovative economists in China and elsewhere, for example Wen Tiejun, are concluding that the narrow thought of Western agricultural economics cannot guide the future of China's 50,000 township governments, 700,000 administrative villages, and millions of surviving natural villages. Worse, the faith that it could inhibits a freer Chinese experimentation with new questions and answers concerning the future of farming.[27] If this is true, the world faces more than just the challenge of overcoming the global vested interests whose behavior threatens to create food shortages. It also faces the challenge of how to reorient human reasoning about economic development in the aftermath of the rise of the "planet of slums."

Such a reorientation would obviously call into question the persistence of an arbitrary and prejudiced definition of what is "modern" in human evolution. This definition, as much extraeconomic as economic, predates the industrial revolution. Ever since the 1500s, Western thinking about evolution has usually defined "modern" as being in a necessary opposition to all sorts of exotic nonmodern otherness, variously categorized as primitive, savage, Oriental, static, or underdeveloped. Unindustrialized farm producers with limited educations have, therefore, been readily conflated with aboriginals; both groups are seen as premodern anachronisms. (A French writer named Marie-Hélène Lafon illustrated this point perfectly in 2007, when she published a novel about France's remaining peasants, explicitly referring to them in the novel's title as "The Last Indians.")[28] The definition could be called an ideology even, in the sense that it confuses empirical truths with normative prescriptions and hides the violence it directs toward peasants behind a front of supposed objectivity.

But such a reorientation would also need critically to examine something else. That would be the nature of the global impact, including its unintended consequences, of a cult of managerialism, the supposed "management sciences." Ever since the American invention of that remarkable term "scientific management" about the year 1910, the world's expanding class of industrial and academic managers has had a vested interest in promoting the arbitrary and prejudiced definition of "modern" just mentioned. After World War II, the managers, both in Soviet bloc countries and in capitalist democracies, promoted the gospel of big farms, which were thought to lend themselves better to intensified techniques of farm mechanization that would economize the use of human labor. They had less interest in the obvious fact that people-land ratios differed greatly in Asia, Africa, and parts of Latin America from those of the Euro-American developmental ideal.

Big farms are a manager's paradise. Small farms—especially small farming enterprises that are fragmented enough to allow the distribution of land to as many members of the community as possible—resist managers. They especially resist managers' passion for standardization, which the industrial revolution generated. Yet even W. Arthur Lewis, the great theorist of dualism, warned that small farms were not, from the view of modern economics, necessarily irrational. Small farmers cultivated the land more intensively than big farmers. They worked harder than hired agricultural workers. And by not requiring managers, they avoided wasteful conflicts between management and its employees.[29]

ENDING THE PEASANTRY AS A MANAGERIAL DREAM

In the twentieth century, at least two different global conferences were planned simply to discuss the matter of how to get rid of "peasants" to embrace "modernity." The first conference was an imaginary one. But it was no less instructive for that. H. G. Wells, the British socialist and science fiction writer, dreamed it up in a 1930s book he wrote called *The Shape of Things to Come*. Wells said that his book was intended to be a short history of the future, from 1929 (the beginning of the world economic depression) to 2105. Wells predicted that the global "Hoover slump" would last from 1930 to 1960, causing the near collapse of many major Western institutions (Harvard University, for example, would degenerate into the condition of a medieval Tibetan lamasery, whose students would have to grow food and make clothes for their teachers: a severe test of faculty-student relations). But Wells hoped that omniscient scientists and engineers, whom he favored, would finally triumph in the 1960s and would climax their victory by holding a conference in Basra, Iraq. Wells wrote that the purpose of this Basra conference should be to assemble "socialistic technicians" from all over the world, so that they could deal with the "primordial peasant civilization which had been the basis of all the barbaric civilizations of the past." The conference would take up "the question of the expropriation of the peasant . . . at the point where Lenin and Stalin had laid it down, defeated." Once peasants had been expropriated, a world state would emerge, Wells fantasized, that would be "socialistic, cosmopolitan, and creative."[30]

The second conference was actually held, in Babelsberg, East Germany in 1977. It amounted to something of a Soviet bloc version of Wells's fictional Basra meeting. The members of this agricultural development conference were law professors and economists drawn from East Germany, the Soviet Union, Hungary, Bulgaria, Poland, Czechoslovakia, and Vietnam, little more than a decade before the Soviet bloc disappeared. The conference stipulated that the basic principle of agricultural growth in socialist conditions was to bring the methods of industrial production to farming. Industry and agriculture should be integrated, through state-run agroindustrial management forms. This integration was not as simple as it seemed. The conference recognized that if industrial production methods were transposed to farming, typical industrial management questions that had previously been unimaginable in peasant villages would now have to be addressed. Questions such as, what sorts of wages should farming people be paid? How many hours of rest should their managers allow them? What types of recreation should they be permitted, and at what age should they be allowed to retire?

The 1977 conference concluded that the complex laws to cover these new questions, once farming was managed industrially, should be created by the councils of ministers of the Soviet bloc countries but in agreement with the ideas of the Soviet Union's Ministry of Agriculture.[31] Peasants scattered from eastern Europe to Vietnam's Mekong Delta were therefore to be subject to a transcontinental legal monoculture, directed from the Union of Soviet Socialist Republics, in which the notion that small food producers might make any creative contribution of their own to growing food, without managerial supervision, was not considered. Is this old Soviet bloc conference merely an eccentric memory from a failed and vanished world? Or is it a distorted funhouse mirror reflection of the world's contemporary farming, with the legal monoculture of the World Trade Organization and its Codex Alimentarius Commission replacing that of the Soviet Ministry of Agriculture?

It is true that some economists have seen elite planners' peasant bashing as little more than an intellectual mistake. In a classic work about the transformation of "traditional" agriculture, published in 1964, Theodore W. Schultz attacked his fellow economists' assumption that one-quarter of the agricultural work force in low-income countries was redundant and should thus be available for urbanization at no cost except the costs of transfer. This "shaky" theory, Schultz wrote, originated in the "bad statistical estimates" generated by the dubious "game" of treating farming as if it could be organized like industry, and thus offer its workers year-round employment, ten hours a day, with no regard for agriculture's peculiar seasonality.

For Schultz, this "game" had distorted elite understanding of farming as early as the global economic depression of the 1930s. Economists then had contrasted the spectacular mass unemployment they saw among Western industrial factory workers with the much less visible unemployment they saw among non-Western farming people. From this contrast, it was treacherously easy to conclude, Schultz wrote, that if non-Western peasants continued to work, at a time of mass industrial unemployment in the West itself, the farm work they were doing must have "a marginal productivity of zero value."[32] Mistakes among Western economists are no laughing matter for the rest of the planet. As the specialists at a 2004 Hangzhou conference about farm management pointed out, the "central subjects of attention" of international agricultural economics are still chosen in the "developed countries" and then transmitted to researchers in the "developing world," more confirmation of Dirlik's theme of globalization as the reconfiguration of colonialism.[33]

But stereotypical thought about peasants is not merely an intellectual mistake. And economists are as subject as everybody else, not just to their own "games" but to the influences of the value divisions in Western history, now spread to the rest of the world. Here, the crucial division between liberalism and socialism on the one hand, associated with Enlightenment Project rationalism and science worship, competes with romanticism and its modern derivatives, some of them pathological, on the other hand. For romanticism and its descendant movements, Enlightenment Project rationalism and the sciences that come with it may seem repressive and alienating.

Even Mike Davis's frightening book about the "planet of slums" belongs to a literary genre. It is the genre that treats the modern city as a sort of moral and economic cancer. In the 1800s, Fyodor Dostoyevsky pioneered the approach with his literary depiction of St. Petersburg as a planned monument to Enlightenment rationalism. Dostoyevsky saw it as a degenerate monument, whose streets were full of murderers, drunkards, and prostitutes. Another version of the capitalist city as cancerous, as a malignancy that devoured the countryside, might be found in T. S. Eliot's famous 1922 poem "The Waste Land."[34] Both Dostoyevsky and Eliot idealized the preindustrial agrarian order and what Davis revealingly and romantically calls its "subsistence solidarities." Unlike Davis, both also thought the solution to the horror of urbanization lay in a return to medieval religion, whether Russian Orthodoxy for Dostoyevsky or Anglo-Catholicism for Eliot. That was because—as the British scholar Raymond Williams put it in a classic work in 1973—such writers were predisposed to attribute the loss of meaning, as capitalist urbanization spread, to the loss of God.[35] How, then, do we distinguish between important wake-up calls of Davis's type, to save our slum-ridden periurbanized planet, and the literary genre of the capitalist city as hell, which rules out the possibility that some peasants at least might want to escape the countryside and move to the cities?

The confusion between developmental economics and ideology worsened in the twentieth century. Fascists, communists, and capitalist utopians pushed the old disagreements about the Enlightenment Project beyond all previous limits. Fascism absorbed and militarized the peasantry-loving traditions of European romanticism, which had seen peasants as embodiments of the national heritage. In the 1930s, Richard Walther Darre, Hitler's Minister of Food and Agriculture in Nazi Germany from 1933 to 1942, preached the need for more natural methods of land management and animal breeding. By such methods, peasants' local knowledge would be selectively encouraged, rather than condemned wholesale by industrial capitalists. This sounded like reasonable environmentalism. But it had a sinister side. Darre was a vicious racist; he was involved in eugenics practices that led to mass murder; and he was the author of German books with titles like "the peasantry as life-source of the Nordic race." Other European countries, under German control, tried to fit in with the Nazi love of tribalism and rural communalism. The Vichy regime in France, for example, celebrated French unity under "the peasant Marshal" Petain.

With the globalization of Fascist influences, the belief that the soil, and farming people of the traditional kind, were the source of good collective racial and political health, spread to Asia. Tojo Hideki, Japan's wartime prime minister and military leader from 1941 to 1944, provided perhaps the most extravagant example. In 1943 Tojo told the Japanese Diet that Japan's very foundations lay in farming, and that "I am determined to maintain the population of the villages at forty percent" of the Japanese whole.[36]

Should we then be surprised that the enemies of Fascism, socialist or liberal, should have reverted, after they had won the war, to the prewar H. G. Wells view that peasants were the basis of "barbaric" civilizations? Some members of the winning anti-Fascist cause even associated rural people with the ready implementation of Nazi genocide. The German exile philosopher Theodor W. Adorno, in an essay titled "Education after Auschwitz" in 1967, repeated the claim that the "tormentors" of Hitler's concentration camps "were for the most part young sons of farmers." Therefore, Adorno asserted, one of the most important goals of post-Auschwitz education in Europe should be "the debarbarization of the countryside."[37] Meanwhile, capitalist futurologists in the United States, like Alvin Toffler, depicted agricultural civilization as simple, authoritarian, and heredity-based, in which "windmills creaked in the fields"; Toffler praised the American Civil War for marking the victory of northern "industrializers" over southern "farmers."[38]

In Asia itself, anti-Fascist nationalists who wished to decolonize their countries could rarely think of economic progress in terms that were independent of the wish for cultural modernization. For them, industry was progressive and conformed to the laws of evolution; farming was "traditional" and had little capacity by itself to evolve toward the modern. As the young Chinese Marxist Qu Qiubai put it in 1924, in a tract devoted to "A General Discussion of Social Science," people who proposed that China should try to be a farming country were defending China's "eternally unchanging" patriarchal despotism and were simply putting the Chinese people into a wooden prisoners' cage.[39] The Sino-Japanese War of 1937–1945 heightened this fear. In 1937, the young Chinese economist Sun Yefang warned his readers that the Japanese empire wished to preserve China as an agricultural satellite, so it could supply raw cotton to industrial Japan's textile factories. Therefore, for China to fail to industrialize would be to surrender to Japanese imperialism.[40]

Similar views could be found elsewhere in Asia. In postcolonial India, according to the Indian sociologist Satish Deshpande, Gandhian economic thought, which had prized the value of farming, was soon eclipsed by the faith that only modern industry could unite the diverse peoples of India into a cohesive nation. Indeed, postcolonial Indian rulers believed that giant dams and giant steel plants were precisely the sorts of monuments that could make the new Indian nation-state visible, in ways that small farms could not.[41]

ENDING THE PEASANTRY AS A MANAGERIAL PROJECT

From H. G. Wells's wish in the 1930s that the peasantry should disappear, the world moved in the 1960s to the discovery by some policy-making social scientists that the peasantry had disappeared, at least in historically favored countries. But to what extent was the Wellsian wish that they should disappear the father of this discovery that they had disappeared, and the optimistic worldview that accompanied it?

In 1967, French sociologist Henri Mendras (1927–2003) published an influential book whose very title—*The End of the Peasants* (*La Fin des Paysans*)—epitomized this whole worldview of postwar modernization theory. Mendras argued that, after 1945, French peasants rapidly changed for the better, into innovative specialists and business people. The massive rural exodus that had accompanied this change was restoring a more "balanced" situation to the French countryside, and France was now seeing the birth of a new, more professional "rural bourgeoisie." This new rural bourgeoisie would place economic and technical arguments ahead of the moral and political debates that had convulsed public life for far too long in France's preindustrial, prescientific past.[42] In making this point, Mendras was clearly—despite his excellent empirical analysis—echoing Cold War hopes, expressed more fully in other "end of" gospels like those concerning ideology and history, that postpeasant rural industrialization would abolish class conflict. Thus, the danger of revolution would fade.

The Mendras theme of the "end of the peasantry" only reinforced a norm-creating global ideology that was already in place. This ideology celebrated bigger, more factory-like farms, whose success was to be measured by increases in labor productivity, not by increases in land productivity. The Massachusetts Institute of Technology Comparative Politics Program quickly translated Mendras's book into English in 1970. The purpose of the translation was revealed in the forward to the book written by the American political scientist Daniel Lerner. Lerner had previously written his own book (1958) about the coming of modernization to Turkey, in which he contrasted the "agrarian, illiterate, isolate life of the Anatolian village" with the millions of Turks who had escaped from it and "now live in towns, work in shops, and have opinions."[43] Lerner, it has been said, was a "nation-building" ideologue during the Kennedy-Johnson Indochina War era in the United States. Now, Lerner praised Mendras's book about the end of the French peasantry, for proving the rightness of the global "thrust toward modernity" being led by the United States. Lerner added that American farmers themselves could feed "hungry humanity around the globe" if this thrust toward modernity had any immediately negative effects on the world food supply.[44]

Lerner's aside about American farmers indirectly raised an awkward question. What would happen to the dream of the end of the peasantry (plausible enough in postwar France) when the dream got transferred to non-Western countries with utterly different people-land ratios and resource conditions?

The Chinese Science Publishers brought out Li Peilin's Chinese language translation of Henri Mendras's book in 1991. Referring to it in 2006, two Chinese agrarian sociologists concluded that Chinese political leaders would have to make the Mendras transformation come true in China. That is, the Chinese state would need actively to create Chinese copies of Mendras's postwar French rural bourgeoisie. This could be done if the government intervened to choose the "outstanding elements" (*youxiu fenzi*) in Chinese villages and then converted them into "new model farmers" skilled in science, management, and entrepreneurship. There would be no need to change the bulk of the Chinese peasantry into new model farmers; many of them were women and old people anyway, and the new creative minority of superior "outstanding elements" would gradually extend their influence over them.[45] This proposal, whatever its merits, conjures up memories of the old prerevolutionary rural gentry elite of China before 1949, once thought to be an obstacle to progress.

Meanwhile, whatever Mendras's original intentions, the now globalized notion of "the end of the peasantry" functions as another means of legitimizing the world's big multinational agribusinesses. Under their regime, farming people are driven into an unprecedentedly severe competition with each other, with the losers being driven out of farming.

Who are the losers? They include American family farmers. As the president of the U.S. National Family Farm Coalition pointed out in 2006, "the American people would not have chosen the type of agriculture we have, diminishing numbers of family farms being replaced by large, chemical-intensive crop farms and polluting, factory-farm livestock operations."[46] The losers also include Latin American union leaders like the Brazilian Chico Mendes, murdered in 1988 for defending the Amazon rainforest, and the rubber tappers in his union, against large cattle ranching operations bent upon deforestation.[47] And the losers include the Thai villagers, threatened by pulp and paper agribusinesses' ambition to replace old forests by fast-growing eucalyptus trees, who try to save their older trees by "ordaining" the trees with yellow robes, sacralizing them as if they were Buddhist monks.[48]

The power of the multinational agribusinesses, in turn, demonstrates their skill at transcending or concealing the innate contradiction between the two postwar global orthodoxies after 1945. These are neoliberal economics on the one hand, supposedly devoted to freer markets, and the manipulative "management sciences," intoxicated by the prospect of expanding the use of the principles of industrial organization, which were thought to have shown their prowess in winning two world wars, on the other hand.

Of all the members of the vast army of Western management sciences gurus after 1945, none is more interesting, because of his candor about the contradiction between the two orthodoxies, than the late Herbert Simon (1916–2001), winner of the Nobel Prize in Economic Sciences in 1978. Simon scoffed at neoliberal economists who ignored "the central role of organizations in economic life," by preferring to analyze markets. Most economic producers did, and should do, their producing within the boundaries of behavior-improving organizations. Yet fashionable economic theory, Simon observed, presented only a "caricature" of this necessary fact, unjustly magnifying the importance of markets and falsely depicting the business firms engaged in marketing as "rudimentary entrepreneurs." Simon praised big organizations. He proposed that they were the perfect antidote to the necessarily limited or "bounded" rationality of individual human beings.[49] Simon's hidden assumption that organization alone could achieve "unbounded" rationality was not very remote from Lenin's faith in a vanguard political party, even if, unlike Lenin, Herbert Simon believed in competing organizations, not in a one-party dictatorship.

Schizoid worldviews, such as the one that combines both neoliberal economics and the passion for management, can survive for a surprisingly long time before their contradictions betray them. Witness Western colonialism in Asia before 1945 and its juxtaposition of an Enlightenment Project "civilizing" mission for everyone with pervasive racial discrimination. But small food producers, in all their immense historical variety, have become a sort of imaginative black hole in managerial or would-be managerial societies whose elites are programmed to think in terms of big organizations, industrial workers, and supermarket-dependent consumers.

The black hole has kept expanding since 1945, as management theory has evolved. Postwar management theory has pretended—as one of its basic defenses of its approach to labor control—that prewar Fordist factory organization was a tyranny. Postwar managers have heralded their new philosophy of "flexible management" as a step toward the greater "democratization" of industrial production. (The first Global Conference on Flexible Systems Management was held in New Delhi in December 2000 on the theme "New Business Paradigm: Global, Virtual, and Flexible.") The real rationale of "flexible management" lies elsewhere. The theory has at least three tasks. The first is to manage the satisfaction of increasingly varied consumer expectations such as did not exist in the depression-ridden period before World War II. The second is to serve the needs of computer-using engineers in rapidly fine-tuning production lines of goods, given the varied consumer expectations. And the third is to explain away the insecurities of work forces made redundant by the greater global mobility of capital. Managing workers themselves was the main interest of management theory before 1945. Managing consumers has increasingly become its obsession more recently. And the transition from worker-oriented managerialism to consumer-oriented managerialism affects peasants adversely. It reflects two historical forces. The first is the emergence of the most far-flung consumer plutocracy in history, ranging from Mumbai millionaires to Russian oil tycoons. The second is the global population boom after 1950, which has made consumers more important and the search for incentives to inspire workers—many of whom are ex-peasants—less necessary, given their greater numerical availability and weaker bargaining positions—hence the misery of Mike Davis's slums.[50]

The states that govern peasants in this increasingly managed world, far from becoming weaker, have merely changed their functions. National elites use the global regulatory mechanisms as much as being used by them, "internationalizing" domestic policy questions in order to overcome domestic vested interests (including the remaining peasantry) of which they disapprove.[51] In the mid-1990s, for example, the United

States had a federal Department of Agriculture with 120,000 or so employees, devoted to implementing government price support plans, directing markets, providing extension services, and increasing international "cooperation"; the fifty American states also had their bureaus of agriculture; and the U.S. Congress, between the 1930s and the 1990s, passed a new agriculture law on average once every five years. Whatever else it might be, this was not the apparatus of a state that wished to practice "free" trade.[52] And few of the poorer Asian and African and Latin American countries can afford to copy the farm management apparatuses of the post-1945 Western and Japanese states on an equal basis, even if they are able, by sheer elite willpower, to turn the "end of the peasantry" from a desired norm into a real-life fact, by stimulating big migrations of rural people into the cities.

In the recent past, the modern bureaucratic state legitimized itself in part by its claims effectively to control contagious human diseases. With the era of the World Trade Organization, this self-legitimizing state control function has extended into farming to protect the international food trade against subversion by "filth," pesticide residues, microbiological contaminations, and mold, in line with the WTO's Codex General Principles of Food Hygiene. But the new managerialism goes far beyond food hygiene. Some states now accept as part of their function the standardization of their domestic farm crops, in line with the demands of big international supermarket chains. The standardization includes the reduction of crop varieties to promote supposed economies of scale and to lower the "market risks" of new products.

The futurologist Alvin Toffler once predicted that the coming "Third Wave" civilization would replace old-fashioned industrial standardization by something Toffler called "the post-standardized mind."[53] No such "mind" is in sight. The goal of such new global management procedures in farming as "farm animal tracking systems" or "documentary files farming" that can trace the whole history of a farm product and the inputs of chemical fertilizers into it may be to safeguard international consumer safety, but such procedures also provide the basis for the emergence of an unprecedented bureaucratic surveillance over food producers. Could any real believer in market freedom, from Adam Smith to Friedrich Hayek, ever have anticipated the authoritarian consequences of an extreme marketing competitiveness doctrine married to the global managerial culture? The danger is that the crop standardization that is occurring at an accelerating rate will lead us back, by a circular process, to the old colonial rice or rubber monocultures, or to the Stalinist overconcentration, in the Soviet bloc, on grain and cotton production. But small food producers are the least readily standardized of people. For this reason, it is not difficult to see why the new managerial civilization welcomes the "end of the peasantry."

NOTES

1. Annette Aurelie Desmarais, "The Via Campesina: Consolidating an international peasant and farm movement," *Journal of Peasant Studies* 29.2 (January 2002): 91–124.

2. Peter F. Drucker, *The Essential Drucker* (New York: Collins Business Edition, 2005), 7.

3. Yin Chengjie, "*Nongye guojihua jingzheng yu tigao woguo nongye guoji jingzhengli* [Agriculture's internationalized competition and the promotion of the international competitiveness of our country's agriculture]," *Nongye jingji wenti* [*Problems of Agricultural Economy*] 1 (2003): 5–10.

4. Ge Maochun et al., *Wuzhengfu zhuyi sixiang ziliaoxuan* [Selected documents of anarchist thought] (Beijing: Beijing daxue chubanshe, 1984), 2 volumes, I: 108–114.

5. Gong Guanyu, "*Tigong 90 yi renkou suoxu de liangshi* [Providing the food that is needed for nine billion people]," *Weilai yu fazhan* [Future and development] 4 (1999): 21–23.

6. E. J. Hobsbawm, *Industry and Empire* (London: Penguin Books, 1968), 157–158.

7. Hu Hengyang, "*Meiguo nongye he zhengfu nongye zhengce* [American agriculture and government agricultural policies]," *Zhongguo nongcun jingji* [*Chinese rural economy*] 6 (1996): 75–79; Wang Dongjing, "*Xifang fazhan shi yimian jingzi* [Western development is a mirror], *Nongye jingji wenti* 6 (2004): 69–74.

8. Tony Judt, *Postwar: A History of Europe since 1945* (London: Penguin Books, 2005), 516–517; Mark Mazower, *The Balkans: A Short History* (New York: The Modern Library, 2002), 134–136.

9. Xu Pinghua, "*Woguo nongcun shengyu laodongli zhuanyi fenxi* [An analysis of the transfer of our country's surplus rural labor force]," *Nongye jingji wenti* 6 (2006): 39–42.

10. E. J. Hobsbawm, *Age of Extremes: The Short Twentieth Century, 1914–1991* (London: Abacus, 1995), 289.

11. Charles W. Hayford, "What's so bad about 'The Good Earth'?," *Education About Asia* (Winter 1998): online.

12. Han Xiaorong, *Chinese Discourses on the Peasant, 1900–1945* (Albany, NY: State University of New York Press, 2005), 4.

13. A. N. Agarwala and S. P. Singh, *The Economics of Underdevelopment* (New York: Galaxy Books, 1963), 408; W. Arthur Lewis, *The Theory of Economic Growth* (Homewood, IL: Richard D. Irwin, 1955), 29–32.

14. Tom Brass, "Latin American peasants: New paradigms for old?," *Journal of Peasant Studies*, 29.3–4 (April–July 2002): 1–40.

15. Tania Li, *Transforming the Indonesian Uplands* (Amsterdam: Harwood Academic Publishers, 1999), xvii.

16. Hobsbawm, *Age of Extremes*, 291.

17. Sun Tao and Huang Guangming, "*Nongcun shehui yanglao baoxian yunxing moshi goujian ji chuangxin yanjiu* [Researching the establishment and innovation of operational models of village society old age insurance]," *Nongye jingji wenti* 1 (2007): 51–55.

18. Chen Xiwen, "*Yinggai renzhen yanjiu nongcun xianshi wenti* [We should study seriously the real problems of the villages]," *Nongye jingji wenti* 4 (2007): 4–8.

19. Anthony W. Pereira, *The End of the Peasantry: The Rural Labor Movement in Northeast Brazil, 1961–1988* (Pittsburgh, PA: University of Pittsburgh Press, 1997), 158.

20. Mike Davis, *Planet of Slums* (London: Verso, 2006), 16–19, 201.

21. Ibid., 19, 33.

22. Gong, "*Weilai yu fazhan*," op. cit.; Lester R. Brown, *Tough Choices: Facing the Challenge of Food Scarcity* (New York: W. W. Norton, 1996); Bruno Parmentier, *Nourrir l'humanite* (Paris: LaDecouverte, 2007).

23. Arif Dirlik, *Global Modernity: Modernity in the Age of Global Capitalism* (Boulder, CO: Paradigm Publishers, 2007), 97–98.

24. John Gray, *Enlightenment's Wake: Politics and Culture at the Close of the Modern Age* (London: Routledge, 1995), 65.

25. Stuart Creighton Miller, *The Unwelcome Immigrant: The American Image of the Chinese, 1785–1882* (Berkeley: University of California Press, 1969), 158.

26. Alexander Gerschenkron, *Economic Backwardness in Historical Perspective* (Cambridge, MA: Harvard University Press, 1969), 8–9, 24–26.

27. Wen Tiejun, *Zhongguo nongcun jiben jingji zhidu yanjiu [A study of the basic economic systems of Chinese villages]* (Beijing: Zhongguo jingji chubanshe, 2000), 22–23.

28. Marie-Hélène Lafon, *Les derniers Indiens* (Paris: Buchet-Chastel, 2007).

29. Lewis, *The Theory of Economic Growth*, 133–136.

30. H. G. Wells, *The Shape of Things to Come* (New York: MacMillan, 1936), 277, 282, 430.

31. Quang Nhu, "*Mot so van de phap ly qua hoi nghi quoc te ve luat nong nghiep hop o CHDC Duc* [Some legal questions encountered at the international conference on farming laws held in the German Democratic Republic]," *Luat hoc* [*Legal Studies*] 4 (1977): 38–41.

32. Theodore W. Schultz, *Transforming Traditional Agriculture* (New Haven: Yale University Press, 1964), 54–70.

33. Dirlik, *Global Modernity*, 97–98; Chen Suijun, "*Nongye jingji guanli xueke qianyan* [The forward positions in the subject of agricultural economy management]," *Nongye jingji wenti* 6 (2004): 75–76.

34. Richard Lehan, *The City in Literature* (Berkeley: University of California Press, 1998), 123–137.

35. Raymond Williams, *The Country and the City* (London: Paladin Books, 1975), 9, 280–296.

36. Maruyama Masao, *Thought and Behavior in Modern Japanese Politics*, ed. Ivan Morris (Oxford, UK: Oxford University Press, 1968), 47.

37. Theodor W. Adorno, *Critical Models: Interventions and Catchwords*, trans. Henry W. Pickford (New York: Columbia University Press, 1998), 195–196.

38. Alvin Toffler, *The Third Wave* (London: Pan Books, 1981), 35–51.

39. Zhuang Fuling, *Zhongguo Makesizhuyi zhexue chuanbo shi [A history of the dissemination of Marxist philosophy in China]* (Beijing: Zhongguo Renmin daxue chubanshe, 1988), 197.

40. Sun Yefang, *Guanyu Zhongguo shehui ji qi geming xingshi de ruogan lilun wenti [Some theoretical questions related to Chinese society and its revolutionary nature]* (Beijing: Zhongguo shehui kexue chubanshe, 1985), 180–188.

41. Satish Deshpande, *Contemporary India: A Sociological View* (New Delhi: Penguin Books, 2003), 65–69.

42. Henri Mendras, *La Fin des Paysans* (Arles: Actes Sud, 1984), 12–14, 291–315.

43. Daniel Lerner, *The Passing of Traditional Society* (New York: The Free Press, 1958), 46.

44. Henri Mendras, *The Vanishing Peasant: Innovation and Change in French Agriculture*, trans. Jean Lerner (Cambridge, MA: The MIT Press, 1970); Michael Latham, *Modernization as Ideology: American Social Science and "Nation-building" in the Kennedy Era* (Chapel Hill: University of North Carolina Press, 2000).

45. Lu Kerong and Zhu Qizhen, "*Shehui zhuyi xin nongcun jianshe yu xinxing nongmin peiyang* [The construction of socialist new villages and the training of new model farmers]," *Weilai yu fazhan* 9 (2006): 27–29.

46. Peter M. Rosset, *Food Is Different: Why We Must Get the WTO Out of Agriculture* (London: Zed Books, 2006), xvi.

47. Pereira, *The End of the Peasantry*, 103.

48. Chris Baker and Pasuk Phongpaichit, *A History of Thailand* (Cambridge: Cambridge University Press, 2005), 214–215.

49. Herbert Simon et al., *Economics, Bounded Rationality and the Cognitive Revolution* (Aldershot, England: Edward Elgar, 1992), 3–6.

50. For a Chinese view, see Yang Jixiong and Wu Jianzu, "*Rouxing guanli: 21 shiji zhiye guanli xin moshi* [Flexible management: The new twenty-first century model of business enterprise management]," *Weilai yu fazhan* 6 (2001): 49–51.

51. Philip McMichael, "World food system restructuring under a GATT regime," *Political Geography* (May 1993): 198–214, 202–204.

52. Hu, "*Meiguo nongye he zhengfu nongye zhengce,*" op. cit.

53. Toffler, *The Third Wave*, 264.

Chapter 3

The Return of the Peasant: Possible? Desirable?

Immanuel Wallerstein

I start with an anecdote and a report made by the United Nations in 2007. The anecdote is this: Recently, I told a European friend that I was going to attend a conference organized around the issue of the future of the peasant. I said to him, "if you were to give me a one-sentence summary of your view on this, what would it be?" He said, "The future of the peasant is the city." His, of course, is the traditional answer of world social science. Almost everyone agrees. And yet a hardy band of academics, especially those who actually study agrarian zones, contest this view as simplistic and misleading—many insist that the most salient feature of the last several hundred years is the survival of the peasant.

Recently, however, the United Nations Population Fund (UNFPA) issued a report entitled "State of World Population 2007: Unleashing the Potential of Urban Growth." Its opening sentences read as follows:

> In 2008, the world reaches an invisible but momentous milestone: For the first time in history, more than half the human population, 3.3 billion people, will be living in urban areas. By 2030, this is expected to swell to almost 5 billion.

This pronouncement about the definitive de-ruralization of the world seems to lend some credence to the traditional view of world social science.

We all know the two factors that have propelled this long-developing trend toward de-ruralization. One is the development of technology that has made it possible to augment the productivity of food production such that it requires a far smaller percentage of the population to engage in this production than had been true for thousands of years, despite the growth in overall world population. This factor is the result of a combination of substituting machines for labor, the development of chemical aids to expanding output, and the advantages of large-scale units of production.

The second factor is that, over the centuries, a growing proportion of erstwhile rural dwellers have found it economically more advantageous to move to urban areas, even when they live as a result in vast urban slums, than to remain in the rural areas. It is irrelevant whether this constant and massive rural-to-urban migration has been the result of someone forcing the rural population off the land or of their choosing on their own to leave the rural zones.

Is there any reason to believe that these two factors will cease to be true in the relatively near future or even that they will be slowed down? The UNFPA doesn't think so. Its report concentrates, therefore, on what can be done to aid the expanding urban populations by getting the world to do three things: "respect . . . the rights of the poor," "reduce poverty and promote sustainability," and "support . . . community organizations, social movements, governments and the international community in improving the nature and form of future urban expansion. . . ."

It seems clear to me that this process of de-ruralization has been a central feature of capitalism as a world-system throughout its history. It seems equally clear to me that both the analytic and organizational reopening of the reality and merits of this process have been part and parcel of opposition to what are regarded as the negative features of capitalism as a system. It requires us, therefore, not merely to place these issues in a developing historical context but to tease apart exactly who has benefited from this process and in what specific ways.

Let us start by looking at the early days of the modern world-system, the long sixteenth century during which capitalist agriculture emerged as a central feature of the modern world-system, one that was limited at the time to large areas of the European continent plus certain parts of the Americas. We observe a system in which many producers in rural areas began for the first time to sell their products on a world market for profit.

These early capitalist agrarian enterprises had many different modes of labor control. In eastern Europe and in the Americas, the enterprises typically controlled relatively large areas and utilized coerced cash-crop labor. Far from de-ruralizing the zones, coercion was used to maintain the labor force within the rural enterprises. The land-controllers sought to prevent rural workers from escaping either to the cities or to unregulated frontier zones, because the productive processes were still labor-intensive and could not be successfully operated if the labor force began to disappear, especially since these were zones of low population density.

In other regions, notably various parts of southern Europe, enterprises typically remained relatively small. While large areas were, in theory, controlled by high-status persons, the actual units of production were operated by small unit holders, tenants who recompensed the large area holders via some form of sharecropping. The output of these small unit holders was often bought by merchants who grouped together export items and thereby profited from the advantages of large-scale market offerings. Here, too, there was no de-ruralization, not only because the production was labor-intensive but also because it was very much in the interest of the sharecroppers to maintain their extended family on the unit. Those who were the primary tenants were maintained in the rural areas by debt mechanisms from which it was difficult for them to escape.

In northwest Europe, the area that began to be the locus of growing capital accumulation, the picture was most complicated. We know that coercive mechanisms that tied laborers to the land began to diminish. We know also that arable production began to become more "efficient" in the sense that the output per acre increased. And we know that pasturage became ever more widespread. The result was indeed some de-ruralization. Let us try to trace how this happened.

In the economic downturn of the late Middle Ages, accompanied by, and in part caused by, the decline of population, this region of Europe saw an increase in the bargaining position of workers both in urban and rural areas. Faced with declining incomes, landowners had two main options. One was to convert some demesnes into leased land with money rents, which gave them more immediate income but involved a gradual transfer of control over the land. The second was the conversion of arable land to pasturage, which required less manpower. Since arable land was now scarcer, the quality of labor became more important to maintain production levels.

In terms of social structure, this need for quality labor resulted in the rise of the yeoman farmer, at the expense of both the large demesne holder and the landless laborer. It was these yeomen farmers who engaged in enclosures to create place for pasturage. The result, as the saying went, was that "sheep ate men." It also, of course, meant less land devoted to raising grain. With the economic and demographic expansion of the sixteenth century, however, the decline in the percentage of land devoted to arable production was compensated by both increased efficiency of production on arable land and grain imports from serf-produced grain from eastern Europe.

Labor could now be increasingly contractual in northwest Europe precisely because, unlike in eastern Europe and the Americas, there was a relatively large labor pool, which had therefore a weak bargaining position. Insofar as more efficient modes of production required more skilled labor but fewer laborers, there were now too many laborers, and landowners wished to rid themselves of the burden of these extra unskilled workers. Some workers left the rural areas because the enclosures made their survival more difficult; some were summarily ejected. They moved to the towns. Or they became vagabonds, and thereby tended to die young.

Yes, some were absorbed by urban industries, but industry was not the main factor in their leaving the rural areas. They were not being ejected to provide cheap manpower for the cities. They were being ejected to provide increased profits for the rural entrepreneurs. This was possible, indeed necessary, because northwest Europe was now located in a world-economy division of labor that made it possible to import grain from eastern Europe and thus permit the increasing specialization of northwest Europe's role in the agrarian production of the world-economy.

To sum up, what we have in the sixteenth-century European world-economy is the development of a division of labor among three different zones, in each of which agrarian production remained the central economic activity. However, the modes of labor control differed quite strikingly among the three zones. In two of them, there was no de-ruralization. On the contrary, the emphasis of the landowners and land-controllers was on keeping rural labor from leaving the land. However, in the third zone, which was the richest zone, a process of de-ruralization began, which, although it remained relatively small in total numbers, was a harbinger of things to come.[1]

The period between 1600 and 1750, unlike the sixteenth century, was one of long relative stagnation in the history of the capitalist world-economy. Once again, let us see what this did to rural labor in the broadest sense. The basic overriding economic reality was that there had occurred a world-economy-wide overproduction in the products that eastern Europe and the Americas had been exporting to northwest Europe. As a consequence, the exporters had to restructure their activities to maintain some profitability, albeit reduced. The basic response was an involution of their sales areas, turning to regional as opposed to world markets.

Since prices had gone down, the seigniors had to sell more if they wished to try to obtain the same level of income. The immediate consequence for the rural workers on the estates owned by seigniors in eastern Europe was an increase in their corvée obligations, such that they no longer had the time to raise products on their own lots. This had the double benefit of increasing the seignior's output while reducing that of the serfs as potential rivals on the regional markets. The net effect was an even harsher tying of the rural worker to his location in the rural zone.

At the same time, the reduction in exports to northwest Europe necessarily led to the reduction of industrial imports from there, for want of the needed money. So the seigniors turned to producing the formerly imported industrial items on their own estates, both to supply their needs and to increase income from local sales of these products. To do this, they had to encourage a movement of artisans from the eastern European towns to their estates. If anything, we saw an increase in the percentage of the population living in the rural areas as a result.

Similar increased pressure on the work requirements on the haciendas in the Americas led to a die-off of Amerindian populations. Therefore, to maintain a work force on the haciendas whose role was now actually expanding, they had to import labor to work in the rural areas. This was done in two main forms: slaves from Africa and indentured servants from northwest Europe. The slaves were, by definition, a coerced work force, who remained in rural areas, except for those who escaped to maroon communities in remote areas that were both rural and self-sufficient. As for the indentured workers, the main attraction for them, since they came with a certain degree of their own free will, was to be released of their bondage after a given number of years and to be rewarded with a small agrarian plot. Once again, the sum effect of all of this was to maintain a rural population at the same, if not greater, level than previously.

In the semiperipheral zones, we see a more complicated pattern. There was agricultural involution as in the periphery but there was also deindustrialization. Spain and Portugal survived by using their American bullion to obtain imports from northwest Europe. But at home, the rural populations remained on the land. In northern Italy, the southern and western Germanies, and the Austrian Netherlands (present-day Belgium)—none of which had bullion-producing colonies—there was instead an exodus of urban industries and artisans to rural areas in the so-called *Verlagssystem*. Artisanal producers worked in rural areas, where labor was cheaper, receiving raw materials from merchants/entrepreneurs who purchased their production at fixed prices. Some rural agricultural workers thereby shifted their employment part-time or full-time into urban-type employments relocated to rural zones. One of the consequences was the usurpation of communal fields, combined with a worsening of peasant exploitation on the land still used for arable production. This was not yet de-ruralization but it was for some de-peasantization.

The decline in world wheat prices in this period led to agricultural diversification, first in the United Provinces and then in England and northern France. In addition, there was a good deal of organizational restructuring, the use of additional fodder to improve efficiency of production, and assarting (bringing less productive lands into cultivation). Above all, there was the combination of arable with either viniculture or animal husbandry.

There was increasing concentration of units, primarily via the enclosure of commons, a method already begun previously. Some of this concentration has been called "bookkeeping centralization," since the units combined were not necessarily contiguous. At the same time, many of the largest land-controllers took to leasing more of their land, thereby increasingly becoming absentee landlords.

The story was different with smaller producers. The squeeze on wheat prices led the less successful ones to lose control of their units, whether they were independent owners or tenants. Others, however, survived and thrived by turning themselves into agents of the large landowners, becoming intermediaries who supervised both landless laborers and small subtenants. As this whole zone was increasing its percentage of world wheat production, there was reorganization of agricultural tenure but largely maintenance of rural populations in place by spreading them over larger areas.[2]

The second half of the eighteenth century and the first half of the nineteenth century marked a further great expansion of the boundaries of the capitalist world-economy, as four major regions that had previously been outside its division of labor were pulled into it—Russia, the Indian subcontinent, the Ottoman Empire, and west Africa. Although there were, of course, very important differences among these regions, their incorporation into the capitalist world-economy had remarkably parallel consequences for their agrarian zones.

Each of these zones saw a creation or expansion of cash-crop products, which were exported to core zones of the world-economy. In each of them, the economic units that engaged in such exports became larger via one of two ways. Landowners could create one variety or another of plantation structures, in which a single large owner had a large workforce at his disposal. Or the land could remain under the control of small unit holders, who sold their output to large merchant exporters and who were bound to these merchants by some form or other of debt bondage. In either case, the production became market responsive, shifting in accordance with the pressures of the world market.

On the Indian subcontinent, the major export crops were indigo, raw silk, opium, and cotton. In the Ottoman Empire, they were mohair yarn, raw silk, cotton, and cereals. In Russia, they were hemp, flax, and wheat. In West Africa, they were at first slaves but then palm oil and peanuts. In all of these zones, the level of exports went up considerably during this period.

One must be aware of what this kind of export-oriented production necessarily meant for agrarian structures. Three things happened. A considerable amount of acreage that had been previously devoted to locally consumed food production had now to be devoted to these crops. In the second place, the workers located in these areas had now to obtain part or all of their food from other acreage that became devoted to specialized food production sold to workers in the export-crop zone to sustain them. And since both the export cash-crop areas and the areas producing food for sale to the first set of areas needed more manpower than they had needed when they produced locally consumed food crops, there had to be a third set of areas that exported workers to the first two zones.

In addition, as has been regularly pointed out, there was a process of deindustrialization in all these four zones, partly under duress and partly because of the profitability to plantation owners and large merchant purveyors of using these areas for cash-crop production. For the most part, this was a shift in the occupational patterns in rural areas.

From the point of view of the agricultural workers, they had less time and less land on which to produce goods for themselves and their well-being. They typically had to work longer hours per day, more days per year, in a system that increased the amount of coercion to remain on the land.[3]

The whole early period of the capitalist world-economy involved a steady reorganization of the tenure systems in rural areas and, over time, a steady reduction in food production for local household consumption. It also involved, in an irregular pattern, the growth of larger-scale units of production or of marketing structures in which the producers were tied to the marketer by debt mechanisms. It did not involve, in this early period, a de-ruralization of the world to any significant extent.

This began to change with a revision of the mode of displacement in times of economic contraction. It had always been the case, long before there was a capitalist world-economy, that there had been an urban-rural alternation between economic upswings and downswings in the location of industrial production. The advantage of an urban location is the advantage of lower transactions costs. The disadvantage of an urban location is that the concentration of workers permits the growth at least of guild spirit, if not of guild structures, which slowly but surely raises the bargaining power of the workforce.

As long as times are good and the producers can find buyers with relative ease, the rising cost of labor seems a minor concern next to the low transactions costs and the low level of worker disruption and sabotage. When, however, times turn bad and markets are tight, the producers seek to reduce costs however they can, and they begin to worry actively about guild spirits and practices.

The solution historically had been to move the operation of artisanal production physically from urban to rural zones. In rural zones, more isolated work forces could be induced to work at lower levels of real remuneration. One favorite mechanism was for an urban merchant to supply the materials to the rural worker against a requirement that he sell the finished product at a price agreed in advance. For the rural worker, the artisanal production became a task added to other household tasks, with perhaps a gendered division of labor. Once involved in such a system, the rural worker was tied to it by a debt obligation out of which it was almost impossible to exit.

It was the urban merchant who would bring the rural location of artisanal production to an end. When times became good again, the attractiveness of lowered transactions costs made its appeal anew. So artisanal production returned to urban areas. This premodern pattern of urban-rural alternation continued in the early centuries of the capitalist world-economy. That is, it was maintained until capitalists figured out how to combine the pluses of lowered guild spirit with some (some, not all) of the advantages of lower transactions costs.

The history of the capitalist world-economy has, from the beginning, been one long effort to create largely monopolized products, which, because they were monopolized, were capable of very large price markups, and therefore of substantial profits. To understand what began to happen to the rural areas, we must discuss the ways in which capitalism as a system is not at all a free market system—quite the contrary.

A market in a capitalist system is both a concrete local structure where individuals or firms sell and buy goods and a virtual institution across the large space in which the same kind of exchange occurs. How large and widespread any virtual market is depends on the realistic alternatives that sellers and buyers have at a given time. In principle, in a capitalist world-economy, the virtual market exists in the world-economy as a whole. But there are often interferences with these boundaries, creating narrower and more "protected" markets.

There are, of course, separate virtual markets for all commodities as well as for capital and different kinds of labor. But over time, there can also be said to exist a single virtual world market for all the factors of production combined despite all the barriers that exist to its free functioning. One can think of this complete virtual market as a magnet for all producers and buyers, whose pull is a constant political factor in the decision making of everyone—the states, the firms, the households, the classes, and the status groups.

This complete virtual world market is a reality in that it influences all decision making, but it never functions fully and freely (that is, without interference). The totally free market functions as an ideology, a myth, and a constraining influence, but it is never a day-to-day reality.

One of the reasons it is not a day-to-day reality is that a totally free market, were it ever to exist, would make impossible the endless accumulation of capital. This may seem to be a paradox because it is surely true that capitalism cannot function without markets, and it is also true that capitalists regularly say that they favor totally free markets. But capitalists, in fact, do not need or want such totally free markets. Rather, they want markets that are only partially free.

The reason is clear. Suppose a world market existed in which all the factors of production flowed without restriction, in which there were a very large number of buyers and a very large number of sellers, and in which there was perfect information (that is, all sellers and all buyers knew the exact state of all costs of production). In such a perfect market, the buyers would always be able to bargain down the sellers to an absolutely minuscule level of profit (let us think of it as a penny), and this low level of profit would make the capitalist game entirely uninteresting to producers, removing the basic social underpinnings of such a system.

What sellers always prefer is a monopoly, for then they can create a relatively wide margin between the costs of production and the sales price, and thus realize high rates of profit. Of course, perfect monopolies are extremely difficult to create, and rare, but quasi-monopolies are not that difficult to achieve. All one needs is the support of the state machinery of a relatively strong state, one that can enforce the quasi-monopoly.

There are multiple ways of achieving such a quasi-monopoly. One of the most fundamental is the system of patents, which reserves rights in an invention for a specified number of years. This is what basically makes new products the most expensive and the most profitable for their producers. Of course, patents are often violated, and in any case, they eventually expire, but by and large, they protect a quasi-monopoly for a rather long time. Even so, production protected by patents usually remains only a quasi-monopoly, since other, similar products that are not covered by the patent may be on the market. This is why the normal situation for so-called leading products (that is, products that are both new and have an important share of the overall world market for commodities) is an oligopoly rather than an absolute monopoly. Oligopolies are, however, good enough to realize the desired high rate of profits, especially since the various firms often collude to minimize competition.

Patents are not the only way in which states can create quasi-monopolies. State restrictions on imports and exports (so-called protectionist measures) are another. State subsidies and tax benefits are a third. The ability of strong states to use their muscle to prevent weaker states from creating counterprotectionist measures is still another. The role of the states as large-scale buyers of certain products willing to pay excessive prices is still another. Finally, regulations that impose a burden on producers may be relatively easy to absorb by large producers but crippling to smaller producers, which then results in the elimination of the latter from the market and thus increases the degree of oligopoly. The modalities by which states interfere with the virtual market are so extensive that they constitute a fundamental factor in determining prices and profits. Without such interferences, the capitalist system could not thrive and therefore could not survive.

Nonetheless, there are two in-built antimonopolistic features in a capitalist world-economy. First of all, one producer's monopolistic advantage is another producer's loss. The losers will, of course, struggle politically to remove the advantages of the winners. They can do this by political struggle within the states where the monopolistic producers are located, appealing to doctrines of a free market, and offering support to political leaders inclined to end a particular monopolistic advantage. Or they can do this by persuading other states to defy the world market monopoly by using their state power to sustain competitive producers. Both methods are used. Therefore, over time, every quasi-monopoly is undone by the entry of further producers into the market.

Quasi-monopolies are thus self-liquidating. But they last long enough (say thirty years) to ensure considerable accumulation of capital on the part of those who control them. When a quasi-monopoly does cease to exist, the large accumulators of capital simply move their capital to new leading products or whole new leading industries. The result is a cycle of leading products. Leading products have moderately short lives, but they are constantly succeeded by other leading industries. Thus the game continues. As for the once-leading industries past their primes, they become more and more "competitive," that is, less and less profitable.

The axial division of labor of a capitalist world-economy divides production into corelike products and peripheral products. Core-periphery is a relational concept. What

I mean by "core-periphery" is the degree of profitability of the production processes. Since profitability is directly related to the degree of monopolization, what I essentially mean by "corelike production processes" are those controlled by quasi-monopolies. Peripheral processes are precisely those that are truly competitive. Whenever exchange occurs, competitive products are in a weak position, and quasi-monopolized products are in a strong position. As a result, there is a constant flow of surplus value from the producers of peripheral products to the producers of corelike products. This flow has been called unequal exchange.

Since quasi-monopolies are dependent on the patronage of strong states, they tend to be largely located—jurisdictionally, physically, and in terms of ownership—within such states. There is, therefore, a geographical consequence of the core-peripheral relationship. Corelike processes tend to group themselves in a few states and to constitute the bulk of the production activity in such states. Peripheral processes tend to group themselves in a large number of states and tend to constitute the bulk of the production activity in these states. Thus, for shorthand purposes, we can talk of core states and peripheral states, provided we remember that we are really talking of a relationship between production processes. Some states have a near even mix of corelike and peripheral products. We may call them semiperipheral states. They have some special political properties. It is, however, not meaningful to speak of semiperipheral production processes.

Since, as we have seen, quasi-monopolies exhaust themselves, what is a corelike process today will become a peripheral process tomorrow. En route, such a production process may locate itself in what is or becomes a semiperipheral state. The economic history of the modern world-system is replete with the shift, or downgrading, of products, first to semiperipheral countries and then to peripheral ones.

The normal evolution of the leading industries—the slow dissolution of the quasi-monopolies—is what accounts for the cyclical rhythms of the world-economy. A major leading industry tends to be a major stimulus to the expansion of the world-economy and results in considerable accumulation of capital. But it also normally leads to more extensive employment in the world-economy, higher wage levels, and a generalized sense of relative prosperity. As more and more firms enter the market of the erstwhile quasi-monopoly, there tends to be "overproduction" and increased price competition, lowering the rates of profit. At some point, this results in a considerably lowered level of profitability, much stock unsold, and consequently a slowdown in further production.

When this slowdown happens, we tend to see a reversal of the cyclical curve of the world-economy. We talk of stagnation or recession in the world-economy. Rates of unemployment rise worldwide. Producers seek to reduce costs to maintain their shares of the world market. One of the mechanisms is by relocation of the production processes to zones that have historically lower wages, that is, to semiperipheral countries. This puts pressure on the wage levels in the units of production still remaining in core zones, and wages there tend to become lower as well.

Effective demand, which was at first lacking because of overproduction, now becomes lacking because of a reduction in earnings of the consumers. In such a situation, not all producers necessarily lose out. There is obviously acutely increased competition among the widened oligopoly that is now engaged in these production processes. They fight each other furiously, usually with the aid of their state machineries. Some states and some producers succeed in "exporting unemployment" from one core state to the others. Systemically, there is contraction, but certain core states and especially certain semiperipheral states may seem to be doing quite well.

The process we have been describing—expansion of the world-economy when there are quasi-monopolistic leading industries and contraction in the world-economy when there is a lowering of the intensity of quasi-monopoly—can be drawn as an up and down curve of so-called A and B phases. These are sometimes referred to as Kondratieff cycles, named for the economist who described this phenomenon with clarity in the beginning of the twentieth century. These Kondratieff cycles have, up to now, been fifty to sixty years in length, adding together the A and B phases. Their exact length depends on the political measures taken by the states to avoid the coming of a B phase and especially the measures to achieve recuperation from the B phase and re-creation of a new A phase on the basis of new leading industries.

Let us now consider the impact of this kind of cyclical shift on the rural zones of the world-system. We can look at some of the major leading industries over the history of the modern world-system: shipbuilding in the seventeenth century, textiles in the early nineteenth century, steel production in the late nineteenth century, and automobile production in the early twentieth century.

Each of these four leading industries followed a similar pattern. For various reasons that are irrelevant to this discussion, the primary locus of production, the quasi-monopolized center, was in each case a particular country, or actually a particular area within some country. For shipbuilding, it was originally Holland, more specifically Amsterdam. For textiles, it was originally England, more specifically Lancashire. For steel, it was again originally England, more specifically Sheffield. For automobiles, it was the United States, more specifically Detroit.

In each case, before too long, the geography of world production began to shift. In the case of shipbuilding, the Dutch were able to maintain their relative monopoly a bit longer by moving shipbuilding to their own nearby rural area, the Zaanstreek, keeping ship repair for Amsterdam. But then, other areas began to compete effectively as shipbuilding centers—most notably North America, especially Massachusetts and later Virginia, but also various English centers, Lisbon and the Algarve, and later many others.

In textiles, the initial shift was to what is today Belgium, the Rhineland, northern France, and Switzerland; much later to Japan and India; and today, of course, to virtually all parts of the world. In steel, the shift was first to parts of Germany and the United States, then to other European loci such as Sweden and Russia, to India and Japan, to Korea, Brazil, and finally, to many other loci. In automobiles, the shift was from the United States to Germany and Japan, then to Canada, Italy, Korea, Malaysia, India, China, and many other loci.

If one studies the recruitment of labor to these new urban centers of production across the world, one notes a steady process of migration from rural areas to these centers. Sometimes, the rural areas from which the migrants come are in the same country. Sometimes, they come to the new centers via interstate migration, but once again from rural areas. Sometimes, the pattern is more complicated. The new industrial processes recruit previously urbanized workers, but then rural migrants come to fill the slots that the transferred urban workers vacated.

What we have here is a steady de-ruralization of the world-system, accompanied by a steady de-peasantization. As the capitalist world-economy expanded its total production, the process accelerated. As late as 1945, the rural population of the world was still quite substantial, and only a few countries had urban populations of over 50 percent. There was considerable acceleration of this process from 1945 to 1970. And it accelerated still faster after 1970. Hence, we arrived at the point where the 2008 United Nations report says not only that the percentage of urban population worldwide is over 50 percent but that it will go up markedly by 2030.

Let us now shift our view from the national and global figures to what has been going on in the rural areas. Obviously, these processes that I have been describing have affected low-ranking persons in the rural areas in different ways. Some profited by them, advancing to the status of yeoman farmer or kulak. Those in a much larger percentage lost some of the limited advantages they had in earlier structures, becoming landless and/or being coerced workers in one form or another.

Naturally, there was resistance. There has always been resistance. It took the form of sabotage, of theft, of rebellion. It also took the form of flight, flight to wilderness or frontier areas, flight to the urban ghettos/*bidonvilles*/*favelas*. And there is no question that, when surveyed over several centuries, the resistance slowed these processes down but never quite stopped them.

What has changed in the last century or so has been the rise of rural social movements, which have sought to transform individual resistance into collective resistance. This rise is, of course, parallel to what has happened in the urban areas. Sometimes, the rural social movements have taken the form of religious sects. And sometimes, they have taken the form of quite secular movements oriented to political action.

What have such movements sought to achieve? I think that, if we cut through the maze of particular demands in particular situations, there have been two basic objectives. One is to reverse the historic pattern of increasing concentration of units of production by establishing or re-establishing control of the land by smaller unit-holders on viable units of production. This call for "land reform" has had some success in some parts of the world-system.

Even where it has been politically successful (in that the state became ready to support some redivision and redistribution of land units), such land reform has run up against the fact that what is viable today involves larger minimal size than what was viable yesteryear. Land reforms that awarded ownership rights meant land units that could subsequently be sold on the market. Land thus divided could be reunited via the market. So, overall, land reform efforts have not been able to reverse the trend toward greater concentration of land ownership/control.

The second thing that rural social movements have sought has been more ambitious than mere land reform. It has been a return to food self-sufficiency. We are living at a moment where most countries in the world have lost national food self-sufficiency—and this has only happened in the last thirty years.

The reasons for this are quite clear. The pressures to open markets have allowed countries with highly efficient food production operations to undercut national food producers in other countries. This undercutting has been combined with pressures on most countries to turn their arable areas to producing export crops other than food. The combination of subsidies to food growers in a few countries such as the United States with world pressure on other countries to eliminate their subsidies made most countries food-import dependent.

This dependence has accelerated de-peasantization in the entire Global South. And into this deteriorating situation huge investment funds have entered to buy farmland, fertilizer, grain elevators, and shipping equipment.[4] One result of this is to subject ever-larger areas of food production to the vagaries of a volatile world financial market. Meanwhile, countries that are no longer food self-sufficient—today the vast majority—encounter wildly rising world food prices that they cannot afford to pay. And those agencies that are specialized in food aid find they are in the same dilemma—unable to pay the increased prices.

This process has also accelerated ecological destruction in two major ways. On the one hand, the increasing transfer of land areas to other uses—deforestation, biofuels, and so on—have, in multiple ways, rendered remaining food-producing areas less productive. And the major solution being offered to increase food output—genetically modified organisms—will have unmeasured and probably quite serious consequences on future production.

So, can the peasant return in some meaningful sense and in meaningful numbers? And is it desirable that the peasant return? It seems clear to me that we are in the midst of a runaway train ride that is carrying the whole capitalist world-economy toward a totally unviable situation far—very far—from equilibrium. What is going on in the rural areas is only a part of the picture, but a very important part.

Let us return to the basic mechanisms of capitalism as an historical system. Capitalism is a system in which the endless accumulation of capital is the *raison d'être* and the bottom line. Let us look at the situation from the viewpoint of entrepreneur—any entrepreneurs, whatever products they are offering on the world market.

Entrepreneurs have three basic costs. They must remunerate their personnel. They must pay for all the inputs needed to produce a finished item. And they must pay whatever taxes are imposed on them. They must then sell their product on a virtual world market. The difference between their total costs of production and the realized sales prices are their profit. Each of the three costs shows long-term secular rises (as proportion of the sales price). They seem each to be coming sufficiently near to their asymptotes so as to lead to wild fluctuations.

The amount of recompense employers pay their employees (from the lowest paid to the high cadres) is a function of the class struggle. The major mode that employees use to foster increased pay levels is some kind of syndical action. Successful syndical action is always difficult to organize, but two things work in its long-term favor. On the one hand, as I have explained, whenever the world-economy as a whole is in an expansionary phase, employers are reluctant to suffer the production interruptions that hostile syndical action would entail and are therefore ready to make some concessions to maintain continuous production. On the other hand, successful syndical action usually reflects more sophisticated political insight by employees and acquisition of tactical knowledge. Both of these increase in any given locale with the passage of time, and therefore, at some point, such syndical action can bear its fruit. In addition, there are advantages to employers collectively, if not necessarily to the individual employer in his or her own firm, in the expansion of the effective demand for commodities. And increasing remuneration to employees increases effective demand in the overall world-economy.

Most employers, however, are primarily concerned with their own short-term profit levels. When various kinds of repressive techniques fail to stem employee demands, the employers have resorted to physical displacement of the process of production, provided the reduced costs of production compensate the costs of change of locale. They have moved the enterprise to areas where employees are ready to accept lower payments and manifest lesser political sophistication and tactical skill. This phenomenon of the "runaway factory" has been a standard technique over the last 500 years. I have explained how this works. But this kind of repeated displacement presumes the existence of these pools of potential employees. And the steady de-ruralization of the world, itself the result of past displacements, represents the asymptotic limit to this process.

A similar difficulty is found in the effort to keep the cost of inputs low. Producers use three main mechanisms to keep these costs low. They do not pay, in large part, for the costs of detoxification. They do not pay, in large part, for the costs of renewing the resources they use. And they do not pay, in large part, for the creation of the infrastructure they need both for obtaining their inputs and work force and for marketing their products. This failure to pay essential parts of the cost of inputs is called the "externalization" of the costs of production.

But as the de-ruralization of the world's work force represents a limit on keeping the price of labor low, so the ecological damage to the biomass represents a limit on externalizing detoxification and resource replenishment. In addition, costs of infrastructure rise steadily because of the rising costs of the work force and lead inevitably to increased taxation. The ecological limits having become quite visible, green movements of various kinds have become politically important and have created pressures both for remedial action (which requires increased taxation) and internalization of these costs (which also means rising costs of inputs for the producers).

Finally, the costs of external payments (taxes plus corruption) have also been rising steadily as a percentage of the sales price. Taxation has risen because of the basic democratization of the world politically. The rising political strength of ordinary people is a function of their collective organization and militancy, which has led, in turn, to the states' seeking to reduce their militancy by some limited redistribution of the surplus value (the "welfare state"). This redistribution had the double advantage of maintaining the political stability of the world-system (by appeasing discontent) and expanding effective demand. Still, the price for this, from the point of view of the individual producer, is a higher tax bill and therefore lower profits. In addition, the costs of corruption have been rising as well because here, too, political sophistication and tactical knowledge on the part of those extorting the benefits have risen steadily.

Countermovements on the part of the producers to reduce the costs of production have not been absent. They occur continuously, and we have seen a large-scale movement of this kind recently. It has been called "neoliberalism" (Thatcherism, Reaganomics) and dominated the politics of a number of countries in the last few decades. However, although such countermovements can achieve some reduction of costs, historically, they have never managed to reduce the costs to the previous low point. It is a pattern of two steps forward, one step backward, or what might be called a ratchet effect. The bottom line is that the curve of the *overall and worldwide* costs of production has been steadily rising. This is the fundamental factor that has produced the structural crisis of the capitalist world-economy in which we find ourselves today.[5]

So here we are today—in the midst of a structural crisis of the capitalist world-economy, of which the historical de-ruralization plus de-peasantization of the world-system has been a central and integral part. If the question is whether we can revive the peasantry as it historically was, the answer is undoubtedly no. Nor would doing so be desirable.

But the crisis of the system takes the form of a bifurcation in which the world is moving toward a reorganization of its basic structure. We can say several things about this process. One is that it is a very chaotic process with enormous and unpredictable oscillations—economically, politically, culturally, and militarily. This chaos will probably include much food suffering, even starvation. The second is that the existing world-system cannot survive, but it is inherently impossible to predict the outcome of the struggle. The third is that there will be new order out of chaos, but whether this new order will be better or worse, we cannot be sure. The fourth is that in such a chaotic situation, every small input has a large effect. We are in a situation of almost perfect free will or, if you will, of the predominance of agency over structure.

Two basic outcomes are possible. One is a world-system that is, like the present one, hierarchical, exploitative, and polarizing. And one is a world-system that is relatively democratic and egalitarian. The structure of the agrarian zones would be quite different under each of these outcomes. In a hierarchical, inegalitarian system, we would undoubtedly see one or another form of coerced labor, even if the percentage of the world population engaged in agrarian tasks remained relatively low. In a relatively democratic, relatively egalitarian world, we might see the return of small, relatively self-sufficient agrarian production units.

Saying much more than this is probably not possible. We can design our utopias as we wish, but there is no guarantee that things will turn out the way we design them. What can be said is that a relatively democratic, relatively egalitarian world has to be one in which the trend is away from, rather than toward, the commodification of everything. This is the repeated theme of the agrarian antisystemic movements today. They are one part—an important part, but not the only part—of a wider coalition of forces in this critical, transnational struggle over the world we are trying to construct in the midst of our uncertain, and let us admit it, rather terrifying world political struggle.

NOTES

1. For a more elaborate discussion of the sixteenth-century capitalist world-economy, see my *The Modern World-System I: Capitalist Agriculture and the Origins of the European World-Economy* (San Diego: Academic Press, 1974), ch. 2.

2. Further details on what was occurring in the agrarian zones of the capitalist world-economy during this period can be found in my *The Modern World-System II: Mercantilism and the Consolidation of the European World-Economy, 1600–1750* (New York: Academic Press, 1980).

3. What happened in these four zones in the period 1750–1850 is discussed in great detail in my *The Modern World-System III: The Second Great Expansion of the Capitalist World-Economy, 1730–1840s* (San Diego: Academic Press, 1989), ch. 3.

4. See Diana B. Henriques, "Food is Gold, and Investors Pour Billions into Farming," *The New York Times* (June 5, 2008).

5. There is a further, noneconomic, element in the process—the apparent success and then the real failure of the world's antisystemic movements, which was crystallized in the world revolution of 1968, has weakened critically the ability of the states to constrain the strength and volatility of the political action of the popular classes. See my analysis in Immanuel Wallerstein, *After Liberalism* (New York: New Press, 1995), Part IV.

Part II

The People's Republic of China

Chapter 4

History, Capitalism, and the Making of the Postsocialist Chinese Peasant[1]

Alexander Day

Much discussion over the years, especially within Western social science, has focused on the definition of the peasantry. China scholars Myron Cohen and Charles Hayford have both suggested that the translation of the term "peasant" into Chinese as *nongmin* early in the twentieth century was part of a process through which intellectuals distinguished themselves from the peasant, often portrayed as a backward and ignorant figure.[2] The discourse on the peasant in the twentieth century thus can be seen as a form of discrimination and marginalization. Cohen has argued that the category "peasant" was an early-twentieth-century cultural invention that helped to legitimate both the politics of the Chinese Communist Party (CCP), founded in 1921, and the privileged status of Chinese intellectuals as bearers of truth and enlightenment. Cohen was writing in the aftermath of the crackdown on the 1989 Tiananmen demonstrations when the reevaluation of the revolutionary and iconoclastic tradition of Chinese politics was at its height following the cultural fever of the 1980s.[3] According to Cohen, an antipeasant iconoclasm was foundational to the mistaken radical politics of twentieth-century China, characterized as antipopular and authoritarian.[4] The introduction of the category *nongmin*—usually translated as "peasant"—into early-twentieth-century political discussions by leftist Chinese intellectuals was a key cultural intervention in this process. Cohen states

> Through the transformation of "farmers" into "peasants," "tradition" into "feudalism," and "customs" or "religion" into "superstition," there was invented not only

> the "old society" that had to be supplanted, but also the basic negative criteria designating a new status group, one held *by definition* to be incapable of creative and autonomous participation in China's reconstruction.[5]

Charles Hayford has made a similar argument, suggesting that the "peasant" was largely constructed during the May Fourth and New Culture Movement (1916–1923).[6] Both Cohen and Hayford tie the term "peasant" (*nongmin*) to the negative historical category "feudalism" (*fengjian*), whereas they see the term "farmer" as a positive category. While Cohen and Hayford do mention that some intellectuals in the 1920s and 1930s were an exception to the dominant antipeasant iconoclasm, noting Fei Xiaotong and rural reconstructionists among others, they stress that at its inception the category *nongmin* carried a negative valence that has influenced understandings of the rural ever since.

Hayford and Cohen are certainly correct in drawing attention to this aspect of the discourse on the peasant: the images of a backward peasant can be found throughout the twentieth century.[7] John Flower brings this justified criticism of elite intellectual attitudes toward the peasantry into the early reform period, arguing that social science in China—as in the West—has constructed the peasant as the backwards other of the intellectual.[8] But the category *nongmin* has from the beginning contained more complex meanings than this focus on antipeasant discrimination implies, necessitating greater attention to historical and political-economic context. Elitism cannot be transcended simply by redefining the "peasant" as a "farmer," somehow evading social science categorization and reaching the real of the rural. Moreover, the term "farmer" is no less problematic or political than "peasant"; it, too, must be understood within the particular historical and political context from which it emerged and in which it operates. Instead, we need to better account for social theorization—the continual reinvention of the peasant—within the context of the political economy of the postsocialist period, for the relationship between the peasant and history remains central to any theorization of the evolution of our global condition.

The postsocialist reconfiguration of Marxist historiography in the early reform period forms an important departure point for all discussions about the peasant in the contemporary moment. Postsocialism is the historical condition of reform period China, in which, as it joined with global capitalism, the historical and political narrative of socialism as an opposition to capitalism lost much of its power. Arif Dirlik argues that postsocialism is a discourse within which arguments over the meaning of socialism are combined with an understanding that the global conditions original to socialism—its antagonistic opposition to capitalism—have changed dramatically. Dirlik uses the term "postsocialism" primarily to understand the "condition of ideological contradiction and uncertainty" produced in the discursive struggle over Chinese socialism during the early reform period. The historical condition of postsocialism centers on socialism's loss of "coherence as a metatheory of politics" resulting from its rearticulation to the capitalist world order.[9] A "metatheory of politics," here, should be understood as an embedding of politics within history, in which the political evaluation of actions and policy is determined through a theoretical elaboration of the relationship between that political act and a narrative of history. During the Maoist period, this historical mode of politics—the explicit embedding of politics within historical discourse—entailed a dialectical understanding of peasant social and political tendencies, meaning that the propensity of peasants to act in a certain way had to be interpreted within the context of concrete historical and social conditions. Peasants could incline toward either egalitarian actions or class differentiation, depending on circumstances. This dialectical conception reached a point of fracture by the time of the Cultural Revolution in the late 1960s, and in the process of postsocialist reform beginning in the late 1970s, it was replaced by a single-sided and static interpretation of the role of peasants in history. Social and political understandings of the peasant lost their dominance, and the economic mode of interpretation became hegemonic. Discussions of intellectual discrimination against peasants tend to miss this dynamic.

Two linked aspects of the postsocialist reevaluation of the peasant by Chinese intellectuals are highlighted here. First, the historical agency of the peasant as a revolutionary subject—a central component of Maoist and dialectical understandings of the peasant—was contested by reform-period intellectuals, and the peasant increasingly was seen in a one-sided manner as backward, ignorant, and the cause of China's supposed slow social and economic development. Second, postsocialism was a revaluation of labor, in which a stress on the differential "quality" of labor replaced the more egalitarian mode of valuing labor that characterized the Maoist period. In other words, the historical agency of the peasantry to transform society was replaced with an individual entrepreneurial agency. While earlier CCP theories of the peasant—which began to be developed in the 1920s and 1930s as Marxist theory was integrated with Chinese conditions—continued as an important point of reference, they were significantly altered within this new context, leading to the end of a dialectical understanding of the peasant. This essay looks at three different categories—agrarian socialism, the Asiatic mode of production, and *suzhi* (quality)—through which the role of the peasant in history was reevaluated during the reform period, introducing a nondialectical understanding of peasant social tendencies. These key categories all link a particular understanding of history, based on the progressive development of the productive forces and technology, to a politics of the peasants, who are understood as needing liberation to develop their capitalist tendencies and transform themselves into entrepreneurial farmers. This understanding in turn undergirds contemporary policy decisions on rural China.

REVOLUTION, CONSTRUCTION, AND THE PEASANT

In general, long-standing Marxist and CCP theorization of peasant character was based on the position of the peasantry within the economy and the contemporary stage of social development through which China was passing. During the revolution, the CCP developed a theory of the peasantry based on its "dual nature" (*liangchong xing*).[10] On the one hand, the peasantry was a rebellious exploited class of rural laborers; on the other hand, the peasantry was also a conservative petty-bourgeois class of "small producers" (*xiao shengchanzhe*) that defended its small plots of land. How this dual class nature was expressed depended on political and social circumstances: it could lead to increasing class differentiation as individual households competed to expand their wealth or peasant fear of landlessness and semi-proletarianization could lead to support for populist egalitarian measures. While its rebellious nature was a key to the Chinese revolution—constituting "the real motive force of historical development in Chinese feudal society," according to Mao[11]—the party always had to worry that, once the rebellion had ended, peasants would return to their conservative and overly egalitarian ways. "Peasant consciousness" (*nongmin yishi*), linked to the petty-bourgeois class position peasants held within society, was a threat to the party's progressive ideals and had to be brought under the leadership of the working class.[12] Early in the revolution, as the party tried to build a disciplined revolutionary army under very difficult circumstances, Mao stated, "The source of such incorrect ideas in this Party organization lies, of course, in the fact that [the Red Army's] basic units are composed largely of peasants and other elements of petty-bourgeois origin."[13] While comprising a rebellious force, peasant subjectivity had to be fashioned into an effective revolutionary weapon by the proletarian party. The success of the revolution depended upon the party's ability to balance the often rather immediate demands of peasants and the long-term historical trajectory of revolution and socialist transformation.

The theory of "New Democracy" (*xin minzhuzhuyi*) was developed during the revolution beginning in 1940 in part to manage the contradictions of a socialist revolution taking place in a country dominated by the peasantry. It stressed a moderate line in which different classes were united in revolution. In the post-war period of construction, New Democracy was to be a period of transition in which, through industrialization, the productive forces would be built up to the point that Chinese society was ready to become socialist. For rural society this meant that a petty-bourgeois economy of small peasants would continue to exist until the Chinese economy could support the industrialization and socialization of agriculture. Politically, during the revolution and early years of construction this policy was designed to maintain the support of middle peasants. Yet there was always a fear of corruption by peasant consciousness, leading to a historical dead end such as "agrarian socialism." The category "agrarian socialism" emerged out of the CCP's revolutionary experience with the peasantry, although soon after the establishment of the People's Republic of China in 1949 the term fell into disuse, only to return during the postsocialist period.[14] In a 1948 speech at a cadre conference in north China near the end of the civil war, Mao maintained the New Democracy line and argued for the need to be vigilant against "agrarian socialism," a form of "reactionary, backward, and retrogressive" thinking based on peasant petty-bourgeois consciousness and leading to "absolute egalitarianism."[15] Agrarian socialism designated an egalitarian socialism that could develop on the material basis of an agrarian peasant economy; this would result in historical stagnation, for peasant egalitarianism would preclude the development of social forces necessary to the expansion and progress of the forces of production. As one journal put it at the time, agrarian socialism was an "attempt to use the standards of the small peasant economy to know and transform the whole world" while avoiding capitalist development—a form of populism.[16] New Democracy, by contrast, was to be a historical transition period in which private ownership, particularly in the countryside, would continue alongside a growing state-run economy, leading to the industrialization of China and finally its socialization, a process that egalitarianism would disrupt.

After the success of the revolution, Daniel Kelliher shows, a party that was intent on industrializing the economy, often at the expense of the peasantry, began to stress the conservative nature of the peasantry and its egalitarian consciousness.[17] Yet the precise nature of the peasantry's historic role at this time of transition from revolution to construction was a matter of debate within the leadership. In April 1951, the Shanxi Provincial Party Committee wrote the Northeast Bureau and the Central Committee cautioning that, while land reform had unleashed the productive power of the peasantry, this spontaneous energy pushed not "in the direction of modernization and collectivization that we demand, but in the direction of a rich peasantry" and the dispersal of mutual aid organizations.[18] They accordingly believed that this spontaneous direction of the small peasant economy toward renewed class differentiation needed to be halted and redirected toward collectivization and a new social form. The Northeast Bureau disagreed with the Shanxi committee, reiterating Mao's earlier New Democracy line on peasant tendencies that was critical of "agrarian socialism," which the bureau saw as a more perilous problem than class differentiation. According to Liu Shaoqi, who agreed with the Northeast Bureau, the shift from an individual ownership system in agriculture to collectivized farms would be inaugurated through a revolution in the mode of production, and could only occur once China was industrialized enough to allow for the mechanization of agriculture. Without such preconditions, restricting the spontaneous tendencies of economic development and encouraging agricultural production cooperatives was a form of "mistaken, dangerous, and utopian agrarian socialist thinking."[19]

At this point, however, Mao contradicted Liu, supporting the Shanxi committee. This marked a departure from the New Democracy line, opening up a wider political space for rural cooperativization and collectivization. As Mao shifted to support a more rapid collectivization in the countryside, the critical term "agrarian socialism" became a political liability, for it could easily be used to criticize rural collectivization, as Liu's comments revealed. It was then edited out of Mao's 1948 speech as it appeared in the fourth volume of his collected works.[20] In the years that followed, as rural policies became more radical, the party was increasingly critical of the peasantry's petty-bourgeois tendency toward class differentiation; discussions of "agrarian socialism" largely disappeared. As the politics of the CCP became more contentious from the late 1950s, within party propaganda, the split between the two poles of the peasantry's dual nature grew wider, bringing the dialectical understanding of the peasant to the point of rupture. Thus, while the ultra-left in the CCP took the stress on the revolutionary nature of the exploited, including the peasants, to extremes during the Cultural Revolution, peasants as "small producers" were at the same time considered to harbor tendencies toward capitalism.[21]

PETTY-BOURGEOIS PEASANT CONSERVATISM AND THE CRITIQUE OF AGRARIAN SOCIALISM AT THE BEGINNING OF THE REFORM PERIOD

A few years after Mao's death in 1976, the Communist Party, now under the leadership of Deng Xiaoping, instigated sweeping reforms of the Chinese economy and society.

A thorough revision of the party's ideological underpinnings was a central part of this process. Intellectuals, many of whom had been targets of the Cultural Revolution but who were now brought back into public life, played an important role. While at first in the late 1970s intellectuals largely returned to the 1950s orthodox Marxist position on the peasantry, stressing the economic determination of consciousness and ideology, over time, establishment intellectuals transformed the earlier understanding of the dual nature of the peasantry. Contrary to the increasingly bifurcated image of the peasant during the 1960s and 1970s[22] and especially the stress on the revolutionary nature of the peasantry, during the early reform period, establishment intellectuals stressed the conservative nature of the peasantry's egalitarian tendencies. Such a conservative peasantry, in turn, was the social foundation for an autocratic state, for dictatorship, and for the cult of personality. Instead of sustaining a "reserve of socialist activism," peasant consciousness formed the social basis for continued feudal influence, the suppression of which was a precondition for modernization. As the reform period developed, peasant historical and political agency was increasingly denied.

In an influential 1979 article, historian Wang Rongsheng argued that historical change in feudalism could not be reduced to the dynamic of rural class struggle and that many rural struggles were between the peasantry and the state, and thus not expressions of class struggle. Wang linked this criticism of peasant historical studies to the stress on class struggle during the Cultural Revolution.[23] Also in 1979, in a major argument for shifting the emphasis in historical research, Dai Yi criticized the singular focus on class struggle and peasant wars during the later Maoist era, particularly during the Cultural Revolution. Consonant with the Party's ideological shift from class struggle to economic development, Dai stated that this misplaced emphasis was because of a misunderstanding of Marxism-Leninism and historical materialism that reached a height during the Cultural Revolution. In contrast, a proper understanding showed that class struggle was only an expression of a deeper contradiction within society, "the contradiction between the productive forces and the relations of production, and the contradiction between the economic base and the superstructure."[24] Peasant wars, while an important aspect of China's feudal society, were not the motive force of history. Thus Dai argued that productivity, not class struggle, "is the most vital, most revolutionary ingredient."[25] In fact, within feudal society "peasant wars could only strike a definite blow at the old productive relationships, could only change certain links of these [relationships], but could not possibly change the old modes of production completely."[26]

These arguments on the peasant were carried even further by Wang Xiaoqiang, an important reformist intellectual, who argued that peasant egalitarian consciousness prevented peasant rebellions from surpassing feudal social relations and rule during the imperial period. At best, a peasant rebellion would simply lead to a new distribution of land and new feudal rulers.[27] The conservative side of the peasantry's dual nature predominated, and the small peasant "utopian fantasy" (*wutuobang shi de kongxiang*) could not truly be established.[28] Under the leadership and education of the proletariat and its party, however, the progressive side could dominate, although the conservative side would not disappear until its social basis in the small "peasant economy" (*xiaonong jingji*) was superseded. Yet as most cadres were from nonproletarian and especially petty-bourgeois backgrounds, peasant consciousness within the party set the stage for the "feudal" methods and incorrect policies of Lin Biao and the Gang of Four, the destruction of internal party democracy, and the ascendancy of an egalitarian "agrarian socialism."[29] By the reform period, therefore, "agrarian socialism" had become a term used by some more radical reformers to criticize Maoist rural policies. In a later article, Wang Xiaoqiang went on to argue that "agrarian socialism" during the Maoist period was a form of populism, linked to peasant consciousness and a "small peasant economy," that short-circuited history by skipping over capitalist development and restoring a natural economy in which all are equally poor. Unlike Russian populism, however, Chinese agrarian socialism was not so directly connected to intellectuals but was a latent energy that was unleashed in peasant uprisings. The clearest example was the Taiping Rebellion (1851–1864), which, according to Wang, suppressed private property, the commodity economy, and the family while it instituted cultural revolution. Scientific socialism, on the other hand, could only be constructed on the foundation of a modern commodity economy,[30] which the New Democratic political and economic policy was intended to provide. While agrarian socialism had a "limited use" during the revolutionary period—notably to motivate the revolutionary force of the peasantry—once the revolution was successful it became reactionary.[31] Feudal rule, built on peasant consciousness, prevented the completion of the two tasks of socialism: the development of the productive forces and the achievement of a democratic revolution.[32]

As the positive image of the peasantry as a rebellious exploited class that could push history forward came under attack by intellectuals, the negative, conservative side of the peasantry as a dependent class, unable to join together and needing the control of an autocratic ruler, was increasingly stressed. This conservative and egalitarian peasant mass was a central figure in the reform-era depiction of Maoist extremism as a populism rooted in the feudal consciousness of a peasant society. Instead of interpreting bureaucracy as a problem of "capitalist restoration" or the rise of a "new bourgeois class,"[33] for example, this discourse blamed the political separation between the state and the people on the lingering effects of an agrarian mode of production, whether it was named feudalism or the Asiatic mode of production. While the former was a social contradiction calling for class struggle, the latter was a stagnant opposition between state and society that required an outside force for modernization. In most formulations of the reform period, the outside force was to be constituted by the intellectuals, who would advise the administrative state on the proper course of modernization.

At a speech at a major party theoretical conference that was to set the stage for reformist theory in the 1980s,[34] Wang Ruoshui, deputy editor-in-chief of the *Renmin Ribao*, attacked the Maoist personality cult that came to be portrayed as the primary cause of the Cultural Revolution, by implication blaming its popularity on peasants:

> The personality cult has deep historical roots in our society. Our country has been primarily dominated by small producers. The small producers' force of habit is very deep-rooted. . . . Marx in his work *The Eighteenth Brumaire* . . . made the following analysis of the small farmers. Due to their dispersed, self-sufficient and mutually isolated nature, they were unable to form a "national bond." As a result, "they can

> not represent themselves, they must be represented. Their representative must . . . appear as their master, as an authority over them, as an unlimited governmental power that protects them against the other classes and sends them rain and sunshine from above." This kind of socio-economic condition nurtures monarchical thinking and produces the personality cult.[35]

The background for Wang's critical position on the peasantry was an attempt to construct a Marxist humanism adequate to critique alienation under socialism. The dependency of the peasant or small producer was portrayed as the social ground for the personality cult, totalitarianism, and political alienation, through which leaders were raised above the masses as saviors. Humanism, in contrast, necessitated the independence of individuals within society.[36] This led to some of the most important intellectual debates from the early reform period to the present.[37]

Similarly, Wang Xizhe argued in 1980 that Mao's peasant background had led to "a type of reactionary utopian peasant egalitarianism."[38] Wang questioned what he saw as the basis of Mao's theory of "agrarian socialism"—a theory, notably, of which Mao was critical, though here Wang names Mao's development strategy itself "agrarian socialism"—the idea that China's peasants had a "reserve of socialist activism" that, once activated by the Communist Party, would lead to socialism.[39] Instead, Wang argued, without the proper historical foundations—namely, a developed industrial economy—this reliance on peasant rebellion led to an autocratic and fascist, not democratic, form of agrarian socialism.[40] As Wang stated,

> Chinese peasants, who had never seen modern heavy industry, let alone had the opportunity to place themselves in its midst, were the very ones who could not possibly have accumulated a reserve of scientific socialist activism. When people used the ideals of socialism and communism to arouse the peasants to revolt, they could instill a consciousness of communism based on the peasants' real mode of existence. This consciousness of communism was of a Heavenly Kingdom of Peace where when the "Great Way" was traveled, there was a spirit of "Cooperation" under heaven. Mao Zedong was able to bring them this kind of heavenly country. So we can understand how they could repay Mao Zedong with fanatic worship![41]

Wang argued, therefore, that the Cultural Revolution was the result of a totalitarian mode of state formed on the basis of peasant consciousness and its corresponding cult of personality.[42] At the time, Wang made a somewhat ambiguous association between "agrarian socialism" and the "Asiatic mode of production" (*yaxiya shengchan fangshi*), a category that has rather different theoretical implications as well as lineage, one to which I will now turn.[43]

PEASANT DEPENDENCY AND THE ASIATIC STATE

In the early 1980s, the linkage between the peasantry and the populist political errors of the Maoist period was deepened by renewed discussion of the Asiatic mode of production (AMP). While the AMP discussion clearly concerned the nature of the Chinese state, it also played an important role in reshaping reform-period understandings of the peasant and its role in history. This focus on the dominance of the Asiatic imperial state shifted attention away from the petty-bourgeois nature of the land-owning peasantry; theoretical concentration on the class nature of the peasantry was replaced by a growing emphasis on state-society relations. It was primarily Wu Dakun, professor of international economy at the People's University of China and a participant in debates on the AMP in the 1950s,[44] who generated this new discussion through his use of this category to criticize the Maoism of the Cultural Revolution.[45] Adopted from Marx, the AMP was a category that allowed intellectuals to discuss multiple lines of historical development. The AMP formulation—designating large-scale agrarian societies with a dominant state—had been largely rejected by Chinese Marxists in the early 1930s because it seemed to place China outside of normal world-historical social evolution.[46]

During the reform era, however, with the reduction of the dual nature of the peasantry to a conservative egalitarianism tendency, the peasant increasingly was portrayed by intellectuals as the cause of stagnation or blockage within society. The historical category of the AMP, likewise, tended to remove all dynamism from Chinese society; the peasantry and its rebellions were no longer the motive force of history; they no longer sustained a revolutionary subjectivity. In 1980 and 1981, Wu argued that the AMP meant that history developed along multiple lines, but that the AMP ended up acting as a block to modernization, in particular because of the problem of bureaucracy.[47] The economic basis of bureaucratism, Wu cites Lenin as arguing, was the "atomized and scattered state of the small producer. . . ."[48] Influenced by the work of Umberto Melotti's *Marx e il terzo mondo*,[49] Wu employed the analytical category of the AMP to argue against the idea that Soviet-style societies were sliding into bureaucratic capitalism, instead asserting that the problem of bureaucracy in the USSR was related to the persistence of the traditional, Asiatic mode.[50]

Wu's application of the category, however, was relatively limited. For Wu, the use of the AMP formulation to criticize bureaucratic rule in China should be largely restricted to the period of the Cultural Revolution.[51] In a logic quite similar to that of Wang Xizhe, Wu stated

> As historical materialists, we cannot consider accidental the degeneration of Russia into a social-imperialist state, or the appearance in China of Lin Biao and the Gang of Four as "feudal fascism." This is certainly permissible as an everyday expression, but scientifically speaking it is not appropriate. Fascism is the autocracy of the monopolistic capitalist class and does not appear in feudal society. The activities of Lin Biao and the Gang of Four in fact revived the Oriental despotism of ancient Asiatic states.[52]

While explicitly arguing against broad anticommunist uses of the AMP concept such as that of Karl Wittfogel,[53] who argued that Soviet-style states were simply a despotic continuation of the AMP, Wu employed the concept more narrowly to criticize the Stalinist personality cult.[54] As Timothy Brook has noted, the category of AMP allowed social contradictions to be understood in terms of incomplete modernization.[55] Clear in

Wu's hesitant treatment, moreover, is an attempt to theoretically preempt the potential for a class-based critique to be arrayed against the reform-period leadership. If political alienation during the Maoist period was the result of the capitalist class's maintaining power and continuing its exploitation through the bureaucracy, then the reformist leadership was open to exactly the same charge. The peasant played a key role, therefore, in rearticulating history and politics so as to defend against just such a critique. The problem of bureaucracy, understood by the ultra-left of the Cultural Revolution as the result of a "new capitalist class,"[56] was here located in the lingering effects of tradition, whether it was considered "feudal" or along the lines of an AMP; reform-period modernization was rendered as its solution. Again, this formulation, produced through a politics of historical rupture, was to result in a temporally bifurcated image of the rural society: both as a cause of stagnation in the past and as a sector whose problems were being solved by Deng-era modernization in the present.

Zhao Lisheng, a professor of history at Lanzhou University and an important historian of rural China in the 1950s, also employed the concept of the AMP. Yet in contrast to Wu Dakun, Zhao used the category to criticize both the Maoist stress on peasant rebellion as an expression of class struggle and the idea that Chinese peasants were petty-bourgeois land owners.[57] Zhao's formulation marked a shift in emphasis from that of Wang Rongsheng, Dai Yi, Wang Xiaoqiang, and Wang Ruoshui, for whom land *ownership* was still understood as the primary social basis for the conservative nature of the peasantry, a nature that dominated "peasant consciousness." On the contrary, Zhao argued that peasants were by nature dependent on the state because of their *lack* of true land ownership. This is the significance of the AMP as formulated by Zhao—it allowed him to shift the focus from the class character of peasant land ownership to the dominance of the state as an explanation for the nature of peasant behavior. Thus Zhao's historical arguments went further than many others in attacking the previously dominant narrative of peasant rebellion as class struggle. As the 1980s progressed, Zhao's formulation came to the fore: the inertial and defensive side of peasant nature was no longer seen as based on the fact of land ownership or their petty-bourgeois nature, but on the lack of independent property ownership and the dependent nature of the peasantry in relation to the state. As a capitalist understanding of property ownership as a general progressive value came to command the intellectual and political scene in the 1990s, therefore, this became the dominant line on the peasantry.

Zhao stressed the oppressive, extractive, and status-based nature of the primitive commune that he discusses under the category of the AMP as an oblique critique of the Maoist commune system.[58] Zhao argued that within the Asiatic commune system, farmers were neither slaves nor serfs, but existed in a commune system with severe restrictions on the individual. Ideologically, Zhao linked the AMP to the Legalist, and not the Confucian, tradition.[59] In the early 1970s, radical Maoists portrayed Legalism as a progressive ideology in comparison to Confucianism, and in the process Legalism and Qin Shi Huangdi, the first Qin emperor, were associated with Mao. By connecting Legalism and an oppressive AMP, Zhao thus furthered his criticisms of Mao. Implied in this critique of Maoism as a form of AMP is a historical narrative in which a stagnant Chinese society is founded on the relationship between an oppressive state and a scattered and dependent peasantry. The peasantry was thus stripped of its agency in two ways: on the one hand, peasant rebellion lost its progressive political character; on the other hand, such a dependent peasant could not be considered economically entrepreneurial either. Only by breaking with state dependency—and thus with the various socio-historical forms of dependency: agrarian socialism, feudalism, and the AMP—could the peasantry help to produce a new historical trajectory for Chinese society. But on what basis might the peasantry break from state to become independent entrepreneurs? This led to the question of peasant "quality" (*suzhi*)—a new formulation of peasant agency.

SUZHI, PEASANTS, AND TECHNOCRACY

It has been pointed out that the discourse of *suzhi* had its beginnings in propaganda campaigns on birth control in the early 1980s. The term *zhiliang* (also "quality") was used in the formulation "population quality" (*renkou zhiliang*) until the mid-1980s, when the term *suzhi* became the dominant term for "quality."[60] At its inception, however, this discourse on population quality was closely linked to a discussion on the "quality of labor" (*laodong zhiliang*), and it is within this context that the emergence of this discourse must be understood.[61] From the late 1970s, in other words, the discourse of *zhiliang/suzhi* was used to understand the position of social groups and individuals within a society in which modernization and development were predicated on technical change, a change in the quality of labor power. In this sense, *zhiliang/suzhi* helped to explain the differential value produced by equal quantities of labor power. From the early 1980s, this understanding of *value* came to imply a particular notion of social and historical development in which the "low quality" of the peasantry explained the supposed stagnation of Chinese historical development. At the same time, the household responsibility system together with population control and increased investment in education opened the potential for raising the quality of the peasantry and the development of a commodity economy.

One of the centerpiece ideological debates of the late 1970s concerned the politics of labor value. During the beginning of the reform period, as we have seen, reformist intellectuals argued that one of the primary errors of the Maoist period was its overly egalitarian remuneration policies—policies that helped to produce the supposed historical error of "agrarian socialism." In 1978, Deng Xiaoping argued that remuneration policies should be linked to both "the quantity and quality (*zhiliang*) of an individual's work,"[62] a policy that was reaffirmed by an important *People's Daily* editorial in January of 1979, which called for the implementation of "distribution of rewards according to work done" over "egalitarianism."[63] The central target of this criticism of egalitarianism was the Dazhai Brigade—the model of egalitarian remuneration policies and the overcoming of the split between mental and manual labor from the 1960s and 1970s—and in 1980 a propaganda campaign to discredit the Dazhai Brigade laid the ideological foundations for the nationwide implementation of the household responsibility system, in which the household was reestablished as the basic unit of agricultural production. Likewise, this shift in remuneration policy was a reversal of the Mao-period advocacy of eliminating the "three great differences" (between workers and peasants, between urban and rural areas, and between mental and manual labor), a reversal that was coupled with the rise in power of a "new class" of technocratic cadre.[64]

This shift in focus from quantity to quality of labor was mirrored in the contemporary discourse on population and birth planning.[65] Within this new structure of value, the contemporary notion of *renkou zhiliang* (population quality) was validated exactly because modernization meant technical progress—modernization was a shift from labor and population quantity to quality. Liu Zhenkun argued in 1982 that "human resources" (*renli ziyuan*) and "population quality" (*renkou de zhiliang*) increasingly conditioned a nation's technical development, the strength of the nation, labor productivity, and economic growth.[66] Likewise, a 1981 article entitled "Labor Power and the Quality of Labor Power" argued that increasing labor productivity "could not be separated from raising the quality of knowledge and skills (*zhishi he jishu suzhi*) of workers," a project that necessitated the controlled growth of population quantity.[67] In an article entitled "Pay Attention to Raising the Quality of Agricultural Laborers," Jin Huishen stated that "so-called *suzhi* principally indicates the production knowledge, labor skills, and scientific culture of the laborer as well his physique and level of health."[68] Jin went on to argue that, in the prereform period, too much attention was paid to raising the quantity of labor power instead of its quality. Subtly equating the Maoist period with pre-liberation traditional agriculture, Jin argued that the origin of this stress was the "'quantity-quality concept' of the small peasant economy" (*xiaonong jingji de 'liang, zhi guannian'*), which viewed having more children as "the fountainhead of wealth."[69] In contrast, while the reformist household responsibility system had released the initiative of the peasants, the key to agricultural modernization was raising "the quality of labor power" (*laodongli suzhi*) and agricultural productivity on the basis of improvements in science.[70] The quality of labor power and the quality of the population were therefore intimately related as this discourse on value emerged at the beginning of the postsocialist period.

Bai Yijin argued that for the "new historical period to solve the peasant question (*nongmin wenti*), it had to solve the problem of peasant quality (*nongmin zhiliang wenti*)."[71] But perhaps the most well-known and influential discussion of the "quality of human resources" (*renliziyuan suzhi*) in rural areas was *The Poverty of Plenty*, authored by Wang Xiaoqiang (critic of agrarian socialism discussed earlier) and Bai Nanfeng.[72] They argued that "China is undergoing the shift from a natural economy towards a commodity economy. In other words, it is changing from an agricultural society to an industrial society."[73] Mirroring Jin Huishen's earlier historical argument, they stated that the main obstacle to this transformation was the *suzhi* of the rural and minority population. As with most reformist intellectuals at the time, Wang and Bai believed that the institution of the household responsibility system for agriculture was a turning point in China's modernization, because it liberated the productive initiative of the peasants. They contrasted the development of the commodity economy during the reform period with the model propagated in the "learn from Dazhai" movement, which they saw as a "simple investment in productive forces" and thus non-transformative quantitative expansion.[74]

Yet according to Wang and Bai, the agricultural reforms sparked "two kinds of enthusiasm, each with a different social content, one geared towards developing the natural economy and the other geared towards developing the commodity economy."[75] Notable is a return to the formulation of the dual nature of the peasantry and the problems it entailed for socialist construction in the early days of the People's Republic; although, in this new formulation, "social content" refers to the technical level and entrepreneurial spirit of the rural population—its *suzhi*—not the dialectical tendencies of the peasant class character. Within postsocialist discourse *suzhi*, as value, displaced class as a way to understand social inequality and peasant agency.[76] In Wang and Bai's postsocialist formulation, therefore, a dialectical understanding of the various tendencies of behavior of the peasantry as a class was replaced by dichotomy between those who are of high quality and those who are not. In other words, the key difference that *suzhi* indicated in this formulation was not determined by the interaction of a dynamic peasantry with concrete historical conditions so much as the lack of a quality that needed to be introduced from the outside.

An increase in the total value produced was possible in backward areas, Wang and Bai argued, even though the quality or efficiency of production did not rise, leading to historical stagnancy in the form of a persistent natural economy.[77] The crucial difference between areas that progressed toward a modern commodity economy compared to those that stagnated in a natural, self-sufficient economy was *suzhi,* or whether or not they had a high "quality of human resources."[78] Labor, here, was not interpreted as a form of social relation so much as an economic resource. For Wang and Bai, *suzhi* referred to "the quality of engaging in commodity production and management."[79] One's *suzhi* was defined by one's aptitude towards functioning in the commodity economy. Most important was a sense of "entrepreneurial spirit," reflected in an "openness to new ideas," a "sense of efficiency," "initiative and drive," and "risk taking." Knowledge and education were essential components of "entrepreneurial spirit," according to Wang and Bai, as one's willingness to break with tradition and use new and efficient agricultural techniques would "raise yields." The discourse of *suzhi*, therefore, not only replaced discussions of class, but it was a reformulation of peasant agency as well. If the early reform period saw a strong critique of the idea of the peasantry having revolutionary or historical agency, *suzhi* as entrepreneurial spirit indicated that particular peasants could have individual agency within the economy.

The narrative of peasant low quality, lack of entrepreneurial spirit, and dependence on the state was most clearly crystallized in the controversial television documentary *Heshang* (*River Elegy*), produced and shown in China in 1988. Primarily written by well-known reportage writer Su Xiaokang, the series located the cause of the turmoil of twentieth-century Chinese history in the agrarian nature of Chinese society. The series built on work of the early 1980s—especially that of Wang Xiaoqiang—that linked feudalism, peasant consciousness, and Maoist excess. With the airing of the series, however, the "dual nature" of the peasantry had become almost completely reduced to a static image of conservative dependency; the once positively valued rebellious side of the peasantry was now converted into a negative, chaotic, and disruptive force that brought about at best no historical progress and at worst regress.[80] In the series, the yellow earth symbolized China's agrarian society, supposedly defensive, inward-looking, despotic, and authoritarian.[81] The West, by contrast, was represented by the blue ocean—an industrial, entrepreneurial, seafaring, outward looking, aggressive, and pluralistic society, one that led to the liberation of the productive forces. The series concluded that, without a bourgeoisie, it would be up to the intellectuals to shift China from a yellow civilization to a blue one.[82] The series also complained that intellectuals got paid less than those who worked with their hands—"mental and physical labor are in an inverse relationship"—and that the "source of all this unfairness is that society lacks a competitive mechanism for ensuring equality of opportunity, it lacks a common yardstick—the market." This reassertion of the value of mental versus manual labor was a direct attack on Maoist egalitarianism and an assertion to pay attention to the quality of labor.[83] The theory of the AMP also played an important role in *Heshang*, although in the series the concept was much closer to that put forward by Karl Wittfogel than its early 1980s formulations: China was an agrarian society based on water control and unable to change. Resistance to change was attributed to an attachment to the soil.

Part four of the six-part series, on "the new era," focused most closely on the figure of the peasant, asking why an industrial revolution had not taken place in China. China, "a large country made up of peasants with small landholdings," was compared to Venice, "the earliest birthplace of capitalist civilization," which was "without agriculture."[84] In China, all land was owned by the emperor, and its "system of centralized power, of a 'great unity' built on the foundation of an agricultural civilization, became a heavy ball and chain weighing down the economy of ancient China and industrial and commercial activities in particular."[85] The environmental-determinist and Malthusian argument of the series was that capitalism could not develop in China because of the stagnant agrarian culture that developed in a society with "too many people crowded onto too little land."[86] This led to China taking its "own path to development" (*yitiao ziji de fazhan daolu*), one which the authors of *Heshang* obviously saw as a disastrous departure from the historical course of modernization. The quintessential example—in fact, the causal foundation—of the culture of China's agrarian civilization was located in peasant "character" or "quality," responsible for holding China back:

> In the vast, backward rural areas, there are common problems in peasant quality (*suzhi*) such as a weak spirit of enterprise, a very low ability to accept risk, a deep psychology of dependency (*yilai sixiang*) and a strong sense of passive acceptance of fate. . . . It's not the lack of resources, nor the level of GNP, nor the speed [of development], but rather this deficiency in the human quality that is the essence of this so-called notion of "backwardness." And the decline in the quality of the general population is caused precisely by the rapid increases in its numbers. This truly is an agricultural civilization caught in a vicious cycle.[87]

Discussions of peasant "quality" in *Heshang* were adopted[88] from Wang Xiaoqiang and Bai Nanfeng. *Suzhi*, the idea of peasant "dependency" (*yilaixing*), and being "fettered" (*shufu*) to the land, were key formulations.[89]

This continued dependence of rural populations on the state, according to *Heshang*, led to the utopianism of the Great Leap Forward and then to famine: "This transition, from economic 'utopia' to political crisis, leading ultimately to the historical tragedy of great social turmoil—can we not say that this is the inevitable end of an agricultural civilization?"[90] Utopianism signaled that "history cold-heartedly passed" China by. Progressive history, in other words, was tied to the technological development of the productive forces and not peasant dynamism or rebellion; any attempt to escape the laws of historical development would invite disaster.[91] As an agrarian civilization, however, China was caught in a cyclical history with no real progress. Commenting on the violence and rebellions that mark a shift from one dynasty to the next, the series stated, "This kind of collapse of the social structure does not possess any 'revolutionary significance,' as some theories would have it." Instead of containing "revolutionary significance," as Mao maintained, peasant rebellions "have time after time unfeelingly destroyed the accumulated wealth of production."[92]

As Jin Guantao, an editor of the important *Zouxiang weilai congshu* (*Towards the Future*) book series and advisor to *Heshang*, stated in the series, social upheavals brought about "the long-term stagnation of China's feudal society."[93] Jin's argument here takes Dai Yi's position on peasant war to its extreme. While Dai argued that peasant war could not "change the old mode of production completely," but only transform certain aspects of it, by the late 1980s, Jin argued that peasant rebellions had an almost wholly negative and stagnant effect on the social and economic development of China.[94] In the series, China's cyclical history is naturalized through the metaphor of the flooding of the Yellow River. Within this metaphor, the "accumulation of sediment" that causes flooding stood in for the role Chinese peasants played within historical turmoil.[95] Beginning with his 1986 *The Philosophy of Development* (*Fazhan de zhexue*), Jin attempted to replace a dialectical understanding of historical development with one based in cybernetic and systems theory, leading to the merging of social science into natural science and a technological model of historical development.[96] Yet the television series also approvingly cited Hegel as noting that in the West, the condition of being fettered to the land and the culture of dependency was broken by seagoing activity, something that Asia lacked.[97] Liberation of the land-fettered population of China consisted not in peasant rebellion but in facing the ocean and opening to the lessons of seafaring civilizations and their science, a task for which only China's intellectuals were suited, for only they could enter into dialogue with the West. In this narrative of stagnation and liberation, the peasant loses all agency and is almost reduced to an inert element of nature—the sediment of earth sinking in the Yellow River—that only science can manage.

CHINESE LIBERALISM AND THE LIBERATION OF THE FARMER

This narrative of stagnation and liberation became the foundation for postsocialist Chinese liberalism, and the Chinese peasant was its foil. During the 1990s, the duality in Marxist and Maoist notions of the nature of the peasant was again transformed; in this iteration the dichotomy between feudal peasant and petty capitalist entrepreneur reached its most extreme form—a split between the dependent peasant and the independent citizen farmer. Peasants were no longer the holders of a revolutionary subjectivity, but the foundation of an anticitizen and anti-rights-based populist politics. It was only when peasants acted in a petty-bourgeois manner as entrepreneurial property owners that liberal intellectuals considered them positively as "citizens." Here, "the citizen" was defined as a person who was independent from the state, an independence primarily derived from their control over private property. In the most explicit forms of this argument, intellectuals portrayed the peasant, a backward subjectivity of dependence and ignorance, as the negation of the citizen.

Qin Hui, a leading Chinese liberal from the 1990s until the present and a historian of rural China who studied with Zhao Lisheng (discussed earlier in conjunction with the AMP), began his historical research critical of the Maoist historical dictum that rural class struggle and rebellion were the motor of Chinese history. Within Qin's narrative, the determining factor of whether one was a peasant is the relationship between collectivities and individuals. To break from being a "peasant," the key to modernization, meant to become independent of large collectivities, the most important of which was the state. "Peasants" are dependent on collectives and are part of organic communities, whereas "farmers" are independent producers who are citizens of a society.[98] Land ownership becomes the primary way to distinguish "farmers" from "peasants." Qin had to reference the English for "farmer" and "peasant" to make this distinction clear, as in the Chinese it is not. In fact, in Qin's work, the Chinese term "*nongmin*" (which he explicitly translates as "peasant" and not "farmer") was sometimes used as a generic category that simply stands in opposition to the category "citizen" (*gongmin* or *shimin*).

In Qin's writings, "peasant" was not simply a category pointing to an empirical social group, therefore, but often operated as a trope for people dependent on collectives, a position that would be eliminated in the modernization process. In this way, even city people might be understood as "peasants" through their position of dependence on the urban work unit system, in which housing, schooling, and food were determined by one's unit. Qin stated in one passage,

> China's so-called nongmin problems of past and present have all been *peasant* problems and not *farmer* problems, and were not merely about those who cultivated the land. . . . Particularly after 1949, the little *citizen* status that existed was gradually eliminated, "city people" were more *peasantized* (or *de-citizenized*) than country people ["peasant," "farmer," and "citizen" are in English in the passage].[99]

Modernization, therefore, is the transformation of "peasant states, agricultural civilizations, and traditional societies" into "citizen states (*shimin [gongmin] guojia*), industrial civilizations, and modern societies." This is a process in which everybody, whether they live in the city or the countryside, had to be transformed from "*peasant* to *citizen*."[100] While in this formulation the peasant is somewhat abstracted from the rural, the main opprobrium of this critique is still directed at rural dwellers. The category "farmer," therefore, emerged in Chinese discourse within a very particular political and historical context: the party's own ideological justification of the rural reforms and the institution of antiegalitarian remuneration policies brought about the effacement of a dialectical understanding of the peasant as a class.

CONCLUSION

While reform-period narratives of peasant characteristics and agency were built on rearticulations of earlier orthodox Marxist and CCP understandings of history and politics, under the new conditions of China's postsocialist reconnection with global capitalism and the reevaluation of labor power that accompanied it, understandings of the role of the peasant in history were dramatically transformed. The dialectical class image of the peasant was slowly replaced by a one-sided and static understanding in which the peasant lost historical and political agency. Under the growing hegemony of economic analysis and evaluation as the 1980s progressed, the petty-bourgeois nature of the peasantry, based on its ownership of the means of production, shifted from a negative to a positive characteristic. Thus, while the peasant was to have no agency in historical change—and no more revolutionary subjectivity—under the new conditions of a commodity economy, the peasant could become an agricultural entrepreneur. The static dichotomy of bad backward peasant and good entrepreneurial citizen-farmer reached its most extreme form in the Chinese liberalism that emerged in the 1990s. For some Chinese liberals, the positive image of peasant potentiality implied that they were no longer peasants; they had the potential to become farmers, for only farmers had the qualities of entrepreneurship and independence necessary to modernity.

Globally, the rural social world is undergoing an immense transformation, and this is more evident in China than most countries. Within this political-economic context, any discussion of the meaning of the categories "peasant" and "farmer" in China—and their adequacy to the present moment—must take place. Yet within this moment of great transformation, it remains difficult to imagine a new future for agrarian society. Understandings of the peasant seem to oscillate between the entrepreneurial farmer operating within a market economy, on the one hand, and the holder of a traditional—and even national—culture under attack by market forces, on the other.[101] The displacement of a class understanding of peasants hampers contemporary Chinese discussions on the position of peasants in Chinese society. As earlier Marxist theorization implied, the petty-bourgeois peasantry has a tendency to class differentiation, one that does not straightforwardly lead to a modern citizenry. While the lack of full property rights over land is an impediment to class differentiation, such differentiation is underway in the contemporary Chinese countryside—a phenomenon for which the blanket term "farmer" is clearly inadequate.[102] At the same time, perhaps the term "peasant" is equally inadequate, also setting limits on our ability to understand contemporary social processes and to imagine a different future for the social space of agricultural production.

NOTES

1. Many people have commented on various incarnations of this essay; I would like to especially thank Gail Hershatter, Arif Dirlik, Chris Connery, Saul Thomas, Dong Zhenghua, Abidin Kusno, Dianne Newell, Alejandro Rojas, Wang Shaoguang, Wang Hui, and Wen Tiejun.

2. Myron L. Cohen, "Cultural and Political Inventions in Modern China: The Case of the Chinese 'Peasant'," *Daedalus* 122, no. 2 (1993): 151–170. Charles W. Hayford, *To the People: James Yen and Village China* (New York: Columbia University Press, 1990) and "The Storm over the Peasant: Orientalism and Rhetoric in Constructing China," in *Contesting the Master Narrative: Essays in Social History*, ed. Jeffrey Cox and Shelton Stromquist (Iowa City: University of Iowa Press, 1998), 150–172.

3. In the same issue of *Daedalus* that Cohen's article appeared, Yu Ying-shih made this direct argument. Yu Ying-shih, "The Radicalization of China in the Twentieth Century," *Daedalus* 122, no. 2 (1993): 125–150.

4. Cohen, "Cultural and Political Inventions in Modern China."

5. Ibid., 154. Notably, here, "farmers" (for which there is no clear Chinese translation), "tradition," "customs," and "religion" seem to be treated as more naturalized and universal categories, somehow less modern or contrived in their historical emergence. This makes one wonder if it is equally Cohen who is partaking in cultural invention.

6. Hayford, "The Storm over the Peasant."

7. See also Xiaorong Han, *Chinese Discourses on the Peasant, 1900–1949* (Albany: State University of New York Press, 2005).

8. John Flower, "Peasant Consciousness," in *Post-Socialist Peasant? Rural and Urban Constructions of Identity in Eastern Europe, East Asia and the Former Soviet Union*, ed. Pamela Leonard and Deema Kaneff (London: Palgrave, 2002), 44–72.

9. See Arif Dirlik, "Postsocialism? Reflections on 'Socialism with Chinese Characteristics'," in *Marxism and the Chinese Experience*, ed. Arif Dirlik and Maurice Meisner (Armonk, NY: M. E. Sharpe, 1989), 363–364, and *After the Revolution: Waking to Global Capitalism* (Hanover: Wesleyan University Press, 1994).

10. Daniel Kelliher, "Chinese Communist Political Theory and the Rediscovery of the Peasantry," *Modern China* 20, no. 4 (1994): 387–415, 390. For a general discussion of Chinese Communist Party theorizations on the peasantry, also see Han, *Chinese Discourses on the Peasant, 1900–1949* and James P. Harrison, *The Communists and Chinese Peasant Rebellions*, Studies of the East Asian Institute Columbia University (New York: Atheneum, 1969).

11. Quoted in Kelliher, "Chinese Communist Political Theory," 392.

12. Ibid., 392–393.

13. Quoted in ibid., 394. Original: Mao Zedong, "On Correcting Mistaken Ideas in the Party," in *Selected Works of Mao Tse-Tung*, ed. Central Committee of the Communist Party of China Committee for the Publication of the Selected Works of Mao Tse-tung (Beijing: Foreign Languages Press, 1965), I: 105–116.

14. According to Bo Yibo, Mao was the first to use this formulation. See Bo Yibo, *Ruogan Zhongda juece yu shijian de huigu* (Recollections of Some Decisions and Events of the Central Committee of the Communist Party of China) *(Shang)*, 2 vols. (Beijing: Zhonggong dangshi chubanshe, 2008), 1: 147.

15. Quoted in Stuart R. Schram, *The Political Thought of Mao Tse-Tung*, Revised and Enlarged Edition (New York: Praeger Publishers, 1969), 341–342. See also Bo, *Ruogan Zhongda juece yu shijian de huigu (Shang)*, 147–148.

16. Bo, *Ruogan Zhongda juece yu shijian de huigu (Shang)*, 147.

17. Kelliher, "Chinese Communist Political Theory and the Rediscovery of the Peasantry," 396.

18. Quoted in Philip A. Kuhn, *Origins of the Modern Chinese State* (Stanford: Stanford University Press, 2002), 104. See Zhonghua Renmin Gongheguo guojia nongye weiyuanhui ban gong ting, ed., *Nongye jitihua zhongyao wenjian huibian* [Collection of Important Documents on Agricultural Collectivization], 2 vols. (Beijing: Zhonggong zhongyang dangxiao chubanshe, 1982) vol. 1 and for a general discussion by a contemporary participant, Bo,

Ruogan Zhongda juece yu shijian de huigu (Shang), 130–149. This incident is sometimes raised in present-day debates that touch on the issue of the relationship between the peasantry and history. For Bo Yibo, whose important book was originally published in 1991, agrarian socialism is a form of populism that has an important but detrimental lineage in twentieth-century Chinese political thought (ibid., 147–148). A discussion on the damage caused by this political lineage ensued after the 1989 Tiananmen demonstrations. See, for example, a series of articles on populism in *Zhanlüe yu guanli* (issue 5, 1994) and Li Zehou and Liu Zaifu, *Gaobie geming: hui wang ershi shiji Zhongguo* [*Farewell to Revolution: Looking Back on Twentieth-Century China*] (Hong Kong: Tian di tu shu you xian gong si, 1995).

19. See Liu Shaoqi, "*Zhonggong Shanxi shengwei 'ba laoqu huzhu zuzhi tigao yibu' de piyu* [Evaluation of Shanxi Provincial Committee's 'Promotion of Mutual Aid Organizations']," in *Nongye jitihua Zhongyao wenjian huibian*, 33. Also noted in Bo, *Ruogan Zhongda juece yu shijian de huigu (Shang)*, 144 and Wang Jun, *Mao Zedong Yu Zhongguo gongyehua* [*Mao Zedong and China's Industrialization*] (Fuzhou: Fujian jiaoyu chubanshe, 2001), 153.

20. Schram, *The Political Thought of Mao Tse-Tung*, 341.

21. Kelliher, "Chinese Communist Political Theory," 397.

22. Ibid.

23. Wang Rongsheng, "*Zhi you nongmin zhanzheng cai shi fengjian shehui fazhande zhenzheng dongli ma*? [Is peasant war the only real impetus for the development of feudal society?]" in *Lishi yanjiu* (1979): 49–56. Wang wrote under the pseudonym Rong Sheng. *Lishi yanjiu* (historical research) was an important site of political discussion at the beginning of the reform period.

24. Dai Yi, "On Some Theoretical Aspects of the Class Struggle as They Relate to Historical Research," *Chinese Studies in History* (1980): 55–74, 58. One of Dai's primary political targets of the article was Qi Benyu, the head of the historical group for the Party theoretical journal *Red Flag* at the time of the Cultural Revolution. Qi was one historian who, at the time, most strongly promoted the idea that peasant rebellion, and thus class struggle, was the motor of Chinese history. His writings on the Taiping Rebellion were particularly prominent, gaining him the attention of Mao. See Roderick MacFarquhar and Michael Schoenhals, *Mao's Last Revolution* (Cambridge: Harvard University Press, 2006), 28–29. For a contemporary analysis of debates on peasant rebellion, see Kwang-Ching Liu, "World View and Peasant Rebellion: Reflections on Post-Mao Historiography," *The Journal of Asian Studies* 40, no. 2 (1981): 295–326.

25. Dai, "On Some Theoretical Aspects of the Class Struggle as They Relate to Historical Research," 60.

26. Ibid., 66. Many of these discussions on peasant rebellion centered on a reevaluation of the Taiping Rebellion (1851–1864). Large historical symposiums on the Taiping were held at the very beginning of the reform era in 1978 and 1979 to facilitate the reorientation of historical work. For a report on a symposium held in Nanjing in May and June of 1979, see Alex Volkoff and Edgar Wickberg, "New Directions in Chinese Historiography: Reappraising the Taiping: Notes and Comment," *Pacific Affairs* 52, no. 3 (1979): 479–490.

27. Wang Xiaoqiang, "Nongmin yu fan fengjian [Peasants and Anti-Feudalism]," in *Lishi yanjiu* no. 10 (Oct. 1979): 3–12.

28. Ibid., 6.

29. Ibid., 9 and 11.

30. The Chinese economy was officially defined as a "planned socialist commodity economy" at the Third Plenum of the Twelfth Central Committee meeting in October 1984. Stuart R. Schram, "Deng Xiaoping's Quest for 'Modernization with Chinese Characteristics' and the Future of Marxism-Leninism," in *China in the Era of Deng Xiaoping: A Decade of Reform*, ed. Michael Y. M. Kau and Susan H. Marsh (Armonk, NY: M. E. Sharpe, 1997), 408–434.

31. Wang Xiaoqiang, "Nongye Shehuizhuyi Pipan [Critique of Agrarian Socialism]," in *Nongye jingji wenti [Problems in Agricultural Economics]*, no. 2 (1980), 9–20.

32. Wang, "Nongmin yu fan fengjian," 12.

33. On the "bureaucratic class," see Kalpana Misra, *From Post-Maoism to Post-Marxism: The Erosion of Official Ideology in Deng's China* (New York and London: Routledge, 1998), 151–182, and Joel Andreas, *Rise of the Red Engineers: The Cultural Revolution and the Origins of China's New Class* (Stanford: Stanford University Press, 2009).

34. This conference was convened by Hu Yaobang in early 1979, shortly after he became the general secretary of the Central Committee. The conference was the scene of a debate between more radical reformers, such as Wang Ruoshui, Su Shaozhi, Yan Jiaqi, and Yu Guangyuan, who were supporters of Hu Yaobang, and moderate reformers around Hu Qiaomu and Deng Liqun. All participants were Marxists. See Misra, *From Post-Maoism to Post-Marxism*, 10–11 and 55–56.

35. Quoted in Bill Brugger and David Kelly, *Chinese Marxism in the Post-Mao Era* (Stanford: Stanford University Press, 1990), 143.

36. Ibid., 142–144.

37. See ibid. The early-1980s debate on humanism resurfaced in the 1990s and became an important ground for debate in the split between the New Left and the Liberals in China. See also Jason McGrath, *Postsocialist Modernity: Chinese Cinema, Literature, and Criticism in the Market Age* (Stanford: Stanford University Press, 2008), especially chapter two.

38. Wang Xizhe, "Mao Zedong and the Cultural Revolution," in *On Socialist Democracy and the Chinese Legal System: The Li Yizhe Debates*, ed. Anita Chan, Stanley Rosen, and Jonathan Unger (Armonk, NY: M. E. Sharpe, 1985), 177–260.

39. Ibid., 187.

40. Ibid., 188.

41. Ibid., 196.

42. Ibid., 196 and 259.

43. Ibid., 193.

44. Many articles on the AMP were published in the 1950s and early 1960s. According to Timothy Brook, in the 1950s, the AMP was usually understood as a form of slave society. This was the viewpoint of Wu Dakun, who was a well-known participant in these earlier debates. Brook suggests that, unlike its use in articles in the early 1980s, the AMP was used during the Maoist period to show that China was not different from the West in its historical development. Timothy Brook, "Introduction," in *The Asiatic Mode of Production in China*, ed. Timothy Brook (Armonk, NY: M. E. Sharpe, 1989), 3–34. The 1950s discussion of the AMP developed in relation to the debates on the "sprouts of capitalism" (*zibenzhuyi mengya*) from the 1950s, which found protocapitalist development in the Song, Ming, and Qing dynasties. Wu Dakun, by contrast, argued that these protocapitalist "sprouts" were no match for the power of the imperial state. See Timothy Brook, "Capitalism and the Writing of Modern History in China," in *China and Historical Capitalism: Genealogies of Sinological Knowledge*, ed. Timothy Brook and Gregory Blue, *Studies in Modern Capitalism* (Cambridge: Cambridge University Press, 1999), 110–157.

45. Brook, "Introduction," 18. While I focus on the political implications of these arguments, I do not mean to imply that they have no historical value. For a very interesting discussion of Wu's argument, see Brugger and Kelly, *Chinese Marxism in the Post-Mao Era*, 23–28.

46. Arif Dirlik, *Revolution and History: The Origins of Marxist Historiography in China, 1919–1937* (Berkeley: University of California Press, 1978), 191–192.

47. Wu Dakun, "Some Questions Concerning Research on the Asiatic Mode of Production," in Brook (ed.), *The Asiatic Mode of Production in China*, 35–46. Interestingly, Wu links

the rise of Lin Biao and the Gang of Four to the persistence of the AMP in China, believing it is a mistake to call their rule "feudal fascism" (p. 43).

48. Ibid., 45.

49. Wu read the English translation, Umberto Melotti, *Marx and the Third World* (London: Macmillian, 1977). For a critical review of Melotti, see Arif Dirlik, "Two Views of Melotti," *Journal of Contemporary Asia* 8, no. 3 (1978): 387–392.

50. Wu, "Some Questions Concerning Research on the Asiatic Mode of Production."

51. Noting Soviet "socialist imperialism" (namely, the Soviet occupation of Czechoslovakia in 1968) and its problem of bureaucracy, Wu argued that Chinese socialism, unlike that of the Soviet Union, did not have such a problem of bureaucracy. Melotti's inclusion of China in the same category as the Soviet Union, argued Wu, was the result of his viewing China during the Cultural Revolution. Ibid., 39–41.

52. Ibid., 43.

53. Karl Wittfogel, *Oriental Despotism* (New Haven: Yale University Press, 1957).

54. Wu Dakun, "The Asiatic Mode of Production in History as Viewed by Political Economy in Its Broad Sense," in *Marxism in China*, ed. Shaozhi Su et al. (Nottingham: Spokesman, 1983), 53–77. Here, Wu walked a fine line between the "scientific" use of the concept to explain "objective historical processes," as he put it, and its politically conservative, anticommunist use. In other words, despite Wu's claims to the contrary, his use of the AMP to criticize the Chinese state during the Cultural Revolution could easily become a general critique of communism in the fashion of Wittfogel.

55. Brook, "Capitalism and the Writing of Modern History in China," 148.

56. See Yang Xiguang, "Whither China?" in *Peking and the New Left*, ed. Klaus Mehnert (Berkeley: University of California Center for Chinese Studies, 1969), 82–100.

57. Zhao Lisheng, "The Well-Field System in Relation to the Asiatic Mode of Production," in Brook (ed.), *The Asiatic Mode of Production in China*, 65–84.

58. Ibid. Other theorists also used the category as an oblique critique of the commune system. Ke Changji did the same; see Ke Changji, "Ancient Chinese Society and the Asiatic Mode of Production," in Brook (ed.), *The Asiatic Mode of Production in China*, 47–64.

59. Brook, "Introduction," 19.

60. Andrew Kipnis, "*Suzhi*: A Keyword Approach," *The China Quarterly*, no. 186 (2006): 295–313.

61. Andrew Kipnis has argued that the discourse of *suzhi* cannot be reduced to neoliberalism; see "Neoliberalism Reified: *Suzhi* Discourse and Tropes of Neoliberalism in the People's Republic of China," *Journal of the Royal Anthropological Institute* 13, no. 2 (May 2007): 383–400, and "*Suzhi*: A Keyword Approach." While he is right that *suzhi* is used in many different ways, some certainly contradicting what is normally meant by neoliberalism, my argument here is closer to that of Ann Anagnost, "The Corporeal Politics of Quality (*Suzhi*)," *Public Culture* 16, no. 2 (2004): 189–208, and Yan Hairong, "Neoliberal Governmentality and Neohumanism: Organizing Suzhi/Value Flow through Labor Recruitment Networks," *Cultural Anthropology* 18, no. 4 (2003): 493–523, and *New Masters, New Servants: Migration, Development, and Women Workers in China* (Durham: Duke University Press, 2008), both targets of Kipnis's criticism. As with any discourse, people may use *suzhi* for many different purposes depending on their own social position and goals. But I argue that the dominant meaning of *suzhi* within postsocialist discourse—as it is used to understand the position of the peasant within society and history—is closely linked to the changing notion of the value of labor power at a time in which China was integrating with global capitalism. Without paying close attention to that frame, the predominance of the discourse of *suzhi* is impossible to understand.

62. Deng Xiaoping, "Adhere to the Principle 'To Each According to His Work'," *Selected Works of Deng Xiaoping, 1975–1982* (Beijing: Foreign Languages Press, 1984), 117–118. This policy contradicted the treatment of distribution by Marx and Engels. See Misra, *From Post-Maoism to Post-Marxism*, 122.

63. Tang Tsou, Marc Blecher, and Mitch Meisner, "Policy Change at the National Summit and Institutional Transformation at the Local Level: The Case of Tachai and Hsiyang County in the Post-Mao Era," in *Select Papers from the Center for Far Eastern Studies*, ed. Tang Tsou (Chicago: University of Chicago Press, 1981), 291.

64. On the "New Class" see Andreas, *Rise of the Red Engineers*, especially chapter 10.

65. Anagnost, "The Corporeal Politics of Quality (*Suzhi*)," 190. See also Bai Yijin, "*Zaojiu xinxing nongmin shi jiejue nongmin wentide zhongyao fangmian* [Making a New Peasant is an Important Aspect of Solving the Peasant Problem]," *Nongye jingji wenti* [*Problems of Agricultural Economy*], no. 2 (1983): 12–14.

66. Liu Zhenkun, "Jiantan zhiyue renkou zhiliangde yinsu ji gaishan renkou zhiliangde tujing [Factors Conditioning Population Quality and Ways to Improve It]," *Henan daxue xuebao (shehui kexueban)* [*The journal of Henan University (social science edition)*], no. 6 (1982): 94–100, 94.

67. Tan Yibin, "Laodongli Yu Laodongli Zhiliang (Labor Power and Labor Quality)," *Qiye jingji* [*Enterprise economy*], no. 3 (1981): 48.

68. Jin Huishen, "Zhongshi tigao nongye laodongzhede suzhi [Pay Attention to Raising the Quality of Rural Laborers]," *Dangdai caijing* [*Contemporary finance and economics*], no. 4 (1983): 85–88.

69. Jin Huishen, "Tigao laodongli suzhi shi nongye xiandaihuade zhanlüe zhongdian [Raising the Quality of Labor is a Key to the Strategy of Rural Modernization]," *Nongye jingji wenti* [*Problems of Agricultural Economy*], no. 11 (1983): 33–35.

70. Ibid.

71. Bai, "Zaojiu Xinxing Nongmin Shi Jiejue Nongmin Wenti De Zhongyao Fangmian," 12.

72. Wang Xiaoqiang and Bai Nanfeng, *The Poverty of Plenty* (Hampshire and London: Macmillan, 1991); Feng Chongyi's *Nongmin yishi yu bainian Zhongguo* [*Peasant Consciousness and Hundred Years of China*] (Hong Kong: Chung Hwa Book Company, 1989) and *Zuochu lunhui: nongmin yishi yu bainian Zhongguo* [*Breaking Out of the Cycle: Peasant Consciousness and Hundred Years of China*] (Changchun: Jilin wenshi chubanshe, 1997) further developed this concept of *suzhi*. For a discussion of this work, see Flower, "Peasant Consciousness," 54–59. Feng, a prominent historian and liberal, is associate professor of China studies at the Institute for International Studies of the University of Technology, Sydney.

73. Wang and Bai, *The Poverty of Plenty*, 2.

74. Ibid., 93.

75. Ibid., 31–32.

76. See Anagnost, "The Corporeal Politics of Quality (*Suzhi*)." On the politics of class analysis in contemporary China, see Guo Yingjie, "Farewell to Class, Except the Middle Class: The Politics of Class Analysis in Contemporary China," *The Asia-Pacific Journal* 26 (2009): 2–9.

77. Wang and Bai, *The Poverty of Plenty*, 32–33.

78. Ibid., 34 and 36.

79. Ibid., 37.

80. See Su Xiaokang and Wang Luxiang, *Deathsong of the River: A Reader's Guide to the Chinese TV Series Heshang*, Cornell East Asia Papers (Ithaca: Cornell University Press, 1991), 187.

81. As Su makes clear in his essay "The Distress of the Dragon Year—Notes on *Heshang,*" it was during Su and cowriter Wang Luxiang's trip to rural Shaanxi during the making of *Heshang* that a conceptualization of rural stagnation, the attachment to the land, and image of the yellow earth came together. This essay was translated in Su and Wang, *Deathsong of the River,* 271–299. See page 279.

82. Ibid., 218.

83. See ibid., 175.

84. Ibid., 163.

85. Ibid., 164.

86. Ibid., 166.

87. Ibid., 169–170, translation slightly modified: the original translation translates *suzhi* as "makeup."

88. At times almost word-for-word, as Richard Bodman and Pin P. Wan point out in their very helpful annotation of the translated script. Ibid., 167 and 170.

89. Attachment to the land, considered the "destiny" of Chinese agrarian civilization because of its geographical nature, is the main theme of the second episode of the *Heshang,* "Destiny" (*mingyun*), written by Wang Luxiang. See Wang Luxiang, "Ming yun [Destiny]," in *Heshang lun* [On Heshang], ed. Cui Wenhua (Beijing: Wenhua yishu chubanshe, 1988), 15–27.

90. Su and Wang, *Deathsong of the River,* 171.

91. The series argued that Plekhanov was correct in his argument with Lenin that "history could not skip its necessary stages of development." Post-Stalinist reforms in eastern Europe, according to the series, showed that "History had apparently once again raised Plekhanov's question. Not that History had gone in retreat; Man, rather, had overtaken it." History, in this narrative, is unavoidable even if it may take its time in passing its judgment: "On the 18th of December, 1978 [the Third Plenary Session of the Eleventh Central Committee of the CCP, which marked the shift to the reform period] this ineluctable current of history finally swept China too into the mainstream of reform among socialist nations." Ibid., 160–161. The metaphor for history, here, is a river: while humans might fight against the current for a short period, this struggle will ultimately result in failure and even disaster. Social Darwinian competition guides the course of history: the industrial revolution in England "forced all nations either to take the path of industrialization or to be eliminated by History." Ibid., 165.

92. See ibid., 187–188. The series quickly linked this "turmoil" to the violence of the Cultural Revolution (page 189).

93. Su and Wang, *Deathsong of the River,* 198.

94. Dai, "On Some Theoretical Aspects of the Class Struggle as They Relate to Historical Research," 66.

95. Su and Wang, *Deathsong of the River,* 192. During the 1980s, the idea that Chinese "feudalism" was stagnant was most famously developed by Jin Guantao and Liu Qingfeng, editors of the *Zouxiang weilai congshu* [*Towards the Future*] book series that published Wang and Bai's *Furao de pinkun* and contributors to the *Heshang.* See Jin Guantao and Liu Qingfeng, *Xingsheng yu weiji—lun Zhongguo fengjian shehuide chaowending jieguo* [*Efflorescence and crisis—on the superstable structure of Chinese feudal society*] (Changsha: Hunan renmin chubanshe, 1983).

96. Hua Shiping, *Scientism and Humanism: Two Cultures in Post-Mao China (1978–1989)* (Albany: State University of New York Press, 1995), 80.

97. Wang Luxiang, "Ming Yun," in *Heshang lun,* 17–18.

98. See Qin Hui and Su Wen, *Tianyuanshi yu kuangxiangqu—Guanzhong moshi yu qianjindai shehui de zai renshi* [*Pastorals and rhapsodies: a new understanding of the Guanzhong model and premodern societies*] (Beijing: Zhongyang bianyi chubanshe, 1996).

99. Qin Hui, *Lun Xiandai Sixiang De Gongtong Dixian* [*The Common Baseline of Modern Thought*], http://www.china-review.com/fwsq/qh.asp (accessed Dec. 17, 2005). Qin notes that this is the opposite of the situation in the West. In the West, city people were more independent than country people. After 1949 in China, city people were less independent than country people. See Qin, "*Nongmin wenti: shenme 'nongmin'? shenme 'wenti'*? [Peasant question: what 'peasant'? what 'question'?]," in *Qin Hui wenxuan: wenti yu zhuyi* (Changchun: Changchun chubanshe, 1999), 15–23.

100. Qin, "Lun xiandai sixiang de gongtong dixian."

101. On the latter, see for example essays in Huang Ping, ed., *Xiangtu Zhongguo yu wenhua zijue* [*Rural China and Cultural Self-Consciousness*] (Beijing: Sanlian shudian, 2007).

102. Qian Forrest Zhang and John A. Donaldson, "The Rise of Agrarian Capitalism with Chinese Characteristics: Agricultural Modernization, Agribusiness and Collective Land Rights," *The China Journal* no. 60 (2008): 25–47.

Chapter 5

China Experience, Comparative Advantage, and the Rural Reconstruction Experiment[1]

Wen Tiejun, Dong Xiaodan, Yang Shuai, Qiu Jiansheng, and Lau Kin Chi

Since China's accession to the WTO in 2001, "China experience" in the Western theoretical discourse could be extracted into two points. First, China's high growth rate, lasting over thirty years, has benefited from institutional change in the four dimensions of privatization, marketization, liberalization, and globalization that are implicated with Western ideology. Second, China's comparative advantage in attracting foreign investment can be mainly attributed to its rich labor resource. Clearly, these two assertions are shaping the world's understanding of China in an increasingly profound manner.[2]

Nevertheless, the assertions above contradict a rarely raised bit of common sense: Most of the developing countries have adopted even more westernized institutional reforms than China did, and all large developing nations have the so-called "comparative advantage" of rich labor resources (e.g., in Asia, there are five developing nations with populations over 100 million). But why did economic phenomena similar to China not take place in those nations? Apparently, the Western mainstream theories cannot explain China's economic growth. In other words, what China possesses is not the experience and comparative advantage in the Western sense.

ONE HUNDRED YEARS: AN ALTERNATIVE READING OF CHINA EXPERIENCE[3]

First of all, we should briefly discuss the historical logic of the China experience. This essay proposes an alternative reading of a century of Chinese history.[4] Since the late Qing Dynasty, under imperialist invasion and continual geopolitical tension in the region, China has made significant impacts in world history. Under geopolitical pressure for over a century, it was able to launch four rounds of endogenous primitive accumulation of capital for industrialization at high costs.

The first round is the Self-Strengthening Movement, which originated in the 1860s. Under the patronage of rising local military power, this movement was later accompanied by the emergence of modern textile and food industries. It was interrupted by the Boxer Uprising and subsequent invasion of the Imperialist Eight-Nation Alliance in 1900.

The second round is the nationalist industrialization campaign after the national reunification in the 1920s–1930s. It was interrupted by the global capitalist crisis in the 1930s (with the drainage of silver in 1934–1936, hyperinflation, and World War II). However, the building of a nationalistic economy by the Nationalist Party's government within or after the war period was another story.

The third round is the primitive accumulation of capital for industrialization in the 1950s after a long period of turmoil. In the 1970s, China resumed diplomatic relations with the West, reconstructed its global geopolitical strategy, and unilaterally introduced Western investments at massive scale. Serious fiscal crises broke out almost instantly, and this round of capital accumulation was interrupted with the transition of power in the ruling party in late 1970s.

The fourth round[5] took place in the 1980s. Under the banner of "reform" and the "open policy," the primitive accumulation of capital for local industrialization resumed, followed by subsequent formation of industrial capital and its structural expansion at high speed. Since the mid-1990s, especially after its accession to the WTO, China has been facing increasing pressure of global surplus financial capital. Today, the tension between domestic and international interests is approaching a critical point of explosion.

In short, despite changes in regime, China has undergone four rounds of endogenous primitive accumulation of capital for industrialization and paid great costs in each round. The nation has finally completed the process of industrialization, being the only Third World economy with an indigenous population over 100 million that boasts such an achievement[6] (see Figure 5.1 and Figure 5.2).

Now, we come to the core mechanism of China's industrialization process, which is this introversive primitive accumulation of capital.

A well-known mechanism of industrialization in former socialist nations is to benefit from the scissors differential between industrial and agricultural products through centralized purchase and distribution. For China in the past sixty years, in addition to the scissors-differential mechanism, another key mechanism of primitive accumulation of capital has been manipulation of labor force. In the name of "socialist transition," state capitalism in substance managed to manipulate the labor force, the richest resource in China, to successfully substitute scarce capital and massively invest

Figure 5.1 Comparison of the economic development

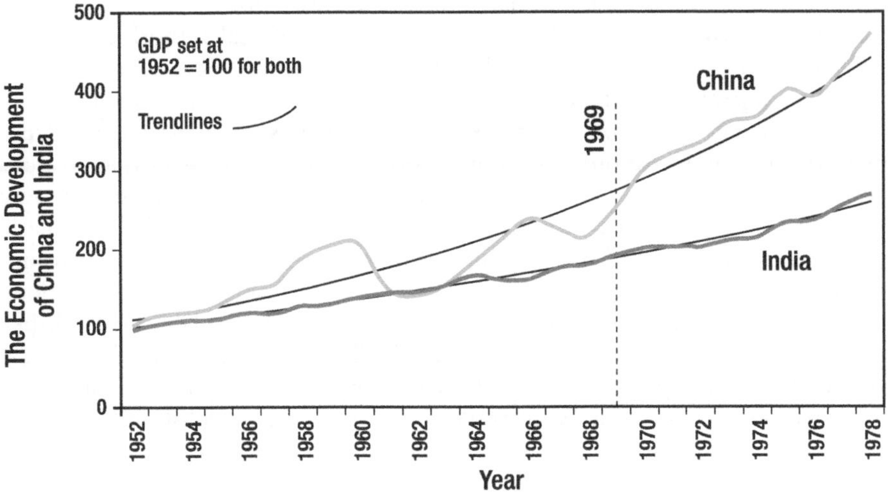

Figure 5.2 Economic structure of China and India

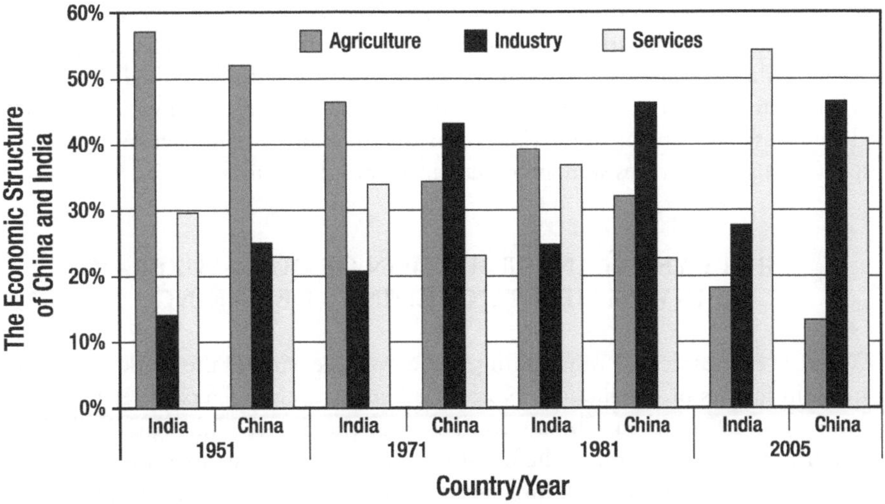

Source: Saumitra Chaudhuri, "Line of Convergence: India-Japan-China & Future of Asia" Sasakawa Peace Foundation and CSDS (Tokyo, Japan, March 6, 2006).

it into gigantic infrastructure building that is necessary for national industrialization with the "Whole People's Ownership."

China, as a continental nation with the largest and still-growing population as well as an extreme scarcity of resources, has completed its late industrialization by taking introversive primitive accumulation of capital as the only available means. As a result, whether necessary primitive accumulation of capital for industrialization could be achieved has become the criterion in judging the success or failure of any political institutions and ideologies in China. This capital-accumulation-based view, in turn, became the intrinsic obstacle that has prevented the political authorities at different levels so far in China from truly implementing the scientific view of development.

This paper suggests that different ways of primitive accumulation of capital will lead to different institutional forms and affect the subsequent path dependence of institutional change. Accordingly, industrialization with Chinese characteristics and its introversive primitive accumulation of capital have led to a relatively centralized institution that is necessarily different from the liberalist system of Western nations, as the latter accomplished industrialization through colonialism and expansion. In the West, centralizing the labor force through massive revolutionary mobilization was inconceivable, with the exceptions of slavery and colonial forced labor. With dispersed labor force, Western capitalism could only gradually develop from individual workshop handicrafts to factory handicrafts and then machine industry. In fact, without colonial expansion overseas, the West would have failed to accomplish industrialization by slowly going through the above three stages of primitive accumulation of capital.

In short, debates about China in the Western academia can be basically attributed to controversies of ideological discourse. What lacks there is a comprehensive understanding of history, not to mention a concurrence of theoretical logic and historical logic. These debates are considered substantial only in terms of ideological struggle but not empirically valuable in terms of social sciences. Both China and the West have marched into the capitalist civilization, yet through very different ways. Under the pressure of external military threats, China, in the early 1950s, rapidly launched the industrial construction through state capitalism. This suggests that the economic bases of China and the West in terms of industrialization were obviously heterogeneous, so that the respective superstructures were predetermined into different forms.

SIXTY YEARS: INTERRUPTION OF QUASI-SUZERAIN INVESTMENT AND CHINA'S DELINKING

In Western economics the functioning of the invisible hand of the market presupposes scarcity in factors of production. Note that here "scarcity" refers to relative scarcity. However, in 1957, when China's conflict with the Soviet Union gradually became apparent, the Soviet Union as the quasi-suzerain called off its investments in China.[7] Hence, the greatest difficulty China faced then was absolute scarcity in capital.

Past experience in international development shows that in cases of industrialization driven by foreign investments, once the dominant factor, namely, the capital, becomes scarce, those developing nations with market economy as economic base and liberalist ideas as superstructure will suffer from interruption of industrialization.

What makes the situation even worse is that during the period of industrial investment by the suzerain, the beneficiary nation usually builds its massive superstructure to fit with the economic base that complies with the industrialization model determined by the suzerain. Once the superstructure and its ideology with implied indoctrination become the dominant discourse of the beneficiary nation, it is difficult to replace it even if the investment is terminated and the economic base gets forced to change. Very often, a reform in economic order changes the previous allocation of interests, so that it will probably face strong resistance and thus the new structure might go into a direction contrary to the goal of the reform. As a result, once the suzerain withdraws their investments, most of the dependent developing nations will be confronted with social turmoil and even humanitarian disasters.

This turmoil may be one of the reasons why, in general, developing nations with comparative advantage of surplus labor resource have failed to accomplish industrialization.

From 1957 to 1960 onward, after the Soviet Union withdrew its investment, China started to experiment with the "delinking strategy,"[8] with guiding principles of "independence, self-reliance, arduous struggle, and diligent nation-building." It continued to successfully mobilize the whole population into localized industrialization through ideological means, which was "continuing revolution" in theory, "class struggle" in popular terms, and nationalism in substance. China has completed the process of industrialization in a much shorter period of time than did the West. In a mere five years (1960–1965), with 800 million people of extreme thrift, and resource products mainly consisting of agricultural staples, China paid off all state debts of the 1950s, including the expenditure for the Korean War. The main mechanism of the success was again primitive accumulation of capital in the name of "ownership by the whole people."[9]

China's autonomous mode of primitive accumulation of capital in this period, if expressed in ideological terms of Eurocentrism, is "faceless human-wave tactics under authoritarianism." Literati like artists and writers, who prioritized sensibility in production process and individualized forms of labor, reacted strongly. This made the ideology responsible for massive mobilization more and more difficult to justify itself among the mass, and needed to rely on political power to consolidate its discursive power. This was the intrinsic reason why Marxism studies that were handsomely financed by the government found it hard to take root in China.

The following basic historical fact should be acknowledged: After the relation with the former Soviet Union tensed up in 1958, China faced great difficulty in implementing the second and third five-year plans alone, as well as in changing the Soviet planned economy model accordingly. In fact, it was no longer possible for China to pursue centralized industrialization. After 1958, China attempted to implement localized industrialization by taking advantage of local small and medium enterprises. In this hastily altered strategy plan, the "five light industries" launched by the People's Commune were the main content.

Under the pressure of decreasing and finally terminated investment from the Soviet Union, Chinese collective leadership unanimously agreed to go on industrializing the country through "mobilizing local initiatives." However, there were disputes on the Great Leap Forward,[10] a massive attempt to run industries by a population lacking experience of industrialization and by local government officials who had experience of guerrilla war only. Following that, in 1960, the Soviet Union cancelled investments completely and withdrew all Russian experts from China. This interruption made a huge impact on China's industrialization project, which had been relying on foreign investments and aimed to develop heavy industries. Correspondingly, China started to reemphasize class struggle, a situation similar to the debates about the Hooligan Movement in the early 1930s and the Marxism in Ravine movement in 1940.

Regrettably, the Three People's Principles (i.e., nationalism, democracy, and the people's livelihood) promulgated by the founder of the Republic of China, Sun Yat-sen, are an imagination that imitates the Western experience. Originating from the Western discursive system, it was unable to mobilize people into revolution. In dire straits, the Three People's Principles in China had no choice but to evolve into nationalism in substance and even made use of triad societies.

The new China born after World War II constructed a socialist imagination that also originated from the West. During the period of industrialization invested by the quasi-suzerain, this socialist imagination had also evolved into means of mobilization for primitive accumulation of the state capital. Since 1960, in the name of this socialist imagination, many occasions of societal-political mobilizations have taken place. It appeared that the superstructure then was a mixture of Chinese characteristics, Stalinist bureaucratism taking shape rapidly in a short term when the quasi-suzerain invested in China, and sectarianism formed during the revolutionary civil war. Therefore, this superstructure could not correspond to the economic reality that was forced to change after the abrupt withdrawal of investment.[11]

THIRTY YEARS: AN ALTERNATIVE READING OF CHINA'S REFORM

Studies of the comparative-advantage theory by Chinese scholars are often defective, because they rarely pay attention to the serious asymmetry between the institutional cost and benefit that is a product of economic growth under Developmentalism. When the governmental officials are formulating policies, they neglect the fact that it is the general population that takes the burden of institutional cost of state industrialization.

For example, the Great Leap Forward industrialization led by local governments in 1958 resulted in economic and political costs much greater and broader in scale than did the central government who accepted investments from the Soviet Union. Nevertheless, no matter how great the cost was, basically that cost was not paid by the government that enjoyed the institutional benefit of industrialization, but was shifted downward to rural areas through the urban-rural dual structure.

One of the authors of this paper has been arguing since the 1980s that different ways of primitive accumulation of capital could lead to different institutions, which will generate different forms of institutional cost and benefit and determine the subsequent path dependence of institutional change in any name of "reform."[12]

Accordingly, China's reform after the 1980s, despite the visage of change in superstructure and ideology, is essentially a consequence of government corporatism that was nurtured during primitive accumulation of capital for state industrialization. Facing waves of fiscal crisis mainly caused by 1970s' more than 12 billion dollars of investments from the West as soon as China regained diplomatic relations with the

West before the 1980s' reform, the state retreated from inefficient economic sectors and managed to transfer its institutional cost to society.[13]

In the late 1970s, under pressure of foreign debts and huge deficiency, the first sector from which the government withdrew was the sector of debt-stricken agriculture that had almost no more surplus value to extract. What emerged afterward was a rural economic base that, in substance, was traditional small-peasant economy plus rural self-governance. In fact, it was the peasants who spontaneously returned to the tradition. Nevertheless, after the superstructure changed from the People's Commune to local governments that had revenue power, the imposed superstructure could not adapt itself to the economic base of traditional dispersed peasant economy. The fundamental contradiction manifested itself as increasingly complicated conflicts between the government officials and the peasants. After the peasants regained autonomy of land use and labor power, rural industrialization and urbanization were complete. Subsequently, the fundamental institutional contradictions, namely, the binary opposition of villages and industrialized cities as well as rural-urban disparities, became increasingly serious.

The government's dissolution of the People's Communes and its withdrawal from the agricultural sector resulted in enormous transactional cost involving 900 million highly dispersed peasants. This institutional cost could only be taken up by agricultural sectors such as rural circulation and agriculture finance. As a result, in the 1980s, these sectors were seriously debt stricken. The government then took its second retreat from those agricultural sectors. Consequently, agricultural sectors such as rural circulation (supplying-purchasing cooperatives) and FCCs (Farmers' Credit Cooperatives) attempted privatization and marketization. Ultimately, institutional cost in the form of high transactional cost between peasants and market was taken up by so-called San Nong Wen Ti translated into "three dimensional agrarian issues" (peasants' rights, village sustainability, and agriculture safety).[14]

After the reform of state-owned enterprises in the mid-1990s, the government still monopolizes finance, insurance, and large-scale state-owned economy that are capable of gaining profits through direct capitalization of resources. These are sectors the government refuses to retreat because of high profits. Therefore, we argue that capital—no matter state-owned, private, or foreign—is the same in essence as long as it is controlled by the state.[15]

Nevertheless, if we agree with Marx's historical perspective that human society has evolved into capitalist civilization and the dialectic perspective that the main contradiction of capitalist economy remains to be capital itself, then from the point of view of enormous pressure and challenge in global competition dominated by international financial capital, China as a developing country must follow the leap from the phase of industrial capital to financial capital and keep its edge in global capital competition. As criticisms both from domestic and Western sources say, China's economic system is state monopolized and has undergone processes of self-monetization and self-capitalization. The system's rapidly expanding money credit is supported by the state political credit that is underpinned by an authoritarian regime intrinsic to a strong sovereignty.

Despite criticisms, the current system could not be easily judged as just or unjust when compared with lessons of the former Soviet Union and eastern European countries. In the latter cases, along with political liberalization came the collapse of national financial systems. In great opportunities offered by the reckless completely open policy, massive national assets created by millions of people in several decades were instantly "capitalized," with Western financial agencies flooding in with enormous surplus liquidity due to the financial bubble.[16]

THE ALTERNATIVE READING OF CHINA'S "COMPARATIVE ADVANTAGE"

To elaborate the cognitive deviation in Chinese academia and clarify our point of view, we take the example of comparative advantage, a concept commonly applied in Western economic theories, to explain problems in developing countries.

In the 1990s, we, the authors, deciphered the law of development in modern Chinese history and then set out to visit other Third World countries. The more we studied rural China as a domestic case of the Third World, the more we became concerned with the Third World problem outside China. We took every chance to compare China with other developing countries. We have visited guerrilla zones in Mexico and India, slums in Bangladesh and Brazil, international hot spots like Cuba, Venezuela, North Korea, Nepal, and Argentina after the financial crisis. After studying policies for over twenty years and visiting over forty countries through field trips, we have developed some thoughts that are alternative to the two oppositional mainstream thoughts introduced into China a century ago, which are socialism modified by the Russians and capitalism modified by the Americans.

Having pondered on the diverse pathways in which different ethnic groups evolved from primitive societies into civilizations and compared the evolutionary tracks of these pathways, we come to realize that pathways to civilizations for ancient human races are strikingly heterogeneous under different resources and environmental constraints. Different modes of production naturally lead to different social-political forms. If one day, scholars in east Asian universities are no longer willing to dogmatically fit Mayan, Incan, and Ancient Chinese civilizations that had lasted for several millennia into the "five stages of civilization" under the historical materialism in Marxism, it may suggest that we start to have our original understanding of the "Asiatic mode" that Marx emphasizes so much.

We need to know, no matter under which banners of "-isms," the core idea of Western mainstream social sciences, which control modern power of discursive construction and decorate its "political correctness," is still monism by virtue of Eurocentrism. Such Eurocentric social sciences are intrinsically implied with theological thoughts of monotheism and clericalism and still serving the global hegemony of unilateralism today.[17]

Located far from Europe, oriental civilizations in the Far East were marginalized and self-marginalized in modern colonial globalization. For the colonizers, the cost to completely colonize the Far East was too high and the indigenous populations there were far too huge to be totally displaced. In short, not only did the Chinese, the largest indigenous population in east Asia, survive the colonizers and their descendants' massacres in the age of colonization, but they also, in the process of modern state building, successfully preserved their gregarious civilization that has been cultivated in millennia of traditional irrigation and agriculture. In fact, the gregarious culture was strengthened through modern state building in two aspects: the arduous war for national independence and the civil war and postwar struggles to defend the state sovereignty. Based on modern state building, a centralized system with oriental characteristics has been formed.

This system possesses two effective mechanisms to integrate social resources: first, making use of the core of historical heritage, namely, gregarious culture (facilitated by kinship systems and geographical bondage), to internalize serious negative externalities caused by market economy; second, making use of unpaid labor investment as substitute for capital or so-called family labor portfolio investment, which is intrinsic to peasant household economy inside the typical oriental village communities with varied and comprehensive economic sectors, such as animal husbandry, home construction, blacksmithing, carpentry, textiles, restaurants, peddlers, and processing. This helps to reduce the institutional cost and relieve development problems under the constraints of extreme capital scarcity.

The above-mentioned two mechanisms allowed China to enter the process of industrialization more easily and faster than did those Third World nations that were once fully colonized by the West and inherited the superstructure constructed by the Westerners even after independence. Anyone can simply find a paradox among developing countries—the more modernized political superstructure, the more institutional cost of the local governance, and the less industrialization (see Figure 5.3).

The so-called Chinese characteristics are results of a combination of a macro politico-economic system from historical heritage and intrinsic mechanisms of micro economic subjects. It was this quality that generated the comparative advantage that allowed China to accomplish the industrialization process and sustain long-term economic growth.

Nevertheless, from the individual standpoint of an alternative scholar, the authors are not willing to take positive roles in discussions of comparative advantage analysis that is overestimated only because of the so-called global competition since the rise of capitalism.[18] Even though the Chinese have fulfilled self-capitalization under premises of state monetarism and financial monopoly and are taking part in mainstream competition of the twenty-first-century financial bubble created by global financial capital excess, we cannot escape from the end game of global financial capitalization and its coming collapse.

"THREE-DIMENSIONAL AGRARIAN ISSUES (*SAN-NONG*)" AND THE "NEW COUNTRYSIDE CONSTRUCTION"

Since the twentieth century, the problem of rural China in the process of industrialization through state corporatism has been nothing but the question of, under strict agrarian resource constraints, how to extract huge surplus from rural areas to support industrialization and, at the same time, ensure that the rural sector would not decline

Figure 5.3 The institutional gains and institutional costs in China's industrialization process

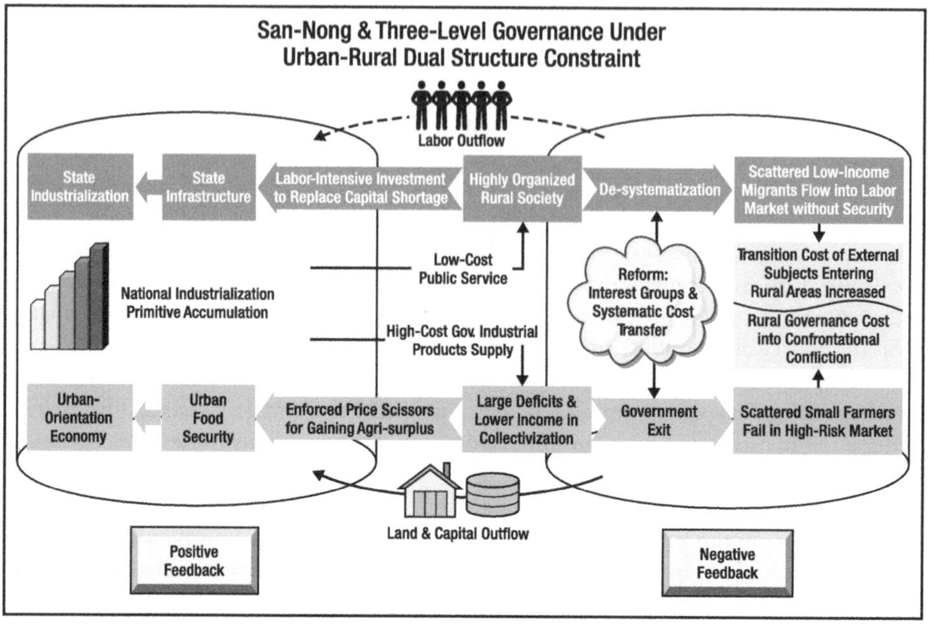

Source: Wen Tiejun's forthcoming book, *Three Rurals and Three Governances.*

rapidly so that the stability of society at large could be guaranteed. The rural sector, being the main carrier of millennia of traditional civilization, has been engrossed in the process of national modernization. In fact, it has been the primary source of primitive accumulation of capital in industrialization under the urban-rural dualism and took the burden of cost transference during several financial crises.[19]

Accordingly, rural development in China is a twofold problem. On the one hand, it is a historical problem of how to inherit and develop an old irrigation civilization that is composed of a huge peasant population with a gregarious culture as a systemic heritage containing internal regulations. On the other hand, it is an inevitable aftermath of primitive accumulation of capital in the specific historical background, in which the goals were to achieve industrialization after national independence and to solve the subsequent problem of the expansion of industrial capital.

In the 1990s, when elaborating this situation, we suggested that the fundamental problem of rural development in China is not simply the problem of agriculture but the "three-dimensional agrarian issues," namely, the "*san-nong*" issues including peasants' rights, rural sustainability, agriculture, and safety under the constraint of the major institutional contradiction of urban-rural dualism. We further proposed that the "*san-nong*" issues are intrinsic to almost all the developing countries where the institutional contradiction of dual structure is commonly found. Moreover, nations with peasant economies, that is, the whole of east Asia including China, Japan, and Korea, have no simple problem of agriculture in the sense of the West. If people in east Asia use the term "farmers" to refer to the peasants with little arable land, hence equating

American farmers who often drive big tractors working for self-owned hundreds of hectares of land with Chinese peasants who work on fragmented and dispersed land with mixed income sources (by part time working in industrial and agricultural sectors) under a small peasant economy, then what follows this basic conceptual mistake is inevitably a series of grave theoretical and policy misunderstandings.[20]

In the late 1990s, China once copied the Western agricultural policy as represented by the United States. This did not only lead to the deterioration of the "*sannong*" problem but also made agriculture the largest polluting industry in China in less than two decades. The problem of unsafe food products became a serious cost of externalities that the society at large has to bear.

Based on the above investigation and reflections, the authors and like-minded people inside China and abroad have worked together and launched the Rural Reconstruction Movement with sustainable development as its substantial contents, including organic farming, ecological architecture, and urban organic consumer cooperatives based on community supported agriculture (CSA) for initiating "fair trade" in China. Accordingly, we have proposed policy recommendations on many occasions.

Fortunately, in October 2005, the Chinese central government specified "building of a new socialist countryside" as a national strategy; in October 2007, "Ecological Civilization" was set as a guiding principle of the whole country; and in October 2008, "resources-conservation and environment-friendly agriculture" was announced as major contents of the long-term strategy in the 2020s.[21]

We hope that in the major changes under globalization, moderate reforms, or as we advocate, innovation instead of reform, can help sustain the stability of rural China, where the majority of the Chinese population lives.[22]

NOTES

1. The research in this paper is sponsored by China National Social Sciences Fund for Major Projects (07&ZD048), the Emergency Project (2009JYJR023) of the Ministry of Education, and the 985-project Phase III Funds of the Renmin University China Rural Development Philosophy and Social Science Innovation Scheme. The first draft in Chinese was published in *Open Times*, February 2008. This version is revised in March 2009. The key author is Wen Tiejun. Wen's assistant Dong Xiaodan drafted the paper, and doctorate student Yang Shuai did research on related materials. Qiu Jiansheng and Lau Kin Chi provided experiences of rural reconstruction both domestic and overseas. The English version is translated by Erebus Wong.

2. The intellectual left in the West has its ideological explanation of China's high growth rate; the influence is almost negligible.

3. The views presented in this essay originate almost totally from China's discursive context, deeply concerned with problems and disputations in China, and effective only in domestic discussions about China's development and the surrounding environment. Please see Wen Tiejun, "China in the Last Century: A Tidal Wave with Four Twists and Turns," in *What Do We Really Want?* ed. Wen Tiejun (Beijing: Huaxia Press, 2004), 3–11.

4. Ibid.

5. Wen Tiejun, "Primitive Accumulation of Civil Capital and Government Behavior," *Economics Weekly* 1 (1988), *Xinhua Digest* (1988); Wen Tiejun and Shouyin Zhu, "Primitive

Accumulation of Governmental Capital and Land Turning into Non-agrarian Use," *The World of Management* 5 (1996): 161–169.

6. In Asia, developing countries with populations over 100 million are China, India, Indonesia, and Bangladesh. Only China has formed an industrial system with a complete structure. None of the African nations has achieved industrialization. In Latin America, only Brazil has achieved industrialization while having a population of over 100 million, of which, however, the indigenous composes only a small proportion.

7. The Soviet Union is referred to as "quasi-suzerain" according to Mao Zedong's assertion in the 1970s that what the Soviet Union practiced was "Socialist Imperialism."

8. We borrow this concept from Samir Amin's Third World Dependence theory. Amin is the first one to use this concept to elaborate China's development.

9. Sources are ambivalent in their explanations of debt repayment to the Soviet Union. One source reports that the repayment period was 14 years, in the first four years in terms of trade by barter and then from 1955 onward from staple supply. A second source (from Zhihua Shen) suggests that in 1964 China had paid back all the debts and interests, one year ahead of agreement. Then in October 1965, the sugar loan and trade arrears were settled. Yet another source (from An Wang) states that according to early agreement, in 1957, China's credit status was negative; that means trading with the former Soviet Union had to be always in surplus.

10. Documents from the Zhengzhou Conference, in January 1958.

11. In public opinion dominated by the Western discourse, these struggles have been labeled as "social turmoil."

12. Wen Tiejun, *Study on China's Basic Rural Economic System: Reflection on a Century of "San-Nong" Issues* (Beijing: China Economic Press, 2000).

13. Please refer to Jean C. Oi, "Fiscal Reform and the Economic Foundations of Local State Corporatism in China," *World Politics* 10 (1992): 99–126.

14. Wen Tiejun, "'San-Nong' Issues: Reflection on the End of the Century," *Dushu* 12 (1999): 3–11. The concept of "three-dimensional agrarian issues" (san-nong: peasants' rights, village sustainability, and agriculture security) was raised by Prof. Wen Tiejun originally in 1996 for addressing China's different agrarian policy thoughts because of a long-term debate inside central policy think tanks since the 1990s. San-nong has been incorporated into China's planning strategy since 2001, including being part of the State's 11th Five-Year Plan in 2005. Based on such policy readjustment, the government initiated "New Socialist Countryside Construction."

15. Wen Tiejun, "Four Issues of Reform," *Phoenix Weekly* (April 2006).

16. Wen Tiejun, "Circulation from Paper to Paper: Rethinking the International Financial Capital Dominated by US Dollar, and Global Economic Crisis and the Trend of China's Crude Growth," in Wen (ed.), *What Do We Really Want?* (Beijing: Huaxia Press, 2004), 91–103. That book collects most of the author's macroeconomic analysis. Three months before the inflation happened in 1988, Wen had posed a theory of economic crisis about China's cyclic economic crises over 40 years, a point of view rare in China's theoretical literature. Then, in late 1988, the price index reached 18.6 percent. What followed the government regulation in 1989 were typical depression and political incidents, and subsequently, two years of depression. In 1993, Wen published "State Capital Redistribution and Private Capital Re-accumulation," which was drafted in 1991, stating that China's economic system before reform basically was of the nature of "State Capitalism." Subsequently, Wen published analyses of cyclic economic crisis after reform. In 1996, "The General Crisis of International Financial Capital System and China Reform" reviewed the impact of global economic crises on China. These macroanalyses are confirmed by successive economic crises, especially by the financial crisis in East Asia impacted by international financial capital.

17. Wen Tiejun, "Globalization, Marginalization, and World Fascism" (a summary of discussion on India's Kerala Experience presented at a seminar in 2001). In 2001, a dozen scholars and writers from mainland China, Hong Kong, the Philippines, and India visited Kerala in India. A few months later, some of the Chinese scholars joining the tour discussed globalization and World fascism. The speakers included Professor Huang Ping, Vice-Director of Sociology Institute of China Academy of Social Sciences; Professor Dai Jinhua of the Institute of Comparative Literature and Cultural Studies of Peking University; and Dr. Lau Kin Chi of Cultural Studies of Lingnan University, Hong Kong. The paper is a summary of discussion and was later published in journals like *Internal Reference for Reform, Tianya*, and *Dushu* in 2001.

18. Natural conscience differentiates human beings from subjects dictated by the "jungle law." We conduct the above logic and explanation only because of painful reflection, and we earnestly hope that one day the theoretical system supporting this essay will collapse.

19. Wen Tiejun, *"San-Nong" Issues and Institutional Transformation* (Beijing: China Economic Press, 2009).

20. Wen Tiejun, "Two Basic Contradictions Which Constrain the 'San-Nong' Issues and 'The Basic Problem of China is Peasantry'," in *Three Dimensional Agrarian Issues and Reflection on a Century* (Beijing: Joint Publisher, 2006).

21. On the other hand, we are annoyed to find that the greatest barrier to the practices and promotion of rural reconstruction is not peasants, who are usually regarded as disorganized as a bag of potatoes or as dispersed as sand, but local governments that are still oriented to Developmentalism, headed toward capital and GDP. It demonstrates that the "central and local relationship" that has undergone difficulty for a very long period is increasingly manifested along with diverse conflicts of interests.

22. Wen Tiejun, "Progressive Reform, Rural Reconstruction and NGO Organizational Cost (C.A.L.S.)," paper presented at the Money, Livelihood and Development Seminar organized by Hong Kong NGOs including China Social Services and Development Research Center and the Community Partnership Project (Beijing, China, July 10, 2001); Wen Tiejun, "We Still Need Rural Reconstruction," in *New Rural Development: Theory and Practice of New Rural Development* (Beijing: Beijing Publishing Enterprise, 2006).

Chapter 6

The Political Economy of Spatial Inequality in China

Shaoguang Wang

Uneven regional development is a universal phenomenon. It exists in almost all large countries, developing and developed alike. Examples include India, Indonesia, Mexico, Brazil, Canada, Great Britain, France, Italy, and the United States. China is no exception. Covering 9.6 million square kilometers, China is the third largest country in the world. Given its gigantic size, it is perhaps inevitable to find significant spatial variations in geographical condition, resource endowment, the sectoral distribution of economic activity, and the level of socioeconomic development.

The purpose of this paper is to explore various key issues related to the spatial effects of China's market-oriented reforms and state intervention in the past decades. It begins the analysis by looking at the historical roots of uneven development and initial attempts to address regional imbalance. It then looks at how and why regional disparities widened in the 1990s. Rather than dealing with regional disparity solely from an economic perspective, the paper takes a political economy approach, investigating both political and economic factors that have shaped regional developments. The paper ends with a brief discussion on how state intervention has helped narrow regional gaps in the last few years.

HISTORICAL OVERVIEW OF REGIONAL ECONOMIC DEVELOPMENT, 1949–1978

When the Chinese communists came to power in 1949, they inherited an extremely lopsided economy. Industrial activities were to a large extent concentrated in what was then called Manchuria (the modern-day northeast provinces of Heilongjiang, Jilin, and Liaoning) and a few major coastal cities such as Shanghai and Guangzhou. Although the coastal provinces accounted for only 11.34 percent of the land, they were the source of 77.6 percent of total industrial output. The rest of the country produced only 22.4 percent of the total industrial output. In particular, western China lagged far behind. Only 8 percent of the total industrial output originated in this region, despite the fact it took up over half of the country's territory.[1]

The new Communist government made a strong commitment to achieving balanced distribution of productive capacity and income. The first Five-Year Plan (1953–1957) of the People's Republic gave high priority to the development of new industrial bases in north, northwest, and central China. Among the 694 industrial projects built during this period, most were located in the inland areas.[2] But Mao hoped to see more changes. In his famous 1956 speech, "On Ten Major Relationships," he again dwelled on the relations between the coast and the interior. In his view, it was both economically irrational and politically unacceptable to keep 70 percent of industry in the coastal areas while leaving the rest of the country more or less untouched by modernization. To speed up the industrialization of the interior, he suggested that new industrial facilities be located in the interior. Only by doing so, he believed, would industrial activities become more evenly distributed.

Indeed, Mao's era was marked by an unprecedented spatial redeployment of productive capacity. Thanks to its strong extractive capacity, the central government under Mao had firm control over the geographic distribution of resources. The investment policy of this period clearly favored backward regions. While more developed provinces experienced substantial outflows of revenues, less developed provinces received enormous infusions of funds for infrastructure and industrial development.

Moreover, in the mid-1960s, out of security considerations, China began a campaign to construct the Third Front, which covered all western provinces and some parts of the central provinces. From late 1964 to 1971, dozens of large- and medium-sized industrial enterprises were moved from coastal provinces to inland provinces, and hundreds more were built on-site. Altogether, between 1956 and 1978, more than 2,000 large- and medium-sized enterprises were established in west and central China. This shift in investment and the establishment of new industrial centers powerfully boosted industrial growth in the traditionally less-developed regions. In 1965, for example, the ratio of agriculture to light industry to heavy industry for central China was 71:15:14. By the end of the fourth Five-Year Plan period (1971–1975), it had become 44:22:34. For the same period, the ratio for west China changed from 69:16:15 to 40:23:37. In addition to financing investments in less-developed regions, fiscal transfers were used to reduce regional inequality in income and the provision of public goods and services.[3] Government transfers made it possible for consumption to be much more evenly distributed than output. As a result, Mao's era witnessed a strong trend toward greater equality in per capita consumption across the country.

In 1978, China changed its policy orientation, shifting the emphasis from *equity* to *efficiency*. The years since have marked a period of rapid economic growth and rising living standards, both of which are unprecedented in Chinese history. Equally important, no province has been excluded from the growth club. Every one of China's provinces has experienced substantial real growth in the post-1978 period. While economic conditions have improved in all provinces in absolute terms, however, performance in relative terms has varied markedly among the regions.

Figure 6.1 shows the changing track of coefficient of variance (CV) of provincial per capita GDP from 1978 to 2007 (in 1978 constant price).[4] It plots two measures of relative dispersion. The top and bottom curves differ only in sample size: the former *includes* Beijing, Tianjin, and Shanghai, whereas the latter *excludes* these three cities. We separate the two curves for a simple reason: although the three metropolitan areas enjoy provincial status, treating them in the same way as we treat other provinces would be problematic, because they are far more urbanized and industrialized than the others. As a result, they enjoy extraordinarily high levels of per capita GDP relative to the national average. For this reason, treating these metropolitan areas as ordinary provinces might greatly bias our analysis of regional disparities. To present an unbiased picture, it is necessary to segregate two sets of statistics—one including the three cities and the other excluding them. As Figure 6.1 reveals, changes in regional disparities display different patterns when the three cities are excluded.

The top curve represents changing coefficients of variation for the whole nation during the period 1978–2007. The time path yields an S curve. In other words, relative dispersion declined sharply between 1978 and 1991, but the falling trend was reversed afterward. The years between 1992 and 2004 witnessed an upsurge in regional inequality before the trend reversed again.

The bottom curve (excluding figures for Beijing, Tianjin, and Shanghai) yields two noteworthy changes in coefficients of variation. First, CVs become much smaller. Rather than fluctuating between 0.80 and 1.05, the curve now oscillates in the

Figure 6.1 Coefficient of variance of provincial per capita GDP (1978 constant price)

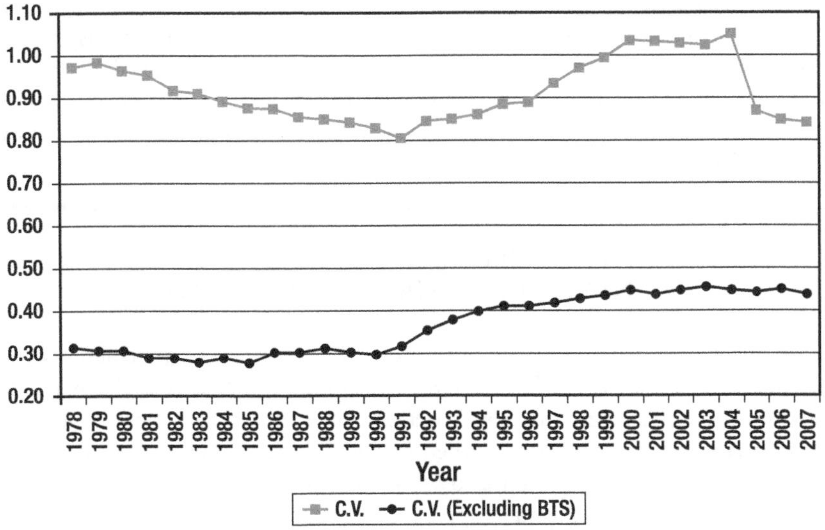

Note: Unless indicated otherwise, all data presented in this paper come from the author's databank.

neighborhood of 0.35–0.45. In other words, once extreme cases are excluded, relative dispersion in per capita GDP does not appear to be alarmingly large in China. Second, the patterns of change in CVs are more or less the same, but the magnitudes of change are much smaller. Regional dispersion decreased only marginally in the initial years of reform, but the years following 1985 saw a steady increase in relative dispersion, especially during the entire 1990s. Consequently, by 2000, CV was 0.14 percentage points higher than that in 1978 (increasing from 0.31 to 0.45). Since then, regional disparity has begun to level off and even shown signs of falling.

Mainstream economists have long argued that regional disparity is an abnormal phenomenon that will not last. Although there is no way for them to deny the presence and persistence of spatial inequality in many parts of the world, they envision a long-term trend toward interregional equality. In 1965, Jeffrey Williamson published a well-known article titled "Regional Inequality and the Process of National Development: A Description of the Patterns." Based on a large set of cross-sectional and time series data, Williamson identified "a systematic relationship between national development levels and regional inequality," or an inverted "U" in the national growth path; that is, regional gaps tended to increase in earlier stages of development and to diminish in later stages.[5] Since then, the inverted-U-shaped pattern of regional development has often been called "the Williamson law." Barro and Sala-I-Martin, for instance, tried to identify a tendency toward convergence among the U.S. states during the period 1840–1980,[6] among Japanese prefectures,[7] and among regions within Western Europe.[8]

Mainstream economists who studied China once also believed that, coupled with economic growth, the operation of market forces by themselves would bring convergence of regional income.[9] This predication has been proved wrong. Neither of the two curves in Figure 6.1 is inverted-U shaped. Instead, they reveal S curves. It seems reasonable to divide the years after 1978 into three subperiods. Before 1985, the general trend was for relative dispersion to fall. But the trend was reversed in the mid-1980s. As market forces were playing a bigger and bigger role in Chinese economy, the country witnessed a sharp upsurge in regional inequality in the 1990s through the first years of the twenty-first century, whether or not the three centrally administered metropolises were counted.[10] Having experienced a secular increase in regional disparity for more than a decade, China seems to have entered a period of stabilization or even convergence in the last few years.

THE POLITICAL ECONOMY OF UNEVEN REGIONAL DEVELOPMENT

Regional disparities change because growth rates of output have varied across provinces over time. Why have provincial growth rates differed? What have been the factors underlying differential economic growth performances among provinces? It goes without saying that economic growth is governed by many determinants. Whatever they are, however, if these diverse factors are to affect economic growth positively, they must somehow help either increase the supply of factor inputs (mainly capital and labor) or enhance factor productivity, or some combination of both. Thus, to arrive at an understanding of the factors behind the growth of output, we must first identify the immediate economic sources of growth.

In the last decade or so, economists in China and elsewhere have conducted extensive research trying to break down the proximate sources of output growth and examine the contributions of labor and capital to output. They generally arrive at two principal conclusions.

First, the contribution of labor input to economic growth was insignificant in China. Here, labor input is measured not only by the total number of working persons but also by such indicators of labor quality as the age and gender composition and the educational and health profiles of the labor force. A World Bank study, for instance, attributed only about 17 percent of growth to improvements in both quantity and quality of the labor force in the Chinese economy as a whole.[11] An abundant labor supply may explain the relatively small contribution of labor in China. It is intuitively plausible that, in a capital-scarce and labor-abundant economy, the injection of more human resources would not increase output very significantly and rapidly.

Second, rapid capital accumulation alone can account for a very substantial part of GDP growth for each and every province of China. This finding confirms the central importance of capital accumulation for growth at early stages of economic development, a position held by such prominent economists as Domar, Harrod, Lewis, and Rostow. It is also consistent with the results of many empirical studies of economic growth. Furthermore, the role of capital in the explanation of growth in China was very similar to that found in other East Asian economies and in developing countries at large.

Since capital investment has been the most important engine of economic growth, regions with greater capital mobilization capacity are expected to grow faster. Then, why are sometimes some provinces more capable of mobilizing local savings and of obtaining capital inflows from other provinces and from other countries? What are the political factors that affected the direction of capital flows? More specifically, we want to explore how the central government's regional policy preference and extractive capacity have affected the spatial distribution of investment resources and ultimately the growth potential of different provinces.

POLICY PREFERENCE

After Mao's death in 1976, his egalitarian regional development strategy was criticized as too costly in comparative advantage, production efficiency, and national growth foregone. Underlying the reform that followed was a fundamental transformation of development philosophy. Chinese policymakers then placed their top priority on rapid aggregate growth. This predominant concern with growth made them less willing to sacrifice growth for such goals as balance and equity. Instead, they were ready to tolerate a certain degree of inequality or widened disparity. They believed that if certain regions were allowed to prosper first, their affluence would eventually trickle down to other regions.

Whereas in the West, believers of the trickle-down theory generally hold that government should not intervene in the course of economic development, their Chinese counterparts actually advocated government intervention on behalf of more developed regions. In their view, China, as a developing country, had to make the best use of extremely scarce capital. Therefore, the government needed to concentrate investment resources where conditions were most suitable for growth.

Since the coastal provinces enjoyed considerable advantages at the beginning of the reform period (a large number of skilled workers, a high level of technology and managerial sophistication, and a relatively well-developed infrastructure), these areas received the government's economic blessing. These provinces also had much easier access to foreign trade and the closest ties to overseas Chinese, an important source of capital and business know-how. Concentrating investment resources in these areas clearly offered the prospect of much more rapid aggregate growth than spreading resources thinly or investing in interior areas where the preconditions for modern growth were still lacking.

For these reasons, a so-called gradient theory (*tidu lilun*) dominated the thinking of Chinese policymakers for much of the 1980s. The theory divided China into three large geographic regions—the eastern (coastal), central, and western—and likened them to steps on a ladder. According to the theory, the government should capitalize on the advantages of the coast first. Only after the coast became sufficiently developed should attention be turned to the central region. The western region, however, would have to wait patiently for its turn. If this strategy had unfavorable implications for equity, its advocates advised people to consider its effects in the long term. In the long term, the theory promised, the fruit of development would eventually come down to everyone in the country.

In the prereform period, nearly two-thirds of state capital investment went to the central and western provinces, whereas the coastal provinces received only 36 percent. Even in the early 1980s, the investment rates were largely identical across the country's four regions (eastern, central, western, and northeastern). Starting from the mid-1980s when the government introduced an asymmetrical development strategy to allow some regions to get rich first, domestic investment began pouring into the eastern coastal region. For the next fifteen years or so, the investment rates in the eastern region were consistently higher, much higher, than those of other regions. The western region especially lagged far behind.[12]

The government's growth-first strategy was also reflected in its decisions to open certain areas along the coast to foreign investors. To encourage foreign investment on the coast, the central government gave coastal areas greater autonomy in a wide range of economic decisions, including the authority to approve large-scale investment projects, the freedom to grant tax concessions to foreign investors, and the right to retain a higher proportion of earned foreign exchange. These privileges enabled coastal areas to offer more incentives to potential investors than interior areas could achieve. Combined with the coast's naturally and historically advantaged position, these policies insured that much of China's foreign investment took place along the coast.

In sum, the bias of the top policymakers explained why the central government directed an increasing proportion of investment resources into coastal provinces and why it went out of its way to help the same provinces to lure foreign investment. The large influx of investment resources, in turn, made growth for coastal provinces possible at faster rates than for others. There was little doubt that the central government's procoastal bias was an important factor contributing to the worsening of regional inequality in the 1990s.

As early as in 1993, deputies from interior provinces, especially those from the west, began to pour out their grievances against the center's procoastal bias at the annual sessions of the National People's Congress. In 1994, even a report by the State Planning Commission sounded a serious warning that if problems caused by growing regional gaps were not settled properly, they might one day become a threat to China's social stability and national unity. Facing growing pressure from interior provinces, the central government decided to reverse its coastal development strategy in 1995. The new guiding principle was to "create conditions for gradually narrowing down regional gaps." This principle was embodied in China's ninth Five-Year Plan (1996–2000), which promised to increase central support to the less-developed regions in the central and western parts of the country. But not until September 1999 did China formally launch the Go West program (*Xibu da kaifa*), which was aimed at narrowing the socioeconomic gap between the coastal and western provinces. Since then, the inland provinces' rates of investment in fixed assets have risen visibly and often surpassed those of the eastern region. Intensive investment has spurred rapid economic growth in the interior regions and increased the income level of the local people. Evidently, the change of the central government's policy preference has played an important role in narrowing regional disparities.[13]

GOVERNMENT EXTRACTIVE CAPACITY

It is clear from the above discussion that, when the central policymakers lack interest in reducing regional inequality, state intervention in resource allocation would only worsen the existing regional disparities. Even if central policymakers have strong interests in pursuing balanced regional development, regional inequality might not necessarily decline, because the other key factor that can affect spatial distribution of resources—government extractive capacity—is equally important.

Government extractive capacity, especially central extractive capacity, is relevant in this context because, as the only institution responsible for redistributing resources among regions, the central government must control an adequate amount of revenue before it can conduct any redistributive policy. Strong central extractive capacity may not be a sufficient condition for interregional redistribution, as in some instances, governments with strong extractive capacity do little redistribution. Nonetheless, it is a necessary condition, because no other institutions, provincial governments included, have incentives to pursue interregional redistributive policies.

The Chinese government's extractive capacity was critically enfeebled during the first two decades of economic reforms. At the core of Deng Xiaoping's reform program was decentralization, which might have been instrumental in generating high economic growth in China over the 1980s and 1990s. The massive fiscal decentralization practiced between 1978 and 1993, however, significantly weakened the government's extractive capacity. As Figure 6.2 reveals, despite its nearly miraculous record of GDP growth, China's ratio of overall government revenue to GDP decreased from 31.1 percent in 1978 to around 10 percent in 1995 and 1996. Moreover, the central government's share of overall government revenue was barely half, or around 5 percent of GDP. Even compared to low-income countries, the extractive capacity of the Chinese central government was extremely weak at the time.[14]

A central government with weak extractive capacity cannot be expected to do much in the way of fighting against regional inequality, no matter how committed it is to achieving this goal. With so little at its disposal in the 1990s, the central government simply did not have much leeway to redistribute investment resources from rich to poor provinces or make large subsidies to poor provinces. Voluntary movement of capital from rich to poor regions also proved unlikely. While the concentration of investment resources in economically prosperous provinces allowed some provinces to gain a good lead in growth, the lack of investment resources dampened the growth potentials of the backward provinces. The result was the continued worsening of regional inequality throughout the 1990s and the first years of the new century.

The government extractive capacity did not rebound until after 1997. Although it is still relatively weak compared with that of most countries in the world, the strengthened state extractive capacity nevertheless provides the possibility of reversing the trend of divergence we have observed in the last decade or so.

Figure 6.2 Government revenue and expenditure as % of GDP, 1978–2007

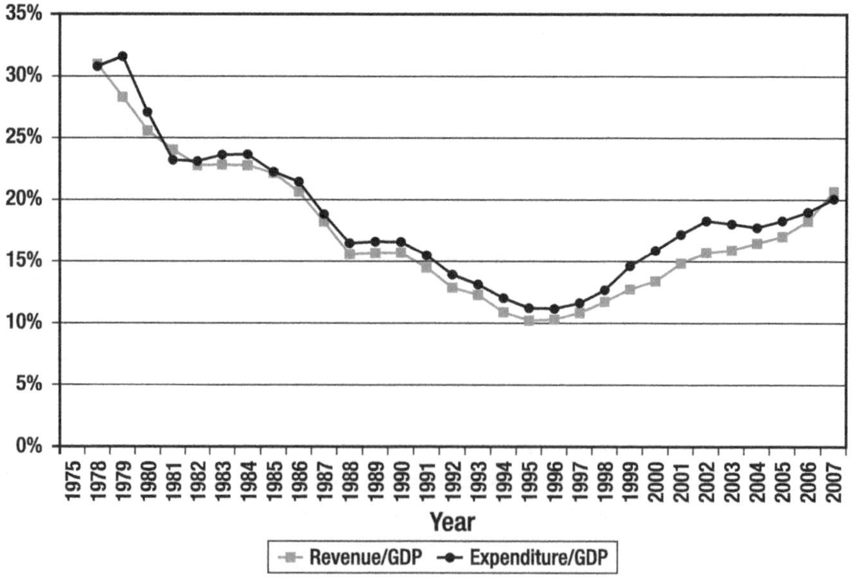

MORE RECENT TRENDS

As pointed out earlier, both the policy orientation and extractive capacity of the Chinese government have changed. In response to growing regional disparities, the Chinese government started to change its skewed regional policies in the late 1990s. Introduced in 1999, its western development strategy, Go West, focuses on infrastructure construction, environmental protection, industrial upgrading, human capital accumulation, science and technology research, and opening the inland provinces to foreign direct investment (FDI). Later, the government also enacted policies to accelerate economic development in the northeastern provinces (2003) and the central region (2005). As the government's development bias toward coastal provinces has been gradually removed, interior provinces now have a real chance to catch up with coastal provinces that enjoy tremendous natural and human capital advantages.

Equally important, to be able to effect equalization across regions, the Chinese government also has made efforts to rebuild its extractive capacity by overhauling the country's fiscal system. Before 1993, China's fiscal system was one of "eating in separate kitchens." This system was beneficial to the developed coastal provinces because they had more fiscal resources and did not have to share tax revenue with other provinces. Without the outside fiscal transfer, the provinces in central and western China, whose fiscal resources were limited to begin with, could not provide similar public services to their people, not to mention construction of new infrastructure or investment in new industries. Clearly, such a "fiscal responsibility system" (*canzheng baogan zhi*) was one of the most important causes of worsening regional disparity in the 1980s and 1990s.[15]

In 1994, the Chinese government changed the fiscal responsibility system to the "tax assignment system" (*fenshui zhi*). This major reform eventually stopped two ratios from decreasing after fifteen years of continuous decline.[16] More importantly, the reform enhanced the central government's ability to extract fiscal resources and thus established the foundation to increase central fiscal transfers (*caizheng zhuanyi zhifu*) to the provinces, especially the economically least developed provinces in central and western China.

Figure 6.3 clearly shows that since 1994 the total amount of the central government's fiscal transfer has increased steadily. Especially after 1999, when the Chinese central government introduced its Go West policy, the amount increased every year and reached nearly RMB 1,600 billion in 2007, which was eight times the amount in 1994.

Which area reaped the most benefits from the fiscal transfer system? According to the statistics of the Ministry of Finance, during the period of 1994–2005, 10 percent of the central fiscal transfers went to eastern costal provinces, 44 percent to central provinces, and 46 percent to western provinces.[17] Central fiscal transfers have helped reduce both vertical and horizontal fiscal imbalance and thereby regional inequalities. Before the 1994 reform of China's fiscal system, the GDP growth rates differed vastly across regions, ranging from 12 percent in the northeastern region to 19.5 percent in the coastal regions. After 1994, the growth rates began to converge. In 2005, the growth rates in the eastern, central, western, and northeastern areas were 13.13 percent, 12.54 percent, 12.81 percent, and 12.01 percent, respectively—the difference became quite small.[18]

Figure 6.3 Fiscal transfers from the national to sub-national governments (RMB billion)

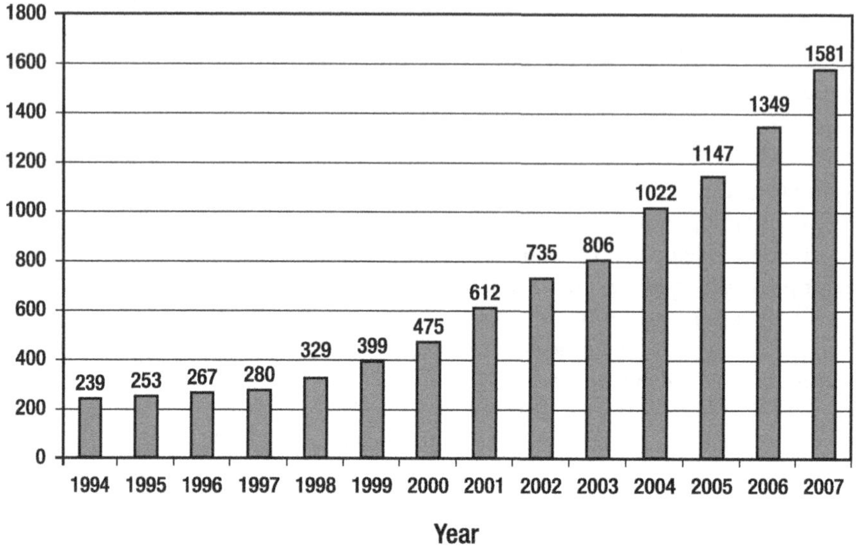

The convergence of economic growth rates in different regions was helpful in preventing regional disparity from growing and may even have helped reduce it. In a long period after 1983, the coefficient of variance of provincial per capita GDP continued to increase. In the 1990s, the regional difference quickly expanded. The turning point was in 1999, when the central government announced the Go West policy. Although regional disparity continued to expand, it leveled off after 2000. In 2004, the expansion tendency was reversed for the first time since 1990. Since then, regional disparity was further reduced (see Figure 6.1).[19] For the fiscal transfer system to bring such notable changes within such a short period of time is miraculous.[20]

NOTES

1. Sheng Bin and Feng Lun, *Zhongguo guoqing baogao* [*Condition of the nation of China*] (Shenyang: Liaoning People's Publishing House, 1991), 666.

2. Bo Yibo, *Ruogan zhongda juece yu shijian de huigu* [*Recollections of certain major decisions and events*] (Beijing: Zhongyang dangxiao chubanshe, 1991), 475.

3. Sheng Bin and Feng Lun, *Zhongguo guoqing baogao*, 667.

4. We use the coefficient of variation (CV) to indicate relative regional disparity, the higher value the larger regional differences. CV = $[(xi - x)2/n]^{1/2}/x$, where "n" (n = 1, 2, 3 . . . n) denotes the number of regions and "x_i" the per capita GDP of the ith region.

5. Jeffrey Williamson, "Regional Inequality and the Process of National Development: A Description of the Patterns," *Economic Development and Cultural Change* 13, no. 4 (1965): 3–45.

6. Robert Barro and Xavier Sala-I-Martin, "Convergence across States and Regions," *Brookings Papers on Economic Activity*, no. 1 (1991): 107–182.

7. Robert Barro and Xavier Sala-I-Martin, "Regional Growth and Migration: A Japan-United States Comparison," *Journal of the Japanese and International Economics*, no. 6 (December 1992): 312–346.

8. Robert Barro and Xavier Sala-I-Martin, *Economic Growth* (New York: McGraw-Hill, Inc., 1995), 398–401.

9. Tianlun Jian, Jeffrey D. Sachs, and Andrew M. Warner, "Trends in Regional Inequality in China," *NBER Working Paper*, no. 5412 (January 1996).

10. Shaoguang Wang and Angang Hu, *The Political Economy of Uneven Development: The Case of China* (Armonk, NY: M. E. Sharpe, 1999).

11. World Bank, *China 2020: Development Challenges in the New Century* (Washington, DC: World Bank, 1997).

12. Shantong Li and Zhaoyuan Xu, "The Trend of Regional Income Disparity in the People's Republic of China," *ADB Institute Discussion Paper*, no. 85 (January 2008): 17–18.

13. C. Cindy Fan and Mingjie Sun, "Regional Inequality in China, 1978–2006," *Eurasian Geography and Economics* 49, no. 1 (2008): 1–20.

14. Wang Shaoguang and Hu Angang, *The Chinese Economy in Crisis: State Capacity and Tax Reform* (Armonk, NY: M. E. Sharpe, 2001).

15. Wang Shaoguang and Hu Angang, *The Political Economy of Uneven Development: The Case of China.*

16. "Two ratios" means the ratio of government revenue to the GDP and the ratio of the central government revenue to the total government revenue.

17. Jin Renqing, "*Wanshan cujin jiben gonggong fuwu jundenghua de gonggong caizheng zhidu* [Enhance and improve the public finance system in equalizing the basic public service]," http://www.zgdjyj.com/Default.aspx?tabid=99&ArticleId=721.

18. Feng Jie and Xuan Xiaowei, "*Woguo quyu zengzhang geju he diqu chaju de bianhua yu yuanyin fenxi* [An analysis on the current situation and causes of unbalanced regional development in China]," *Development Research Center of the State Council Working Paper*, no. 138 (2006).

19. A number of recent researchers have confirmed this finding. See C. Cindy Fan and Mingjie Sun, "Regional Inequality in China, 1978–2006"; Shantong Li and Zhaoyuan Xu, "The Trend of Regional Income Disparity in the People's Republic of China"; United Nations Economic and Social Commission for Asia and the Pacific (ESCAP), *Economic and Social Survey of Asia and the Pacific 2008: Sustaining Growth and Sharing Prosperity* (New York: ESCAP, 2008): 48–57. See also Kam Wing Chan and Man Wang, "Remapping China's Regional Inequalities, 1990–2006: A New Assessment of de Facto and de Jure Population Data," *Eurasian Geography and Economics* 49, no. 1 (February 2008): 21–55.

20. Feng Jie and Xuan Xiaowei, "*Woguo quyu zengzhang geju he diqu chaju de bianhua yu yuanyin fenxi.*"

Chapter 7

Reserve the Land for Family Farming

On the Use of Farmland and the Future of Peasantry in China[1]

Dong Zhenghua

PEASANTS AND FAMILY FARMING: HISTORY AND THEORETICAL BACKGROUND

The argument of this paper is based on the simple historical fact that the trinity of peasantry, farmland, and the family farming system has long existed in history, no matter what forms of peasantry there have been: peasant proprietor, half-tenant, or tenant peasants. The fate of the peasants is also the fate of the family farming system. If one day the peasants have to leave their farmland and the family farming system is defeated, peasantry, as a specific social stratum, will inevitably become extinct. This breakup of the trinity may lead to the real "end of peasantry," as Henri Mendras described it in the 1960s.

Early in the nineteenth century, there was a series of discussions on whether the end of peasantry would come. Both Adam Smith and David Ricardo excluded the peasant from their blueprints of modern economy. Karl Marx also argued that both the "mode of production of peasantry" and the peasants themselves would disappear inevitably. Nonetheless, history has its own logic, which was sometimes unexpected. By the end of the nineteenth century, large-scale industry had already dominated the production system in Europe, yet the family farming system did not disappear. So, what is wrong with the theories of modern capitalism? The social democrats in the late years of the nineteenth century put great effort toward solving this puzzle, among the outcomes of which were the discussions between Karl Kautsky and Werner Sombart in Germany, as well as the argument between Lenin and the populists in Russia.

In the twentieth century, the small-scale family farming system continued to dominate the world. In some regions, there was the combination of, and conflicts between, the majority of small family farms and a small number of capitalist farms, which owned a huge amount of acreage and hired a good many farm laborers. In the Soviet Union and China, there were the socialist experiments in agriculture, that is, mandatory or semimandatory collectivization of farming and farmland that eliminated the family farming mode. During the campaign of the People's Commune, Chinese peasants were labeled as "members of the Commune," although there was no real change in their social and economic statuses.

Many scholars have maintained to admit the born nature of agriculture and the peasant as a unity of modern economy and have opposed driving peasants off the land, no matter if it is via mandatory collectivization, the setup of wage-labor farms, or concentration of land at the hand of superior landlords. At the 1979 United Nations International Conference of Rural Reforms and Developments, delegates from about 150 countries and national liberation movements agreed on the notion that "the equal distribution and efficient utilization of land are the prerequisites for rural developments and for improving productivity in the elimination of poverty."[2]

Theodore Schultz also promotes the family farming system that combines peasants' property rights and their right to operate the land.[3] However, in his theory, the peasant in the medieval era was formulated as a rational agent. Such a rational-choice and utilitarianism-based theory is renounced by the Chayanovian School and some others. However, some points in their criticisms are not fair to Schultz. For example, Schultz is criticized for neglecting the relations of production in his analysis. Quite on the contrary, Schultz argues for the elimination of the landlord-tenant peasant system and supports rural reform, which aims to give land to the tillers, and advocates for ownership based on residence. Another point for which Schultz has been attacked is his opposition to "the nationalization of land." Among the developing countries and regions, as represented by east Asia in the postwar era, "he who farms shall have his own land" and "farmland should be used by farmers" are the two principles of land reform. Specific regulations under these principles prohibit tenant farming or the conversion of farmland into land for other uses. These policies can be regarded as state control over peasants' possessing or distributing land and as alternatives for nationalization of the land. In my opinion, Schultz seems to have underestimated the importance of state power and its functional roles in multiple aspects of land and agriculture, such as strengthening the bargaining power of farmers in international trade and protecting farmers from the negative impact of the international market. It seems that all these functions of the state should be eradicated, given the current logic of liberalism that defends private ownership and international free trade. However, if this were true, namely, if there were no such state interventions, perhaps agriculture in east Asia and many other areas in the world would not be able to sustain itself.

Chayanov inherited Marx's viewpoint, which holds that in order to survive, some peasants of small-scale family farming would sell their products at the production price.[4] He tries to explain the surviving mechanism of peasants and their family farming by making distinctions between the labor model of family-based corporate and the model of wage-labor corporate. However, Chayanov's account looks unconvincing. In addition, his theory only addresses regions with limited land, excessive labor force, and little chance to migrate for employment. This makes his theory especially irrelevant to areas such as the United States, Australia, and Canada, where land resource is abundant and labor resource is comparatively scarce.

To explain the surviving advantage of peasants and family farming, a better theory should be based on the nature of agriculture per se. Yujiro Hayami and Vernon W. Ruttan's arguments make more sense here.[5] They argue that the mechanization process in the industrial sector has standardized the working process and hence made it easier to control, but such upgrading does not apply to the agriculture sector, because there are many more uncontrollable ecological and biological variables in the process of agricultural production. It is very important for the human actor in this process to supervise the producing process. In consequence, the quality of work in such a producing process becomes very hard to control or to supervise. Also, widespread, scattered working fields make supervision even more challenging.

There have always been disputes on the issues of self-sustained farming and family farming among Chinese scholars. Many consider the small-scale farming system as the major contributor to ancient China's backwardness and emblematize the peasant as the symbol of poverty and backwardness of China. In their discussions, peasants of ancient China are clearly distinguished from modern peasants who enjoy personal freedom and the legitimate right to utilize and operate their farmland. In ancient China, the emperors could enslave the peasants, tax them, and make them migrate, or restrict them to certain areas. As long as a peasant was documented in the register, he would have to live for, produce for, and offer human labor to the emperor; and to not register was to directly violate the Law of the Empire. Hence, although there had been more than one time of "equal distribution of land" (*jun tian*) during the dynasties, and several scholars in the late Ming and early Qing period had already raised the notion that "he who farms shall have his own land," and maintained that "he who owns the land should farm by himself, so that only peasants can own the land,"[6] peasants under such policies were still registered labor without practical or personal freedom.

Yifu Lin proposes a similar argument to Hayami and Ruttan: The most crucial factor that contributed to the failure of the People's Commune was the difficulty to supervise the Commune members, who were usually passive in working.[7] On the contrary, the superiority of the family farming system lies in the fact that the peasants who work are producing for their own interests, so they are usually more active in production. Note that Lin's argument differs from Hayami and Ruttan in that, whereas Lin describes supervision in the process of agricultural production, Hayami and Ruttan talk about the supervision of the quality of work. It is widely known among people who have rural experiences in China in the 1960s and 1970s that the intensity of laboring in the People's Commune was by no means low. Pushed by the class-struggle notion, the Commune members had to work for the collective from early morning until evening, especially in the busy seasons. But this was not enough. They were continuously forced to "cut off the tail of capitalism." The real crux here was not the lack of human effort, but the ineffectiveness of the labor, substantial waste of labor force, and production without returns, which gave birth to the "poor production team with ironically high 'productivity.'" In his investigation of agricultural history in the Yangzi Delta, Philip Huang[8] shows that the irrigation projects and the increase of multiple crop indexes during the People's Commune period had greatly raised the yield of per unit area, and yet such projects also led to problems such as extreme labor force intensification and growth without development.

At any rate, the history of the People's Commune in China demonstrates that the biological and ecological factors in agricultural production and the comparatively scattered nodes in the process of production could not match an organization system that is extremely concentrated and uniform.

As described above, contrary to the wish of the social democrats, who expected large-scale production to replace the small-scale family system and then to finally wash over the rural areas, the late nineteenth century saw a surprisingly increased number of small-scale family producers in western Europe. Such phenomenon was termed "an astonishing and mysterious force." Today, many people are still confused, possibly even more confused, by the survival of peasantry economy. Some who do not have or cannot be bothered to gain comprehensive knowledge about agriculture and the peasant both in history and in the real world still share the beliefs of social democrats, as K. Kautsky has mentioned. They believe that "peasants are mysterious, unthinkable, and sometimes calamitous."[9] In mainland China, the launch of the Rural Household Contracted Responsibility System actually restored the tradition of family farming. This restoration was welcomed by peasants and also benefited the state. However, during the thirty years of this reform, the peasants' rights to lease and use the land were threatened from time to time. Also disagreements arose on the contract responsibility system per se. For example, some people argue that the household contract system is no longer a mercy to the peasants but has become the shackle on millions of peasants. This argument is a deadlock: If peasantry was not eliminated, the "three-*nong*" problem (referring to agriculture, village, and peasant) would not be solved. So, is the household contract system a necessary condition for the development of agriculture, or is it just a step back to nowhere? How can we ensure the peasants' rights on their land so that it will not be seized or deprived? And through what kind of institutions could we make sure that land is used by the peasants (or farmers, as in the economic professional category today) and for farming purposes only? These are all urgent questions with regard to the current situation of agriculture and peasants in China, and are, of course, the major issues to be addressed in this paper.

THE DANGER OF THE LARGE-SCALE ENCLOSURE OF FARMLAND

Since 1982, the Central Committee of the Chinese Communist Party and the PRC State Council have released a total of ten "Number 1 Documents" regarding agricultural issues.[10] All ten documents have fully demonstrated how important the agricultural problem is to the PRC government. The first and foremost issue among these documents is peasants' rights and interests over their land property. In the five "No. 1

Documents" issued between 1982 and 1986, for example, the Rural Household Contracted Responsibility System was repeatedly stressed and promoted as an alternative for the former production team system. The documents acclaimed the new system as "the great innovation of Chinese Peasants," and the contract term has been extended repeatedly. In the subsequent fifth of the "No. 1 Documents," from year 2004 to 2008, although the focus was shifted to the peasants' burden relief and infrastructure constructions in rural areas, land policy still remained a big concern. Take the 2004 document for example. It states that "governments at all levels must strictly carry out the policy on agricultural land protection; for the sake of protecting peasants' rights and interests, and of controlling the scale of land requisition, they should strictly follow the standard approval procedure in issuing permits for non-agricultural farmland uses, and comply with the general plan of land use." Again, the 2008 document reiterates that "[we should] be unswerving in constantly sticking to the land policy that is based on the 'family contracted responsibility system,' to accelerating the launch of the register system on the right of land management, to ensuring the license of the land management right be successfully designated to every individual family, and to preventing any malpractice from peasants' rights over contracted-land."

The documents above reveal that protecting the peasants' rights as well as the total amount of farmland is a problem in today's China. As it is often said, the most crucial economic, social, and political problems in contemporary China all have something directly or indirectly to do with the land system. In recent years, many scandals involving government officials were related to land issues as well. Between October 2006 and early 2007, about 1,500 government officials were accused of unlawful land requisition.[11] As the economy develops, farm acreage gradually expands, and land transactions inevitably increase. If the current land problem cannot be solved properly, land-related disputes will deteriorate.

The primary problem that lies at the heart of China's land system is this dilemma: On the one hand, the population is too large; on the other hand, the land is quite limited, with the acreage per capita only one-third of the world's average. The arable land in China has been cultivated at the maximum level, among which farmland, however, is only 0.1 hectare per capita (as of 2006), which is less than half the world average. Moreover, this number is dropping year by year. According to Mr. Chen Xiwen, an official in the Central Leading Group of Finance and Economy, the farmland shrank by net 114 million Chinese acres (i.e., 7.93 million hectares) within eight years from 1997 to 2004. Consequently, the average annual output of grain in China was reduced from 497.5 million tons between 1995 and 1999 to 454.4 million tons between 2000 and 2004.[12]

For the 1.3 billion Chinese people, grain is their daily staple and is much more important than any other strategic materials such as steel or oil. Given that there have not been any effective regulations on the global grain market so far and speculation takes place very often, China's food supply must not depend on the world market for security reasons; it must be self-reliant. That there is no grain supply crisis today does not mean that there will not be a crisis in the future. In March 2008, several deputies to the NPC and commissioners of the CPPCC drew attention to China's "grain security." Commissioner Li Yuefeng, for example, pointed out that, in ten years, the gap between the demand and the supply of grain in China will reach 100 to 150 million tons per year, which means the shortage will be 25 percent *higher* than the grain security alert line.[13] At the same time, the spokesman of the Ministry of Agriculture acknowledged that, to ensure its grain security, China should produce 500 million tons of grain every year. To achieve this goal, China has to keep a minimum acreage of 1.8 billion *mu* or 120 million hectares, as well as to put effort into increasing the output per hectare.[14]

But the cost of the increase of per acre output has been higher and higher, since output depends on the use of a great deal of chemical fertilizer that is destructive to the ecological environment. One news article in 2008 reported that the Han River in Hubei Province was so seriously polluted that 200,000 people had difficulty accessing unpolluted drinking water.[15] One of the main causes of pollution was the massive use of fertilizer by a large state-owned farm in the basin of the Han River. Therefore, if we want to ensure food security and protect the environment at the same time, the most practical means is to secure total farming acreage.

Besides the land usage problem per se, we cannot ignore the problem of social instability in the rural area either. Just as Chen Xiwen said,

> In the process of large-scale land requisition, serious infringement of peasants' legitimate land rights occurred in many places. Because the compensation was too low and the resettlement policy was not properly implemented, many landless farmers have lost their means of livelihood and the hidden danger of social instability was hence seeded.[16]

In fact, every year a large number of peasants appeal to the higher authorities about land requisitions. Organized mass protests are also observed.

The governments at various levels are supposed to take major responsibility in securing the farmland acreage, protecting the peasants' rights and interests, and promoting rural social stability. Yet, ironically, the main cause for the shrinking of farmland is related to government intervention. It is exactly the local government that requisitions farmland for nonagricultural purposes. By 2003, the number of research and development (R & D) regions (*kaifa qu*) all over the country had reached 6,015, of which 70 percent were illegal. If this situation continues unchecked, the 120-million-hectare security line set by the central government will soon be broken. To deal with this issue, the Third Plenary Session of the Sixteenth CCPCC passed the motion that the current land requisition system should be reformed in accordance with the principle of protecting the peasant's rights and interests and of placing the land requisition under strict control. Nevertheless, as Chen Xiwen observes, since this reform "required the readjustment of the interests of diverse interest groups," it ran into "extreme difficulty."[17]

THE PROBLEMS OF THE CURRENT COLLECTIVE FARMLAND OWNERSHIP SYSTEM

The current Chinese constitution prescribes that any organization or individual is prohibited from dealing in land ownership. The legitimate farmland ownership transfer should go through governmental requisition. Unfortunately, since the current "collective ownership" system does not define clearly who has land ownership, the local government at multiple levels, in collaboration with real estate companies, could very easily abuse land requisition for non-farming uses by paying little to the farmers in the name of public demand.

Under the People's Commune system that originated in the late 1950s, land ownership was divided into multiple layers. Before the family contracted responsibility policy, the collective ownership had followed the Working Regulations in Rural People's Commune, or the Sixty Regulations for short, under which land ownership was defined on three levels with the production team as the primary base. The second regulation in chapter 1 stipulates that "the basic working unit of the People's Commune is the production team." And the twenty-first regulation in chapter 4 states that "all pieces of land in the domain of a production team belong to this team." Moreover, there was the rule of Four Fixed Attachments: Human labor, livestock, tools, and land are all fixed and attached to the production team. According to these principles and rules, under the collective land ownership, the production team is the principal entity to claim the basic rights over a given piece of farmland. Meanwhile, under the policy of three-level ownership, the People's Commune and the general production team (*shengchan dadui*) also have partial land ownership. Nowadays, however, with the dissolution of the People's Commune, such three-level ownership does not exist.

In 1994, the Ministry of Agriculture promulgated the document entitled the "Opinions on Stabilizing and Improving the Land-contracted Relationship." It is stipulated that

> when the land use is adjusted, it is prohibited to mandatorily change ownership; In addition, it is not allowed to transfer the ownership that originally belonged to the group-level collective economic organization (formerly called "the production team") to the village level by making it contracted evenly at the village level.

The PRC Land Administration Law (effective January 1, 1999) prescribes that "the collective land owned by the farmers of one village should be operated and administrated by the village economic organization or by the villager committee. If the collective land is owned by two or more economic units within a village, the land should be operated and administrated by the according economic units or by the villagers' groups. If the land is collectively owned by the farmers of a *xiang* ("township"), that land should be operated and administrated by the *xiang* collectives." The PRC Rural Land Lease Law (effective since March 1, 2003) reiterates the above law but changes "management and administration" into "contract-distribution with the peasants."

In fact, according to policies and laws, neither the villager committee nor the villager group is a collective economic organization of the peasants. By law, they are authorized to operate, administrate, or lease the land, but they themselves have no land ownership. With regard to the relationship between the villager committee and the village collective economic organization, The PRC Villager Committee Law, effective since 1998, stipulates that "the villager committee is a self-administered, self-learned, and self-served grass-roots autonomous organization" (clause 2); that "the villager committee should respect the collective economic organizations' legitimate rights to have independent economic activities . . . and should protect the legitimate property rights and other interests of the collective economic organizations, the leasehold, joint leaseholds or other partnerships" (clause 5); and that "the village committee should set up several villager groups in accordance with the situation of the villagers' settlements" (clause 10). Therefore, the law stipulates clearly that the villagers' committee should "respect" and "safeguard" the village collective economic organizations. In this sense, at least at present, both the production team, which was originally granted the collective land ownership, and the "collective economic organization," such as an administrative village or town, are merely nominal entities.

As the entity of collective ownership is separate, divided, and nominal, land ownership and administration become very chaotic and frequently altered. Even the government departments in charge have difficulty in sorting them out. "Some Opinions Regarding Land Ownership Determination" issued in 1998 by the National Land Administration Authority is a case in point. This document was specifically promulgated in order to better implement the PRC Land Administration Law. Clause 7 stipulates that before the "Notice of Enhancing Farmland Administration and Preventing Arbitrary Occupation of Farmland" was issued by the State Council, all the land leased by various units of the whole people ownership, the urban collective ownership, or town and village ownership should be registered in accordance with regulations concerned. If permanent buildings are constructed on the land site, the responsible land occupants should make a supplementary land requisition application in accordance with the given length of limited period, and the land should be owned by the state. Clause 8 stipulates that before the Sixty Regulations were publicized in September 1962, all land (including land privately owned before the cooperative period) that was originally owned by the peasants collectively but was now used by various units of the whole people ownership, the urban collective ownership, or the returned overseas Chinese collective farms should return to the peasants; yet, if lands had not been returned after the Sixty Regulations were promulgated, the land ownership should belong to the state. Clause 11 stipulates that if a group of peasants has collectively leased land from another group of peasants and the continuous tenancy has exceeded a period of twenty years, the land ownership should belong to the current occupants. However, if the continuous term of tenancy has not reached a period of twenty years, or if the original owners request the current tenants to return the land concerned or lodge a complaint to the authorities against the current tenants within a period of twenty years, then the claim of land ownership should be submitted to the county government for arbitration. The above clauses reveal that whenever land ownership disputes arise, in most cases, the government departments in charge usually uphold the status quo. If the dispute is raised between state ownership and collective ownership, the arbitration is usually to the advantage of the former.

Of course, no matter how the ownerships are defined, no individual peasant household is entitled to such right. The No. 1 Document of 2008 raised that "various infringements upon the land lease rights and interests of the peasant households should be prohibited." As Chen Xiwen points out, "to lease and make use of farmland and to decide whether and how the rights over farmland use is transferred is the peasant's legitimate right granted by law."[18] This statement is based on the PRC Rural Land Contract Law, under which the first clause of the general rules stipulates that "peasants are granted long-term secured rights over farmland use." Nevertheless, under the current circumstances of vague land ownership and merely nominal collective ownership, neither the "operation and administration rights" nor the "use rights" is ensured, not to mention the fact that the so-called long-term lease still has an end date, especially when local government requisitions large tracts of farmland in the name of economic development. According to relevant rules, the "township" and "town" (*xiang* and *zhen*) governments take over the administrative functions concerned from its predecessor, namely, the People's Commune, and are entitled to administer its collective land ownership on behalf of the towns, although town governments are not entities for the collective economic ownership.[19] In fact, some town administrations still function like the previous People's Commune, arbitrarily dividing and even dominating peasants' collective land ownership. The consequence is that local governments in collaboration with developers and some village cadres often require farmland for nonagricultural use. Moreover, this use is often conducted against the will of peasant households, and the compensation is usually much lower than market price. Covered in the name of "lease," the fraudulent land requisitions have deprived many peasants of basic rights, and thereby allowed corrupting officials to make huge amounts of money.

FINDING A SOLUTION TO FURTHER AGRARIAN SYSTEM REFORM

What are the possible solutions to the nominal collective ownership of farmland? Some scholars and policymakers advocate for returning to the system of the People's Commune. They argue that the family-contracted responsibility system was a sudden return to a backward precapitalist mode of small-scale production and that the autonomous small farmers no longer have value in the economic system. Obviously, this point of view does not correspond with the reality of great changes both in agriculture and in rural areas over the three decades since the abolishment of the People's Commune, during which the gross output of agricultural production grew rapidly and a large sum of concealed surplus labor left the villages for other jobs. According to the data released by the National Bureau of Statistics, by early 2006, China's rural population amounted to 940 million, and actual permanent rural residents numbered around 750 million.[20] It is unknown whether the rural population of 750 million people includes the large number of peasant workers employed by the village and township enterprises. However, it is, by any means, a miracle that in less than three decades nearly 200 million people have flowed from the countryside into urban areas.

Three decades after the rural reform, a number of villages in China have achieved remarkable economic success since they adhered to or resumed the collective management and administration system. Some villages have become famous worldwide, such as the Nanjie Village in Henan province. In the context of urban and rural institutions being separate from each other, these villages serve as the models of rural industrialization. They are indeed another model of industrialization and urbanization with Chinese characteristics, and their lessons deserve careful investigation. The grand agenda of China's economy and society is to strive out of the traditional agricultural pattern. In this sense, it would be better if there are hundreds of towns like Huaxi Village, *Daqiu Zhuang*, and Nanjie Village continuously emerging from everywhere in China. Nevertheless, it would be hardly realistic if most villages in Henan, the nation's premier food production province, follow the steps of Nanjie to achieve rural industrialization. As a matter of fact, without the family-contracted rural reform or the extensive traditional agricultural economy in surrounding areas, there would not be such a huge supply of raw materials, food, cheap labor, and market, as required by the agricultural processing industries in Nanjie. For the sake of rural economic diversification, the traditional and the industrial development patterns complement each other. However, to promote industry is not equal to running diversified agricultural economy. In addition, with regard to legal issues, the ownership entities of these collective industrialized villages like Nanjie are still unclear, and many villages have already divided their assets into shares distributed among villagers. Given the facts above, it is unconvincing and unsound to use Nanjie Village's industrialization as a case to argue that the rural family-contracted land reform is inferior to collective management and administration. However, at any rate, the emergence of these industrialized villages and towns demonstrates that *nongcun* ("rural areas") in the "three-*nong*" problem does not imply "villages" that are engaged in traditional agriculture. Instead, these "villages," where the overwhelming majority of villagers are not peasants anymore, have developed into large-scale industrial and trading corporations, with a number of small towns becoming new industrial centers. In making overall plans for urban and rural development, the state should encourage and support the construction and development of these new industrial villages and vigorously create better conditions to urbanize them. Once urbanization is achieved, the former rural villagers will become urban residents. And through legitimate economic compensation, what was originally farmland can be changed into urban land. Only under these circumstances can migrant workers from other areas enjoy the same legitimate residential and working status as the local villagers do.

While some others endorse farmland privatization, Wen Tiejun holds that China is not prepared for farmland privatization, because it is impossible for Chinese government to provide 900 million rural people with social security. In fact, the limited farmland in the countryside undertakes the responsibility for providing peasants with the basic livelihood. I agree with Wen's conclusion. While Wen may worry about the bankrupt peasants' livelihood after farmland privatization, here I will discuss the impracticability of privatization from two different perspectives.

First, as the land per capita in rural China is less than 0.15 hectare, land privatization will result in smaller-scale and even more fragmented management of land for a long time. Many people are concerned that land annexation and social polarization, which appeared repeatedly during the preindustrial period, will lead to social instability. In my opinion, things will go the opposite way. As urbanization and industrialization are rapidly expanding and the total amount of farmland is continuously decreasing in China, the land price will continuously go up. In this case, most farmers will firmly hold their small private lands and will not easily sell them. Hence, land privatization will only make business expansion more difficult. Japan, South Korea, and Taiwan have all been facing this dilemma after decades of "land to the tiller" reform.

China's household contract responsibility system is similar to the so-called unimodal strategy, which is carried out in some countries in east Asia. The singular difference between them lies in the land ownership system. For example, after land reform in Japan, private landowners reached 90 percent of the total number of owners, while sharecroppers reached 88 percent. Japan implemented the Agricultural Basic Law in 1961, trying to expand the operation scale, promote management cooperation, improve the efficiency of family agriculture, and increase the income level of farmers. Then, the government repeatedly amended the law, promoting land circulation by loosening restrictions on the maximum area of land ownership. But by 1980, 71 percent of the peasants still had land with area size below 1.0 hectare and three-fifths of these peasants had land with area below 0.5 hectare. In 1999, the Japanese government replaced the Basic Agricultural Law with the Basic Law of Food, Agriculture and Village for the same purpose. In 2001, it implemented the Agricultural Land Law Amendment to promote the establishment of corporate systems of agricultural production and further weaken the state control over agricultural land. These policies made it very difficult to transfer land by purchase, because according to this amendment, it is illegal to buy land and force peasants to leave that land. The increase of land prices and recessions occurring in the agricultural economy made land transfer even less frequent. To promote land transfer, Japan replaced purchase with tenancy. In doing so, the government set up a variety of exceptions to the restrictions on tenancy. Similar to the "entrusted to manage" provision in Taiwan, Japanese law allows peasants in peasants' associations to commission land to other members. Even so, the total area involved in the circulation of ownership and use rights is only about ten thousand hectares.[21]

Second, another argument in favor of farmland privatization maintains that privatization helps capital enter agriculture and thus can promote land transfer as well as expand the scale of land management. In doing so, privatization can accelerate capital-intensive agricultural development and thus further the marketization of the rural economy. However, what really takes place might be quite the opposite. After privatization, part of the land will probably be concentrated in the hands of powerful corporations. These pieces of land might not be utilized for farming but for house building, hotel construction for tourism, or even be hoarded for higher prices. Some private capitalists may invest in some economic planting, such as cocoa, coffee, and rubber trees, but are less likely to invest in grain planting. Such a situation is caused by the biological nature of grain planting and consequently by the rate of return on capital, which is much lower than those in nonagricultural industries (including agricultural production supplies and agricultural product processing industry). The international agricultural academia has already had many discussions on this point and the international experience of agricultural development can also support this observation.

Du Runsheng, one of the pioneers of China's rural reform, has already noticed that family management and agricultural modernization can be compatible. The United States, Germany, Japan, and other developed countries are examples.[22] Nowadays, family farms rather than large capitalist farms are more prevalent in the world. The reason is as follows. First, capital entering agriculture is influenced by the ecological characteristics of agricultural production, for example, drought and flood disasters, restrictions of sunshine and irrigation, long production cycle, and lack of continuity. Therefore, it is strategically better for the capitalist to control agricultural products and the production of farm tools than to take part in the agricultural production process directly. Second, family farmers share the good tradition of working hard from dawn to night. Meanwhile, education and technical training as well as those "scale-neutral" supplies (such as small- and medium-sized farm machinery, irrigation facilities, fertilizers, pesticides, and new varieties of crops or livestock and so on) could improve the efficiency of family farming more than they can large-scale land management. Third, the low level of industrialization has led to limited nonagricultural employment and small-scale land per capita. That is the reason why the average scale of land for agricultural management is so small in many developing countries. When the Industrial Revolution took place, the agricultural population in western Europe had dropped considerably, to about 50 percent of the total population. However, agricultural population still occupied 70–80 percent of the total population when industrialization started in developing countries. Thus it will be a very long process to transfer agricultural population to the urban space.[23]

Given the dilemma that the peasants' right to farmland management must be protected, while the ownership of farmland could not be privatized, it cannot be considered a bad choice to "be unswerving in sticking constantly to the land policy that is based on the 'family contracted responsibility system.'" In the long run, the sole way out may be to reduce the agricultural population gradually while making the remaining peasants expand their managing scale step by step. Following this, capital investments need to be expanded and agricultural technology innovation needs to be fostered to improve productivity and accelerate the process of rural modernization. As small-scale family farms are still prevalent in China and other eastern Asia countries now, this change will be a long and gradual process.

Yang Yao argues that the possibility of diversification of the current farmland system has resulted from the instability of farmland ownership and nonintegrity of family farmers' usufruct of their farmland. He stresses the importance of balancing efficiency, equity, and social stability. He also emphasizes the sharp regional difference within the existing farmland system, considering the degree of individualization in land ownership as the crux. He points out that it is necessary to take comprehensive considerations on three aspects, as follows. First, the stability of the agricultural land system complements the allocation of resources. Stable land ownership could attract investment and more rights over the disposal of land could elevate the efficiency of resource allocation. Second, social security and unemployment insurance are important to the agricultural land system. Although a more "highly individualized" farmland system may reduce the efficiency of agricultural production, this loss may be compensated by its functions as social security and unemployment insurance. These two functions, far beyond the role of agriculture itself, will have a far-reaching impact on the entire national economy and national stability. The last point is about the equality of rights. The collective ownership system gives every legitimate member of the village an equal right to use the land. The pursuit of equality will consequently lead to land adjustments. Yao points out that any state interference with the collective ownership of land runs counter to the constitutional principle that prescribes rural land to be owned by collectives. The government should not interfere with farmers' self-management but should only give them economic and administrative guidance. In addition, to prevent village cadres from abusing their power, the state must take responsibility to have them supervised.[24]

Yao's analysis is convincing and crucial, although the "inductive system innovation" that he discusses does not break away from the current framework of the nominal collective ownership. Is there any alternative to the existing system? In my opinion, to protect farmers' rights firmly, it may be feasible to confer peasant families' complete permanent usufruct as prescribed by the constitution. Meanwhile, state policymakers should abandon the rigid and merely nominal collective ownership and instead support farmers' cooperatives organized on a voluntary basis. Such an organization should be autonomous, owned by farmers, and used for them only. This is a "supply and marketing cooperation," too. What we want to achieve is the initiation of a new pattern of "small government (to streamline the township government) and big society (varieties of farmers' economic cooperatives and communal self-government organizations)." For this purpose, a wide range of legislation is necessary and three actions should be taken immediately.

First, it is urgent to formulate a new law to protect agricultural land and basic agricultural law. Any illegal arrogation on land ownership must be forbidden. Meanwhile, to expand the operation scale, we must encourage the circulation of farmland in agricultural use and prohibit behaviors such as "deserting and segmenting agricultural land, or converting it into construction land." The government should be only responsible for examining and approving plans of land expropriation and levying land tax and value-added tax. In short, the government should just take the role as an arbiter or as a supervisor. Developers must bargain with farmers directly, expropriating land at reasonable prices.

Second, we must initiate the law of agricultural cooperation and then help farmers establish their own economic cooperatives and autonomous communal organization, which has similar "self-management, self-education, and self-service" as the village committee has. Meanwhile, it is necessary to strengthen the state's functions in law enforcement and supervision and to reduce the administrative functions of grassroots government.

Third, we should initiate a series of laws, including agricultural credit, agricultural insurance, agricultural disaster compensation, and the rural social security laws. It is the government's duty to help farmers resolve the difficulty of agricultural loans and small-scale loans through dedicated national financial institutions and to strictly limit loan sharking. The government should also implement antimonopoly laws in the production and marketing of farm tools, as well as in the processing of agricultural products, to encourage peasants to sell their products directly. Only in this way can farmers withstand natural and manmade disasters.

Moreover, we must also initiate an agricultural technology promotion act, which will help farmers manage their land with the latest technology and science, thus increasing agricultural productivity. The research and development sector for agriculture should be invested in mainly by the government.

"Ownership" means that property is at the legal owner's disposal completely. By this definition, farmers today do not have complete rights of free disposal. To protect farmers' rights effectively, it is plausible to extend the term of land use (usually thirty or fifty years) indefinitely and to make the permanent usufructs from a commonsense right to a constitutional one. The distinction between this proposed policy and the privatization policy is clear, since in the latter, the peasants' rights and interests over land are protected but also restricted by law. There are many differences between the farmers' economic cooperation that I described above and the People's Commune system. In economic cooperation, there is an exit mechanism, and members will not be punished for their exits. Even production cooperation, which should be formed voluntarily, is likely to appear in villagers' groups but may also appear as an intergroup or even intervillage organization. Thus the scale of organization may continue to expand, or shrink because of the withdrawal of farmers.

The law is a manifestation of the will of the state. Implemented in 2007, the PRC Property Law regulates that the property owner has the right to establish usufructuary right in regard to real or movable property. According to this law, once peasant households have obtained the permanent utilization rights of a piece of land, they are entitled to the usufructuary rights of this land. Here, although the phrase "usufructuary rights" does not refer to the full right to possess the land, it includes rights to occupy, utilize, and profit from the land, to request compensation if the land is damaged by others, and to transfer the above rights. The new system of land ownership I discussed above can be regarded as a new type of state ownership, the essence of which is to split agricultural land ownership between the state and the farmers. It is different from the concepts of local state-owned and cadres economy. Some scholars have demonstrated the necessity of land nationalization from the perspective of China's socialist nature. Actually, nationalization has nothing to do with socialism. There have been varieties of advocacy of state ownership in history. Henry George in America held the single-tax theory of land in nineteenth century. Lenin, following Marx, also proposed to establish "a truly free economy of farmers," which would guarantee the free exchange of land, freedom of moving and of expanding section, thus replacing the outdated *mir* (a tax paying unit) with new free collaborations.[25] Just as the collective economy in the People's Commune period eventually became a cadres' economy, the collective ownership has been a system controlled by the local government from the very beginning (especially since the dissolution of the People's Commune) to the extent that this collective ownership could be described as local or semistate ownership. The most urgent task is to establish the principle of rule of law. Nowadays, as political power allies itself with capital to occupy large-scale land in the pretense of public interest, it is time to fix the related areas in the legal system.

There is no need to consider the concept of state ownership as a taboo. The crux of the problem is strong administrative interference. The most important issue is that farmers' rights should be protected firmly. As for the ownership, it is just a facade and means nothing without real interests. In order to protect farmers' rights, every level of the government must abide by laws and regulations. To my understanding, such a new system of land ownership should be qualified as follows: The land ownership is shared by farmers and the state under the rule of law. The policy that farmland should be used by farmers must be maintained, and farmers' rights must not be violated. Today, as the representatives of the collective owners, many cadres are encroaching farmers' rights. I hold the opinion that fighting against the alliance of political power and capital should be prioritized.

To protect farmers' rights as well as farmland, we should not only legislate strictly but also timely punish those offenders. Reconstruction of the legal system is urgent and important today. As Du Runsheng points out, "the rule of law, but not the rule of man, is the most exigent."[26] It may be predicted that in the long run, with the change of the labor-land ratio, the scale of agricultural units will expand, the farmers' economic strength will be enhanced, the situation of peasant cooperatives in the market will improve, and state intervention will be limited. Right now, it is the responsibility of the state to formulate laws to protect farmers' rights and to nurture the agricultural industry.

NOTES

1. I am grateful to Professor Arif Dirlik, Professor Wu Xiao-an, and two graduates, Ms. Yige Dong and Mr. Kun Liu, for their comments and English editorial assistance.

2. Carl K. Eicher and John M. Staatz, *Agricultural Development in the Third World* (Baltimore: Johns Hopkins University Press, 1984), 263.

3. Theodore Schultz, *Transforming Traditional Agriculture,* trans. Liang Xiaoming (Beijing: The Commercial Press, 1987), 125–126.

4. Alexander V. Chayanov, *The Peasant Farm Organization*, trans. Xiao Zhenghong (Beijing: Zhongyang Bianyi Publishing House, 1996), 233, 237.

5. Yujiro Hayami and Vernon W. Ruttan, *Agricultural Development: An International Perspective,* trans. Guo Xibao et al. (Beijing: Chinese Social Sciences Publishing House, 2000), 389–393.

6. Gong Li, *Ping Shu Ding* (Beijing: Commercial Press, 1937) volume 7, section 5, part 1.

7. Yifu Lin, *System, Technology and the Agricultural Development in China* (Shanghai: Shanghai People's Press, 1995).

8. Philip Huang, *The Peasant Family and Rural Development in the Yangzi Delta, 1350–1988* (Stanford: Stanford University Press, 1990).

9. Karl Kautsky, *The Agrarian Question,* trans. Liang Lin (Beijing: Joint Publishing Company, 1955), 14.

10. "The 10 'No. 1 Documents' on Agriculture Issued by The Central Committee of the Chinese Communist Party and the State Council, PRC." Available: http://xinnongcun.agri.gov.cn/counter.asp?id=20846&IClass=0003, http://news.xinhuanet.com/fortune/2004-02/09/content_1304399_3.htm and http://nc.people.com.cn/GB/6843047.html (accessed April 15, 2008).

11. Qiu Feng, "China's Land Reform Is at the Critical Point," *China News Weekly* (January 4, 2008).

12. Xiwen Chen, "Problems of Agriculture, Rural Villages, and Peasants in Today's China," *Study and Research* 1 (2006). Available: http://nc.people.com.cn/GB/116210/116211/116212/6902331.html (accessed April 15, 2008).

13. Dong Yang, "There Might Be 100 Million Tons Shortfall in the Supply of Grain in Ten Years in China," *Chinanews*. Available: http://www.chinanews.com.cn/cj/hgjj/news/2008/03-18/1195062.shtml (accessed March 18, 2008).

14. Runfeng Yao, et al., "China's Grain Import Is Not the Main Factor of the Rise of Price in the International Grain Market," *Xinhua News,* March 10, 2008. Available: http://news.xinhuanet.com/misc/2008-03/10/content_7761644.htm (accessed April 2, 2008).

15. Yiping Wei, "The Other Side of the Pollution of Han River," *Sanlian Life Weekly,* March 6, 2008. Available: http://news.sina.com.cn/c/2008-03-06/170815091232.shtml (accessed April 15, 2008).

16. Xiwen Chen, "Problems of Agriculture, Rural Villages, and Peasants in Today's China," *Study and Research* 1 (2006).

17. It is mainly the interest of local governments. Since the reform of the taxation system in 1994, the local governments, given the power of total taxation on land income by the central government, have taken land as the bank that means to get a huge sum of money from expropriating the farmland with a little compensation to the peasants.

18. Xiwen Chen, "Problems of Agriculture, Rural Villages, and Peasants in Today's China," *Study and Research* 1 (2006).

19. "Notice on Promoting to Issue Licenses for the Collective Land Ownership" issued in 2001 by the Department of National Land and Resources stipulates that the town government has the power to manage the town-level collective land.

20. Chong Xiao, "The Number of Peasants Is Decreasing," *Net of China,* February 22, 2006. Available: http://www.china.com.cn/chinese/EC-c/1131488.htm (accessed April 15, 2008).

21. Sekiya Syunsaku, *The Agrarian System in Japan* (Beijing: Joint Publishing Company, 2004).

22. Du Runsheng, *Autobiography of Du Runsheng* (Beijing: People's Press, 2005), 112, 203.

23. For detailed discussion, see Zhenghua Dong, "On Two Theoretical Questions Regarding the Development of Modern Agriculture," *Marxism and Reality* 28 (2006): 145–152.

24. Yang Yao, "Chinese Farmland Ownership System: A Framework for Analysis," *Social Science in China* 56 (2000): 54–65.

25. Vladimir Lenin, *Complete Works* (Beijing: People's Press, 1968), volume 16, 390–391.

26. Du Run-sheng, *Autobiography of Du Run-sheng* (Beijing: People's Press, 2005), 21.

Chapter 8

Awaiting Urbanization

Urban Village Redevelopment in Coastal Urban China

Leslie Shieh

AWAITING URBANIZATION

Urbanization describes the shift from rural to urban and is often expressed as percentage increases in urban population, urban land uses, and nonagricultural outputs. This paper examines the normative dimension of urbanization—how government policies seek to guide and condition the integration of villagers into the city. It draws attention to the agrarian society at the interstices between city and countryside where the complex boundaries of rural and urban are being constantly negotiated. As the built-up city sprawls rapidly outward, farmland and village settlements at the periphery have been requisitioned to make way for apartment buildings, shopping centers, warehouses, and factories. The rural to urban transition, as experienced by village communities, is an ongoing process of shifting livelihoods and seeking new ways to retain control over their land. In this dynamic process, urban land uses engulf lingering portions of indigenous villages and leapfrog beyond, leaving the fragmented villages as islands in the urban landscape, referred to in Chinese as *chengzhongcun* ("urban villages" or "villages in the city"). Contending with ways to bring these rural exceptions under the regulatory regime of urban planning has become a pressing issue for many large coastal cities. What draws my attention to urban village redevelopment is the question of how these villages become part of the city, not only in terms of land or administrative transition from rural to urban, but the ways through which villagers are reconstituted as urbanites.[1]

In particular, this paper examines how the nationwide community building initiative, "*Shequ* Construction" (*shequ jianshe*), works in tandem with local urban village redevelopment plans to facilitate the integration of villagers into the city. Piloted by the Ministry of Civil Affairs, *Shequ* Construction aims to strengthen cellular and place-based governance by creating standards for a neighborly environment and building the capacity of "residents' committees" (*jumin weiyuanhui*) to undertake administrative functions, maintain public order, and manage social welfare needs. Divided into four parts, this paper begins by problematizing the urban village phenomenon in terms of integration. Next, it presents an overview of the urban village redevelopment plan proposed in 2005 by the Nanjing Municipal Government. Then, through comparing the experience of two village communities, it examines the role of *Shequ* Construction in the redevelopment process. In the first, as relocated villagers adjust to urban neighbors and the urban way of life in apartment blocks, *shequ* programming transmits appropriate ways of living in an urban neighborhood and expected behavioral norms. In the second, more remote village, officials have decisively adopted urban-based neighborhood standards. The concluding discussion considers the interactive effects of the two policies and the ways in which *Shequ* Construction functions as an instrument of normative urbanization.

The research is based on fieldwork conducted in Nanjing, Jiangsu Province in 2006 and 2007. It draws on government documents and interviews conducted with officials in the planning bureau on the city's urban growth and village redevelopment plans and with officials in district-level civil affairs bureaus on local implementation of the nationwide agenda to construct communities. To understand how policies unfolded on the ground, interviews were conducted with the villagers' committee and residents of Rivertown Village[2] and Willow Village, and the residents' committee and residents of White Blossom *Shequ*, an urban neighborhood where some of the city's villagers have resettled after land acquisition. Repeated visits were made to the two villages to observe and document their redevelopment process. I also had the opportunity to visit three villages in the city's two counties that have established profitable enterprises, presenting a contrasting course of development whereby urbanization of the countryside occurs in situ as opposed to arising from the outward expansion of the city.[3]

INTEGRATION: FRAMING THE URBAN VILLAGE PHENOMENON

The straightforward explanation for the formation of urban villages is found in the particular circumstances of Chinese land laws. Under the Chinese constitution and China's Land Management Law, administratively designated urban lands are defined as state lands, with property rights ultimately controlled by agencies of the state. Administratively rural lands, on the other hand, are defined as collective lands, with property rights, though limited, assigned to rural villages.[4] Only state-owned land can be leased and land use rights transferred from state to work units or development companies.[5] Thus, rural land has to be first acquired by the municipality from the rural collective to be developed for urban land uses; it then becomes urban and state owned.[6]

Being less troublesome than "settlement land" (*zhaijidi*) to compensate and convert, farmland, throughout the 1980s and 1990s, was typically requisitioned first, leaving village settlements as pockets in an increasingly urban landscape. In such circumstances, land use controls and decision making remain in the hands of villagers' committees, with the resulting spatial development outcomes often at odds with stipulated objectives of municipal urban planning goals. Consequently, as cities now try to capture and redevelop village land, the process is often long and drawn out, first with resistance over land acquisition and compensation, and then with resolving the livelihood hardships villagers face after relocation.[7] The redevelopment of urban villages is thus more complicated than facilitating the transformation of rural (collective) lands into urban (state) lands through processes of state expropriation and reassignment. Understanding urban villages solely in terms of land governance suggests that they are temporarily at an in-between phase in the process of rural to urban land conversion, awaiting urbanization. Such processes are accompanied by the social and economic ramifications of also facilitating the transformation of former villagers into urban citizens. As such, urban village redevelopment must be recognized as a social phenomenon as much as a land-use issue.[8]

The social policy discourse that has arisen in English scholarly writings on the urban village phenomenon in China frames the villages as sites of resistance and questions why they persist despite redevelopment efforts. This literature centers on the enclave nature of urban villages and the informal economy within them. It explores the relationships on which urban villages are built—the tight internal networks and well-defined hierarchies between migrants and migrant leaders and between villagers and migrant renters, as well as working relationships between villagers' committees and local governments.[9] Rather than viewing urban villages as simply an outcome of the land conversion process, these studies seek to decipher the more complex community dynamics that have rooted the urban villages in place and empowered villagers to resist relocation and demolition. Urban villages are regarded as entities separate from the "formal" city, as unique sites of self-help and resistance.

Extending this discussion by taking the view from the city, this paper is concerned with the problematic of integration. By questioning villagers' integration, as opposed to their resistance, it seeks to examine how urban-centered redevelopment policies intend to absorb villagers as residents and, conversely, how villagers interpret the plans for their incorporation. To facilitate this inquiry, I examine the interaction between two different policy-driven integrative mechanisms: (1) the directive to forge strong neighborhood-based community bonds under *Shequ* Construction and (2) urban village redevelopment plans that seek to expedite the process of rural to urban conversion. These two policies, the former implemented by the civil affairs bureau and the latter by the planning bureau, are often analyzed separately.

In broad terms, *Shequ* Construction, an urban policy program, seeks to strengthen neighborhood governance by two means: building strong grassroots leadership to manage social welfare needs and setting standards for a neighborly environment of low crime rate, volunteerism, and green spaces.[10] *Shequ*, in official discourse, is defined as "a social collective formed by those who reside within a defined geographic boundary."[11] Initiated in the 1990s at the height of state-owned enterprise restructuring, *Shequ* Construction's practical goal is to draw urban residents out of the cellular work units and into community-based social services administered by the reconstituted residents' committees. The housewives and grandmothers of the socialist neighborhood institution have been replaced by a younger and more professionalized staff. On an emotional level, the nationwide agenda also aims to foster a sense of neighborhood-based community in an increasingly stratified and commodified urban society.

In the context of urban village redevelopment, *Shequ* Construction plays a significant but overlooked role in urbanizing the city's hinterland. First, for villagers relocated to apartments in urban neighborhoods, *shequ* programming serves as an integrative devise in conditioning their everyday cultural practices. Second, at a wider scale, a recent initiative under experimentation in Nanjing intends to extend the policy program from urban neighborhoods into rural villages. From its beginnings in aiding the transition of urbanites' sense of community from workplace to home, the policy has also come to be an instrument for transferring urban standards and reforming rural practices. The policy has had both positive and negative impacts on village communities. In these new sites undergoing "community construction," the articulation of *Shequ* Construction with urban village redevelopment initiatives raises many as yet unasked questions about its rationale and appropriateness as a means of bringing about social order.

NANJING'S URBAN VILLAGE REDEVELOPMENT

Nanjing municipality encompasses eleven urban districts and two rural counties. At the grassroots level, there are currently 799 residents' committees and 587 villagers' committees (VCs). The villages are within the two counties (230 VCs) and the five suburban districts (326 VCs), and on the fringe of the six urban districts (31 VCs).[12] In the broadest sense of the term "urban village"—that is, urbanizing villages of mixed rural and urban activities and land uses in an urban jurisdiction—one could say that there are 587 urban villages in Nanjing. However, it is necessary to differentiate between them, as the city's redevelopment schemes specifically target villages that are now within the urban core. With planning issues that differ from those confronting villages farther away in the countryside, these villages do not face the city's encroachment but are already engulfed by it.[13] With land use controls and decision making in the hands of villagers' committees, what happens in these villages largely falls outside the scope of urban administrative bureaus. Sanitation trucks that spray and sweep the city streets every morning drive past them. Villagers have self-built low-cost housing to cater to the needs of thousands of rural migrants, many of whom either cannot afford or lack the proper registration papers to take up residence in the formal city. Overcrowded and underserved by public infrastructure, these self-built structures are vastly incongruent with the new development projects that surround them. Many researchers have cautioned that redeveloping urban villages demolishes a significant source of low-income housing.[14] However, from policymakers' perspectives, urban villages are sites of ungovernability with substandard housing, deficient infrastructure, an abysmal environment, and high crime rates.

In 2005, the Nanjing Municipal Government announced an aggressive urban village redevelopment plan to requisition seventy-one urban villages within the city's ring road and to dissolve their villagers' committees within four years. The redevelopment was estimated to add about 67 square kilometers of urban land.[15] This presented a significant amount relative to the size of the city's urban core, which is about 243 square kilometers. And, as the city had already used up its designated construction land quota to 2010, redevelopment would provide an important source of land.[16] A survey conducted by the city estimated that redevelopment would entail the relocation of 104,000 villagers and provisions for their social welfare as they become urban residents. In addition to the number of villagers impacted, the survey estimated the displacement of 136,000 migrants, or about 10 percent of the city's migrant population. In economic terms, redevelopment would require close to 100 million RMB of collectively owned assets to be compensated or reorganized into share-holding companies or collectives.[17]

The redevelopment plan outlined a three-phase process for implementation by district governments. Phase 1 (2005 to 2006) would consist of requisitioning the residual pieces of collectively owned land within the six urban districts. With regard to villages in the suburban districts, the plan directed local officials to focus, for the time being, on improving the living environments. Phase 2 (2007 to 2008) would involve demolishing all illegal self-built structures in villages, particularly in the suburban districts. Given the large number of people and the amount of collective assets implicated, the objective, at this moment in time, would be to lay out the necessary infrastructure such as roads, water and sewer lines, and telecommunication to promote future growth and development. Phase 3 (2009), planning ahead for their future incorporation, would focus on strengthening the management of urban village communities according to urban standards.[18]

In addition to this working timeline that proceeds outward from the urban core, the plan further categorizes the seventy-one urban villages into three types according to their method of redevelopment. Type A villages, accounting for forty-seven of the seventy-one, are those in areas already approved for development projects and slated to proceed with land requisition and relocation. Eight villages labeled Type B are located in areas designated for open green space in the city's land use plan. When opportunities arise, these villages will be incorporated into planning projects and redeveloped accordingly. For villages farther out that may be difficult to attach to projects within the plan's four years, the municipal government plans to gradually incorporate them into the construction land reserve to acquire for urban uses in the future. Type C includes the residual portions of fourteen villages left over from previous development projects. Those in the urban core are to be listed as areas for urban renewal and will proceed by acquisition and resettlement. For those farther out in the suburban districts with the village form basically intact, city planners do not object to postponing action so long as control and management over the living environment is strengthened.[19] In reality, each phase required much more time than the plan allowed, and the efforts overlapped and waned depending on the negotiations and available funding.

In the following sections, I explore the nuances of Nanjing's redevelopment plan through the experiences of two villages located within the urban core. Both are slated for immediate attention under Phase 1; however, their categorization—Rivertown Village as Type A and Willow Village as Type C—has rendered them at different points in the process with different strategies and options available to them.[20]

REDEVELOPMENT THROUGH DISSOLUTION: LAND ACQUISITION AND RELOCATION

Rivertown Village is located on the western edge of Nanjing's urban core, just outside the Ming Dynasty city wall. Nanjing began its westward expansion in the 1980s to accommodate the numerous returning youths who were sent to the countryside during the Cultural Revolution. In native Nanjing residents' mental map, the area to the west across the Qinhuai River that runs through the urban core is perceived as peripheral—crossing the river meant leaving the city.[21] In the 1980 to 2000 master plan, this area to the west, known as Hexi (literally "west of the river"), was not yet part of the urban core.[22] During this period, in addition to the appearance of six-story low-rise work-unit housing, farmland was also being requisitioned to build factories, mostly those producing construction materials such as lumber and concrete. Gradually, small wholesale markets and warehouses for construction materials also moved in.

Subsequent master plans, forecasting growth, have designated Hexi as a secondary urban center, conceiving of it as the city's center for culture and sports.[23] In the early period of trying to bring projects to the area, city officials had difficulty attracting developers on whom they relied to help finance and build basic infrastructure. Therefore, officials were lenient and developers bought land that was easiest to compensate. Consequently, agricultural land was expropriated and developed first, leaving village settlements standing next to towering commercial high-rises. Then, in preparation to host the 2005 Tenth National Games, city planners, aided by the emergent housing market, undertook a concerted effort to transform this area.[24] Block upon block of newly built commercial housing, shopping centers, landscaped parks, and Olympic-sized sports stadiums are now connected to the urban core by the subway line and a road system of wide boulevards. In this suburban landscape, lingering village settlements like Rivertown sit in jarring contrast.

As construction went on around it, the village was itself in a construction furor that had, until the recent emphasis on redevelopment, escaped tight scrutiny from the planning bureau. City planning at the time gave officials limited oversight and responsibilities for administratively rural land. In seeking compromises with rural villagers within their purview, officials allowed the retention of land for "self-use" (*ziliudi*) and approved certain development projects.[25] Much of the construction centered on shifting toward a nonagricultural livelihood based on rental income. Its proximity to the city and the concentration of construction factories and warehouses drew many rural migrants to rent informal housing in Rivertown. Migrant workers account for about 80 percent of the residents living there today.[26] Many occupy dilapidated housing with shared water taps and latrines self-built by landlord-villagers. In a process aptly described as "house planting" (*zhong fangzi*), villagers subdivided their homes into individual rooms and built basic boarding houses on vacant lots, bringing in 150 to 200 RMB per room a month. On average, each family receives 2,000 RMB a month in rental income, with some receiving as much as 7,000 RMB. Most can recoup construction costs within one year. As the locals say, it takes one year to cultivate the seedling but it yields a sizable harvest every year afterward.[27]

Over time, as less farmland remained and more villagers moved out, villagers stopped putting money into infrastructure improvements. Inevitably, the living environment has become terribly degraded. When it rains, inadequate drainage causes the roads to flood. In the summer heat, the smell from the poorly constructed public latrines is overwhelming. Rather than street numbers, the signs above doors read "rental unit 1," "rental unit 2," and so on. Many migrants make their living as scavengers, and their sorted recyclables, from scrap metal to cardboard boxes to plastic beverage bottles, are piled high in the alleyways. Given these inhospitable conditions, the Rivertown villagers I managed to meet—a few of whom were still living there but most of whom were only returning to collect rent—agreed that redevelopment is necessary. However, because they feel uncertain about their future and they know the great difference between the compensation they will receive and the price developers will pay the city, they want to get as much as they can from their land while they still have the opportunity.

Dissolving the Village Collective

Decisions at the village level are made by villagers' committees and other village governing organizations.[28] Villages, as "mass organizations of self-management at the grassroots level,"[29] create their own financial base from collective assets and revenues. The collective resources pay for social services (such as schools and clinics), administrative operations and salaries, and economic development. While Rivertown, like all villages on the periphery of large cities, benefited financially from participating in the exchange flows of people and capital, it never had the opportunity to accumulate great wealth. In wealthy villages in Nanjing's two rural counties, collective revenue has been used to build new homes for every member of the village and provide tuition for children to attend university in the city.[30] Nevertheless, Rivertown villagers would prefer their rural or agricultural "registration status" (*hukou*). The once-treasured urban or nonagricultural *hukou* had meant guaranteed employment, food provision, and access to social services, but their rise in income from rents and collective dividends and their proximity to the city had long afforded them an urban lifestyle. Rather than benefits, I was told that a change to urban status would mean giving up the rural advantages of early marriage with the possibility of having two children. Furthermore, they felt at a disadvantage to compete in the urban knowledge-based labor market. A resident remarked that while the urban *hukou* makes them eligible for low-income social assistance should they face difficulties, 300 RMB per month per person is a dramatic reduction from the rental income they currently receive.[31]

Rivertown no longer appears in the Nanjing administrative roster of rural villages and urban *shequ*. The villagers' committee continues to monitor and look after the remaining villagers who have yet to receive their urban registration status and to manage the few parcels of collectively owned land. It works out of a two-story village service center that it now shares with a neighboring village in similar circumstances. A committee member explained that when villages dissolve, collective assets are either sold or reorganized into a share-holding company or cooperative. In the case of Rivertown Village, not much land remains in collective ownership. Without large amounts of assets, and thus requiring less complicated negotiations, Rivertown is in a weak position to resist redevelopment plans that seek its dissolution. What will likely happen is that collectively owned assets, such as warehouses, rental housing, valued crops and livestock, and land will be converted into cash and apportioned to village members. A portion will be given to the street office to manage any remaining affairs related to Rivertown residents, such as contributions to their social security.[32]

With regard to compensating and resettling villagers, according to the *Nanjing Land Acquisition Compensation Relocation Regulations*,[33] compensation essentially involves four calculations:

1) *Crops on agricultural land*: Compensation is based on the value of one season's yield. Trees with economic value are calculated separately.
2) *Housing*: Compensation is calculated from the number of family members and the size and cost of current housing and additions.
3) *Land*: Compensation is calculated based on its land category. Land in China is given a category number determined by the quality of the land/soil and the locality's socioeconomic level.
4) *Labor relocation*: All working-age villagers receive a one-time payment, with variations among districts.

While the calculation appears formulaic, in practice, discrepancies arise in the total amounts of compensation received among villages within the same district and among households within the same village. Early compensation standards made further distinctions as to whether land was acquired for municipal projects, priority constructions, and nonmunicipal projects, which, as one study estimates, caused compensation prices to vary significantly by between 10 and 40 percent.[34]

Moreover, compensation packages have been assessed and agreed to on a household-by-household basis and are not publicly disclosed. In the two cases recounted to me by a villagers' committee member, the discrepancy boiled down to a matter of timing and unexplainable bad luck. One villager had held out longer in hopes of receiving more compensation, but in the end, as part of a later wave of residents to be relocated, his family paid more for their apartment in the affordable housing project to which they have been assigned. In another case, two villagers found out after the fact that for their comparable stone houses, one had been compensated at the low end of the stipulated range whereas his neighbor had, for undocumented reasons, received the high end, which allowed him to resettle into a larger and better located apartment.[35]

Relocation and Social Integration into Urban Neighborhoods

With their compensation, Rivertown villagers have been resettled into affordable housing projects across the city. While villagers may have long begun to acquire the commodities that signify an urban lifestyle, such as television sets and washing machines, adjusting to the realities of daily life after relocation is difficult. For most families, a lack of job security and stable income are reasons for their low level of life satisfaction. Economic hardship is often felt some time after relocation, after the monthly rental income ends and monetary compensation has been spent on moving and resettling.

A recent survey conducted by Nanjing Normal University of relocated villagers in an affordable housing neighborhood reported that the unemployment rate rose from 1.8 percent to 16.3 percent after relocation. While 43 percent of the relocated villagers reported an increase in income, many did not meet even the minimum urban livelihood standards. About 40 percent of the residents fell below the city's minimum living standard of 220 RMB per month; and half of those working had monthly earnings below the city's minimum wage of 540 RMB.[36]

Villagers I met talked about the considerably higher expenses of urban life. Most daily necessities now need to be store-bought at urban prices. In the city, a simple daily task such as cooking rice means using metered water from the tap and electricity for the rice cooker. Because farming is no longer an option for children who do not do well in school, families feel obligated to spend money on education so their children can keep up with their urban classmates. They were not faced with these realities suddenly as their lifestyle has been constantly changing in the urbanization process. However, these expenses multiply the overall financial pressures they feel. Gainful employment has been difficult to secure, particularly for those in their mid-40s and older. Many of them lack the education needed to compete in the urban labor market because schools in the countryside tend to be inferior to those in the city and members of this generation came of age during the Cultural Revolution when school curriculums were disrupted. They also face the setback that, being close to retirement age,[37] potential employers are less willing to hire them and invest in their training.[38]

Socially, the resettled villagers, or "land-loss farmers" (*shidi nongmin*) as they are typically referred to in the city, are looked down upon by their neighbors, who often regard them as "uncivil" (*bu wenmin*) or "uncultured" (*mei wenhua*). White Blossom *Shequ* is a mixed-income neighborhood where relocated villagers live among the urban working class, teachers, and college professors, but each group lives in separate apartment blocks. Within the enclosure, villagers, unlike their urban neighbors, have planted chives and vegetables instead of grass and flowers. Director Li recognizes that many of the older relocated farmers may not find interest in the activities that the residents' committee organizes, such as choir groups, book clubs, and calligraphy classes. In the past, she sought to mitigate complaints the residents' committee received about the smell of fertilizers, the pests being attracted, and the unsightliness of the neighborhood open space being taken over by relocated farmers who brought elements of rural life with them. But, with the emphasis on *Shequ* Construction and the accompanying evaluation measures handed down from above with standards on neighborhood greening and beautification, Director Li is compelled to respond. She had them unearthed once, but in the spring, the elderly farmers sowed new seeds.[39]

Shequ Construction, which began with the goal of strengthening local capacity to provide social services to laid-off workers, must now respond to all those dislocated by urban change—farmers who have lost their land as well as workers who have lost their jobs. The vegetable garden incident, while trivial, calls attention to the greater implications of *Shequ* Construction as a valuation system where resettled villagers and their rural practices are perceived as backward. The former villagers must alter their conduct in accordance with the higher-valued urban status. In this way, their integration is linked to the broader *suzhi* discourse that sees the "low-quality" rural populace as hindering the country's advancement.[40] In the context of relocation, *Shequ* Construction is thus no longer a policy project solely about laid-off *danwei* workers—their sense of belonging and the provision of their social services. Seen more broadly, the policy seeks coherence and defines what it means to be an urbanite living in an urban neighborhood. For the resettled villagers, membership in the urban *shequ* means regulations and changed expectations—where to go, what procedures to follow to seek assistance, and what activities and behaviors are acceptable. The list of dos and don'ts on the bulletin board clearly outlines the rules to live by: "Do not sun-dry sheets on the *shequ* commons. Do not burn garbage. Do conserve electricity and water. Do report suspicious activities to the residents' committee." The low regard for the villagers' "backward" ways and the specificities of what constitutes a "pleasing environment" (*huanjing youmei*) in evaluation measures prevent the accommodation and inclusion of villagers' practices.

REDEVELOPMENT THROUGH INTEGRATION: CONFORMITY OF INTERESTS

With seventy-one villages undergoing redevelopment, acquisition and relocation depend in large part on infrastructure projects or commercial development to initiate and finance the process. An alternative redevelopment method that city officials would like to explore is to temporarily retain the village settlement, with a focus, at least for the time being, on managing the living environment. This option is considered viable for what they deem as intact villages farther out in the periphery, where much of the farmland remains and where the incoming migrants do not yet outnumber the out-migrating villagers.[41] Recent experiments with extending the *Shequ* Construction policy program into villages will facilitate an assessment of whether this redevelopment model is feasible for a greater number of villages.

Despite being an urban village listed for redevelopment, Willow Village villagers' committee has been working to bring its village up to urban *shequ* standards with the expectation that its redevelopment will follow this model. Willow Village sits on the northern edge of Nanjing's urban core. Its evolution into an urban village took a similar path to that of Rivertown. In the 1980s, following the return to the household responsibility system and the decollectivization of agriculture, their village production brigade was dissolved and replaced by a villagers' committee. At that time, as China's economy was gradually taking off, nearby state-owned industries, the largest being Nanjing Automobile, acquired agricultural land for factory expansion and employee housing. Those who were employed by the industries were given urban registration status. Since, at most, only a few members of each household were eligible for urban *hukou*, families retained their village housing. Residents have not been moving out, but their main source of livelihood has shifted from agriculture to renting housing to migrant workers. Today, Willow Village has about 2,000 permanent residents and 6,000 migrant renters.[42]

Coexistence of Villagers' Committee and Shequ *Residents' Committee*

In 2006, the municipal and district governments readjusted the street office and *shequ* jurisdictions to reflect the changes from nearby road construction and housing developments. Willow Village and portions of a neighboring village left untouched by redevelopment were grouped together to form Willow Village *Shequ*. For the time being, due to a lack of compensation funds, the amount of collectively owned assets, and the adequate condition of the existing infrastructure to support the existing density, memorandums issued by the municipal planning department support Willow Village's redevelopment through infrastructure upgrades as opposed to demolition and relocation. Planning officials will, however, incorporate Willow Village into the city's land reserve for prospective commercial housing development—a move that will allow future development projects to finance land acquisition.[43] In fact, the use of land reserves has become a crucial planning strategy. It places land with good prospects, such as along light rail constructions in which the government has invested heavily, in the hands of the government. This prevents developers from negotiating joint development projects with villages and allows the city to undertake multiphase projects.[44]

The establishment of Willow Village *shequ* has created the unique circumstance of a villagers' committee coexisting with a residents' committee. But in fact, members of the two committees are the same group of people; they simply hold different positions in each committee. They assist residents according to their residency status: agricultural (rural), nonagricultural (urban), or temporary (migrant). As long as the village is not dissolved, the villagers' committee remains in charge of collective assets and is responsible for the welfare of its remaining hundred or so rural *hukou* residents, mostly pensioners. The residents' committee is responsible for servicing and managing the urban and temporary *hukou* holders. Their joint appointment in the residents' committee has increased the workload of the villagers' committee members. The *shequ* vice-director explained that under the mandate of *Shequ* Construction, the residents' committee's main responsibility is providing social service, with funding and direction coming down from the street office. In contrast, the villagers' committee focuses primarily on economic development and meets its needs from its own collective assets. Furthermore, they are expected to keep records of migrants' employment and legal status in the city and carry out the seemingly impossible task of overseeing the transient population's family planning.[45]

As the members of the residents' committee and the villagers' committee are the same and as the majority of the residents were born in Willow Village, the administrative shift to an urban neighborhood has not changed the villagers' sense of place. Willow Village is still being referred to as a village and not a *shequ*. This may change in the future as redevelopment proceeds and new housing developments alter the area's landscape and bring in residents from other parts of the city.

Standardization and the Village Community Construction Program

In June 2006, Nanjing municipal civil affairs bureau issued a working proposal for each district and county to set up pilot villages in which to extend the urban-based *Shequ* Construction policy. A year later, it followed with the document *Recommendations for*

Strengthening the Construction of Standards for the City's Shequ Residents' Committees and Villagers' Committees, with similar but separate measures to evaluate each urban neighborhood and rural village on a one-hundred-point scale.[46] While service standards can lead to greater accountability, the service areas being standardized under Village *Shequ* Construction carry wider implications. They raise questions with regard to how the urban-based programming is being extended to rural villages, and more critically, how the initiative seeks to prescribe norms of "good" urban governance to the "unruly" urban villages.

In accordance with the broader state agenda, Nanjing's experiments with expanding the urban-based *Shequ* Construction policy to villages came at a time when rural affairs dominated state policies. In January 2006, the No. 1 Document[47] (*yihao wenjian*) issued by the central authority raised specific social policy directions for the "Construction of a New Socialist Countryside." The state committed to restructuring rural taxes and fees as well as increasing its spending on rural health care and education. Interestingly, however, the Village Community Construction standards do not address any of these social issues. Kelliher (1997) observes that when it comes to self-government, the concern for officials on both sides of the debate, whether they are for or against village elections, centers on controlling rural "lawlessness" rather than on the ideal of autonomy. In a similar way, self-governance under Village *Shequ* Construction centers on establishing the state's rural presence, with intentions of curbing corruption and enforcing state policies over tax collection. The 2007 standardization checklist defines qualities of grassroots self-governance, outlining specific functions of villagers' committees. The highest scoring categories include adherence to village election regulations (22 points) and lawful reporting and auditing of affairs and finances (24 points). As many village leaders hold joint appointments in the Party branch, residents' committee, and villagers' committee, this emphasis on elections has them constantly preparing for elections. When I interviewed Willow Village's *shequ* vice-director (who is also a member of the villagers' committee and Party branch), the election for the villagers' committee had just concluded, and preparations were about to begin to elect the village Party secretary.

Despite intentions of elevating rural quality of life to urban standards, the urban-centric evaluation measures disregard important differences between residents' and villagers' committees. Villagers' committees have long been responsible for handling crucial matters of property administration, taxes, and welfare provision. In comparison, until recently, the residents' committee was secondary to the workplace in importance for urban families. The policy's starting point is based on achievements in urban neighborhoods, as opposed to what rural social issues are and how to improve rural community life. The working proposal for Village *Shequ* Construction pilot sites highlights the following three objectives: (1) to impart urban thought and practice toward *shequ* services, specifically the construction of in-community service stations to assist those most in need and bring convenience to residents' everyday life; (2) to foster the development of social organizations and intermediary service organizations, such as seen in the proliferation of seniors' associations, book clubs, dance groups, and disability support groups in urban neighborhoods; and (3) to increase the level and capacity of residents' participation in neighborhood affairs, establishing similar volunteer organizations as those in urban *shequ*.[48]

As the *Recommendations for Strengthening the Construction of Standards* was only approved in 2007, the results of how well neighborhoods and villages fared were not yet available to me.[49] I assumed that Willow Village would be measured as an urban neighborhood. However, still regarding itself as a village, the *shequ* vice-director referred to the village standards and was hopeful that Willow Village would do well. With the expectation that the municipal and district governments will follow through with their commitment to improve the water and sewer, electricity, and gas connections, the village leaders themselves have, working with the *Shequ* Construction standards, undertaken several capital improvement projects. They have built a three-story service center that is just as big and well-equipped as those in urban core neighborhoods. The village has also repaved all the main roads. On my first visit, residents and village officials were planting trees along the street that led to the service center.

Land politics and strategic calculations underlie the integration and *Shequ* Construction of Willow Village as much as they do the land requisition and residents' relocation of Rivertown Village. For civil affairs bureau officials, standardization serves the purpose of facilitating the future incorporation of suburban villages. At the very least, standardization would ensure that the villages are not concentrations of crime, poverty, and poor living environment.[50] Furthermore, the implementation of standards has given the government indirect use of village finances to fund major infrastructure improvements, such as road paving, whereas in urban neighborhoods, similar improvements must be authorized and funded by the district or street office budget.

Villagers seemed satisfied with the status quo, whether labeled as an urban village or a *shequ*. Land tenure and improvements made in the interim will provide the villagers some leverage when they need to negotiate land acquisition and compensation. When asked whether it might be possible for the village to remain intact in the city and what that might look like, a villagers' committee member replied that he did not know how it would work out procedurally. But, he said, it may happen if Willow Village becomes recognized as a successful case study of village *shequ* construction. He commented further that the resulting media attention and visits by government officials would make demolition and relocation much more difficult to carry out. The ever-changing circumstances that villagers have been living through have demonstrated to them that there may be new arrangements in the future. In the meantime, villagers are not passive participants. They continue to invest in infrastructure improvements and look for opportunities to respond to and self-protect from land appropriation and relocation.

CONCLUSION: NEGOTIATING URBANIZATION

This paper has examined urbanization through the ways in which policies seek to incorporate urban villages into the city and reconstitute villagers as urbanites. It demonstrates that becoming urban is not marked by a particular point in time when collective land is requisitioned and administratively reclassified as urban and villagers receive their nonagricultural registration status. Rather, villagers' integration into the city is a protracted process that requires them to continually find new ways to participate in new systems. *Shequ* Construction is primarily regarded as a welfare decentralization policy aimed at shifting the responsibilities for social services onto local governments as urban workers are turned out from their once life-long, all-providing positions in state-owned enterprises. The ballooning demands on local governments are, where possible, transferred to residents' committees. The context of urban village redevelopment highlights the normative underpinnings of *Shequ* Construction to guide behavior and instill values. It governs by way of clearly stipulating favorable practices and providing an evaluation system to measure adherence to them. "Becoming urban" involves livelihood transitions and administrative shifts but also the everyday habitual practices of being *shequ* residents.

On an individual level, living in an urban *shequ* requires learning new behaviors and practices spelled out by the *shequ* evaluation measures. Villagers both internalize and resist the values and judgments placed on them.[51] They may internalize their "backwardness" as the explanation for the frustrations they feel in their dealings with the *shequ* director. At the same time, they resist attempts to destroy their vegetable gardens. In the homogeneity of urban neighborhoods, particularly as workers from the same work unit traditionally lived together, the normative values of what constitutes a "good" *shequ* are largely shared. The greening of the public spaces would not be taken to mean vegetable gardens but rather flowers, trees, and grass.

While in urban neighborhoods the policy aims to build up the capacity of residents' committees to be self-governing, in villages, which have largely relied on collective revenues to pay for public goods and services, Village *Shequ* Construction, said to elevate rural quality of life to urban level, has limited their relatively broad discretion by dictating certain areas of spending. Even though it is too early to determine their effectiveness, officials view conformity to standards to be instrumental for their future incorporation, particularly in a redevelopment process that is fraught with conflicts of interest. In Willow Village, village leaders accept the rationales behind the policy because it has brought improvements to the service infrastructure. Urban villages, as villagers define the interstitial spaces in which they live, are not characterized by incongruent land uses but places that encompass both urban and rural advantages.

NOTES

1. I am grateful to the villagers' and residents' committee members who took the time to share their experiences. I would also like to acknowledge the Institute of International Research at Hopkins-Nanjing Center for sponsoring my stay in Nanjing. I thank participants of the UBC Peter Wall Summer Institute for Research 2008, members of the UBC China Studies Group, and my dissertation supervisory committee and examiners for their critical comments on earlier drafts.

2. All the names of people and places in this paper have been changed to ensure anonymity.

3. Yu Zhu, "In Situ Urbanization in Rural China: Case Studies from Fujian Province," *Development and Change* 31, no. 2 (2000): 413–434.

4. People's Republic of China, *Zhonghua renmin gongheguo tudiguanlifa* [Land Management Law of the People's Republic of China], adopted 25 June 1986, revised 29 December 1988 and 29 August 1998, article 10; People's Republic of China, *The Constitution of the People's Republic of China*, adopted 4 December 1982, amended 14 April 1988, 29 March 1993, 15 March 1999, and 16 March 2004, article 10.

5. Anthony G. Yeh and Fulong Wu, "The New Land Development Process and Urban Development in Chinese Cities," *International Journal of Urban and Regional Research* 20, no. 2 (1996): 330–354; Qingshu Xie, A. R. Ghanbari Parsa, and Barry Redding, "The Emergence of the Urban Land Market in China: Evolution, Structure, Constraints and Perspectives," *Urban Studies* 39, no. 8 (2002): 1375–1398; George C. S. Lin and Samuel P. S. Ho, "The State, Land System, and Land Development Process in Contemporary China," *Annals of the Association of American Geographers* 95, no. 2 (2005): 411–436.

6. More recent rural land reforms have sought to restrict rural land acquisition by local governments and affirm the land-use rights of farmers. Specifically, the Law on Land Contract in Rural Areas (2002) stipulates that rural households could transfer the use right to their contracted land to other farmers, a right not contained in the Land Management Act. In 2008, at the Third Plenum of the Seventeenth Central Committee, the CCP issued the Decision on Certain Issues Concerning the Advancement of Rural Reform and Development, which introduced the possibility for collectively owned "construction land" (*jianshe yongdi*) to be traded without being first acquired by the government. For a discussion on the main changes, intentions, and shortcomings of recent rural land reforms, see Sarah Y. Tong and Gang Chen, "China's Land Policy Reform: An Update," *Background Brief No. 419* (Singapore: East Asian Institute, National University of Singapore, 2008); Robin Dean and Tobias Damm-Luhr, "A Current Review of Chinese Land-Use Law and Policy: A 'Breakthrough' in Rural Reform?" *Pacific Rim Law and Policy Journal* 19, no. 1 (2010): 121–159.

7. To prevent the emergence of urban villages, rural land is now typically requisitioned in large tracts with settlement and agricultural land together. Many cities, particularly coastal ones, are redeveloping urban villages that resulted from earlier land conversion processes. Nanjing Land Management Bureau official, interview by author, Nanjing, 10 April 2006.

8. Michael Leaf, "Chengzhongcun: China's Urbanizing Villages from Multiple Perspectives," in *Urbanization in China: Critical Issues in an Era of Rapid Growth*, ed. Chengri Ding and Yan Song (Cambridge, MA: Lincoln Institute of Land Policy, 2007).

9. Xiaoli Liu and Liang Wei, "Zhejiangcun: Social and Spatial Implications of Informal Urbanization on the Periphery of Beijing," *Cities* 14, no. 2 (1997): 95–108; Laurence Ma and Biao Xiang, "Native Place, Migration and the Emergence of Peasant Enclaves in Beijing," *The China Quarterly* 155 (1998): 546–581; Li Zhang, *Strangers in the City: Reconfigurations of Space, Power, and Social Networks within China's Floating Population* (Stanford: Stanford University Press, 2001); Li Zhang, Simon X. Zhao, and J. P. Tian, "Self-help in Housing and Chengzhongcun in China's Urbanization," *International Journal of Urban and Regional Research* 27, no. 4 (2003): 912–937; Michael Leaf and Samantha Anderson, "Civic Space and Integration in Chinese Peri-urban Villages," in *Globalization, the City, and Civil Society in Pacific Asia: The Social Production of Civic Space*, ed. Mike Douglass, K. C. Ho, and Giok Ling Ooi (New York: Routledge, 2008).

10. Nationwide *shequ* reform began with the promulgation of Document 23 issued by the General Offices of the Central Committee and the State Council (2000). The English literature on China's community-building experience under the *Shequ* Construction policy is expanding to cover aspects such as the decline of work-unit-based social services, experimentation in different cities, perspectives of residents' committee directors, and cultivation of grassroots democracy. See James Derleth and Daniel Koldyk, "The *Shequ* Experiment: Grassroots Political Reform in Urban China," *Journal of Contemporary China* 13, no. 41

(2004): 747–777; Linda Wong and Bernard Poon, "From Serving Neighbours to Recontrolling Urban Society," *China Information* 19, no. 3 (2005): 413–442; David Bray, "Building 'Community': New Strategies of Governance in Urban China," *Economy and Society* 35, no. 4 (2006): 530–549; Yong Gui, Joseph Y. S. Cheng, and Weihong Ma, "Cultivation of Grassroots Democracy: A Study of Direct Elections of Residents Committees in Shanghai," *China Information* 20, no. 1 (2006): 7–31; Miu Yan and Jianguo Gao, "Social Engineering of Community Building: Examining Policy Process and Characteristics of Community Construction in China," *Community Development Journal* 42, no. 2 (2007): 222–236; Leslie Shieh and John Friedmann, "Restructuring Urban Governance: Community Construction in Contemporary China," *City* 12, no. 2 (2008): 183–195.

11. People's Republic of China, General Offices of the Central Committee and the State Council, *Guanyu zhuanfa Minzhengbu guanyu zaiquanguo tuijin chengshi shequjianshe de yijian de tongzhi* [Memorandum from the Ministry of Civil Affairs on Promoting Urban Shequ Construction Throughout the Nation], 2000, Document 23.

12. Nanjing Municipal Statistics Bureau, *Nanjing Statistical Yearbook* (Nanjing: Nanjing Municipal Statistics Bureau, 2009), table 1-1.

13. Within the extended metropolitan region, villages can more appropriately be distinguished according to their distance from the urban core and the standard of living of their residents. See Terry G. McGee, "The Emergence of Desakota Regions in Asia: Expanding a Hypothesis," in *The Extended Metropolis: Settlement Transition in Asia*, ed. Norton Sydney Ginsburg, Bruce Koppel, and Terry G. McGee (Honolulu, HI: University of Hawaii Press, 1991), 6–7. Following this model, Nanjing's urban villages can be categorized into three types. The first type describes villages that are now part of the urban core. These villages are without farmland, but the land use rights remain with villages' committees. Urban villages located in the suburban districts belong to the second type. These villages have some remaining farmland, but the majority of residents no longer work in agriculture as their main source of income. The third type of urban village is one to two hours' commute from the urban core where a large amount of farmland still exists. Although some villagers are engaged in agriculture, their ways of life and livelihood are heavily impacted by their proximity to the city. Redevelopment in Nanjing targets villages of the first type.

14. Weiping Wu, "Migrant Housing in Urban China: Choices and Constraints," *Urban Affairs Review* 28, no. 1 (2002): 90–119; Zhang, Zhao, and Tian, "Self-help in Housing"; Yan Song, Yves Zenou, and Chengri Ding, "Let's Not Throw the Baby Out with the Bath Water: The Role of Urban Villages in Housing Rural Migrants in China," *Urban Studies* 45, no. 2 (2008): 313–330.

15. Nanjing Municipal General Affairs Research Office, "*Guanyu Woshi Chengzhongcun qingkuang de diaocha ji qigaizao jianyi* [Assessment and Other Redevelopment Recommendations Concerning Our City's Urban Village Conditions]," *Selected Works from 2005 Investigation and Research* (Nanjing: Nanjing Municipal General Affairs Research Office, 2005).

16. "Chengzhongcun sinian gaizhao [Redevelopment of Chengzhongcun in Four Years]," *Jinling Evening Post*, December 13, 2005. To protect agricultural lands, the 1998 Land Management Law placed a mandatory cap on the amount of farmland that can be converted to construction land. The provincial government reviews, approves, and reports to the State Council applications from lower levels to convert agricultural land to construction land. In some cases State Council approval is required, particularly with the conversion of primary farmland. See Samuel P. S. Ho and George C. S. Lin, "Emerging Land Markets in Rural and Urban China: Policies and Practices," *The China Quarterly* 175 (2003): 694–696.

17. Nanjing Municipal General Affairs Research Office, "*Guanyu Woshi Chengzhongcun* [Assessment and Other Redevelopment Recommendations Concerning Our City's Urban Village]."

18. Nanjing Municipal Government, *Shizhengfu guan yu jiakuai tuijin "Chengzhongcun" gaizaojianshe de yijian* [Recommendation from the Nanjing Municipal Government Concerning the Acceleration of Chengzhongcun Redevelopment], 2005, Document 214.

19. Nanjing Municipal General Affairs Research Office, "*Guanyu Woshi Chengzhongcun* [Assessment and Other Redevelopment Recommendations Concerning Our City's Urban Village]"; Nanjing Municipal Government, Document 214.

20. Although the redevelopment process is similarly contentious, Nanjing's urban villages are quite different from their counterparts in southern Chinese cities of the Pearl River Delta, such as Guangzhou, Dongguan, and Shenzhen, which have been the focus of many recent studies on the phenomenon. See Li Zhang, Simon X. Zhao, and J. P. Tian, "Self-help in Housing and Chengzhongcun in China's Urbanization," *International Journal of Urban and Regional Research* 27, no. 4 (2003): 912–937; Junfu Li, *Chengzhongcun De Gaizao* [*The Redevelopment of Urban Villages*] (Beijing: Kexue Chuban She, 2004); Zhikui Xie, *Cunluo Xiang Chengshi Shequ De Zhuanxing – Zhidu, Zhengce Yu Zhongguo Chengshihua Jinchengzhong Chengzhongcun Wenti Yanjiu* [*The Transition from Village to Urban Community: A Study of Institution, Policy and the Urban Village Problem during the Urbanization in China*] (Beijing: Zhongguo Shehui Kexue Chuban She, 2005). For instance, in Shenzhen, a city formed out of a conglomeration of fishing villages, urban villages were formed through an in situ process. Consequently, they have a stronger hold on their land interests through greater involvement of the village collective as developers of commercial buildings and market housing.

21. Nanjing Planning Bureau official, interview by author, Nanjing, 30 March 2007.

22. Nanjing Municipal Planning Bureau, *Nanjing chengshi guihua* [*Nanjing Urban Planning*] (Nanjing: Nanjing Municipal Planning Bureau, 2001), 17–18.

23. Nanjing Municipal Planning Bureau, *Nanjing chengshi guihua* [*Nanjing Urban Planning*] (Nanjing: Nanjing Municipal Planning Bureau and Nanjing Urban Planning and Research Center, 2004), 14.

24. Nanjing Planning Bureau official, interview by author, Nanjing, 30 March 2007.

25. Qingfang Fang, Xiangming Ma, and Jinsong Song, "*Chengzhongcun: woguo chengshihua jinchengzhong yudaode zhengce wenti* [Chengzhongcun: Policy Challenges of China's Urbanization Process," *Chengshi Fazhan Yanjiu* [*Urban Studies*], 1999, no. 4, 19–21.

26. Rivertown Villagers' Committee member, interview by author, Nanjing, 27 February 2006.

27. Field notes, 14 March 2007.

28. Village governance is composed of the villagers' committee, Party branch, village representative assembly, and economic management committee. The villagers' committee handles the day-to-day administrative tasks such as dispute mediation, public safety, tax collection, and family planning. Party branch members will typically sit on the villagers' committee. The economic management committee manages the collective assets and operates the township and village enterprises (TVEs). The village representative assembly is the ultimate overseer of village affairs; both the villagers' committee and the economic management committee are answerable to it. For a detailed discussion of village governance structure, see Allen Choate, "Local Governance in China: An Assessment of Villagers Committees," *The Asia Foundation Working Paper Series*, Working Paper No. 1 (New York: The Asia Foundation, 1997). In this paper, the term "villagers' committee" is used to refer to village governing organizations collectively, unless specified.

29. People's Republic of China, *The Constitution of the People's Republic of China*, adopted 4 December 1982, amended 14 April 1988, 29 March 1993, 15 March 1999, and 16 March 2004, article 111.

30. Field notes, Gaocheng County, Nanjing, conversation with a villagers' committee member, 22 April 2006.

31. Field notes, 13 April 2007.

32. Rivertown Villagers' Committee member, interview by author, Nanjing, 14 March 2007.

33. Nanjing Municipal Government, *Nanjingshi zhengdi chaiqian buchang anzhi banfa* [Nanjing Land Acquisition Compensation Relocation Regulations], 2004, Document 93.

34. Dongxiang Chen and Shenglu Zhou, "*Nanjingshi nongcunfangwu chaiqian buchang zhengceyanbian ji gaige yanjiu* [Study on Evolvement and Reform of Compensation Policy for Rural House Removal in Nanjing]," *Zhongguotudi kexue* [*China Land Science*] 19, no. 6 (2005): 8–11.

35. Rivertown Villagers' Committee member, interview by author, Nanjing, 14 March 2007.

36. Jingjuan Guan, "*Qianxi anzhi junmin de shehui rentong – yi nanjingshi m shequ weili* [Preliminary Analysis of the Social Identity of Relocated Residents: Case of M Shequ in Nanjing]," Selected graduating thesis, Nanjing Normal University, Department of Sociology and Social Work, *Shijing* [*Perspectives*], no. 4 (2007): 10–11.

37. The retirement age in China is not uniform; it depends on the physical demands of the work and the length of time an employee has been working. Typically, for factory workers, the retirement age is fifty for women and fifty-five for men. For officials and professionals, it is fifty-five for women and sixty for men. Many state-owned enterprises permit and even encourage employees to retire in their forties to cut labor costs and make openings for new college graduates.

38. Field notes, 27 April 2007.

39. White Blossom *Shequ* director, interview by author, Nanjing, 18 June 2007.

40. The word *suzhi* is usually translated into English as "intrinsic quality." Reform-era birth planning, rural planning, and education policies have linked the word to China's development and created a discourse around raising the quality of the population. For instance, regulating births was framed around raising fewer children of higher *suzhi*. Similarly, the low *suzhi* of the country's large rural population was said to have attributed to the country's failure to modernize. See Borge Bakken, *The Exemplary Society: Human Improvement, Social Control, and the Dangers of Modernity in China* (Oxford and New York: Oxford University Press, 2000), chapter 2; Rachel Murphy, "Turning Peasants into Modern Chinese Citizens: 'Population Quality' Discourse, Demographic Transition and Primary Education," *The China Quarterly* 177 (2004): 1–20; Andrew Kipnis, "Suzhi: A Keyword Approach," *The China Quarterly* 186 (2006): 295–313.

41. Nanjing Planning Bureau official, interview by author, Nanjing, 16 March 2007.

42. Villagers' committee member, interview by author, Nanjing, 18 May 2007.

43. Nanjing Planning Bureau official, interview by author, Nanjing, 16 March 2007.

44. Youtien Hsing, *The Great Urban Transformation: Politics of Land Property in China* (Oxford and New York: Oxford University Press, 2010): 107–108.

45. Willow Village *Shequ* vice-director, interview by author, Nanjing, 18 May 2007.

46. Nanjing Municipal Civil Affairs Bureau, *Guanyu jiaqiang quanshi shequ juweihui he cunweihui guifanhua jianshe de yijian* [Recommendation Regarding the Strengthening of Standardization Construction of Shequ Residents' Committee and Village Committee], 2007, Document 10.

47. Conventionally, the first document issued by the central authority (Chinese Communist Party Central Committee and the State Council) every year is interpreted as what the leadership considers to be the most important issue for the country. Since 2004, rural development has been the topic of the first document, demonstrating its urgency and the government's determination to address problems in rural areas.

48. Nanjing Municipal Civil Affairs Bureau, *Quanshi nongcunshequfuwu yushequjianshe shidiangongzhuo fangan* [Working Proposal for the Pilot Studies for Village Community Service and Community Construction in the City], 2006, Document 118.

49. As of the time of this writing (late 2011), it remains unclear whether all urban neighborhoods and rural villages have been assessed following the proposed standardization measures and points system. Village *shequ* construction has remained an important initiative for the City, particularly the Civil Affairs Bureau. For instance, at the recent Nanjing Municipal Communist Party Congress in October 2011, the Civil Affairs Bureau reported the implementation of the governance model "one-party, one-residents' (villagers') committee, one-service station, and one-management office," which was an objective of the standardization measures. According to the report, the model has been implemented in 86 percent of urban neighborhoods and 67 percent of rural villages. Nanjing Municipal Communist Party, Municipal Civil Affairs Bureau, "Strengthen Livelihoods and Promote Social Harmony," 12 October 2011, available online at http://www.njsw.gov.cn/site/swww/dbdh13/wnphz_mb_a3911101254635.htm, last accessed 25 November 2011.

50. Nanjing Civil Affairs Bureau official, district level, interview by author, Nanjing, 21 June 2007.

51. I draw on Rachel Murphy's (2004) discussion on rural education and her observation that rural parents both accept and challenge the biases against their children in the education system. Murphy, "Turning Peasants into Modern Chinese Citizens."

Chapter 9

Public Regulation of Private Relations

Changing Conditions of Property Regulation in China

Pitman B. Potter

The development of property rights in the People's Republic of China reflects tensions between liberal legal models and socialist principles associated with other areas of China's socioeconomic and legal development policy. The globalized international discourse of private property ideals associated with liberal capitalism serves as context for understanding legal reform efforts in China.[1] In the international liberal discourse of property rights, ideals of efficiency and individual liberty privilege private property discourses of economism and republicanism, and result in the entrenchment of private property into law and popular culture.[2] The expansion of these regimes through the process of globalization promotes local acceptance of liberal standards of property law by developing economies even as it invites conflict over assimilation of underlying norms and values. The development of China's legal regime for protecting property rights reveals dynamics and outcomes of ongoing normative tensions between globalized liberal ideology and local legal and political culture. Challenges also arise around the organizational structures and processes for implementing property rights in China.[3]

EMERGING REGIMES FOR PROPERTY RIGHTS IN CHINA[4]

Under the rubric of internationalization of property rights, Chinese jurists have called for greater reference to be made to foreign law from Japan, Europe, and the Anglo-North

American tradition as precedents for property rights reforms in China.[5] Chinese civil law notions of "property behavior" (*wuquan xingwei*) have been influenced in particular by German law (either directly or through the forms adopted from Japan and Taiwan).[6] Taiwan law scholars, such as Wang Zejian, have been particularly influential in the transmission of German civil law concepts to China.[7] The recently enacted Property Rights Law of the PRC is particularly influenced by liberal ideals of private property rights, albeit qualified by imperatives of socialist regulation.

Transitions Toward Ideals of Private Property

While the economic reform policies enacted beginning in 1978 granted enterprises greater autonomy in decision making and permitted increased diversity of economic actors and transactions,[8] doctrinal norms continued to emphasize the importance of state interests in the enforcement of private law relations. The 1982 constitution extended protection to property but only to the extent that it would constitute "lawful property," the definition of which remained the exclusive province of the state.[9] Constitutional requirements that the exercise of citizens' rights, including the right to own property, do not conflict with the state or social interest[10] effectively granted the state a monopoly to interpret those interests and thus to determine the extent to which private property rights would be recognized and enforced. During the period of accelerated reform following Deng Xiaoping's 1992 "Southern Tour" (*nanxun*), property policy and legislation emerged as important agenda items for both academics and government officials. While conventional norms of public ownership and protection of public interest remained well represented,[11] increased attention was also paid to reforming the system of state ownership. Existing discourses on management rights were expanded to address not only issues of managerial autonomy but also managerial responsibility to conserve state property.[12] Problems of corruption and mismanagement of state property (particularly in state-owned enterprises) gave rise to calls for tighter regulation.[13] However, policy changes supporting the transition to a market economy meant that state ownership rights must also evolve and in some instances give way to diverse alternatives.[14]

The PRC constitution was amended in 1993 to affirm the socialist market economy as the foundation for economic policy.[15] The transition from the socialist commodity economy meant that increased market autonomy for economic actors (including individuals as well as enterprises) could extend beyond the realm of transactions in goods. This invited changes to the existing property rights regime to extend protection not only to immovable property such as land and movables such as personal property but also to intangibles such as intellectual property.[16] In 1995, a semiofficial proposal on property legislation was published, which suggested that conventional boundaries for property rights as set forth in the General Principles of Civil Law should be reexamined.[17] Jiang Zemin's speech to the CPC Fifteenth National Congress in October 1997 supported the development of property rights in corporations—an essential precursor to expanded private property regimes generally.[18]

Efforts to draft a code of property law in 1998 under the aegis of a Civil Code drafting team revealed ongoing disagreements over the proper scope of private property rights. On one hand, by clarifying property as a civil law relationship, the drafters emphasized the importance of limiting state intrusion. Thus, the draft property law contained a principle that property rights could not be interfered with by third parties (including government organs).[19] On the other hand, the draft retained the basic principles of protecting "lawful" rights and interests and safeguarding social and economic order and socialist modernization, as well as a prohibition against property rights harming the public interest.[20] Explanations of this section make specific reference to the constitutional provisions on the market economy—and by extension the limits on full marketization imposed by the Party's policy imperatives on socioeconomic order.[21] Thus, even as renewed efforts are made to enshrine property rights into legal codes, the rights that resulted unavoidably remained subject to the general tenor of constitutional provisions favoring socialist public ownership over private property rights.

Confronting those who argued for more expansive private property rights protections in the constitution, opponents of expanded constitutional protection suggested that this would contribute to problems of corruption and misuse of state property.[22] This reflected the extent to which norms of public ownership remained deeply ingrained in the normative and institutional framework for China's property law regime.[23] Indeed, the importance of conforming to China's particular "conditions" (*tedian*) remains a powerful orthodoxy governing the scope and terms of property rights reform.[24] Doctrinal norms continued to emphasize the importance of state interests in the enforcement of private law relations.[25] The centrality of public ownership was part of this orthodoxy and inhibited the recognition of private property rights.[26]

The 1999 revisions to the constitution did not ultimately include a provision on the sanctity of "private property rights" (*siying caichan shensheng*)—instead the language provided that the self-employed, private, and other nonpublic sectors constituted an important component of the socialist market economy, whose lawful rights and interests would be protected by the state.[27] The constitutional amendment originated nominally with the CPC Central Committee,[28] although the CPC Politburo Standing Committee and its politics and "law system" (*zhengfa xitong*) remain the key arbiters on issues attendant to the constitution and other key enactments. The 1999 amendment confirmed that, although the socialist market economy would permit individual enterprises and private firms to play an important role, ultimately property rights would remain subject to the policy priorities of the Party/state and would not receive unlimited constitutional protection. While this confirmation was touted as a major step forward in China's reform process,[29] the reference to state protection of lawful rights and interests signaled that the private sector would remain subject to significant state control. Parallel provisions were to be found in the newly enacted Contract Law of the PRC (1999), which confined contracts to notions of "lawful rights and interests of the parties," and subjected contracts to the imperative to protect "state and social interests."[30]

The limits of the 1999 constitutional revision reflected a continuing policy position that privileged socialist public property. While China's socialist system might tolerate or even encourage private property, this would still depend on the policy direction and dispensation of the Party/state.[31] Indeed complaints about the phenomenon of "unit crimes" (*danwei zui*), such as bribery and tax evasion, committed by enterprises suggested further limits to official tolerance of private businesses.[32]

The constitution was amended yet again in 2004 to provide in Article 13 that lawful private property "shall not be violated" (*bu shou qinfan*). The language of protection for private property contrasts with the provisions in Article 12 that socialist public property is "sacrosanct and inviolable" (*shensheng bu qinfan*), underscoring the continued privileging of public property.[33] The proposed application of the term "sacrosanct" (*shensheng*) to private property was rejected yet again, although the constitutional affirmation of an expansive role for private property rights signaled an important change in official orthodoxy on relations between public and private ownership. These constitutional developments, in turn, paved the way for completion of a draft property law, work on which had begun in the early 1990s.

Property Relations in Land

Property rights in land are a key feature of China's property rights regime. The post-Mao reforms associated with Deng Xiaoping saw far-reaching changes in PRC land policy. While the constitution and the General Principles of Civil Law continued to provide that ownership of land remained the exclusive province of the state and the collective, land use rights were increasingly granted to private farming and business operations in rural and urban areas.

The Land Administration Law enacted in 1986 reiterated constitutional principles of public ownership of land and clarified the jurisdictional arrangements for land administration.[34] Revisions in 1988 to the constitution and the Land Administration Law of the PRC permitted broader land use rights to be conveyed to private entities. In 1990, China enacted regulations permitting businesses to take long-term interests in land for the purpose of subdivision and development.[35] Local governments began enacting regulations for their own real property markets,[36] giving rise to concerns over jurisdictional conflicts and administrative problems in the system of land administration.[37] The Law of the PRC on Urban Real Estate was enacted in 1994, in an effort both to expand the possibilities of private acquisition and management of land use rights and to tighten state control over perceived abuses.[38] Land registration rules were enacted shortly thereafter.[39]

As a result, investment in real property for residential and industrial purposes soared, although speculation and flipping of property leases was common.[40] Judicial decisions in disputes before the People's Courts reflected confusion over a range of issues, such as the rights of lessor and lessee regarding leased property,[41] real estate valuation,[42] unauthorized sales and leasing of real estate,[43] disregard for licensing requirements,[44] and disputes over building quality.[45] Rights to inherit real estate also arose,[46] as did questions concerning cooperation between agencies and compatibility across regulatory regimes on such issues as resolving real estate issues for firms in bankruptcy.[47] Since real estate transactions involve transfers of two kinds of property interests—ownership of buildings and fixtures and use rights to the underlying land—the regulatory system struggled to deal effectively with each of these transfers and the rights that underlie them.[48] The focus of law and regulation was increasingly moving beyond the traditional focus of clarifying the respective scope of state and collective ownership to manage transfers and registration of land use rights.[49] While obligatory recitation of principles of socialist public ownership was unavoidable, increased attention was being paid to the problem of legal protection for land use rights as a property right.[50] With land use rights recognized as enforceable and transferable, mortgages and other ancillary relationships could begin to proceed more easily.[51]

Policy recommendations for resource use, transportation, and pollution in urban areas reflected changing approaches to sustainable land use.[52] Recent decisions to rationalize and diversify land use, relocate industrial sites outside the cities, and legalize the status of migrant workers suggest a growing appreciation of sustainability issues in some coastal cities.[53] However, interior cites, provincial and prefecture capitals often lag behind. Sophisticated models already exist for achieving sustainability goals through balancing of social and economic needs in land use policy,[54] but systemic implementation remains elusive. Conflicting land use claims—particularly the conflict between preserving agricultural land and the conversion to industrial and residential uses—remains a major point of conflict in rural and periurban areas.

In the rural areas, land use policies often conflicted initially with local collectivist sentiments, leading to violence in some cases.[55] The acceleration of agricultural reform, based in part on the appearance of private family farming, did not diminish the importance of collective ideals about land use, leading one prominent observer to describe the result as "redistributive corporatism."[56] Reflecting the policies of the CPC Politburo committee from which it emerged, the revised Land Administration Law (1999) reiterated the importance of safeguarding socialist public ownership of arable land.[57] This had particular implications for mining enterprises and other activities where ownership rights affect the value of land and operations licenses.[58]

Land use issues have come particularly to the fore as development and urbanization efforts intrude on local agricultural communities.[59] The resiliency of rural poverty in the midst of China's urban economic boom remains a major concern.[60] Displacement of agricultural communities in periurban areas to accommodate suburban economic development zones continues, with attendant problems of land use conflicts and social dislocation.[61] Possible outcomes for China's rural communities depend on resolution of local problems of land use, industrialization, and social cohesion (particularly the issue of migrant workers) through planning processes that are informed and responsible to local needs.[62] The Rural Land Contracting Law (2002) permitted limited transfers of land use rights under "household responsibility" (*chengbao*) contracts with approval of the local authorities.[63] In October 2008, the Seventeenth CPC National Congress approved a rural reform package that removed the government approval requirements for certain land use rights transfers.[64]

Although the increased flexibility of land use rights and the more recent discussions of the possibility of establishing an actual land ownership system suggest a transition toward a more private-oriented property rights regime, the state continues to play a critical role. Registration agencies permit state intrusion in the transfer of property interests in land.[65] The state's Land Administration Bureau (*tudi guanli ju*) remains firmly in control of the approval of land use and the creation and assignment of leases in land. As well, ancillary administrative organs have direct interests in land management. The Environmental Protection Bureau, for example, oversees environmental management on all urban and rural land. The Ministry of Civil Affairs oversees the relocation of families and individuals resulting from changes in land use. Moreover, the residual ownership rights held by the state and the collective mean, in effect, that rights to land remain subject to the discretion and consent of the state. Rather than beginning with a presumption of individual rights to private ownership of property in land, the Chinese system proceeds from the assumption that the state holds the basic rights of ownership, and that all subsequent uses, transfers, and so forth, depend on state approval. Thus, individualized notions of liberty and economic utility continue to yield to the Chinese state's conception of public responsibility and collective interest.

The Property Rights Law

The 2007 Property Rights Law of the PRC attempts to formalize and expand legal protection for private property interests by imposing regulatory procedures on the requisition and transfer of property rights in land.[66] Enabled in part by the 2004 revisions to the PRC constitution that enshrined a right to own private property, preparation of the law accelerated with a public release of a draft statute in July 2005. A "fifth reading" draft was considered in August 2006. While intended originally to provide greater protection for private property and to lend greater certainty to financing arrangements, the draft law was subject to late-coming criticism from traditionalist intellectuals such as Gong Xiantian of Peking University, who stated that it contravened socialist principles and would empower and legitimate land requisitions by local officials for private gain.[67] Other opponents expressed concern that the draft would contravene constitutional provisions distinguishing between public and private property.[68] Proponents of the draft's principles of "equal protection" for private and public property claimed that while the constitution affirmed the distinction between public and private property, it nonetheless granted equal legal protection for both forms.[69] The draft was withdrawn in mid-2006 and underwent significant revisions that entrenched the importance of protecting public and state property and protecting rural land use rights by restraining the authority of officials to engage in or approve property transfers (including land acquisition and reallocation). The draft was reconsidered by the NPC Standing Committee throughout late 2006 and submitted to the full NPC for approval in early 2007 after lengthy debate and delay.[70] The Property Rights Law of the PRC came into effect October 1, 2007.

Described as a "basic civil law," the Property Rights Law acknowledges the increased autonomy of property relations between private social and economic actors, while also underscoring the state's continuing role to regulate these relations.[71] The Property Rights Law aims to "uphold the basic socialist economic system" and to "regulate the order of the socialist market economy"[72] by regulating more effectively rights that are already entrenched or implied in China's existing property regimes. Nonetheless, through its emphasis on providing "equal protection to the property of the state, the collective, and the individual," the law clearly signaled further support for property rights in the private economy.[73] The Property Law clarifies the rights and obligations attendant to a wide range of property relationships involving real property, movable property, and intangibles. While the statute does not purport to create new property rights, it does clarify the powers of rights holders in matters such as usufruct and condominium relationships. Property security is dealt with at some length, such that mortgages, liens, and charges are now more likely to be clearer and more enforceable, and hence more acceptable to lenders.

Of particular importance are the new law's provisions limiting the authority of local officials to expropriate land without lawful process and requiring compensation of villages for land converted from agricultural uses. Such provisions are intended to protect local community interests in cultivated land. The Property Rights Law affirms state interests in natural resources such as water and imposes penalties on local officials for unlawful transfer of state assets, while also providing for procedural limits on transfer of collective property, which includes rural land. Parties with property interests in land will be required to attend more fully to issues of due diligence on property ownership and on the question of a party's authority to transfer property rights in land.

As a result of its procedural requirements that officials specifically review and approve registrations and transfers of property interests in land, the law brings into play the Administrative Litigation Law's provisions on judicial review of specific administrative actions.[74] This may work to impede the patterns of arbitrary and often corrupt abuses of regulatory authority to facilitate conversion of agricultural land to private residential investment. However, the increased emphasis on private interests may also work to insulate private property relations from state intrusion to the extent that registrations and approvals become ritualized practices devoid of serious regulatory scrutiny. Hence, integrity in implementation will be key to achieving the policy goals underlying the new legislation.

By affirming public ownership of land while also allowing for expanded recognition of private interests in land use, the Property Rights Law will undoubtedly raise a host of issues over the boundaries of public and private property relationships. The debate that characterized the last year prior to enactment is certainly not over, as those who seek more public scrutiny over property relations continue to pressure for limits on private autonomy. Implementing regulations and Supreme Court interpretations will be key indicators of the policy direction of private property rights in China under the new regulatory regime. In both process and substance, the Property Law attempts to balance goals of efficiency and fairness in China's attempts to expand property rights in the course of its tumultuous economic growth process. The Property Rights Law represents a major new development in China's property rights regimes, although it remains to be seen whether it can achieve the policy goals for which it was enacted. As former Zhao Ziyang advisor Bao Tong seems to suggest, we cannot yet know whether this latest effort will auger well for a sustained prospect of limiting the intrusion of the state into the social economy of China.[75]

UNDERSTANDING PROPERTY REGIME PERFORMANCE: NORMS AND STRUCTURES

The application of globalized liberal models on property law and regulation to China's circumstances is affected by local contexts, particularly sociocultural norms and political and administrative structures. The performance of such arrangements may be anticipated through use of the paradigms of Selective Adaptation and Institutional Capacity, which allow better understanding of the normative and organizational dimensions of regime performance.[76]

Normative Interchange and the Role of Selective Adaptation in China's Property Rights Regime(s)

The reception in China of transplanted legal models entails an interaction between their underlying norms and local values. In contrast to expectations about convergence that suggest development toward a globally unified system of institutional practices and values,[77] Selective Adaptation explains variations in local reception of nonlocal standards by reference to the extent of normative consensus.[78] Selective Adaptation suggests that local implementation of nonlocal standards depends on the extent to which those standards' underlying norms are received by local interpretive communities.[79] Interpretive communities comprised of government officials, socioeconomic and professional elites, and other privileged groups exercise authority of political and/or professional position, specialized knowledge, and/or socioeconomic status to interpret nonlocal standards for application locally.[80] In the course of this process, interpretive communities interpret nonlocal legal standards in light of their own normative outlooks. Such interpretation is not necessarily a conscious process of matching foreign models to local interests but also involves subliminal dynamics of perception, complementarity, and legitimacy.

Perception of the content and operation of international law standards determines the ways that interpretive communities will interpret and apply them.[81] China's reception of international legal standards on trade and human rights, for example, depends significantly on perceptions by local interpretive communities of academic and policy specialists about issues of legal development generally,[82] historical contexts for China's participation in international regimes,[83] and challenges of globalization.[84] *Complementarity* between international and local practices and values informs the dynamics of local accommodation and resistance to international standards.[85] Factors of complementarity are evident in local analyses of China's participation in the international system and tend to emphasize the need for compatibility with China's systemic and substantive requirements.[86] *Legitimacy* concerns the extent to which both interpretive communities and their local audiences accept the purposes and consequences of transplanted legal forms.[87] Dynamics of legitimacy are evident in China's academic and policy discourses explaining China's increased participation in the international legal system.[88] Working together, these elements inform the process of Selective Adaptation that characterizes the interplay between acceptance on nonlocal rule regimes and assimilation of underlying norms.

China's property rights regime reflects the influences of Selective Adaptation. The process for enactment of China's Property Rights Law involved a conscious process of borrowing from international sources.[89] In the course of the process, interpretive communities of specialists reviewed international property law models and considered how they might apply in part or in full to China. Such adaptation, however, involves not only conscious efforts at review and comparison of globalized legal standards on property but also less conscious engagement with underlying norms. This, in turn, involves dynamics of perception, complementarity, and legitimacy.

Perception

Perceptions about the utility of globalized liberal doctrines on private property rights for economic development are evident in the writings of law specialists on the foundations of property law in China.[90] Lockean themes depicting property as an appropriate mechanism for establishing production and labor incentives and promoting economic accumulation[91] are evident in the attention paid to notions of economic utility in the early drafting efforts on the Property Rights Law.[92] The final version of the Property Rights Law was explained in part by reference to economic and social utility.

> In order to meet the requirements of materializing in an all-round way the scientific concept of development and building of a socialist harmonious society, it is necessary to enact a property law . . . to stipulate the questions of a general character in the property system and questions in real life calling for urgent regulation, thus further defining the attribution of things to avoid disputes, bring into full play the usefulness of things, protect the property of obligees and improve the Chinese-style socialist property system. . . . As the reform and opening-up and the economy develop, people's living standards have improved in general, and they urgently require effective protection of their own lawful property accumulated through hard work, of the right to land contractual management they enjoy in accordance with law, and of their other lawful rights and interests. Enactment of the property law will serve to define and protect private ownership, condominium right, right to land contractual management and house-site-use right, for the propose of protecting the immediate interests of the people, stimulating their vigor to create wealth and promoting social harmony.[93]

However, perceptions about liberal concepts of property seldom extend to the entire reach of liberal discourses on property relations. In contrast to liberal principles derived from Roman law supporting private land tenancy and the natural law foundations for private property realms independent of the state,[94] prominent specialists in China emphasize the priority of state policies and interests in public property.[95] Limited perceptions about international liberal discourses of property law are evident in efforts to condition expanded property rights protections under the Property Rights Law to the needs of socialist development.[96] Hegel's call for attention to be paid to the material realities of social and economic life as a basis for restraining the unfettered application of abstract concepts of absolute rights to private property[97] is evident in the application of Hegel's philosophy of law to legal reform in China more broadly.[98] In contrast to liberal discourses extolling the political utility of private property rights for protection of individual liberty,[99] authoritative commentary from China emphasizes the role of collective property in strengthening "democratic management."[100] Thus, the perception of property specialists concerning international liberal discourses on property remains somewhat partial and selective, drawing on notions of economic utility but also avoiding embrace of the political implications for individual and private rights.

Complementarity

The factor of complementarity is evident in the relationship between the regulatory norms of the international property system and regulatory norms in China. Liberal notions of law as a restraint on state power and social ideals of individualism that have informed many of the legal forms derived from Europe and North America are not endemic to China. The liberal regulatory ethos[101] may be conceived in terms of *responsible agency*, a typology by which regulators and their political superiors are accountable to the subjects of regulation and, as a result, are expected to exercise regulatory authority broadly in accordance with norms of transparency and the rule of law. By contrast, local norms informing China's official regulatory culture[102] may be described in terms of *patrimonial sovereignty*. Drawing on traditional norms of Confucianism combined with ideals of revolutionary transformation drawn from Marxism-Leninism and Maoism, regulatory culture in China tends to emphasize governance by a political authority that remains largely immune to challenge. To the extent that China's property rights regime entails use of legal forms drawn from abroad, their normative foundations of responsible agency are often in conflict with local norms of patrimonial sovereignty. Issues of complementarity are also evident in tensions about the locus of rights. The orientation of liberal property rights regimes toward individual rights invites conflict with local norms of collectivism, while private rights discourses of liberalism conflict with the public law norms of Chinese tradition and PRC policy.[103]

Yet, the development of property rights in the PRC has long been a process of building complementarity in normative regimes governing private and public interests.[104] Recognizing the centrality of public ownership orthodoxy, proponents of expanded private property rights focused on changing the terms governing standards of public ownership by distinguishing public ownership of natural resources from collective ownership of land by private economic entities.[105] The market economy is seen by some commentators as requiring diversity in the means of distributing wealth and thus might permit expanded private property rights.[106] Thus, broader civil law autonomy for individuals need not displace the collective imperative of state-centric economic law.[107] The debate of relations of public and private rights continued in the context of the Property Rights Law, as critics and supporters debated the constitutionality of provisions on equal protection of public and private property rights.[108] By bringing this debate within the discourse of constitutional rights and purposes, the interpretive community of legal specialists commenting on the Property Rights Law seems to suggest that, rather than operating in conflict, the two paradigms of private and public rights could become mutually sustaining, thus supporting complementarity in the Selective Adaptation of international property rights standards. Thus, the extent of complementarity between globalized norms of private property rights and local norms of socialist public ownership appears limited, as acceptance of globalized legal standards on property is not accompanied by assimilation of underlying norms.

Legitimacy

Legitimacy dimensions of Selective Adaptation may be appreciated in light of tensions around property rights and the right to development. As a signatory of and advocate for the 1993 Bangkok Declaration on Human Rights,[109] China places strong emphasis on the right to development over requirements of civil and political rights. In its 1991 Human Rights white paper, the PRC explicitly adopted a position supporting the primacy of economic growth by stressing the right to subsistence as the primary right from which all other rights derive.[110] In explaining the 1991 white paper, the Director of the State Council Information Office stressed the primacy of the state's management of economic conditions as the basis for development: "[W]e enable our people to have the economic foundation upon which they can enjoy political rights."[111] The 1995 and 1997 Human Rights white papers underscored the regime's commitment to the primacy of the right to development.[112] Achievements in satisfying human rights to subsistence and development were given prominence yet again in the 2000 Human Rights white paper, subordinating civil and political rights.[113] The 2004 Human Rights white paper formally integrated themes of subsistence and development, drawing on the international discourse of the right to development to complement China's ongoing emphasis on the right to subsistence.[114] These perspectives are reiterated in the 2008 white paper on the rule of law that affirms the centrality of Party leadership and asserts China's "basic stand" on human rights as "placing top priority on people's rights to subsistence and development."[115]

The continued emphasis on the people's right to development has contributed to growing popular rights consciousness, particularly in areas of property rights. Public demonstrations over a range of concerns have continued to expand in recent years, such that the Public Security Bureau reported 87,000 public order disturbances in 2005, up from 74,000 in 2005, and 58,000 in 2003.[116] Many of these concern disputes of rural land use policies.[117] As well, urban and rural residents alike have gradually begun to use legal mechanisms to achieve redress. By the early 2000s, expanded public participation in the legal process is widely evident.[118] Villagers seeking compensation for expropriation of their land in favor of public and private development and neighborhood residents in urban areas seeking redress for allegedly unlawful relocation and expropriation of housing and other areas suggest the growing awareness of property rights among the populace.[119]

The growing trend of public citizens using the law to enforce their rights against government abuse and against abuse by privileged citizens suggests a new and dramatic phase in China's legal development. This poses a significant dilemma for the governing regime, which has, to a large extent, based its legitimacy on a commitment to the rule of law. If the legitimacy of the regime comes to be compromised to the extent that it fails to deliver on commitments regarding the rule of law,[120] an entirely new calculus of political authority may emerge. Although the Party staffing and discipline systems are powerful mechanisms for ensuring compliance by judges and lawyers, the regime's ability to control outcomes is weakened to the extent that the law becomes part of the public domain. The newly enacted revisions to the Lawyer's Law reveal the extent of concern by the government—as new and more stringent requirements are imposed on lawyers upholding the interests of the state in the face of popular rights claims.[121]

To the extent that the state is implicated in denying people access to redress for infringements of property rights that the state has publicly affirmed, legitimacy for the property rights regime is diminished. The Chinese government's support for the right to development invites popular criticism when the benefits of such rights are not delivered. To the extent that both property rights and the socioeconomic benefits attached to them are not forthcoming to wide segments of the populace, the resulting legitimacy deficit not only affects government's authority to rule but the capacity of the property rights regime to modify property relations behavior effectively is undermined. The challenge of legitimacy, combined with the challenges of perception and complementarity already discussed, raises important questions about the sustainability and effectiveness of China's emerging property rights regimes.

Organizational Performance and Institutional Capacity in China's Property Regime(s)

Distinct from but not unrelated to normative interchange, institutional capacity is an important factor in legal regime performance.[122] The operation of the Chinese legal regime depends on the Party/state's instrumentalist use of law to pursue policy goals and to maintain political dominance. Law is not intended as a limit on state power but rather is a mechanism by which state power is exercised. As a result the capacity of institutions to implement legal rules is critical. Institutional Capacity describes the ability of institutions to perform assigned tasks in the context of local political and socioeconomic conditions.[123]

Elements of institutional purpose, location, orientation, and cohesion are particularly important indicators of Institutional Capacity. *Institutional purpose* concerns the goals of institutional behavior, and the way these reflect consensus and conflict among communities in which institutions operate. Thus, the capacity of local governance institutions to implement new standards on property relations depends on the degree of clarity and consensus regarding policy objectives. Institutional capacity also depends on issues of *institutional location*, particularly the question of balancing central authority with local power.[124] In China, practical divisions of power and authority between local and central government departments permit a degree of policy interplay between the central and sub-national governments that reveal marked differences of perspective and practice and affect institutional capacity.[125] Institutional capacity also depends on *institutional orientation*, namely, the priorities and habitual practices of institutions. Tensions between formal and informal approaches to recognition and enforcement of property rights standards are important examples of institutional orientation.[126] Finally, institutional capacity depends on issues of *institutional cohesion*, involving the willingness of individuals within institutions to comply with edicts from leaders and to enforce institutional goals. In the context of implementing newly enacted property rights standards at the local level, institutional cohesion often reflects issues of human resource management and administrative discipline. Thus, the structural features of institutional capacity provide an organizational counterpoint to the normative features of Selective Adaptation.

Institutional Purpose

As with virtually all PRC legislation, implementation of the Property Rights Law will continue to depend on policy imperatives of the Party/state. Yet these are often far from clear or unified. While the Property Rights Law can hardly be said to create new private rights in property where none had existed previously, the statute's provisions clarifying transactional procedures and limiting the authority of officials to intervene echo policy priorities favoring greater autonomy in property relations. Yet the extent of consensus on these issues remains obscure. Challenges against the constitutionality of the law are not simply the abstract discourses of isolated academics, but rather reflect deep-seated disagreements over the purposes and practices of property law and the implications for Chinese socialism and socialist development.[127] The depth of disagreement is evident as well in Wang Zhaoguo's introductory speech on the law, whose effort to balance economic utility goals with priorities on socialism and fairness was mandated by the extent of political controversy around the basic policies and purposes of the Property Rights Law.[128]

The struggle for consensus has been heightened by disagreement over rural development policies. The CPC's Document No. 1 for 2008 affirmed the importance of rural reform,[129] but policy debates continue as to how this should proceed. The effort by no less than Hu Jintao to press forward at the Third Plenum of the Seventeenth CPC Central Committee with a major rural reform initiative to grant peasants broader powers to transfer land use rights was partially stymied by conservative opponents.[130] While rural reforms were passed at the Plenum after some forty-one revisions,[131] the intended scope of land use rights transfers appeared to be limited to "nonagricultural development land" (*feinong jianshe yongdi*).[132] While this small step challenges the monopoly held by government departments on transfers of land use rights, clearly a consensus has not yet emerged in support of unfettered powers of alienation of property rights for rural land users. For the Property Rights Law to fulfill its intended goals of supporting expanded autonomy in the ownership and use of property while still entrenching the supervisory role of the Party/state, a sustainable consensus will need to emerge in favor of expanding the rights of land use holders to register, protect, and transfer their rights. At present, this prospect seems remote.

Institutional Location

Debates over the Party's decision on rural development reflect contending perspectives on local conditions. Opponents of expanding land use transfer rights have pointed to the iconic role of land as a foundation for social insurance, questioning whether the purported economic efficiencies to be gained from expanded transfer rights will still protect social needs in rural areas.[133] The reforms are expected to increase migration of surplus agricultural labor to the cities (potentially reaching 700 million by 2020), raising concerns of urbanites over local capacity and social conditions.[134] Still other opponents have expressed doubts that a liberalized land use transfer system will benefit peasants in areas where land quality is poor and access to markets and transportation is limited.[135] Proponents of expanding land use transfer rights have tended to adhere to conventional economic theories extolling the virtues of capital liquidity and mobilization.[136] While such an approach resonates with the experience and training of development and planning officials in Beijing and various provincial capitals, it remains uncertain as to whether it suits the realities of local conditions. Indeed, critiques of the proposal have urged greater attention be paid to local conditions.[137] Demographics also appear to play a role, as older villagers apparently tend to prize landholdings as social security, while younger people seem more eager to leave the land to move to the cities.[138]

Coordination with local conditions is an essential component of institutional capacity. While some attention is paid to the need to facilitate economic growth for the decentralized communities of rural areas, development goals of private property rights are often constructed in terms that conflict with local social arrangements. Basic policy goals underlying rural land reform seem to privilege perspectives on economic organization and behavior more reminiscent of urban rather than rural realities. Indeed the current world food crisis suggests that conventional economic perspectives on efficiency and comparative advantage may lead to market distortions and unsustainable burdens for rural residents.[139] Resulting dislocation and migration of the peasantry to urban areas may well be a "natural" consequence of economic imperatives about efficiency but may also contribute to breakdown of social relations in both the countryside and the cities. Neoliberal economic approaches centered on accumulation, institutionalization, and urbanization, with little attention to preserving local cultures and traditions, pose challenges for implementation of the new Property Rights Law and, in the long term, challenge traditional patterns of rural life.

Institutional Orientation

The government's continued reliance on formal systems of regulation at the central and local levels is evident in the new Property Rights Law, with its processes for registration and administration of property rights. State policy decisions and responses to issues of property relations remain subject to the limitations of formal institutionalism, which reflect the influences of liberal property models as well as the state's imperative to ensure (or appear to ensure) regulatory control. Yet the predominance of informal relations in local socioeconomic and political life is well known.[140] The formal regulatory ethos that pervades the Property Rights Law poses significant challenges for inhabitants of rural society, whose reality of socioeconomic and political relations is often far removed from the practices of legal formalism.

This tension has the potential not only to impede the effectiveness of the Property Rights Law in controlling unauthorized creation and transfer of private property rights in land but also to put institutional pressure on traditional social relations in rural areas. To the extent that enjoying the benefits of property rights protection requires compliance with formal regulatory models, this privileges people already adept at communicating and acting in the formal regulatory world, while excluding and marginalizing those who are no so adept. In the short term, this state of affairs has the potential to aggravate rather than relieve socioeconomic tensions and, in the longer term, may undermine traditional patterns of socioeconomic and political relations. The orientation of China's Property Rights Law remains focused on formal processes of project approvals, licenses, formalized regulation, and the "legalization" of economic relations. In China's rural societies, however, much economic activity is conducted through informal family networks and market networks. Local merchants often consider formal requirements of licensing to be mechanisms for state control, as indeed they are. The new law reveals dynamics of regulatory formalism by the way it confers on local officials authority to approve registration and transfer of property rights in land. Yet, more often than not, basic decisions on property-related issues of allocation, development, and land use are made informally at the family or community level with little attention to regulatory formalities.[141]

Institutional Cohesion

The Property Rights Law and its extension to land use relations in rural China will depend heavily on implementation by local officials who put the policy purposes of the law ahead of their own parochial interests.[142] Enforcement of property transfer requirements by disinterested officials, the availability of impartial judicial review of administrative action in respect of land use rights, and the effective implementation of remedies (particularly compensation) for unlawful expropriation of land all will depend on a cohort of local officials committed to achieving the policy goals underlying the new regime. A key element of this involves the experience and training of local officials to support relative autonomy in property relations. However, as indicated by the broader lack of consensus on policy goals, the tradition of Party rule is one that has repeatedly denigrated the role of private property.[143] Training materials and seminars at the Central Party School and regional Party training facilities (even in the cosmopolitan center of Shanghai) often extol the importance of the public ownership system's socialist ideals.[144] At the local level, officials will require comprehensive retraining to shed predispositions against private property relations, and it remains uncertain as to whether there is the political will or the capacity to bring this about.[145]

Effective constraints on administrative action by local officials either restraining legitimate autonomy in land use transfers or engaging in arbitrary expropriation of land will require more effective judicial review under the Administrative Litigation Law. While courts in the urban areas are well disposed to grapple with the intricacies of property rights relationships, rural courts remain understaffed and often incapable of exercising effective supervision over local Party officials. Surveys of local courts reveal their embeddedness in local communitarian society and their dependency on local political authorities.[146] Acting more like magistrates or justices of the peace, local judges often have neither the training nor the experience—let alone the political protection—to effectively confront administrative abuses by local officials. This further undermines the capacity for institutional cohesion in local property regime institutions.

As well, corruption is a well-known feature of regulatory life in China, particularly at the local level, with significant costs for economic growth and social well-being.[147] As China's property regime purports to empower government departments to oversee property relations, China's property system also privileges local business interests. Local Party cadres are often invested either personally or for policy reasons with large business interests who are seen as a major component of China's economic growth miracle and are also viewed as essential to maintaining satisfactory levels of employment. Assessments of local cadre performance in rural development are heavily influenced by the imperative to maintain levels of economic growth and employment. As a result, local officials have little incentive to respond to issues of preservation of social relations in land or popular calls for sustainable land use, instead often opting to maintain economic growth at all costs and to protect enterprise autonomy from intrusive regulation.[148] The symbiotic relationship between local officials and large business interests invites problems of corruption and particularly the tendency to place the parochial interests of officials ahead of the policy goals of the new Property Rights Law and associated regulatory regimes. Thus, issues of institutional cohesion, combined with those of institutional purpose, location, and orientation, suggest that implementation of the Property Rights Law faces ongoing organizational challenges that augment the normative dynamics of Selective Adaptation.

SUMMARY

In contrast to the models of Western liberalism, where the norms of individual liberty and economic efficiency constrain the state to limit its regulation of private property, in China the state continues to occupy a central role in mediating property relations. The contours and consequences of debates over inclusion of a private property protection clause in the 1999 constitutional amendments suggest the extent of opposition to liberal private property rights regimes. The 2004 amendment to the Chinese constitution and the 2007 Property Rights Law reveal that, although liberal notions of expanded private property rights are taking hold among certain legal and policy elites, norms about protecting state and social interests remain strong. Selective Adaptation analysis suggests that assimilation of globalized liberal norms of property remain partial, while Institutional Capacity analysis reveals that operational obstacles continue to confront policy initiatives on property rights reform. The outcomes from these processes will determine the ability of the Party/state to manage increasingly private property relations effectively so as to prevent economic development from undermining the security, health, and well-being of society.

NOTES

1. He Qinghua, "*Fa de yizhi yu fa de bentuhua* [Legal transplanting and localization of law]," *Zhongguo faxue* [*Chinese legal studies*] no. 3 (June 2002): 3-15.

2. See generally, Hugh Gibbons, "Justifying Law: An Explanation of the Deep Structure of American Law," *Law and Philosophy* 3, no. 2 (August 1984): 165–279. For discussion of the dilemmas attendant to challenging liberal private law regimes, see, e.g., Alan Brudner, "Hegel and the Crisis of Private Law," Kenneth Casebeer, "The Crisis of Private Law Is Not an Ideal Situation," and Charles Yablon, "Arguing from Necessity: A Comment on 'Hegel and the Crisis of Private Law'," *Cardozo Law Review* 10, no. 5–6 (1988-1989): 949–1000, 1001–1018, and 1019–1030, respectively.

3. This paper appeared originally as Pitman B. Potter, "Public Regulation of Private Relations: Changing Conditions of Property Relations in China," in *Developments in Chinese Law,* ed. Guanghua Yu (London: Routledge, 2010).

4. This section updates the author's "Globalization and Local Legal Culture: Dilemmas of China's Use of Liberal Ideas of Private Property Rights," *Asian Law* 2 (2000).

5. See e.g., Qian Mingxing, "*Lun woguo wuquanfa de jiben yuance* [On the basic principles of our civil law]," *Beijing daxue xuebao* [*Beijing University Journal*] no. 1 (1998): 29–38; Zheng Chengsi, "*Minfadian zhong de jige gainian xianyi* [Various basic ideas in the civil code]," People's University Social Sciences Information Centre, *Minshang faxue* [*Civil and commercial legal studies*] no. 7 (1998): 14–15; Yu Nengwu and Wang Shenyi "*Lun wuquan fa de xiandaihua fazhan qushi* [The development of modernization of property law]," *Zhongguo faxue* [*Chi-

nese legal studies] no. 1(1998): 72–80; Zheng Ruikun, "*Lun woguo de wuquan lifa* [Legislation of our country's property rights]," *Faxue [Legal studies*] no. 3 (1998): 18–19, 16; Guo Mingrui, "*Guanyu woguo wuquan lifa de san dian sikao* [Three perspectives on our country's property legislation]," *Zhongguo faxue* [*Chinese legal studies*] no. 2 (1998): 21–26; Liu Jingwei, "*Cong woguo tudi zhidu zhi biange kan wuquanfa zhi feixing* [Viewing the abandonment of property rights from the transformation of the land system]," *Zhengzhi yu falu* [*Politics and law*] no. 3 (1996): 47–48.

6. See e.g., Liang Huixing, *Zhongguo wuquanfa caoan jianyi gao* [*Outline of opinion on a draft Chinese property law*] (Beijing: Social Science Manuscripts Press, 2000); Sun Xianzhi, "*Wuquan xingwei lilun tan yuan yiqi yiyi* [Exploring the origins and significance of theories of property behaviour]," *Faxue yanjiu* [*Research in law*] no. 3 (1996): 80–92; Wang Liming, "*Wuquan xingwei ruogan wenti tantao* [Inquiry on several issues of property rights behaviour]," *Zhongguo faxue* [*Chinese legal studies*] no. 1 (1997): 58–70. Also see Edward J. Epstein, "The Theoretical System of Property Rights in China's *General Principles of Civil Law*: Theoretical Controversy in the Drafting Process and Beyond," *Law and Contemporary Problems* 52, no. 2–3 (1989): 179–216.

7. See e.g., Qian Mingxing, *Wuquan fa yuan li* [*Principles of Property Law*] (Beijing: Peking University Press, 1994); Ji Yibao, "*Lun wuquan gongshi de xingzhi he zhidu jiazhi* [On the character and systemic value of property public notice]," *Zhong wai faxue* [*Chinese and foreign legal studies*] no. 3 (1997): 47–51. Also see Wang Liming, "*Wuquan xingwei ruogan wenti tantao* [Inquiry on several issues of property rights behaviour]," *Zhongguo faxue* [*Chinese legal studies*] no. 1 (1997): 58–70.

8. See generally, He Guanghui, "Continue to Deepen Reform by Centering on Economic Improvement and Rectification," *Zhongguo jingji tizhi gaige* [Reform of the Chinese Economic Structure] no. 2 (1990), translated in *FBIS Daily Report: China*, March 23, 1990, 21.

9. See *Constitution of the PRC* (1982), Article 13.

10. See *Constitution of the PRC* (1982), Article 51.

11. See e.g., Li Yunhe, "*Dui gongyouzhi we zhuti de yi dian kanfa* [A view on the centrality of public ownership]," *Zhongguo faxue* [*Chinese legal studies*] no. 5 (1993): 37–38; and Wang Shenyi, "*Lun wuquan de shehuihua* [On the socialization of property rights]," *Faxue pinglun* [*Legal studies commentary*] no. 1 (1999): 56–61.

12. See e.g., Xie Zichang and Wang Xiujing, "*Guanyu chanquan de ruogan lilun wenti* [Several theoretical questions about property rights]," *Faxue yanjiu* [*Research in law*] no. 1 (1994): 42–47.

13. See e.g., forum comments in "*Jiaqiang guoyou zichan guanli duse guoyou zichan liushi luodong* [Strengthen management of state property and block the runoff and leakage of state property]," *Zhengzhi yu falu* [*Politics and law*] no. 1 (1996): 22–25, 45; Wang Jueyu, "*Ezhi guoyou zichan liushi de falu duixiang* [Legal objectives of halting the losses of state owned property]," *Faxue* [*Legal studies*] no. 6 (1995): 35–37.

14. See e.g., Zou Xi and Shu Sheng, "*Shichang jingji shehui zhong de guojia caichan suoyouquan* [State property ownership rights in the market economy society]," *Zhongguo faxue* [*Chinese legal studies*] no. 4 (1996): 56–62.

15. See "Draft Amendments to Constitution Discussed," Beijing *Xinhua* English Service, March 22, 1993 in *FBIS Daily Report: China* (FBIS-CHI-93-054) March 23, 1993, 13–14.

16. See Gong Xiangrui and Jiang Mingan, "*Zai lun gongmin caichanquan de xianfa baohu* [Again, on constitutional protection for citizens' property rights]," *Zhongguo faxue* [*Chinese legal studies*] no. 2 (1992): 70–73; Hu Jingguang, "*Shichang jingji huhuan due gongmin caichanquan de xianfa baozhang* [The market economy calls for constitutional

protections for citizens' property rights]," *Zhongguo jingji ribao* [*China economy daily*], June 18, 1998, 4.

17. See Property Law Research Program of CASS Law Institute, "*Zhiding Zhongguo wuquanfa de jiben sikao* [Basic perspectives on enacting Chinese property law]," *Faxue yanjiu* [*Research in law*] no. 3 (1995): 3–10.

18. Hu Xiaobo, "Informal Property Rights and Their Formalization in 1997: A Political Economy Analysis," in Joseph Cheng, ed., *China Review* 1998 (Hong Kong: Chinese University of Hong Kong Press, 1998), 314–338, 323.

19. See "*Zhongguo wuquan fa (caoan)* [Chinese property law (draft)]," Article 2, in Liang Huixing, *Zhongguo wuquanfa caoan jianyi gao* [*Outline of opinion on a draft Chinese property law*] (Beijing: Social Science Manuscripts Press, 2000), 5.

20. See "*Zhongguo wuquan fa (caoan)* [Chinese property law (draft)]," Articles 1, 5, page 5.

21. Ibid., 95–97.

22. See Huang Rutong, "*Shi fou yiding yao ba 'Siying caichan shensheng bu ke qinfan' xiejin woguo xianfa* [Do we really want to write 'the sanctity of private property is inviolable' into our constitution]," *Dangdai faxue* [*Contemporary legal studies*], no. 4 (1998): 5–7.

23. See Qian Mingxing, "*Woguo wuquanfa de tiaozheng fanwei, neirong tedian ji wuquan tixi* [The scope of adjustment, special contents and property system in our property law]," *Zhong wai faxue* [*Chinese and foreign legal studies*], no. 2 (1997): 88–90.

24. See Guo Mingrui, "*Guanyu woguo wuquan lifa de san dian sikao* [Three perspectives on our country's property legislation]," *Zhongguo faxue* [*Chinese legal studies*], no. 2 (1998): 21–26, 23–24.

25. See e.g., Yu Nengwu and Wang Shenyi "*Lun wuquan fa de xiandaihua fazhan qushi* [The development of modernization of property law]," *Zhongguo faxue* [*Chinese legal studies*] no. 1 (1998): 72–80, 73.

26. See generally, Wen Zhiyang, "*Zhanlun Zhongguo minfa wuquan tixi* [Sketching China's civil law property system]," *Faxue* [*Legal studies*], no. 6 (1997): 37–40. For a poignant example of a reformist scholar responding to orthodox perspectives in times of conservatism, see Wang Liming, "*Lun guojia suoyouquan zhuti de quanminxing wenti* [On the issue of the mass character of the bulk of state ownership rights]," *Zhongnan zhengfa xueyuan xuebao* [*Journal of the Central South Political Legal Institute*], no. 4 (1990): 17–24.

27. See "Text of PRC Constitutional Amendment," Beijing *Xinhua* Domestic Service, March 16, 1999 in *FBIS Daily Report: China* (FBIS-CHI-1999-0316); "Tian Jiyun on Constitutional Amendments," Beijing *Xinhua* Domestic Service, March 13, 1999 in *FBIS Daily Report: China* (FBIS-CHI-1999-0316), March 13, 1999; "Li Peng Presides over Closing of 9th NPC," Beijing *Xinhua* Domestic Service, March 15, 1999 in *FBIS Daily Report: China* (FBIS-CHI-1999-0326), March 15, 1999.

28. See "More on NPC Third Plenary Meeting," Beijing *Xinhua* English Service, March 9, 1999 in *FBIS Daily Report: China* (FBIS-CHI-1999-0308), March 9, 1999.

29. See "Constitution Amendment Gives Solid Legal Support to Private Business," *China Economic News: Special Supplement for the Second Plenary Session of the Ninth National People's Congress* (April 19, 1999), 2–3; "Constitutional Amendments Propel China's Reform and Opening-up," Beijing *Xinhua* English Service, March 15, 1999 in *FBIS Daily Report: China* (FBIS-CHI-1999-0315), March 17, 1999.

30. See *Contract Law of the PRC* (1999), Articles 1 and 52.

31. See Zhang Guangbo, "*Lun caichan de shensheng bu ke qinfan* [On the sanctity of property is inviolable]," *Faxue zazhi* [*Legal studies*], no. 4 (1999): 10–11.

32. See e.g., Dai Jiabing, "For Public Interest: Breaking the Law and Not Being Punished," *Beijing fazhi ribao* [Beijing Legal System Daily] Feb. 23, 1998, 7 in *FBIS Daily Report: China* (FBIS-CHI-98-114), April 24, 1998.

33. See generally, Zhang Qianfan, *Xianfa zue daolun* [*Guiding theory on constitutional law*] (Beijing: Law Press China, 2008), 501–502.

34. See Land Administration Law of the PRC (1986, rev. 1988). Also see "*Nongmuyu bu fubuzhang Xiang Zhongyang xiang quanguo renda changweihui zuo guanyu tudi fa caoan de shuoming* [Vice Minister of Agriculture, Livestock, and Fisheries Xiang Zhongyang delivers an explanation of the draft land law to the NPC Standing Committee]," *Zhongguo fazhi bao* [*China Legal System Gazette*] March 19, 1986, 2.

35. Pitman B. Potter, "China's New Land Development Regulations," *China Business Review* (March-April 1991): 12–14.

36. See e.g., "Shanghai Municipality, PRC Land Administration Law Implementing Measures," *China Law & Practice* (December 15, 1994): 32–49.

37. See Cao Fengying, "*Fangdichan lifa ruogan wenti sikao* [Perspectives on several questions of real estate legislation]," *Zhengzhi yu falu* [*Politics and law*], no. 3 (1994): 50–52.

38. See "People's Republic of China, Administration of Urban Real Property Law," *China Law & Practice* (October 3, 1994): 23–38. For a review of regulatory conditions leading up the enactment, see William D. Soileau, "Past is Present: Urban Real Property Rights and Housing Reform in the People's Republic of China," *Pacific Rim Law & Policy Journal* 3 (February 1995): 299–387.

39. See Donald C. Clarke and Nicholas C. Howson, "Developing P.R.C. Property and Real Estate Law: Revised Land Registration Rules," *East Asian Executive Reports* (April 15, 1996): 9–17. Also see Supreme People's Court Administrative Tribunal, ed., *Xingzheng susong yu tudi guanlifa: Xin jie* [*Administrative litigation of land administration law: New interpretations*] (Beijing: Current Events Press, 1999).

40. See, generally, Anthony Walker, *Land Property and Construction in the People's Republic of China* (Hong Kong: Hong Kong University Press, 1991).

41. See cases discussed in Wang Liming, ed., *Zhongguo minfa anli yu xueli yanjiu—Wuquan bian* [*Studies in Chinese civil law cases and theory*] (Beijing: Law Publishers, 1998); An Conghua et al., eds., *Renmin fayuan yinan panli pingxi: Minshi zhuan* [*Evaluation of difficult cases of the People's Courts: Civil Volume*] (Changchun: Jilin Chubanshe, 1999), 201, 205, 211, 217, 226.

42. See e.g., Case no. 15, in *Shanghai fayuan anli jingxuan—1997* [*Carefully selected cases from the Shanghai Courts—1997*], ed. Li Changdao (Shanghai: Shanghai People's Press, 1997), 50.

43. See e.g., Case no. 17, in *Shanghai fayuan anli jingxuan—1999* [*Carefully selected cases from the Shanghai Courts—1999*], ed. Qiao Xianzhi (Shanghai: Shanghai People's Press, 2000), 81.

44. See e.g., Case no. 6, in *Shanghai fayuan anli jingxuan—1996* [*Carefully selected cases from the Shanghai Courts—1996*], ed. Li Changdao (Shanghai: Shanghai People's Press, 1997), 16.

45. See e.g., Case no. 9, in *Shanghai fayuan anli jingxuan—1999*, ed. Qiao Xianzhi, 44.

46. See e.g., Case no. 6, in *Shanghai fayuan anli jingxuan—1997*, ed. Li Changdao, 43.

47. See e.g., Qian Weiqing and Guo Yuyuan, "*Pochan qiye fangdichan chuli yi ji youguan wenti de tantao* [Inquiry on resolution of real estate of bankrupt enterprises and related questions]," *Zhengzhi yu falu* [*Politics and law*], no. 1 (1995): 51–53.

48. See, generally, Qian Mingxing, "*Woguo wuquanfa de tiaozheng fanwei, neirong tedian ji wuquan tixi* [The scope of adjustment, special contents and property system in our property

law]," *Zhong wai faxue* [*Chinese and foreign legal studies*], no. 2 (1997): 88–90. Also see Wang Yongxia, "*Lun budongchan wuquan biandong zhong zhaiquan he wuquan de baohu* [Safeguarding creditor and property rights in the transfer of immovable property rights]," *Faxue pinglun* [*Legal studies commentary*], no. 2 (1998): 121–125.

49. See Chen Jian, *Zhongguo tudi shiyongquan zhidu* [China's system of land use rights] (Beijing: Machinery Industry Press, 2003); Zhang Shuanggen and Zhang Xuezhe, "*Lun woguo tudi wuquan zhidu* [On our land property rights system]," *Zhongguo tudi kexue* [*China land science*], no. 3 (1997): 7–10, 6.

50. See Wang Lanping, "*Lun woguo tudi shiyongquan yu yongyi wuquan* [On rights of use and property rights in usage of land in China]," *Shandong shida xuebao* [*Journal of Shandong Normal University*], no. 2 (1997): 28–30.

51. See e.g., Zhang Shaopeng, "*Guanyu fangdichan diya falu zhidu ruogan wenti de yanjiu* [Research on various questions in the legal system for real estate mortgages]," *Zhongguo faxue* [*Chinese legal studies*], no. 2 (1997): 71–78; Shi Diao, Wang Jin, and Du Xueyi, "*Wanshan woguo diya zhidu de ji dian lifa sikao* [Considerations on perfecting various items of legislation in our mortgage system]," *Zhongguo faxue* [*Chinese legal studies*], no. 4 (1997): 45–49.

52. John Whitelegg, John Barrett, Dabo Guan, and Klaus Hubacek, "Resource Consumption in China, Beijing, and Shanghai," (CCICED, 2005).

53. "Shanghai to test land use measures," *China Daily,* Dec. 4, 2006, http://www.china.org.cn/english/government/191109.htm; *Shanghai shi tudi liyong zongti guihua 1997–2010* [*Comprehensive plan for land use in Shanghai municipality 1997–2010*] (Shanghai: Shanghai Municipal Government, 1999).

54. Tian Shi and Roderic Gill, "Developing effective policies for sustainable development of ecological agriculture in China: the case study of Jinshan County with a systems dynamics model," *Ecological Economics* 53 (2005): 223–246.

55. See Elizabeth J. Perry, "Rural Collective Violence: The Fruits of Recent Reforms," in *The Political Economy of Reform in Post-Mao China*, ed. Elizabeth J. Perry and Christine Wong (Harvard University Asia Center, 1985), 175–192, 179 et seq.

56. See Jean C. Oi, "The Fate of the Collective After the Commune," in *Chinese Society on the Eve of Tiananmen: The Impact of Reform*, ed. Deborah Davis and Ezra F. Vogel (Cambridge, MA: Harvard University Press, 1990), 15–36.

57. See "The Law of Land Administration of the People's Republic of China," Articles 1, 2 & 8, in *China Economic News* (Oct. 26, 1998), 8–12, and (Nov. 2, 1998), 8–11. Also see Supreme People's Court Administrative Tribunal, ed., *Xingzheng susong yu tudi guanlifa: Xin jie* [*Administrative litigation of land administration law: New interpretations*] (Beijing: Current Events Press, 1999), 108–109.

58. See Cui Jianyuan, "*Tudi shang de quanliqun lungang* [Theoretic outline of the cluster of rights in land]," *Zhongguo faxue* [*Chinese legal studies*], no. 2 (1998): 14–20. Also see Wen Zhiyang, "*Zhanlun Zhongguo minfa wuquan tixi* [Sketching China's civil law property system]," *Faxue* [*Legal studies*], no. 6 (1997): 37–40.

59. Edward Cody, "In the Face of Rural Unrest, China Rolls Out Reforms," *Washington Post,* Jan. 28, 2006.

60. Shaohua Chen and Martin Ravallion, "China Is Poorer Than We Thought, but No Less Successful in the Fight Against Poverty," Policy Research Working Paper no. WPS 4621 World Bank Development Research Group (May 2008); Calum G. Turney and Rong Kong, "Vulnerability, Trust, and Microcredit: The Case of China's Rural Poor," United Nations University Research Paper, No. 2008/52 (May 2008).

61. Wong Siu-wai and Bo-sin Tang, "Challenges to the sustainability of 'development zones': A case study of Guangzhou Development District, China," *Cities* 22, no. 4 (2005): 303–316.

62. Karl Hallding et al., "Policy Option Scenarios for Sustainable Urbanization in China," (CCICED, 2005).

63. Law on the PRC on Land Contract in Rural Areas (Order of the President No. 73), Oct. 9, 2005, http://www.gov.cn/english/2005-10/09/content_179389.htm.

64. "*Tudi zhidu gaige bianchu guanjian yibu* [Land system reform takes a key step]," *Caijing* [*Finance*], Oct. 20, 2008.

65. See Ji Yibao, "*Lun wuquan gongshi de xingzhi he zhidu jiazhi* [On the character and systemic value of property public notice]," *Zhong wai faxue* [Chinese and foreign legal studies] no. 3 (1997): 47–51; Sun Xianzhi, "*Lun budongchan quan dengji* [On the registration of rights to immovable property]," *Zhongguo faxue* [*Chinese legal studies*], no. 5 (1996): 51–62.

66. "*Zhonghua renmin gongheguo caiquanfa* [Property Rights Law of the PRC]," *China Economic News*, Mar. 16, 2007, Supp. No. 9–10.

67. Gong Xiantian, "A Property Law (Draft) that violates the constitution and basic principles of socialism," trans. Eva Cheng, *Links*, no. 29 (Aug.12, 2005); Gareth Powell, "Not everyone supports law on privatization," *China Economic Review*, February 25, 2007, http://www.chinaeconomicreview.com/property/2007/02/25/not-everyone-supports-law-on-privatization/html; Mure Dickie, "China delays property law amidst rights dispute," *Financial Times*, March 9, 2006; Tracy Quek, "China delays passage of property rights law," *Straits Times*, March 10, 2006. For subsequent indication of Professor Gong's views, see Gong Xiantian, "*Guanyu di liu ci shenyi hou de 'Wuquanfa (caoan)' reng zai wuge zhongda yuanze wenti shang weifan xianfa bixu renzhi xiugai de yijian* [Opinion concerning five important questions of principle in the draft property law following the sixth debate, which violate the constitution and must be conscientiously revised]," (Dec. 9, 2006).

68. Hao Tiechuan, "'*Wuquan fa (caoan)' weixian wenti zhi wojian* [My perspectives on the issue of the 'Property Rights Law (draft)' contravening the constitution], *Faxue* [*Legal studies*], no. 8 (Aug. 10, 2006): 41–42; Zhou Gangzhi, "*Gongwu gainian ji qi zai woguo de shiyong* [The concept of public property and its application in our country]," *Xiandai faxue* [*Modern legal studies*] 28, no. 4 (July 2006): 62–67.

69. See e.g., Gao Fei, "*Ye tan wuquan fa pingdeng baohu caichanquan de xianfa yiju* [Speaking again about the constitutional foundation for equal protection of property rights under the property rights law]," *Faxue* [*Legal studies*], no. 10 (2006): 128–138; Liu Zhigang, "*Lixian zhuyi yujing xia xianfa yu minfa guanxi* [The relationship between constitution and civil law in the context of constitutionalism]," *Faxue pinglun* [*Legal studies commentary*], no. 2 (2007): 20–31.

70. Wang Zhaoguo, "Explanation on Draft Property Law" (Delivered at the Fifth Session of the Tenth National People's Congress), March 8, 2007, http://English.people.com.cn/200703/08/print20070308_355491.html.

71. Ibid.

72. Ibid.

73. Ibid.

74. "*Zhonghua renmin gongheguo xingzheng susong fa* [Administrative Litigation Law of the PRC]," *Chinese Law and Practice* 3, no. 5 (June 5, 1989): 37.

75. Bao Tong, "Of Kings and Bandits," March 31, 2007, http://rfaunplugged.wordpress.com/2007/03/31/bao-tong-of-kings-and-bandits/html; Bao Tong, "China Has Come Full Circle," March 16, 2007, http://rfaunpkugged.wordpress.com/2007/03/17/china-has-come-full-circle-baio-tong-on-the-enlightment-ushered-in-by-chinas-new-property-law/html.

76. Pitman B. Potter, "Legal Reform in China – Institutions, Culture, and Selective Adaptation," *Law & Social Inquiry* 2, no. 4 (Spring 2004): 465–495.

77. Ugo Mattei, *Comparative Law and Economics* (Ann Arbor: University of Michigan Press, 1997); David Trubek et al., "Global Restructuring and the Law: The Internationaliation

of Legal Fields and the Creation of Transnational Arenas," *Case Western Reserve Law Review* 44, no. 2 (1994): 407–498.

78. For discussion of the intersection of norms with identity and community, see Roberto Unger, *Knowledge and Politics* (New York: Free Press, 1975). Also see Amitai Etzioni, "Social Norms: Internalization, Persuasion, and History," *Law & Society Review* 34, no. 1 (2000): 157–178.

79. For discussion of interpretive communities, see Stanley Fish, *Is There a Text in This Class: The Authority of Interpretive Communities* (Cambridge, MA: Harvard University Press, 1980).

80. For discussion of formation of political groups based on organizational experience, see Jurgen Domes, "Intra-Elite Group Formation and Conflict in the PRC," in *Groups and Politics in the People's Republic of China,* ed. David S. G. Goodman (Cardiff, England: University College Cardiff Press, 1984), 26–39. For discussion recognizing that organizational priorities influence political decision making, see Kenneth Lieberthal and Michel Oksenberg, *Policy Making in China* (Princeton: Princeton University Press, 1988), 404, et seq. and sources cited; and Susan L. Shirk, "The Politics of Industrial Reform," in *The Political Economy of Reform in Post-Mao China,* ed. Elizabeth J. Perry and Christine Wong, (Harvard University Asia Center, 1985), 195. For a contrary view, see Lucien Pye, *The Dynamics of Chinese Politics* (Cambridge: Oelgeschlager, Gunn & Hain, 1981). In the China context, see H. Lyman Miller and Liu Xiaohong, "The Foreign Policy Outlook of China's 'Third Generation' Elite," and Joseph Fewsmith and Stanley Rosen, "The Domestic Context of Chinese Foreign Policy: Does 'Public Opinion' Matter?," both in *The Making of Chinese Foreign and Security Policy,* ed. David M. Lampton (Stanford: Stanford University Press, 2001), 123–150 and 151–187.

81. See e.g., David Kennedy, "Receiving the International," *Connecticut Journal of International Law* 10, no. 1 (1994), 1.

82. See e.g., Zeng Lingliang, "*21 shiji falu fuwu maoyi de fazhan qushi yu Zhongguo faxue rencai peiyang de yong you gaige* [Development trends in 21st century trade in legal services and needed reforms in training of China's legal talents]," *Faxue pinglun* [*Legal studies commentary*], no. 1 (2001): 3–8; Xiao Yongping, "*Falu de jiao yu xue zhi geming* [Revolution in teaching and studying law]," *Faxue pinglun* [*Legal studies commentary*], no. 3 (2003): 153–160.

83. See e.g., Li Baojun, *Dangdai Zhongguo waijiao gailun* [*Treatise on contemporary Chinese foreign policy*] (Beijing: People's University Press, 1999); Wang Yinzhou, *Quanqiu zhengzhi he Zhongguo waijiao* [*Global politics and China's foreign policy*] (Beijing: World Knowledge Press, 2003).

84. Rao Geping and Huang Yao, "*Lun quanqiuhua jincheng yu guoji zuzhi de hudong guanxi* [On mutual impacts of globalization processes and international organizations]," *Faxue pinglun* [*Legal studies commentary*], no. 2 (2002): 3–13; Liu Shuguang, *Quanqiuhua yu fan quanqiuhua* [*Globalization and anti-globalization*] (Changsha, Hunan People's Press, 2003), 103–166. For response to such resistance, see He Qinghua, "*Fa de yizhi yu fa de bentuhua* [Legal transplanting and localization of law]," *Zhongguo faxue* [*Chinese legal studies*], no. 3 (2002): 3–15.

85. Okifira Seliktar, "Identifying a Society's Belief System," in *Political Psychology,* ed. Margaret Herman (San Francisco: Jossey-Bass, 1986).

86. See e.g., Li Dexi, Qian Zhen, and Lin Zhe, *Quanqiu beijing xia de Zhongguo minzhu jianshe* [Development of democracy in China under the global background] (Chongqing: Chongqing Press, 2005), based on a policy conference at the authoritative Central Party School. Also see Gao Gangjun, "*Zhongguo de heping fazhan yu guoji fa de jiazhi tixi* [China's peaceful development and the value system of international law]," *Faxue pinglun* [*Legal studies commentary*], no. 3 (2006): 104–110; Zhang Shaodong, "*Ye lun guoji tiaoyue zai woguo de*

shiyong [Again examining the application of international treaties in China]," *Faxue pinglun* [*Legal studies commentary*], no. 6 (2001): 73–79.

87. Max Weber, *Economy and Society*, ed. Guenther Roth and Claus Wittich (Berkeley and Los Angeles: University of California Press, 1978); F. Scharpf, "Interdependence and Democratic Legitimation," in *Disaffected Democracies: What's Troubling the Trilateral Countries?* ed. Susan J. Pharr and Robert D. Putnam (Princeton: Princeton University Press, 2000); Stephen P. Turner and Regis A. Factor, *Max Weber: The Lawyer as Social Thinker* (London and New York: Routledge, 1994).

88. See e.g., Jiang Xiyuan, "An Analysis on Changing International System and Its Acceptance of China," *International Review* 39 (Summer 2005): 19–36.

89. See e.g., Jiang Ping and Li Guoguang, eds., *Wuquanfa yinan wenti jingda* [*Explanation and responses to difficult questions on the Property Rights Law*] (Beijing: Falu chuban she, 1997).

90. See e.g., Zhu Guanxin, "*Lun wuquan huntong guize ji qi zai woguo wuquan fa caoan zhong de yingyong diwei* [On provisions for commingled property and the proper place in our property law draft]," *Faxue* [*Legal studies*], no. 7 (2006): 49–55; Wang Liming, *Wuquan fa lun* [*Property rights theory*] (Beijing: China University of Politics and Law Press, 1998); Guo Mingrui, "*Guanyu woguo wuquan lifa de san dian sikao* [Three points for consideration in China's property rights legislation]," *Zhongguo faxue* [*Chinese legal studies*], no. 2 (1998): 21–26; Zheng Ruikun, "*Lun woguo de wuquan lifa* [On China's property legislation]," *Zhongguo faxue* [*Chinese legal studies*], no. 3 (1998): 18–19; Yu Nengwu and Wang Shenyi, "*Lun wuquan fa de xiandaihua fazhan queshi* [On the phenomenon of modernization development in China's property law]," *Zhongguo faxue* [*Chinese legal studies*], no. 1 (1998): 72–80.

91. See Carol M. Rose, "Property as a Keystone Right?" *Notre Dame Law Review* 71, no. 3 (1996): 329; S. Coval, J. C. Smith, and Simon Coval, "The Foundations of Property and Property Law," *Cambridge Law Journal* 35, no. 3 (1986): 457–475.

92. See, generally, Liang Huixing, *Zhongguo wuquanfa caoan jianyi gao* [*Opinion draft of China's property law*] (Beijing: Social Science Abstracts Press, 2000).

93. Wang Zhaoguo, "Explanation on Draft Property Law" (Delivered at the Fifth Session of the Tenth National People's Congress), March 8, 2007, http://English.people.com.cn/200703/08/print20070308_355491.html.

94. See Boudewijn Bouckaert, "What Is Property?" *Harvard Journal of Law & Public Policy* 13, no. 1 (1990): 775–816, 785 et seq.

95. Li Kaoguo, "*Lun woguo chengshi jianshe yongdi de xianzheng houyong yuanze* [On the principle of expropriation first, use second in China's urban development land use]," *Xiandai faxue* [*Modern legal studies*] 29, no. 4 (July 2007): 37–43; Ji jianye, "*Nongmin quanli baozhang yu xin nongcun jianshe* [Safeguarding peasants' rights and the construction of the new countryside]," *Faxuejia* [*Jurists*], no. 1 (2007): 11–14; Zhou Gangzhi, "*Gongwu gainian yi qi zai wuguo de shiyong* [The concept of public property and its application in our country]," *Xiandai faxue* [*Modern legal studies*] 28, no. 4 (July 2006): 62–67.

96. See *Zhonghua renmin gongheguo wuquanfa shiyi* [Interpretation of the Property Rights Law of the PRC] (Beijing: China Economy Publishing House, 2007); Han Dayuan, "*You 'Wuquanfa (caoan)' de zhenglun xiangdao de ruogan xianfa wenti* [Considering various constitutional issues in light of the debates over the "Property Rights Law (Draft)"]," *Faxue* [*Legal studies*], no. 3 (2006): 24–32.

97. See Peter G. Stillman, "Hegel's Analysis of Property in the Philosophy of Right," *Cardozo Law Review* 10, no. 5–6 (1989): 1031–1072.

98. See Lin Zhe, *Hei-ge-er de faquan zhexue* [*Hegel's philosophy of legal rights*] (Shanghai: Fudan University Press, 1999).

99. See James E. Krier, "The (Unlikely) Death of Property," *Harvard Journal of Law & Public Policy* 13, no. 1 (1990): 75–83.

100. Meng Qinguo, "*Wuquanfa ruhe baohu jiti caichan* [How does the property law protect collective property?]," *Faxue* [*Legal studies*], no. 1 (2006): 72–77.

101. See e.g., Will Kymlicka, *Liberalism, Community and Culture* (Oxford: Clarendon Press, 1991).

102. See, generally, Stanley Lubman, *Bird in a Cage: Legal Reform in China After Mao* (Stanford: Stanford University Press, 1999); Pitman B. Potter, *The Chinese Legal System: Globalization and Local Legal Culture* (London: Routledge, 2001); Randall Peerenboom, *China's Long March Toward Rule of Law* (Cambridge: Cambridge University Press, 2002).

103. Yin Tian, "*Wuquan zhuti lungang* [Treatise on the locus of property rights]," *Xiandai faxue* [*Modern legal studies*] 28, no. 2 (March 2006): 3–11.

104. See e.g., Qian Mingxing, "*Woguo minshi fazhi sishi nian de bianqian* [Changes in forty years of our civil law system]," *Zhongwai faxue* [*Chinese and foreign legal studies*], no. 5 (1998): 1–8; Wang Jianrui, "*Wanshen siyou caichan baohu zhidu de falu sizao* [Legal perspectives on perfecting the system of protecting private property]," *Faxue zazhi* [*Legal studies magazine*], no. 2 (1999): 25–26; and "Law on Private Economy Called For," *China Economic News,* Aug. 23, 1999, 1–2. Also see Hu Jingguang, "*Shichang jingji huhuan dui gongmin caichan de xianfa baohu* [The market economy cries out for constitutional protection for citizens' property rights]," *Zhongguo jingji ribao* [*China economic news*], June 18, 1998, 4.

105. See Guo Mingrui, "*Guanyu wo guo wuquan lifa de san dian sikao* [Three perspectives on Chinese property legislation]," *Zhongguo faxue* [*Chinese legal studies*], no. 2 (1998): 21–26, 24–25.

106. See e.g., Qu Maohui and Li Qiang, "*Xianfa ying queren duozhong fenpei fangshi* [The constitution should acknowledge many forms of distribution]," *Hunan shifan daxue shehui kexue xuebao* [*Social science journal of Hunan Normal University*], no. 5 (1998): 22–25.

107. See Liu Shuilin, "*Jingji fa yu minfa de shichang jingji guannian jichu yanjiu* [Basic research on concepts of the market economy of economic law and civil law]," *Faxue yanjiu* [*Research in legal studies*], no. 1 (1997): 34–39.

108. See articles by Tong Zhiwei, Han Dayuan, Zhang Qianfa, and Jiao Hongchang in "*Xianfa xuezhe ping 'Wuquanfa (caoan)' de weixian yu hexian zhizheng* [Constitutional scholars assess the debate over the constitutionality of the 'Property Rights Law (Draft)']," *Faxue* [*Legal studies*], no. 3 (2006): 2–41.

109. See "Final Declaration of the regional meeting for Asia of the World Conference on Human Rights," Bangkok Declaration, Article 8, *Human Rights Law Journal* 14 (1993): 370.

110. See "Text of Human Rights White Paper," *FBIS Daily Report: China* (supplement), November 21, 1991.

111. See "Interview with Zhu Muzhi, Director of the State Council Information Office," *Xinhua,* November 2, 1991; *FBIS Daily Report: China,* November 4, 1991, 15–16, 16.

112. See "The Progress of Human Rights in China," Xinhua Domestic Service, December 27, 1995, *FBIS Daily Report: China,* December 28, 1996, 8–26; See "Quarterly Chronicle and Documentation (April–June 1997)," *The China Quarterly* 151 (September 1997): 698.

113. State Council Information Office, "White Paper: Fifty Years of Progress in China's Human Rights" (2000). The 2000 White Paper noted that China's conditions require "putting the rights to subsistence and development in the first place under conditions of reform, development and stability."

114. State Council Information Office, "China's Progress in Human Rights in 2004" (April 2005).

115. State Council Information Office, "China's Efforts and Achievements in Promoting the Rule of Law," (February 28, 2008): 11, 31.

116. Ching-Ching Ni, "Wave of Social Unrest Continues Across China," *Los Angeles Times*, Aug. 10, 2006; Richard McGregor, "Data show social unrest on the rise in China," *Financial Times*, Jan. 29, 2006.

117. See e.g., Esther Pan, "China's Angry Peasants," *Council on Foreign Relations Backgrounder*, December 15, 2005, http://www.cfr.org/publication/9425/.

118. Neil J. Diamant, Stanley B. Lubman, and Kevin J. O'Brien, *Engaging the Law in China: State, Society, and Possibilities for Justice* (Stanford: Stanford University Press, 2005).

119. John Pomfret, "Chinese Fight a New Kind of Land War," *Washington Post*, September 13, 2003, http://www.washingtonpost.com/ac2/wp-dyn/articles/A6761-2003-Sep13.html.

120. Pitman B. Potter, "Riding the Tiger—Legitimacy and Legal Culture in Post-Mao China," *The China Quarterly* no. 137 (1994): 325–358.

121. Law of the PRC on Lawyers and Legal Representation, October 2007, http://www.chinanews.com.cn/gn/news/2007/10-28/1061502.shtml. Also see Human Rights Watch, "China: Curbs on Lawyers Could Intensify Social Unrest—New Regulations Cast Doubt on Legal Reforms," (December 12, 2006); Human Rights Watch, "'Walking on Thin Ice': Control, intimidation, and harassment of lawyers in China," (April 2008).

122. Pitman B. Potter, "Selective Adaptation and Institutional Capacity: Perspectives on Human Rights in China," *International Journal* 61, no. 2 (2006): 21–37.

123. P. Healey, "Building institutional capacity through collaborative approaches to urban planning," *Environment and Planning* no. 30 (1998): 1531–1546; Lisa L. Martin and Beth A. Simmons, "Theories and Empirical Studies of International Institutions," *International Organization* 52 (1998): 729–757; Ernesto F. Betancourt, "A New Approach to Developing Institutional Structure," *Studies in Comparative International Development* 32 (1997): 3–29; J. A. Desveaux, *Designing Bureaucracies: Institutional Capacity and Large-Scale Problem Solving* (Cambridge: Cambridge University Press, 1995).

124. James S. Wunsch, "Institutional Analysis and Decentralization: Developing an Analytical Model for Effective Third World Administrative Reform," in *Polycentric Governance and Development: Readings from the Workshop in Political Theory and Policy Analysis*, ed. Michael D. McGinnis (Ann Arbor: University of Michigan Press, 1999).

125. S. Dougherty and R. McGuckin, "Federalism and the Impetus for Reform in China," *China Law and Practice* 15, no. 4 (2002): 36–53; S. Dougherty, R. McGuckin, and J. Radzin, "How Federalism—Not Just Privatization—Is Driving China's Economy," *Zhongguo jingji pinglun* [*China economic forum*] 1, no. 2 (2002): 7–19.

126. Pitman B. Potter, "China and the International Legal System: Challenges of Participation," *The China Quarterly*, no. 191 (2007): 340–365.

127. See notes 65–67 and accompanying text. Also see Huang Rutong, "*Shi fou yiding yao ba 'Siying caichan shensheng bu ke qinfan' xiejin woguo xianfa* [Do we really want to write 'the sanctity of private property is inviolable' into our constitution]," *Dangdai faxue* [*Contemporary legal studies*], no. 4 (1998): 5–7; "*Xianfa xuezhe ping 'Wuquanfa (caoan)' de weixian yu hexian zhizheng* [Constitutional scholars assess the debate over the constitutionality of the 'Property Rights Law (Draft)']," *Faxue* [*Legal studies*], no. 3 (2006): 2–41.

128. Wang Zhaoguo, "Explanation on Draft Property Law" (Delivered at the Fifth Session of the Tenth National People's Congress), March 8, 2007, http://English.people.com.cn/200703/08/print20070308_355491.html.

129. "China vows to deepen rural reform in 2008," *Xinhuanet*, January 31, 2008, http://news.xinhuanet.com/english/2008-01/31/content_7532861.htm.

130. See, generally, Joe Fewsmith, "Tackling the Land Issue – Carefully," *China Leadership Monitor*, no. 27 (Winter 2009): 1–8, http://www.hoover.org/publications/clm/issues/

37361849.html; Edward Wong, "China May Let Peasants Sell Rights to Farmland," *New York Times*, October 10, 2008; Edward Wong, "Hints of Discord on Land Reform in China," *New York Times*, October 16, 2008, www.nytimes.com/2008/10/16/world/asia/16china.html; Mark Magnier, "China land reform disappears from radar," *Los Angeles Times*, October 15, 2008, http://latimes.com/news/nationworld/world/la-fg-land15-2008Oct15 ,0,362260.story.

131. See "*Zonggong zhongyang guanyu tuijin nongcun fazhan ruogan zhongda wenti de jueding* [Decision on Major Issues Concerning the Advancement of Rural Reform and Development]," *Xinhua*, October 19, 2008; "CPC Closes major meeting with decision on rural reform, development" *People's Daily* (English), October 13, 2008, http://english.peopledaily.com.cn/90001/90776/90785/6513620.html; "Chronology of the CPC's decision on rural reform, *People's Daily* (English), October 20, 2008, http://english.people.com.cn/90001/90776/90785/6518136.html.

132. "*Tudi zhidu gaige bianchu guanjian yibu* [Land system reform takes a key step]," *Caijing* [*Finance*], October 20, 2008.

133. "*Jingti tudi liuzhuan zhong de bu liang xianxiang* [Beware of bad trends in land transfers]," *Banyuetan* [*China Comment*], October 28, 2008, http://news.xinhuanet.com/legal/2008-10/28/content_10264151.htm.

134. "China extends rural reform and development in new Party document," *People's Daily* (English), October 20, 2008, http://english.peopledaily.com.cn/900001/90776/90785/6517482.html.

135. Sim Chi Yin, "China to double rural income by 2020," *Straits Times*, October 13, 2008.

136. See e.g., comments from CASS research fellow Li Chenggui in "China extends rural reform and development in new Party document," *People's Daily* (English), October 20, 2008, http://english.peopledaily.com.cn/90001/90776/90785/6517482.html.

137. "Jingti tudi liuzhuan zhong de bu liang xianxiang [Beware of bad trends in land transfers]," *Banyuetan*, October 28, 2008, http://news.xinhuanet.com/legal/2008-10/28/content_10264151.htm.

138. Mark Magnier, "China land reform disappears from radar," *Los Angeles Times*, October 15, 2008, http://latimes.com/news/nationworld/world/la-fg-land15-2008Oct15,0,362260.story.

139. See e.g., Penelope Simons, "Binding the Hand that Feeds Them: Sovereignty, the Agreement on Agriculture, Transnational Corporations, and the Right to Adequate Food in Developing Countries," in *Redefining Sovereignty in International Economic Law,* ed. W. Shan, P. Simons, and D. Singh (Oxford: Hart Publishing, 2008).

140. Thomas Gold, Doug Guthrie, and David Wank, eds., *Social Connections in China* (Cambridge: Cambridge University Press, 2002).

141. Ni Guoliang, *Zhongguo xibei diqu xiandaihua zhong de jingji yu wenhua guanxi* [*Relations between economy and culture in the course of modernization in China's northwest*] (Lanzhou: Gansu People's Press, 1998).

142. For early examples, see Jean C. Oi and Andrew G. Walder, *Property Rights and Economic Reform in China* (Stanford: Stanford University Press, 1999).

143. Bao Tong, "Of Kings and Bandits"; Bao Tong, "China Has Come Full Circle."

144. See e.g., Zang Zhifeng, "*Woguo gongyouzhi yu fei gongyouzhi jingji xiangtongyi de genju* [The foundation for economic integration of our public and non-public ownerships systems]," *Xuexi shibao* [*Study times*] (April 26, 2004): 3; Chi Fulin, "*Yi ren wei ben wanshan shehui zhuyi shichang jingji tizhi* [Humanism: Perfect the socialist market economic system]," *Xuexi shibao* [*Study times*] (September 22, 2003): 4.

145. See e.g., Willy Lam, "CCP Campaign for a New Generation of 'Red and Expert' Officials," *China Brief* 9, no. 13 (June 23, 2009), http://www.jamestown.org/programs/chinabrief/single/?tx_ttnews[tt_news]=35170&tx_ttnews[backPid]=25&cHash=a0aad095c4.

146. Zhu Suli, *Song fa xia xiang* [*Taking law down to the villages*] (Beijing: Chinese University of Politics and Law Press, 2000).

147. Xie Ping and Lu Lei, *Zhongguo jinrong fubai de jingjixue fenxi* [*Economic analysis of financial corruption in China*] (Beijing: CITIC Publishing House, 2005).

148. Breffini O'Rourke, "China: Rural Discontent Spotlights Those Left Behind," *Radio Free Europe* (February 1, 2006).

Part III

Tricontinental Perspectives

Chapter 10

Primitive Accumulation and the Peasantry in the Present Era of Neoliberalism with Reference to the Indian Experience

Utsa Patnaik

The proposition that the advanced country constitutes for the developing one a mirror of its own future is not true as regards the fate of the peasantry. The Third World peasantry will not disappear but will resist successfully the current attacks on it. In today's advanced countries, petty production virtually did disappear as agricultural relations were capitalistically transformed in the course of the eighteenth- and nineteenth-century "agricultural revolution" preceding and accompanying industrialization. One can question whether the term "revolution" can be applied at all given that capitalist agrarian transformation was accompanied by increasing import dependence for vital primary products. A striking fact of history is the endemic inability of large-scale capitalist agriculture to meet to an adequate extent the needs of expanding industry for wage-goods, raw materials, and energy, hence an endemic inability to maintain Northern living standards without some form of forced or induced trade, both in the past and at present. Today's advanced countries historically relied heavily for wage goods and raw materials on primary imports from colonially subjugated areas, where slave-based and indentured-labor-based plantation systems were developed to export to Europe the tropical crops that it could never produce. In the Indian case, there was heavy taxation of peasants and direct use of taxes to purchase export goods. These primary imports into Europe, vital for its industrial growth and for diversifying consumption, were the commodity equivalent of taxes and rents wrung from subjugated Third World populations and so represented unilateral transfers, not normal trade. The export of capital from Europe to develop North America and other areas of recent European migrant settlement was also crucially dependent on the balance of payment flexibility imparted by the control over exchange earnings of the colonies. Further, capitalist industrialization inevitably implied rising domestic unemployment as technical change rapidly displaced labor, but because large-scale out-migration took place from industrializing Europe to regions of recent settlement, economic crisis and political tensions at the core of capitalism were defused. Today's advanced countries exported their unemployment in the past not only through out-migration but also through the export of goods to colonially subjugated markets, inducing deindustrialization in them. I have argued elsewhere that Ricardo's theory—that mutual benefit for both trading countries necessarily arises from specialization and trade—contains a fatal logical error and represents an intellectual rationalization of an international division of labor that was not voluntarily entered into by today's Third World countries.[1]

The historical conditions under which today's advanced countries industrialized are so specific and indeed unique, that Third World countries cannot possibly replicate them. The unemployment situation these nations face is worse today owing to the ever-falling labor intensity of production, which implies not only jobless growth but also job loss growth in the most advanced manufacturing sectors. Unemployment is endemic to capitalist production driven by technical change in today's developing countries, but millions of peasants today have nowhere to migrate to and little possibility of absorption into the secondary sector. Large labor-surplus developing economies like India and China, in particular, do not have the choice of seizing entire continents from indigenous inhabitants to export their population increment abroad or of financing their capital formation through transfers from other nations without impacting their own domestic mass consumption. They have to solve their unemployment and livelihood problems primarily through expansion of their own internal market in forms that represent a drastic modification of the classical capitalist paradigm. The unemployment problems of developing nations cannot be solved through standard forms of industrialization, which destroy small-scale production, because in a trade open world, competitiveness demands highly capital-intensive technology with very low or zero elasticity of employment with respect to output.[2]

The old primitive accumulation of capital concerned seizure of primary resources, including energy resources, from today's Third World countries and the lone temperate colony, Ireland. A new phase of primitive accumulation of capital is visible today with a renewed thrust from advanced nation corporations to access tropical lands through contract systems formally subsuming the peasantry under capital, or through outright land acquisition. This thrust complements the struggle to control world energy resources. From exclusive reliance on fossil fuels, capital is turning once more to the land to fill energy supply deficits. All this necessarily entails an attack on both the food security and asset possession of petty producers, and it generates bitter resistance from them. This paper briefly documents the developments in India under neoliberal reforms and argues at the end that the peasantry is resisting the attacks on it, with responses that are beginning to turn from passive forms of resistance like suicides to active forms like opposition to acquisition of their land by the government and corporations. These forms have the potential of undermining the political stability of Third World countries. Therefore, democratic governments will be obliged to modify their present uninformed and unwise pursuit of a growth strategy that seeks to imitate today's advanced nations with no regard to the specificity of their own livelihood and unemployment problems. Alternative strategies that generate livelihoods and genuine development for the majority must necessarily incorporate the preservation of petty production but on the basis of cooperation permitting higher productivity.

THE EXPORT OF UNEMPLOYMENT UNDER CAPITALISM

The nature of capitalist growth has always been, and continues to be, such that it engenders unemployment daily, hourly, and on a mass scale. The objective of capitalist production is to maximize profits for capitalists, not to provide employment to the existing unemployed or the underemployed, nor are capitalists or the state they control usually concerned with ensuring minimum livelihoods for the laboring poor. Two major features as regards employment marked classical industrialization in Britain, France, and other countries in Europe in the eighteenth and nineteenth centuries. First, wages were kept to the minimum possible level by capitalists to maximize profits, taking recourse to the extensive exploitation of labor through raising absolute surplus value, namely, the lengthening of the working day for the same daily wage and the widespread use of the underpaid labor of women and children. The resulting raising of the rate of surplus value (the ratio of surplus labor to necessary labor), however, led to a contradiction. The restriction on mass labor earnings, in the very process of maximizing profits, meant that the internal market for capitalism could never grow rapidly enough to stave off the problem of inadequately expanding demand and maintain the economic incentives for accumulation, as long as the economy was considered to be a closed one. Although much theoretical attention was devoted to the problem, it did not exist in practice for the early industrializing countries, for the very inception of the capitalist mode of production was preceded and accompanied by a high degree of exploitative trade integration arising from conquest and forcible subjugation of other societies that were made to serve both as providers of resources and as markets.

Second, from its inception, capitalist industrialization was marked by labor-displacing mechanization, perhaps because the main industries involved were import-substituting industries (imported cotton textiles and bar-iron for example). Textiles in Europe could not compete with the much cheaper imported handicraft textiles of Asian artisans as long as mechanization did not reduce unit labor costs of yarn and cloth, nor could iron ores be extracted and reduced profitably until innovations were applied. Once introduced, however, innovations spread and affected not only import-substituting goods but also domestic employment in every traditional sphere. Extensive methods of labor exploitation gave way to intensive methods, in which there was a rise in relative surplus value through a dual route—reduction in necessary labor through decline in the cost of wage-goods, in which colonial exploitation played a major role, and rise in labor productivity through the substitution of dead labor (machinery) for living labor.[3] This latter route provided a means of partially overcoming the contradiction affecting accumulation, by absorbing more investment in the form of capital-intensification. However, with mechanization inevitably came labor displacement at a faster rate than the increase in labor demand arising from expansion of the domestically absorbed part of total output, giving rise to social discontent and to Luddite movements for breaking machinery.

Such unemployment has been often labeled "frictional" unemployment, as though it is always a short-run problem, which ignores the fact that had today's advanced economies been closed economies, the unemployment owing to mechanization would have reached abnormally high proportions not commensurate with the concept of a reserve army of labor, and created social tensions not manageable within the capitalist system. In Britain, for example, despite the highest rate of manufacturing growth seen in its history, as well as rapidly growing exports in the early period of industrialization, by the 1840s, the discontent and social tensions owing to rising unemployment and bad conditions of work and life of the laboring poor combined with rapidly increasing income inequality had reached such a pitch that the fledgling working class movement under the banner of Chartism was ready for a general insurrection, and the ruling classes were in fear of revolution. The insurrections of the 1840s in Britain, France, and other countries in Europe were militarily suppressed, but the social instability of the capitalist system had been exposed within a mere six decades of the inception of industrialization. The early industrializers overcame the problem of growing unemployment inherent in their capitalist growth and technical change simply by exporting their unemployment abroad, an option which is not open in any serious way to today's large labor-surplus economies like India and China. The export of unemployment (a phrase first used by J. M. Keynes) took place through colonization and imperialism and appeared in multifarious forms. The most direct form of export of unemployment was the physical migration of population. The precondition for this was the seizure of enormous tracts of land by western Europeans from indigenous peoples in the Americas, South Africa, and Australia and those lands' permanent occupation by the in-migrants. "Land" in this context means not just land with the capacity for producing crops but includes all the natural fauna, rich water, timber, and mineral resources of these occupied regions. In Britain, nearly 2 percent of the domestic labor force every year was migrating for permanent settlement abroad by the mid-nineteenth century, while the nation got rid of large numbers of criminals and members of the potentially riotous underclass by transporting them to Australia.

Second, unemployment was exported by industrializing countries like Britain by flooding the subjugated colonies with its cotton textiles and other manufactured goods under discriminating commercial policy that kept these markets compulsorily completely open to imports, while the metropolitan market was protected from their handicraft manufactures for nearly 150 years. Export of unemployment by this route meant import of unemployment by the colonized artisans. While employment and wages rose in the industrializing country with output expanding at about double the rate of domestic absorptive capacity, the other side of the coin was that, in the colonies, manufactures employment went down sharply resulting in deindustrialization. The process was a prolonged one in vast countries like India and China, since the limitations of early transport protected the poorly connected hinterland that was penetrated by imports only after the railways became important.

Third, unemployment was exported by the leading imperialist country through a more complex route in which areas of recent white settlement, including North America, were developed through capital exports, the bulk of which the tropical colonies were made to finance. The then-leading imperialist power, Britain, did so through the systematic annual appropriation of the foreign exchange (forex) earnings from rising export surplus of its many colonies—the largest being India—to the rest of the world. These forex earnings, mainly from exports of primary goods and simple manufactures, became very substantial during the quarter century before World War I (WWI) and were used to meet the deficits on the balance of payments of the metropolis, allowing it not only to export capital and earn dividends but pari passu increase its capital goods exports. Britain, the world capitalist leader, not only shored up incomes in the European continent, the United States, and regions of white settlement (Argentina, Brazil, and South Africa) by running continuous current account deficits vis-à-vis them but also developed them rapidly by exporting capital, thus incurring ever increasing balance of payments deficits with these regions. Sustaining this system under the prevalent regime of fixed exchange rates (the gold standard) without itself suffering gold outflow, was only possible through its appropriation of the vast export surplus earnings of India and other colonies from these very same regions to offset its own deficits as Saul has shown in his *Studies in British Overseas Trade*.[4] By 1910, India alone was obliged to provide 60 million pounds sterling in its exchange earnings from these areas, all appropriated by Britain.[5]

In the colonies, the peasants and artisans producing rising exports were paid in local currency, out of tax revenues they themselves had paid in to the state. Therefore, no new purchasing power was injected; rather, their rising export surplus became the commodity equivalent of rising taxes extracted from them. The strong deflationary impact of the mechanism (which involved one-quarter to one-third budgetary surpluses in India) led to higher net unemployment in the economy. Export-led growth of unemployment was the result. The Great Depression that started with the agricultural depression from the mid-1920s was the coup de grace and pauperized large segments of the peasantry in India—the percentage of rural labor force dependent on wage-paid work leapt from 26 to 38 percent comparing the 1921 and 1931 censuses. China fared even worse with not only deep agricultural depression but also foreign invasion, both civil war and anti-Japanese war, the latter entailing the loss of 6 million lives.[6]

It might be argued that today's developing countries are getting their own back in the current era because their cheap labor leads to relocation of labor-intensive segments of metropolitan industry, whose products are exported back to advanced countries. Deindustrialization in the advanced countries is the result. However, this process is not symmetrical to the previous one. Certainly, some local employment is generated, but since production is in the hands of the advanced country corporations, they benefit by maintaining high rates of surplus value and mainly repatriate profits. They pressurize governments to set up special economic zones where domestic labor laws are relaxed to enable them to raise the rate of surplus value via draconian terms of contract for local labor and reduced standards of work safety and pollution control. The other beneficiaries are advanced country consumers enjoying cheapening imported consumer goods from developing countries.

Further, ultimately the resulting import surplus and current account deficit of rich advanced countries especially of the world capitalist leader, the United States, paradoxically continue to be substantially financed through the rapid reserves build-up and lending to them by poor developing countries—China and India, among others—and involve transfer in a new form, with the latter lending (in the form of purchase of U.S. government securities) at a much lower rate than the rate at which they borrow from the world. About 2.5 to 3 percent of India's GDP is the estimated cost to the Indian economy of such borrowing short and lending long, which effectively is a transfer to advanced countries. Such transfer is increasing owing to the recent spurt in debt-creating capital inflows into India, far in excess of what is justified by the small deficit on India's current account, leading to a sudden increase in the rate of buildup of reserves, which reached well over US$300 billion by mid-2008, second only to the mountainous Chinese reserves. As domestic rural hunger and poverty rise, poor countries help to finance the import-dependent consumption boom of the United States.

THE FAILURE OF CAPITALIST AGRICULTURAL TRANSFORMATION TO MEET THE WAGE GOODS AND RAW MATERIALS REQUIREMENTS OF INDUSTRIALIZATION

As B. H. Slicher van Bath[7] has documented, in the late feudal period, the population of today's advanced countries had a very limited and monotonous diet, and cotton clothing was not available for mass wear. Very low agricultural productivity in Europe compared to Asia arose from a multiplicity of factors—a single growing season in their cold temperate lands compared to year-round cropping in tropical Asia, high seed-yield ratio ranging from 0.25 to 0.33 compared to 0.10 in Asia, and the vicious cycle of an intense human food–livestock feed competition in Europe entailing the inability to carry livestock through the barren winter, reducing, in turn, the availability of manures and thus keeping yields low. The consumption basket of European populations improved and diversified dramatically only after colonial expansion and forcible acquisition of access to tropical lands with their relatively higher productivity and highly diverse output vector. Even to this day, the United States, which has three times India's cultivated area and practices capital-intensive agriculture as a business, ends up producing a smaller volume of agricultural output than India. The near-complete elimination of seasonality, however, is a modern phenomenon: advanced country supermarkets carry the entire range of temperate and tropical products year-round as the giant food transnational companies have been integrating poor peasant farmers in more and more developing countries through contract systems into a global food chain serving advanced countries.

Trade in primary products is an absolute imperative for advanced country populations that rely heavily on imports from warmer lands to provide the physical elements of their high living standards entailing highly diversified consumption baskets far beyond the capacity of local agriculture to supply. It is surely of little use to be a millionaire in Canada if one can never drink coffee, wear cotton clothes, use a teak or mahogany escritoire, or buy flowers in winter. Such trade is far from essential, however, for the majority of developing countries, which can meet all their primary sector requirements from their own lands. Some of these countries that are food-import dependent have been brought to that position only owing to the incessant demands on their best lands to grow export crops.

Economic theory has ignored the heterogeneity of primary resources and productive capacities available to different societies. It has ignored the fact that tropical countries produce a large range of primary products that can never be produced under field conditions in cold temperate advanced countries. Rather, it has said that benefit from free trade always follows from product specialization, according to the principle of comparative cost, and exchange through trade—which is assumed to be voluntarily entered into by both trading partners. To this day, the Ricardian theory of comparative advantage is invoked in northern universities and the WTO to urge developing countries to open their economies to freer trade and investment, promising them large gains from doing so. However, there is a logical fallacy at the heart of Ricardo's theory with its two-country, two-goods model. The conclusion of mutual benefit from trade depends crucially on his assumption that "both countries produce both goods" in the pretrade situation for only then can the cost of production of the goods, and hence relative cost in each country, at all be defined and compared.

But the assumption "both countries produce both goods" is materially untrue. Say Canada imports coffee from Brazil and exports machinery to it. Since Canada cannot grow coffee, the production cost of coffee in Canada is fictitious; it cannot be defined at all, and hence, relative cost cannot be defined. Let us remember that relative cost is the number of units of coffee that can be produced by withdrawing the labor required to produce one unit of machinery and putting it instead into coffee production. Relative cost has to be calculated for both countries in the pretrade situation and then compared to determine which country has the comparative cost advantage, that is, produces more coffee from the labor transferred from producing a unit less of machinery. Since cost information does not exist for the cold country unable to produce the tropical good, the trade cannot be explained in terms of comparative advantage.

Similarly, Indian economic historians have fallaciously argued that India ceased to export cotton cloth and exported raw cotton while importing its cloth from England, because the latter country's "comparative cost advantage" lay in cloth production and India's in raw cotton. Now, relative cost (the amount of cloth producible by transferring the labor going into producing one unit raw cotton to producing cloth instead) could certainly be defined for India that could produce both raw cotton and cotton cloth. But England, with its cold climate, could not produce raw cotton. The "production cost of a unit of raw cotton" is fictitious; it could not be defined for England, so nor could the relative cost (the amount of cloth producible by transferring the labor going into producing one unit raw cotton to producing cloth instead). The precise type of material fallacy involved in Ricardo's theory is the "converse fallacy of accident" in which a highly specific assumption is made (both countries produce both goods), and from this, a general conclusion of mutual benefit from trade is improperly drawn and applied to all cases, including those where the assumption itself is not satisfied. Ricardo's fallacy is a variant of Aristotle's *A dicto simpliciter ad dictum secundum quid*,[8] and the reader who may be interested is referred to my more detailed discussion available elsewhere.[9]

The entire argument of necessary mutual benefit from specialization and trade is logically incorrect and an exercise in apologetics, an intellectual rationalization of and justification for what actually happened in history. We know that the history of capitalist accumulation starting from its western European centers proceeded in a far less idyllic fashion than is portrayed by the theory of voluntary trade for mutual benefit: it saw the forcible colonial subjugation by a handful of western European nations of the peoples mainly of tropical and subtropical regions; it saw the promotion of slavery and indentured labor for running vast plantation systems producing tropical consumption goods and raw materials to satisfy the requirements of these European industrializing societies. Where slavery did not exist, as in India, the population was taxed heavily, a large part of the tax revenues being used to purchase from the peasant taxpayers primary products for export. The direct link established between the fiscal system and the trade system (taxes paid by peasants being converted to export goods produced by the same peasants) marks the specificity of the exploitative metropolis-colony relationship. *The export goods became the commodity equivalent of taxes*; their export represented transfer, not normal trade. When these export goods reached the metropolis for direct use as wage goods and raw materials or were reexported to earn foreign exchange, the original colonized producers were not required to be paid anything since they had already been "paid" in their own country out of their own tax contributions. Such costless access to these valuable tropical goods, or *transfers*, substantially aided the first industrialization in Britain and that country's rise to dominance as an imperial power. An estimate of transfers from Asia and the West Indies relative to Britain's GDP during the Industrial Revolution has been attempted by this author.[10] The entire imperialist global system of trade and capital flows depended crucially on forced specialization in primary product exports by subjugated populations.

Why was such forcible subjugation and trade at all necessary for capitalist accumulation? Why did today's formerly colonized developing countries not enter voluntarily into specialization in primary products and their export in exchange for manufactured goods, if indeed it was of great mutual benefit as the standard Ricardian theory argued? The answer lies in the fact that specialization and trade cannot be of mutual benefit and were not of mutual benefit where primary production was concerned. The major adverse impact of specialization is on food production and availability in the tropical country, lowering the level of nutrition and in extreme cases resulting in famine.

INVERSE RELATION BETWEEN PRIMARY EXPORTS AND DOMESTIC FOOD OUTPUT AND AVAILABILITY

There is ample evidence, some of which I have discussed and summarized elsewhere, that both under colonial systems and in modern times, as primary exports from developing countries grow over time always, there is a fall in domestic food grains output and availability and hence declining nutritional standards for the population—no exceptions are to be seen. *In short, there is an inverse relation between agricultural exports and maintaining domestic food security.*[11] In British India during the half century before independence food grains output virtually stagnated while exported commercial crops grew ten times faster (the respective annual compound rates being 0.11 percent and 1.31 percent) while per capita food grains availability declined about 29 percent in the interwar period.[12] In Java, under the Netherlands, the main export crops of sugarcane and rubber boomed, while per capita rice production declined by one-fifth over the same period. Colonized Korea was made to export 60 percent of its rice to Japan by the late 1930s, and the calorie intake of its own population fell substantially. Colonized Ireland experienced the inverse relation with a vengeance, resulting in a massive famine.

In Mexico during the two decades after the late 1960s, the share of total grain output going as animal feed to meet burgeoning export demand for meat went up from 5 to 30, while the output per capita of the food staples of the ordinary people, maize and beans, declined. The six largest countries in sub-Saharan Africa, accounting for three-fifths of the region's population, saw a one-third decline in per capita cereals output over the decade 1980 to 1990 when their primary exports were growing fast, and the decline has continued at a slower rate since then.[13]

An obvious proposition bears repetition, for it is never theoretically recognized by economists. Agricultural land is a resource that is not produced by human labor (though its productivity can be improved by investment), and once the technological limits to productivity within a given social production system are reached, it becomes conceptually on par with nonrenewable energy resources. *There is a struggle by advanced capitalist countries for control over the productive capacity of limited tropical land resources all over the world, just as there is a struggle for control over fossil energy resources. Moreover, energy resources are, once more, sought to be produced from crops.* After a century and a half of reliance on fossil fuels and with spiraling oil prices as the imperialist United States fails to "pacify" Iraq, the matter is again coming full circle, back to the land. Agriculture is under-renewed and there is strong pressure today to grow biofuels and devote a rising part of grain and sugarcane output to conversion to ethanol. A rising fraction of food grains is again being used as fuel. This development is a recent, very serious addition to the threat to food security in developing countries already posed by growing external demands by advanced countries for procuring traditional and new export crops from limited tropical lands. The more advanced societies demand the use of the productive and biodiverse tropical lands of developing countries to underpin their rising living standards and energy needs, the less land is available for meeting the essential requirements of local poor populations.

The entire matter becomes a zero-sum game. Increasing areas of food grains growing land are diverted to export crops, and over time, a rising share of the food grains is used as animal feed and biofuel, which are mainly consumed by the rich or exported. Even where absolute food grains output does not decline or continues to rise, since it rises slower than the population is rising and its end uses change from direct consumption to animal feed, industrial consumption, and biofuels, we find that there is decline in the domestic availability of food grains for direct consumption, per head of population ("availability" is defined as output minus both net exports and net addition to public stocks). In extreme cases, this can become a steep absolute decline in domestic availability. All this leads to declining nutritional standards of the poor in the country engaging in this type of specialization and increases in mass hunger, since food grains alone account for seven-tenths or more of the energy intake of the poor. Any type of shock to the system (e.g., severe drought, rapid food price rise) can precipitate visible famine. Even without this extreme outcome, declining nutrition levels are bad enough. Such "hidden famishment" is the price that poor developing country populations are made to pay as the cost of free trade, but it is a cost that is neither recognized nor addressed by their own governments, which pretend that poverty is declining and continue to follow the same policies increasing mass hunger and malnutrition. Today, international organizations talk of the problems of child and maternal malnutrition, but the fact of increasing undernutrition within the general population as a whole in India, including at least 250 million men, is never recognized or mentioned. This strange reverse gender bias is to be seen in the writings of even progressive Indian academics taking their cue from the discourse of the international organizations.

To summarize, given the nature of tropical land as a limited resource that cannot be augmented by human labor as regards its extent, and whose supply is thus virtually fixed, external demands lead to a decline in domestic food production for local populations to accommodate rising exports. The economic mechanisms urged by developed countries, through which this is brought about, include trade openness, specialization in export crops, reduction of government's intervention to maintain domestic food security systems, and, most important, macroeconomic deflation hitting the mass of the population even as incomes for a minority rise fast. These issues are discussed briefly in the following sections in the context of India's experience under neoliberal economic reforms.

RISE IN UNEMPLOYMENT AND POVERTY UNDER NEOLIBERAL REFORMS

India is widely projected abroad as a shining success story of economic reforms, an important "emerging market" for northern goods and services, and an attractive destination for investment, all this in view of the high annual GDP growth rate, which has been averaging 6 to 7 percent, second only to China. This portrayal of a dynamic economy is indeed partially true, and it carries benefits for a small well-to-do minority, but it is entirely misleading as regards the welfare implications for the majority of the population. A high growth rate by itself conveys no information at all either about the composition of this growth or its income distribution effects.

Agriculture and industry, the material productive sectors supporting together over four-fifths of the population, have gone into stagnation or decline as regards contribution to GDP and to employment. There has been a severe depression in agriculture in particular for over a decade, marked by falling per-head real incomes. Unemployment rates in both rural and urban India have been rising, and average food grains absorption within the country has declined to a historic low comparable to the colonial period, with the brunt of the increased hunger being borne by rural

India. For a decade now, there has been unprecedented agrarian distress manifesting itself in rising farm indebtedness, loss of assets including land, and many thousands of farmer suicides in excess of normal numbers. Official figures and claims of decline in rural poverty, figures that are reproduced in World Bank publications, are misleading because they are based on a logically incorrect method of poverty estimation. Correct estimates show poverty to be high with an increase in the depth of poverty during the period of economic reforms.

An observer of Indian society and economy today would not be able to avoid a sense of deep unease as dualism becomes more blatant: on the one hand, there is a visible real estate and share market boom; on the other hand, many thousands of farmers in excess of "normal" numbers are committing suicide.[14] On the one hand is fast burgeoning consumption by the urban middle classes, more varied high-protein diets, and modern consumer durables and electronic goods. On the other hand, food grains absorption in rural India is today lower than before WWII, and the depth of hunger is growing with declining energy intake for the majority of the population in villages and more recently in towns as well.

The one sector of the economy that has been expanding rapidly is the services sector, which now contributes over half of the gross national product (see Figure 10.1). A small segment is high-income information-technology-enabled and financial services, but the bulk remains low-income personal and catering services for the benefit of the small minority of rich Indians, a minority that has enjoyed rapid rise in real incomes under reforms. There is rising income inequality of a very specific and disturbing kind:

Figure 10.1 Contribution of economic sectors to GDP, 1982–83 to 2006–07 (%)

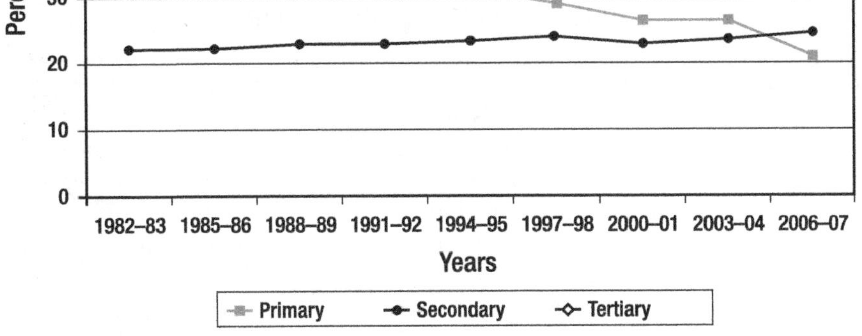

Source: Chart updated from Patnaik 2007.

an absolute decline of real income for the vast majority of the population and very rapid rise in real incomes for a small minority. This has fed the real estate and tourism boom and fast-growing demand for high-end consumer durables and electronic goods by this minority seeking to emulate northern lifestyles. On the other hand, for the majority of the population, it has meant higher unemployment, indebtedness, land and other asset loss, and hunger—in short, growing immiserization.

The rapid changes in its economy and society are the direct outcome of adopting neoliberal economic policies and trade liberalization. India started implementing reforms and seriously opening up to free trade from 1991, after taking an Extended Financing Facility from the IMF of US$5 billion following the temporary difficulties created by the first Gulf War. The sum borrowed was small and soon repaid, but it was the entry point for the international financial institutions' agenda pushing for a complete reversal of the strategy followed up to that date of Nehruvian dirigiste strategy of development, in which the state had been a major investor, banking had been nationalized, and public sector enterprises had been set up in a range of industries.

The basic questions are, why should rapid growth under neoliberal reforms and trade liberalization, advised by the Bretton Woods Institutions (BWI) and under the WTO discipline, be accompanied by agricultural depression and acute distress in particular regions, and why should there be an adverse impact on food security and poverty? The answer can be summarized as follows: The core of neoliberal reforms advised by the international financial institutions is expenditure-deflating policies that are applied in the main to the population in the unorganized sector, the peasantry. These macroeconomic deflationary policies lead to rising unemployment and falling incomes. Second, the peasantry is exposed to global demand patterns with trade openness, and the structure of land use starts to change away from crops mainly entering into consumption of the local poor and toward greater exports for supplying the consumption needs of foreign populations. At the same time, trade openness also means that the peasantry is exposed to the volatility of global prices, which, in their downward phase, ruin small producers exporting cash crops.[15]

DECLINING FOOD GRAIN OUTPUT AND AVAILABILITY UNDER REFORMS

A severely adverse impact on food security, following adoption of greater trade openness in India, was to be expected on the basis of the past and current experience of present-day developing countries discussed earlier, and I have been warning of this outcome since 1992. That is, indeed, what has happened: 8 million hectares of land have been diverted away from food grains production mainly to export crops within a total gross sown area that is stagnant or somewhat declining, and the end use of grain is also changing with a higher share going to animal feed, industrial use, and biofuels. Yield rise having slowed down has not compensated for area decline, and the growth rate of food grains output halved in the 1990s compared to the 1980s and has declined further since 2000, falling well below the population growth rate (see Figure 10.2). Per capita grain output

Figure 10.2 Annual food grains output growth and population growth, 1980–81 to 2007–08

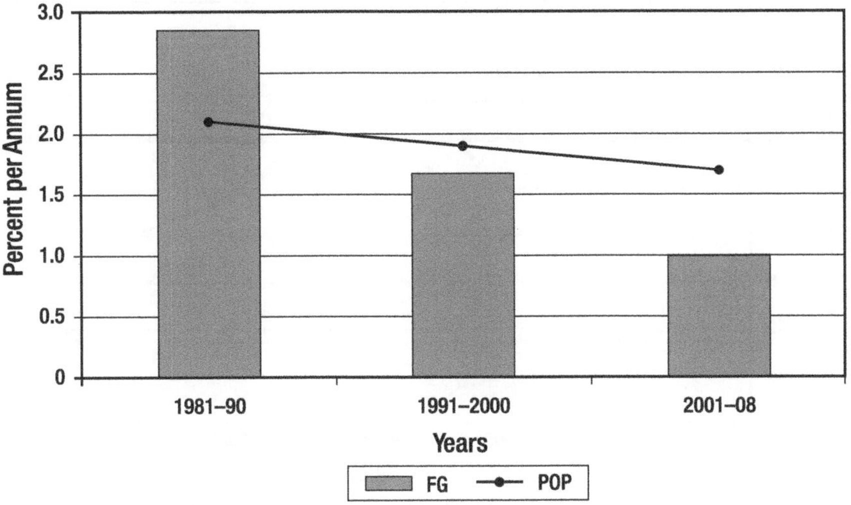

Source: Chart updated from Patnaik 2007.

has been declining more steeply than before and has touched a historic low of 155 kg per head annual average in the triennium ending 2004–2005 (see Figure 10.3). This output is the same level as fifty years ago during the First Plan and actually lower than the prewar average during 1937–1941, which was 157 kg.[16]

Availability fell even faster than did output between 1998 and 2002. The large gap between the two trends reflects the fact that, by July 2002, public food grains stocks of 64 million tonne had built up, 40 million tonne in excess of the normal buffer stock for that time of year. The reason was the severe contraction in purchasing power of the mass of the mainly rural population, discussed a little later. At the same time, private grain exports also rose. Unlike every previous short episode of per head domestic output decline, which had been always compensated by net imports and drawing down of public stocks to maintain domestic availability, this long period was highly abnormal in seeing the opposite—as per head output declined, more stocks built up and more was exported, reducing availability to a historic low. The majority of Indian economists as well as the Indian government ignored the real reason for the lower absorption that was loss of purchasing power and demand deflation and wrongly argued that the problem was "overproduction." It put the blame on allegedly "too high" minimum support price to farmers that allegedly gave "the wrong signals" leading to a higher output than the market demanded. Instead of putting purchasing power and food back into the hands of the poor, which the situation required, the government proceeded, instead, to export 22 million tonnes of grain out of stocks during 2002 and 2003 and to freeze procurement price and reduce public procurement, allowing

Figure 10.3 Food grains output and availability per capita in kilograms per annum, triennial average centered on specified years, 1990–91 to 2004–05, India

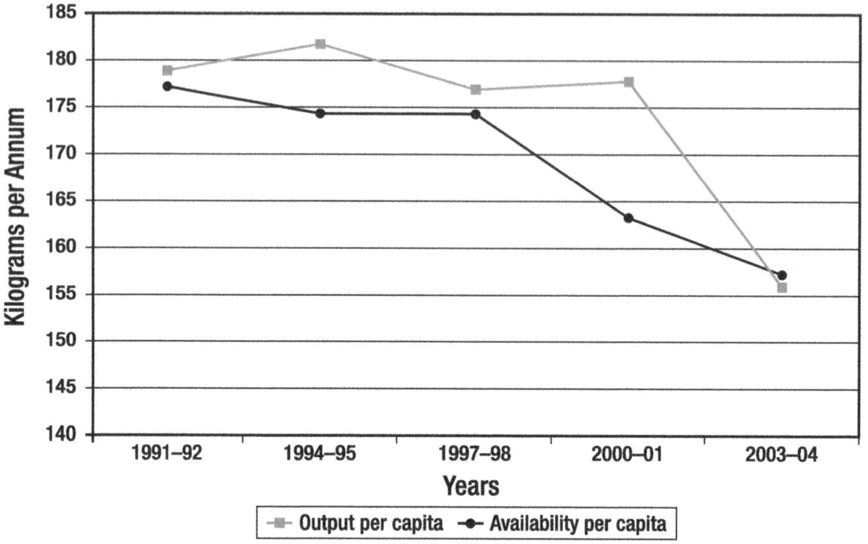

Source: Chart updated from Patnaik 2007.

transnational companies like Cargill to come in to purchase from the distressed farmers. After only two years of recovery, the same story of abnormal stock buildup combined with large private grain exports has been repeated during 2007 to 2010, as global food price inflation combined with recession has impacted mass demand adversely. By 2007, the per head grain demand in India had already declined below the average level of the least developed countries (see Table 10.1).

Farmers have been repeatedly urged to "diversify" output away from food grains to the horticultural and other products required by the global food corporations for supplying supermarkets in advanced countries. The entry of these corporate entities, both foreign for contract farming and domestic for supply retail outlets in cities, has been facilitated by state governments. The trend of falling grain output and availability per head, which I anticipated in 1992 and have been writing about since then, reached crisis proportions by 2001 with availability per head dropping to 151 kg, compared to 178 kg in the early nineties. This is what led me to title a public lecture delivered in early 2004 "The Republic of Hunger." I pointed out that the average Indian family was absorbing 115 kg less of food grains per annum by the three years ending 2002–2003 compared to a mere six years earlier, the triennium ending 1997–1998. I also pointed out that official poverty estimates were gross underestimates, because they took a food basket that was over thirty years old and that poverty measured by applying the official nutrition norm directly to the consumption data showed that 75 percent of the rural population did not reach the norm by 1993–1994 (see Table 10.2). By 2004–2005, this had risen to 87 percent, an all-time high.

Table 10.1 Per head direct, indirect, and total cereal supply/demand, India in the world economy, 2007

		QUANTITY (million tonne unless otherwise stated)						
Country/Region	*2 Production*	*3 Net Imports and Stock Changes*	*4 Total Supply*	*5 Food (DIRECT use)*	*6 Feed, Seed, Processing, Other (INDIRECT use)*	*7 Per head Direct Kg*	*8 Per Head Total, Kg*	*9 Percent of Indirect to Total*
INDIA	212.4	–9.5	202.9	177.7	25.2	152.6	174.2	12.4
LEAST DEVELOPED	125.9	14.5	140.4	105.5	34.9	136.9	182.1	24.9
AFRICA	130.8	58.1	188.9	138.7	50.2	144.1	196.4	26.1
CHINA	395.3	–8.9	386.4	203.8	182.6	152.5	289.1	47.3
EUROPEAN UNION	261	14	275	61.7	213.3	125.1	557.3	77.6
USA	412.2	–137.6	274.6	34.5	240.1	111.6	889.5	87.5
WORLD	2121.3	54.6	2066.7	966.2	1100.5	146.6	313.6	53.2

Source: Food and Agriculture Organization, *FAO Statistical Yearbook 2009*, Food Balance Sheet.

Table 10.2 Poverty estimate 1993–1994 and 2004–2005, all India rural

Direct Estimate				
Levels of calorie intake per day	*2,400*	*2,200*	*2,100*	*1,800*
Required monthly per capita expenditure in 2004–2005 to access nutrition levels, Rs	800	575	515	342
Percent of persons below specified nutrition level, 2004–2005	87.0	69.5	60.5	25.0
Percent of persons below specified nutrition level in 1993–1994	74.5	58.5	49.5	20.0
Official Estimate	***1993–1994***	***2004–2005***		
Official Poverty Line OPL (Monthly per capita expenditure, Rs.)	206	356		
Percent of persons below OPL	37.3	28.5		
Daily calorie intake at OPL	1,980	1,820		

Sources: Official estimates from Planning Commission. Direct estimates calculated by author from NSS, Report No. 513, *Nutritional Intake in India*, A-18, A-90. (U. Patnaik 2007)

However, both academics and the government seemed oblivious to the hard reality of a food and nutrition crisis that every data source revealed. In retrospect this "conceptual blindness" probably arose mainly because the inflation rate had reached a historic low and they inferred that, therefore, the poor were becoming better off. While the consumer price index for agricultural laborers, heavily weighted by food, rose by 60 percent between 1993–1994 and 1999–2000, it rose by only 11 percent in the next five years to 2004–2005. However, economists seemed to forget that the inflation rate can go down not only when supply increases faster than demand but also when demand falls faster than supply does, and it was this latter scenario that was operative. In Keynesian terms, it was a severe squeeze on aggregate effective demand and a fall in mass purchasing power, which was showing up as lower inflation despite the fall in output per head. The adjustment to lower per head supply was taking place through increasing hunger, which the government refused to recognize. Its wrong policies led to an even faster decline in output per head, and strong inflationary trends emerged in 2007.

Reality does not go away when policymakers bury their heads in the sand. The National Simple Survey (NSS) consumer expenditure data show that 58.5 percent of rural persons could not access even 2,200 calories (lower than the official rural energy norm) in 1993–1994, while the figure reached nearly 70 percent by 2004–2005. The percentage below the lowest level of 1,800 calories, the poorest of the poor, rose from 20 to 25 percent over the period. Official estimates are much lower because they do not apply the nutrition norm directly to the current data but update the cost of a thirty-one-year-old fixed consumption basket using a price index. This strange procedure is "convenient," for it cumulatively underestimates the poverty line—these poverty lines allow the consumer to access nutrition levels that are lower and lower over time—a fact not mentioned to the public. By 2005, the official poverty line (OPL) was less than Rs.12 per day (US 27 cents per day), so low that only one bottle of water could be purchased with it. Some academics estimated from the data that "extreme poverty" defined as those spending less than half the OPL, had become zero—positive sounding indeed, until an examination of the same data showed that there were no observations at such levels of spending. People ceased to exist before reaching these levels! For the reader who is interested in poverty measurement questions, my critique and alternative estimates are published in Patnaik 2007. China's rural poverty lines appear to be as unrealistically low as India's—800 yuan per annum, or 2.2 yuan per day, is equal to about Rs.12 at the current exchange rate.

Macroeconomic deflationary policies advised by the international financial institutions include reduction in state expenditures, monetary austerity and high real interest rates for producers (but easy consumer credit), reduction in the ratio of budget deficit to GDP, caps on wages aided by labor retrenchment policies, and currency devaluation. All these together add up to a strongly deflationary package that has been implemented by successive Indian central governments since 1991, regardless of their political composition. The pattern has been that three years or more of severe contraction immediately after a general election are followed by two years or less of more expansionary policies as governments try to regain electoral support eroded by the hardships they have inflicted on the people. The main target of the expenditure-deflating policies has been the unorganized sector, in particular agriculture. Public investment in agriculture was already declining in the 1980s, but the decline has become steeper since 1991. Plan development expenditures including on irrigation, vital for the primary sector, were nearly 4 percent of net national product in the pre-Reform period but halved to 1.9 percent by 2001 and continue to be far below the pre-Reform level in 2007–2008. This decline in autonomous expenditures was the main reason for the drop in growth rates of both output and employment, leading to income deflation suffered by the peasantry, in turn leading to a fall in induced investment. By 2003, only a paltry Rs.124 per month ($3) was being invested per farming family at the all-India level, and in many states, the figure was negative according to the National Sample Survey (Report No. 497).

When public investment rates and public development expenditures in the primary sector are actually declining, there is not the slightest possibility of reconciling an export thrust from farming with maintaining domestic food grains availability. The consumption of the mass of the poor is then sacrificed to meet the demands of the external sector and the local rich. A remarkably similar outcome is seen in China under its internally driven market reforms, where export thrust has entailed declining per capita food grains output for the rural masses since 1990, with particularly sharp decline after 1996. Average calorie intake has been falling in rural China as well, though the absolute level continues to be higher than in rural India. Even though it was the agrarian crisis that propelled the UPA government to power in the 2004 general elections in India, the government, by immediately enacting the Fiscal Responsibility and Budgetary Management Act, reiterated its commitment to a strongly deflationary fiscal stance as advised by the international financial institutions. Under the Act it is mandatory for the government to reduce the fiscal deficit, and this means further expenditure deflation. From around 6 percent in 2001 the gross fiscal deficit as percent of GDP has been reduced to 3.7 percent by 2007 and further to 2.5 percent by 2008.The irrational policy of expenditure deflation remains the Vedas and the Upanishads for the government whose thinking is dominated by the global moneylenders' economic dogmas advocating deflationary policies, dogmas that are privileged over the question of livelihoods and food security of the poor. Yet the worsening situation to be addressed effectively requires exactly the opposite policy, namely, a strongly expansionary fiscal stance. While India's National Rural Employment Guarantee (NREG) Act of 2006 might seem to go against this, it is to be noted that budgetary allocation to this has been paltry, a mere 10 percent more than was being spent earlier under various employment generation schemes (which were consolidated and merged with the NREG program), and this allocation was cut in the 2007 budget, even though it was announced that the scheme was to be extended to more districts. It was only in 2008 with deepening agrarian crisis that the allocation was raised.

The reason for such relentless attacks on employment and mass incomes is that cropping pattern shifts and supply shifts alone will not do the job for the advanced countries wishing to see such specialization on the part of developing countries, for desired supply shifts in modern market economies need corresponding *demand shifts* to succeed. An essential element of the mechanism is to reduce the purchasing power of the masses, usually the unorganized rural population, so that mass demand for basic necessities including food grains reduces to release land resources for growing more export crops and for the greater diversion of food grains itself toward more commercial and industrial use demanded by the local and foreign well-to-do classes. Under colonial systems where there was direct control, such reduction in mass purchasing power was directly made through imposing heavy taxes and using a part of taxes to buy up export goods.

Under modern conditions where there is no direct control, the same mechanism works through *public expenditure deflation*. Thus the attack is both on the supply side reducing output growth via reduced investment, and simultaneously on the demand side through expenditure deflation, that sets in motion reverse multiplier effects on incomes. Every Rs.100 less of such public spending reduces incomes by a multiple of 4 to 5, that is, by between Rs.400 and Rs.500 (assuming as it is reasonable to do that only one-fifth to one-quarter of every incremental rupee earned is saved and hence three-quarters to four-tenths is spent). Public expenditure deflation has been severe in the primary sector, and it is this that is the main cause of not only lowered levels of activity but associated rise in unemployment and decline in incomes and purchasing power. Rise in unemployment under every status (daily, weekly, and usual status) has been much greater in rural compared to urban areas. The NSS consumption expenditure data clearly indicate a fall in real spending on both food and cloth in rural India between 1993–1994 and 2004–2005, as well as falling energy intake (calorie intake per head per day).[17]

APPROPRIATION OF LAND AND WATER RESOURCES OF THE PEASANTRY

Since 1998, a few years after global prices of primary products started falling and rendered export crop farmers insolvent, particular states (Andhra Pradesh, Vidarbha region of Maharashtra, Punjab, Kerala) have seen a very high incidence of indebted farmer suicides and these suicides are continuing at present except in Kerala.[18] Suicides have been regarded historically as a passive form of peasant resistance. Such passive forms, turning despair into self-destruction, have been changing into active forms of resistance over the last two years, precipitated by a new phase of aggressive land acquisition by the corporate sector with the help and mediation of state governments. The present new phase of primitive accumulation, of land-grab from the peasantry, is on account of diverse causes. First, the largest areas are involved in the setting up of Special Economic Zones (SEZs), of which several hundred have been approved in India. Bitter resistance by the peasantry notified that their crop-bearing land will be acquired for SEZ has been spreading throughout the country from Goa and Maharashtra to Bengal and Orissa.[19] Second, foreign and domestic corporate entities acquire land for their industrial and other projects that also put pressure on water resources for cultivation and drinking for the rural population. Third, foreign and domestic companies want land at many locations for setting up collecting points of agricultural products to supply their retail marketing chains.

It is often argued that, since peasant farming is not remunerative, there should not be such resistance to giving up land where state governments are negotiating compensation packages that are much better than peasants received in the 1960s. However, these compensation rates are too low, for they capitalize only the present unusually depressed incomes from farming, and they exclude the displaced owners completely from future capital gains. It is forgotten, first, that agriculture is not inherently badly paying but has been made so by misguided deflationary public policy: the current agrarian depression can and must be countered by reversing those policies. Second, it is forgotten that the prospects for finding employment other than in agriculture are far worse for displaced peasants than three decades ago, owing to the capital intensity of production techniques rising further in the interim. Then, too, for the peasant his land provides a minimum assured, even if inadequate, income today, and no cash package can actually compensate for the loss of such a valuable productive asset. Third, it is forgotten that displaced farmers have nowhere to go: analogies with primitive accumulation in today's advanced countries are entirely misplaced. There is no New World to which our peasants can migrate in vast numbers, nor is there the prospect of gainful absorption into nonagriculture on the required scale.

The solutions to the unemployment and livelihood problems of the peasantry and rural labor lie in innovating and following an alternative trajectory of development that will address the specific problems discussed so far. The revival of agricultural and particularly food grains output growth to at least the pre-Reform rate of 3 percent annually is a priority, for only then will the employment rate also revive, entailing a simultaneous revival in both the supply of food and the demand for it from the poor as mass purchasing power rises.

The urgency of a revival of food production is underscored by the currently unfolding global food crisis. The thinking behind the pattern of specialization deliberately promoted by the Bretton Woods Institutions and the WTO in Third World countries from the 1970s was to reinstate free trade and the old international division of labor, in which developing countries would supply advanced country supermarkets with a variety of crops only they can produce, while importing food grains and dairy products from the latter. This model has already produced increasing food insecurity and deepening hunger in developing countries, for macroeconomic contraction combined with growing exports led to land diversion, declining domestic food output, as well as declining demand as mass incomes fell, in virtually every developing country implementing neoliberal reforms and trade liberalization.

The average annual world cereal output in the triennium 1979–1981 was 1,573 million tonnes for a 1980 population of 4,435 million according to FAO data. By the triennium 1999–2001, cereal output had increased only to 2,084 million tonnes for a population of 6,071 million in 2000. *Thus world per capita cereal output declined from 355 kg in 1980 to 343 kg in 2000.* Given the facts that, during this period, per capita income increased significantly and that the income elasticity of demand for cereals (consumed both directly and indirectly via processed food and animal feed) is positive, such a stagnant or declining per capita cereal output should have spelled significant shortages leading to a rapid inflation in cereal prices.

However, the long-term increasing imbalance of decelerating food output growth in the world economy during the 1980s and through the 1990s was suppressed, and no unusual inflation was seen; on the contrary, price deflation occurred in many countries, precisely owing to the Fund-guided income-deflating mechanisms depressing rural mass incomes and hence effective demand discussed in this paper. Owing to this suppression, most observers did not understand the gravity of the situation. A shock or trigger was required to make the long-term decline in nutrition explicit, and this shock has come from the sudden global oil price rise, which has little chance of being reversed, and consequent diversion of grain to biofuel production in advanced countries.

The model of free trade and export specialization has been discredited explicitly with the large-scale diversion of food grains to fuel production in the north, the disappearance of global food stocks, and spiraling food price inflation. In thirty-seven countries out of the many that have been made food import dependent by Fund-guided, or rather misguided, policies over the last thirty years, food riots have taken place over the last year mainly in their urban areas. With food inflation rates of 15 to 25 percent, the poor are hard hit. In India, food price inflation since mid-2006 has been averaging 7 to 8 percent with spikes in particular commodities, and urban discontent is growing. While India, in the last fifteen years of neoliberal reforms and trade liberalization, has gone quite a long way along the same slippery path of reforms and export thrust other smaller countries have followed for three decades, it is still in a position to retrieve a worsening situation provided the goal of "grow more food" is addressed on an urgent basis and mass purchasing power is restored. This requires appropriately higher procurement prices for crops including the commercial crops and the active setting up of cooperative groups to reclaim waste land and to cultivate jointly for food production, as is being done with positive results at present in Kerala, a traditionally food-deficient state. Farmers seem to be responding to the substantial rise in the central procurement price for wheat and rice, belatedly announced last year, and there was some, though so far inadequate, revival of food grains output during 2007–2008.

The alternative trajectory requires, second, the proper funding and effective extension nationwide of the National Rural Employment Guarantee Scheme, under which a hundred days of employment on various types of rural infrastructure projects are provided to every family asking for work. The resulting rise in purchasing power and mass demand would raise the food grains demand to more normal levels from the present nadir and so reduce hunger. Some evidence is available to show that distress out-migration from villages has reduced considerably wherever the NREGS is being properly implemented. The alternative trajectory requires the revival and expansion of the Public Distribution System, which had been unwisely allowed to run down, and an end to targeting given that there is deepening undernutrition with over seven-tenths of the population unable to access minimum energy needs. The data show that urban poverty, too, has been rising during the period of neoliberal economic reforms.

Finally, higher levels of autonomous investment in irrigation, rural infrastructure, crop research, and extension work would lead to more induced investment on the part of the peasantry and put the overall revival of the rural economy, including nonfarm activities, on a firm basis. Industrial growth is necessary, but no matter how high the growth rate, demonstrably it has not and cannot solve the unemployment and income problems in developing countries that need to find their solutions within the labor-intensive activities of agriculture and small-scale manufacturing.

SUMMARY AND CONCLUDING REMARKS

In the present era of the dominance of finance capital, we see a new process of primitive accumulation, in which the resources of the Third World peasantry, and in particular its land assets, are sought to be appropriated by large-scale corporate capital for diverse purposes including speculation. A segment of this capital that is interested in accessing primary goods to supply domestic and foreign retail chains is seeking to formally subordinate the Third World peasantry under capital using contract systems, without the real subsumption of labor under capital, namely, without necessarily instituting direct wage-labor-based large-scale capitalist production.

This paper has argued that it would be an incorrect reading to see these processes as signifying the "end of the peasantry" or "the disappearance of the peasantry" and the development of purely capitalist relations of production based on wage-paid labor. It bases the argument on a radically different reading of the historical role of the primary sector in the rise of industrial capitalism in Europe and in the European population's extended territories in North America, from the conventional reading of history. The conventional or mainstream reading says that the end of the peasant as peasant and the transition to capitalist agriculture ("agricultural revolution") successfully provided from *domestic* sources the increased wage good and raw materials requirements of industrialization. Rejecting this conventional view, this paper says that successful "agricultural revolution" in today's advanced capitalist countries is a myth, and the transition to large-scale capitalist agriculture in these countries did not, in practice, ever provide in adequate volumes the required wage goods and raw materials for industrial development and so entailed increasing import dependence. From their very inception and throughout their rise to dominance through imperialism, capitalist economies constituting today's advanced countries have relied on sharply rising volumes of imports of basic wage goods and raw materials from the Third World countries with most of these imports not being paid for, since they were tax financed or rent financed. The advanced countries continue, in the present era, to make heavy, increasing demands on the varied productive capacity of tropical lands to maintain and improve the import-dependent lifestyle of its population. It is taken for granted that importing primary goods from Third World countries is good for them, too, which is a false proposition based on the logically incorrect Ricardian theory of comparative advantage.

Because land is not a product of human labor, diversion of tropical lands from food grains to export crops to keep supermarket shelves in distant lands stocked throughout the year has always entailed a decline in both food production and access to food for the poorer mass of Third World populations. Such a trend of decline in food security is clearly visible in the last quarter century as well, since neoliberal reforms, including trade liberalization, were introduced in virtually all developing countries to smash protective barriers to trade, to pry open agriculture to a renewed round of exports, and to formally subsume peasants under international capital. This has again brought about a crisis of food production and of increasing undernutrition for the majority of the rural population. These propositions have been illustrated in this paper using the specific case of India.

Although neither economic theory nor the extant histories of industrialization cognize this basic reality, the very rise and stability of the capitalist system in advanced countries has historically entailed its exploitative coupling with peasant agriculture in distant lands and has entailed, under certain conditions, the famishment of the peasantry. This coupling is not about to end today, first because if the Third World peasantry is completely torn asunder from its means of production, it has nowhere to go, unlike the displaced peasantries of Europe who were absorbed into alternative employment or migrated to lands seized from indigenous populations elsewhere. Second, nonagricultural employment opportunities are not expanding adequately given the high levels of labor-displacing technical change that are mandatory under modern competitive globalized manufacturing. For these reasons, the peasantry is fiercely defending its right to retain its land and to continue its cycle of petty production.

Large-scale capitalist agriculture in advanced countries is unable to produce even temperate primary goods cheaply and cannot produce a vast range of tropical primary goods at all. Advanced countries whose populations depend on imported primary products to provide a large part of the physical basis of their high living standards, therefore, need to continue the coupling of their economies with distant peasant agriculture, a coupling marked by a dialectic of deteriorating the living conditions of the peasantry without absorbing them into alternative productive employment at the global level. The immediate prognosis is a continuation under conditions of increasing distress for the peasantry, of the exploitative coupling between advanced country consumption patterns and Third World peasant production. The long-term prognosis is a strong revival, as a reaction to increasing distress, of alternative radical paradigms of development in the Third World based on stabilizing and improving peasant production through cooperative effort, rather than continued passive subservience to the ongoing processes of the formal subsumption of the peasantry under international capital.

NOTES

1. U. Patnaik, "Ricardo's Fallacy," in *The Pioneers of Development Economics*, ed. Jomo K. S. (Delhi: Tulika, 2005).

2. P. Patnaik, *Accumulation and Stability under Capitalism*, (Oxford: Clarendon Press 1994) discusses these issues in detail.

3. K. Marx, *Capital, Vol.1, XV.* Tr. by Samuel Moore and Edward Aveling (New York: International Publishers, 1967).

4. S. B. Saul, *Studies in British Overseas Trade* (Liverpool: Liverpool University Press, 1960).

5. U. Patnaik, "The Free Lunch—Transfers from the Tropical Colonies and Their Role in Capital Formation in Britain during Industrial Revolution" in *Globalization Under Hegemony*, ed. Jomo K. S. (Delhi: Oxford University Press, 2006).

6. The figure of 6 million lives lost during the anti-Japanese war is from Jon Halliday, *A Political History of Japanese Capitalism* (New York: Monthly Review Press, 1975).

7. B. H. Slicher van Bath, *The Agrarian History of Western Europe AD 1600–1850* (London: Mathew Arnold, 1963).

8. J. Barnes, *Complete Works of Aristotle* vol.1 (Princeton: Princeton University Press, 1984); C. L. Hamblin, *Fallacies* (London: Methuen, 1970).

9. U. Patnaik, "Ricardo's Fallacy." See also Ralph Davis's brief critique along similar lines in *The Industrial Revolution and British Overseas Trade* (Leicester: Leicester University Press, 1985).

10. U. Patnaik, "The Free Lunch—Transfers from the Tropical Colonies and Their Role in Capital Formation in Britain during Industrial Revolution."

11. U. Patnaik, "On the inverse relation between primary exports and domestic food absorption under liberalized trade regimes," in *Work and Well-being in the Age of Finance*, ed. J. Ghosh and C. P. Chandrasekhar (Delhi: Tulika, 2003).

12. G. Blyn, *Agricultural Trends in India—Output, Area and Productivity 1891–1947* (Philadelphia: University of Philadelphia Press, 1966).

13. For supporting references, see U. Patnaik, *The Republic of Hunger and Other Essays* (Delhi: Three Essays Collective, 2008).

14. K. Nagaraj, provides the most systematic recent analysis of suicide rates and their regional incidence using police records. K. Nagaraj, *Farmers' Suicides in India: Magnitude, Trends and Pattern*, 2008. www.macroscan.org.

15. U. Patnaik, "Global Capitalism, Deflation and Agrarian Crisis in Developing Countries," Social Policy and Development Programme, Paper Number 13, United Nations Research Institute for Social Development (UNRISD) October 2003; shorter version under same title in *The Journal of Agrarian Change* (January–February 2003).

16. G. Blyn, *Agricultural Trends in India—Output, Area and Productivity 1891–1947* (University of Philadelphia Press, 1966); U. Patnaik, *The Republic of Hunger and Other Essays.*

17. National Sample Survey Organisation, Report No. 402, *Level and Pattern of Consumer Expenditure 1993–94*; Report No. 405, *Nutritional Intake in India 1993–94;* Report No.

497, *Income, Expenditure and Productive Assets of Farmer Households, 2003;* Report No. 508, *Level and Pattern of Consumer Expenditure 2004–05*; Report No. 513, *Nutritional Intake in India 2004–05*. Available at www.mospi.nic.in.

18. The act passed in 2007 by the state assembly setting up a Debt Relief Commission empowered to adjudicate private moneylender debt has produced a dramatic decline in suicides.

19. So far, it has been successful in Bengal and Goa, where proposals for setting up SEZ were withdrawn.

Chapter 11

Peasants in Indonesia and the Politics of (Peri)Urbanization[1]

Abidin Kusno

The nature of Asian urbanization has been the object of theoretical attention for almost two decades. A central theme in the discussion revolves around the dissolution of the city and countryside divide, and it seems the focus is largely on questioning whether the city is winning (through urbanization) or if the countryside is losing in the development game.[2] Such issues, however, are much more complex in Asia. For Terry McGee, (who is among the first to consider the specificity of the region), urbanization and the process of urban spread means "the emergence of regions of highly mixed rural and non-rural activity surrounding the large urban cores of many Asian countries" that are "significant foci of industrialization and rapid economic growth."[3] McGee calls this region *desakota* from the Indonesian words *desa* for "village" and *kota* for "town." The term signifies an attempt to revise the conventional or Eurocentric view of urbanization as a process, which assumes a distinction between rural and urban. It broadly signifies an extended-urban region, which includes the "periurban" (*pinggiran kota*) zones and an extensive area of mixed rural-urban land use along two large urban cores linked by transportation routes.[4] The periurban areas thus, in Phillip Kelly's words, are not only "new and enduring urban form . . . which is neither rural nor urban but incorporates distinctive elements of both,"[5] but they are also the spaces undergoing rapid urbanization. In these "transitional landscapes or a dramatic new species of urbanism,"[6] Jonathan Rigg proceeds to argue that "people cannot easily be squeezed into single categories like 'rural/agricultural' when their work not only crosses the agriculture/industry divide but they have also led 'split' lives in terms of where they live."[7] Similarly, Gregory Guldin argues that the migration of people from rural to the urban in China came in tandem with urbanization of and by the rural in situ via, among others, rural industrialization.[8]

This in situ urbanization of the rural raises the questions of not only "what's a peasant to do?" but also who the peasant is today, and where the peasant has been staying and moving around.

These studies have importantly identified and captured some central features of urbanization with "Asian characteristics" that perpetuates, rather than challenges, the capitalist world system. Yet, with studies mostly centered on the *processes* of urbanization, very little attention has been given to the *political* formation of *desakota*, or "periurban."[9] Also very little attempt has been made to place these extended spaces in their historical context to understand the political processes that have made their formation possible.[10] This essay, with a particular focus on Jakarta, is intended to fulfill, however imperfectly, these purposes. I argue that periurbanization stemmed from the postcolonial state's attempt to eliminate the political identity of the peasant (along with its memories of mass political mobilization) and to form a new subjectivity via multiple occupations and labor mobility (instead of isolation) even as these practices have been well established during the colonial and even precolonial periods.[11] Central to this governing strategy is the formation of the extended urban region beyond the administrative boundaries defined by the capital city, such as the "periurban" (*pinggiran kota*) of Jakarta. The rapid urbanization in this area could be seen as stemming from the nonagricultural job opportunities opened up by the state policy of industrialization and economic growth of capitalist countries in the region, but, as I will argue, the periurban is also a political space for the transformation of the peasants' identity. This paper thus aims to open inquiries on the largely unnoticed relations between the politics of *urban* planning and the transformation of the peasant world in the Southeast Asian region. I organize the essay into three parts, each consisting of different sections representing the rural, the urban, and the periurban.

There are a few caveats to note at the outset. First, it is not the intention of this paper to problematize existing studies that have finely shown that the rationale for rural-to-urban migration is rural poverty and the perceived economic opportunities in cities. The aim of this paper is to offer a different way of seeing centered on the interplay between politics and space that would help to unravel the formation of the periurban as a space of governmentality specific to Indonesian history. Second, I shall confine my attention to Indonesia and its capital city, Jakarta, and hope readers with knowledge of a wider geographical stage of Southeast Asia would offer inputs for the interest of comparative studies and a more global approach to the issue. Third, on terminology and classification: I use the words *desakota* and "periurban" interchangeably, assuming that they both refer to a similar characteristic even though each designates different geographical propinquity to the city. Both terms, in any case, designate what Guldin called "a partially urbanized countryside." I use the term "peasants" and the "floating mass" to designate an "imagined community" constructed either by the state or by the peasants themselves in their engagement with politics of identity and identification.[12] In reality, the notion of "peasants," like "the village," is problematic since the social group is neither monolithic nor unchanging. Instead, it has been characterized by internal class, gender, ethnic differentiation, tension, and conflict. The category of floating mass is harder to explain and identify. It is constructed in the shadow of popular radicalism of the 1960s. The term refers to people, largely underclass rural-to-urban migrants, who could be turned into productive subjects as long as they refrained themselves from any engagement with politics or political parties. As will become clear, floating mass is both a "real" and "imagined" category created by the state to govern bodies and imaginations. As such, members of the floating mass could not be shown statistically, but their presence could be *felt* through the voice of the state. Finally, the use of "space" here is not metaphorical, instead it is practical for only then can it function as a spatial technology of governance. As will become clear, it is through space that the movement of the floating mass to the periurban area—designated as economic space—is managed and controlled (almost) without the use of force.

PROLOGUE

Earlier Vision after Decolonization

In 1962, Kenneth Watts, formerly a Town Planning Advisor under the United Nations Assistance Program, published his proposal for the greater Jakarta region to the Ministry of Public Works and Power for which he worked from 1956 to 1959. Watts started by saying,

> The problems attending rapid growth in tropical cities cannot be resolved within the boundaries of the cities themselves. . . . For, by enhancing the attractiveness of the city to the would-be migrant, they will only accelerate the rate of inward migration. . . . An alternative policy has often been urged—that of preparing complementary programmes for the surrounding region. They would have as their objective the improvement of conditions both in the rural area as a whole, which might encourage the prospective migrants to remain where they are, and in the smaller towns of the region, which might have the effect of deflecting migrational flow from its main objective. How valid are these arguments?[13]

Watts was then facing an unprecedented rapid population growth in the city where he worked. The flow of migrants to the city was due to many factors, but among the most pivotal reasons was the political insecurity of the countryside in the aftermath of the Indonesian revolution. The social and political unrest that plagued the surrounding regions of Jakarta, the economic difficulties in the villages, and, not least, the "modernity" of Jakarta, led many "migrants" to abandon the memories of ruin in order to occupy the city of the future.[14] J. M. van der Kroef wrote in 1954 that "Life in a *kota Parijs* like Djakarta has cast a magic spell even on those who live far from the city's crowded, bustling roar. A modern city, with modern ways and urban conveniences is a concretization of revolutionary aspirations, affording education, material comforts and an escape from ennui, or so it is hoped."[15]

Confronted by "the magnitude of the rural-urban movement [which] is now so great . . . that attempts to halt it—far less reverse it—are quite futile," Watts suggested the development of "small towns" at the outskirts of Jakarta to "create counter-magnets to the pull of the big city,"[16] and he said, "if effort were made to stimulate industrial growth in the smaller towns, the chances of attracting more migrants to them might be much better than is usually supposed."[17] Watts believed that his 1959 outline plan for a small "tropical" town in the greater Jakarta region was a "short-term" solution for the city. This temporary solution ended up haunting Jakarta's future twenty years later as the New Order of Suharto (1966–1998) consolidated its power by producing (with assistance from the World Bank in the 1970s and 1980s) a new, yet similar, urban development plan.[18]

These plans were politically designed and used as a mechanism to create order and peace after the 1965 massacre of individuals (mostly peasants) who were accused of having communist ties.[19] The terror aimed (though not exclusively) at the annihilation of the left and the political (as well as the physical and mental) body of what the communist leader called "the majority in the villages in our country . . . the poor peasants together with the agricultural laborers [who made up] the largest force pushing the revolution forward."[20] In this aftermath of killing and detention, the New Order of Suharto found resolution in the periurban areas of the greater Jakarta region as a way to manage the "mass subject" in both the city and the village. The idea of creating countermagnets of small towns around Jakarta thus goes back to the era of early decolonization,[21] but the aftermath of 1965 and its pervasive concern over security could be seen as the turning point for the implementation of such spatial politics of urbanization.

THE RURAL

The Political Economy of Governing the Peasants

The coup of October 1, 1965 and the charges against the Communist Party as the generator of the event served to change the social life and institutional direction of rural Java, and by extension, Indonesia. The Communist Party, with remarkable success in mobilizing peasant interests in land reform, was decimated; many of its members were killed and imprisoned in a series of frightful terrors. The slaughter of over 500,000 people, many of whom were peasants, workers, and activists supportive of the Indonesian left mostly in rural areas of Java and Sumatra, had radically changed the village and prompted waves of migration to the city. Ali Sadikin, the governor of Jakarta who served in the first decade of the Suharto regime noted in his memoir that the influx of migrants (permanent or temporary) to the capital city was overwhelming especially when many of them had become "vagrants" (*gelandangan*) and "sex workers" (*wanita P*).[22] This may not be true, for many of them were gradually absorbed into the informal sector, but the violence of category suited Sadikin's need to demonize the poor migrants from villages for the "cleaning up" of the capital city. As I will argue in the next sections, during the mid-1970s, the formation of the periurban became a space for the containment of migrant labor from the countryside, and this move was due, in large measure, to the aftermath of the 1965 terrors, in which the governing rural bodies became heavily monitored by rapid spatial and political disciplinary actions. I will return to this issue, but for now, it is sufficient to say that Sadikin was appointed by Sukarno (1950–1966), but he worked in the force field of Suharto who assumed power in 1966. The urbanization that the governor witnessed was different from that of Kenneth Watts, for the influx of migrants of his time stemmed from the "cleaning up" of the village from "communist infiltration" and the "restoration of order" under military control.[23]

"Directly after the coup," Gary Hansen points out, "nearly every 'district head' (*bupati*) on Java was replaced by an officer from the army, usually of colonel rank. Likewise, many 'village heads' (*lurah*) were replaced by veterans or recently deactivated members of the army. To further buttress government hegemony in the countryside, the army created its own hierarchical structure parallel to the territorial units of local and regional government. Thus, all levels of civilian government from the province down to the village area are now complemented by a counterpart army command with functioning authority over the respective territorial jurisdiction."[24] This systematic alteration of political and institutional life within the village fundamentally reorganized the political economy of rural life to a degree that there were "no 'peasants' lobbies at either local, regional, or national level."[25] The restructuring, as Gary Hansen reported, "had served to cast a heavy pall over rural Java, and most peasants and rural leaders were much less inclined to risk involvement in any form of organized political activity, let alone opposition to government programs."[26]

The agrarian land reform program initiated under the Sukarno regime was soon regarded as "communist inspired."[27] In place of agrarian reform, the Green Revolution was introduced, under which peasants were transformed into farmers' groups and cooperatives in order to carry out state-controlled "intensification" of food production, a strategy that had resulted in national self-sufficiency in the 1980s. While this was acknowledged as successful (receiving international acclaim), it was also an expression of the top-down approach, in which farmers of the government group could obtain "fertilizer, insecticides, and pesticides at the 'official' prices, credits to pay their input, loans . . . and better prices for their produce."[28] Those who remained independent producers of their own land were never quite left alone, for they, too, held no power in the system that sought to undermine their agencies. In *Agrarian Transformations*, Hart, Turton, and White indicate just how the mechanism of creating agrocommodity relationship is linked to the control of the peasantry.[29] The Green Revolution has taken away the peasants' control of their means of production (both land and tool) even though they have gained productivity and larger income.[30] In this sense, the Green Revolution, while increasing productivity, has its goal of dismantling the political base of the peasants and hence protecting the regime from the possibility of rural unrest.

The Green Revolution thus was part of the attempt to depoliticize the village by ways of intensification and commercialization of the rural economy under the disciplinary control of rural elites and, behind them, the military. The program was part of the national "stabilization and rehabilitation" program in the aftermath of 1965. In 1968, two years after the regime change, President Suharto laid out his new development plan on agriculture:

> For the next five years, industrial development will be concentrated on those industries supporting agricultural development, such as manufacture of fertilizer, insecticide and farm implements. . . . Increased use of fertilizer and insecticides will

> require outlays by farmers. Since their resources are very limited, finance may be a major obstacle. To meet this problem, plans have been made to establish village banks and village warehouses. . . . Government rural credit facilities will also be strengthened and extended. Additional finance may be provided by private domestic and foreign capital. Such companies could assist farmers by supplying fertilizers, insecticides, and farm implements on credits, and by providing training in the use of these implements, repayment to be made by delivery part of the additional production made possible by this assistance. A start has been made in this co-operation between farmers and private entrepreneurs.[31]

What underlies this state patronage mechanism of agrocommodity relations is not only the attempt to alleviate rural poverty and to promote rural employment but also to control the peasants by integrating them into a network of agricultural labor dependent on the "patron-client." With technology of production and lands in the hands of corporations, managers, and entrepreneurs, middle-lower-end poor peasants have lost the capacity to control their own agricultural base.[32] In this mechanism, the rural elites ran the show while serving the state by becoming not only the beneficiaries but also the "police" of the countryside. And with social hierarchy in place, the countryside "police" were able to monitor and control the type of labor that many were engaged in within the local space. Often, many peasants on the lower end of the rural hierarchy were thereby displaced if the police suspected them to have communist loyalties. The political capacity of the state and its rural elite was based on the mobilization of the militaristic and ideological discourses of stability and security. Through the discourse of "cleaning up" the rural from the communist threat, political activities of villagers thus were eliminated.

This technique of governance that seeks to clean the social environment of the rural from the "communist threat" by working under the network of the Green Revolution has fragmented the peasantry as a relatively autonomous unit of sociopolitical force and ended what Ben White called the "self-organization and resistance" of peasants and rural poor.[33] With local civilian government and its military counterpart standing out as the sole representative of organized power and with many peasants losing control of institutions and land and unable to afford inputs on the Green Revolution, the peasants became what Foucault would call "docile bodies" available for elimination and transformation. Thus, programs to eliminate peasantry and to reduce the number of peasants could spontaneously initiate with ease by the state. For instance, as recorded by Ben White,

> In August 1984 Minister of Agriculture Affandi announced, seemingly out of the blue, that small farms of less than half a hectare (and in a later phase, those of less than one hectare) would be abolished: there were too many farmers in Indonesia, and the numbers were ideally to be brought down from 60–70 percent to 8 percent of the population. They would be encouraged to sell their farms or amalgamate with other farmers, to join one of the government's Transmigration or Nucleus-Estate programs outside Java, or to shift to non-agricultural occupations.[34]

The Ministry of Agriculture basically expressed the general strategy of the nation's security measure. He recalled the concern of Major-General Ali Moertopo (1924–1984), a key member of the President's advisory board, who had long been preoccupied by the political arrangement of Indonesian population as a prerequisite for accelerated economic growth. In 1972, Moertopo (then head of OPSUS, a special operations unit linked to the army under the Suharto regime), helped formulate a state ideology, which was to be applied "to every aspect of life, to every government institution and state organization, as well as to all levels of urban and rural society."[35] One of his most important concepts was the "floating mass" (*massa mengambang*)—"a demobilized and depoliticized population"—which became the central pillar of Suharto's political system.[36] The floating mass is essentially a policy of population control pursued in the aftermath of the terror, murder, and massive arrests of people accused to have had association with communism or leftist ideas and their affiliated mass organizations. In Lane's word, it is "a policy of political restructuring aimed at making permanent the end of any form of open mobilization politics."[37] To ensure the death of "popular radicalism," the military established bureaus, which screened citizens to make sure that they were clean of communism. A citizen who passed the screening of the "clean environment" (*bersih lingkungan*) program could obtain a certificate of good behavior needed for a job and membership application. However, regardless of whether citizens passed or failed the screening, they remained members of floating masses. In Slamet's words,

> The deprived rural masses are floating politically because the government wants them to stay unorganized. They are floating because they are more and more cut off from the land and even from work opportunities as labourers, as a result of changes in technology favourable to the richer peasants, to landed members of the bureaucracy and to agro-business. . . . [38]

The Floating Mass and Its Spatial Governance

The floating mass essentially referred to people in the villages who, after the events of 1965, were seen as a potential threat to the stability of the New Order. Under the category of floating mass, the people in and from the villages were condemned to have no affiliation with any political party. Eliminated of political adversaries and identities, the floating mass could be moved around as "productive labor" to support national development.

Ali Moertopo's 1972 doctrine reads as follows:

> It is worth remembering that in the past the people in general, particularly those in the villages with their own, often national, ways of thinking, were played upon and involved in the political and ideological conflicts of the parties. . . . The mass of people, especially those in the villages, always fell prey to the political and ideological interests of those parties. Their involvement in the conflicts of political interests had as its result the fact that they ignored the necessities of daily life, the need for development and improvement of their own lives, materially as well as spiritually. Such a situation should not repeat itself. . . . Therefore it is only right to attract the

> attention of the mainly village people away from political problems and ideological exclusiveness to efforts of national development through the development of their own rural societies. . . . Here lies the meaning and the goal of the *depolitisasi* (the process of freeing the people from political manipulation) and the *deparpolisasi* (the process of freeing the people from political party allegiances) in the villages. . . . In this way people in the villages will not spend their valuable time and energy in the political struggles of parties and groups, but will be occupied wholly with development efforts. Through this process there emerges the so-called "floating mass" i.e.: people who are not permanently tied to membership of any political parties. This concept of "floating mass" should lead to increased development efforts. . . . [39]

In the mind of the state, the idea of dislodging villagers of the right to participate in any party politics—except voting only at national election time—was to force individuals to be preoccupied "wholly with development efforts." Nothing could translate better the idea that everyone should be "wholly occupied" in their life for developmental efforts than flexibly diversifying occupations for survival. Uprooted from their base, members of the floating mass were made to earn their livings from various occupations ideally moving around different places, in Moertopo's words, "to improve their own lives, materially as well as spiritually." In a crucial way, Moertopo's vision was in line with the diversification and multiplication of job opportunities and the dream for a better life away from the village. The extended era of "stabilization and rehabilitation" (1966–1975) could be seen as the period that set the foundation for the transformation of the political subjectivity of peasants in the village into politically passive but productive floating masses drifting in and out of the city and the countryside in search of jobs. While villagers were moving in and out of the rural areas, military command posts were stationed permanently at all villages to ensure the nonexistence of political activity in the rural areas. Intended for villagers, the concept of the floating mass was to create a condition that would "let them live in calm, to work and construct" even if they had to move around as opportunity arose.[40]

The floating mass concept in some ways sets villagers free from their rural base, but it also brings the peasants back into the fold of the state. It creates a condition for diversification of job opportunities in the village and encourages both circular and permanent migration to the city, which needs their labor power. The de-politicization of the village and the engineering of the "floating mass" came in tandem with the opening up of the village for the labor market. The "floating mass" concept thus not only encouraged peasants to leave the countryside and seek nonfarm-related occupations, but it has also changed the social relations of the peasant world and has led to the rapid decline of the peasantry as a political force.

By the 1970s, identifying the peasants in terms of their place, occupation, and status was no longer easy, because they were marked not only by diversity but also by mobility. Attached to the peasants are often other categories such as workers, traders, and "migrants" in the city. Indonesian anthropologist, Koentjaraningrat, indicated, for instance, the difficulty of categorizing the peasants and migrants as two separate categories given the high frequency of migration in the rural ring around Jakarta.

> It was apparent that not all of [villagers] were landless peasants. Some were landowners who sharecropped their land or who only harvested the kinds of fruit which required the least care, thus freeing them for work in construction or road-building projects in the city or elsewhere, allowing them to earn a substantial amount of cash in a short period of time. Some even left their land uncultivated and speculated on rising land prices while working in the city. Naturally, many landless peasants would not leave the village if they could earn money by setting up foodstands, cigarette stands or the like, right in the village.[41]

Koentjaraningrat did not discuss the political displacement of the peasants and the formation of the floating mass in the Suharto era, but he pointed to a new subjectivity emerging out of the changing condition of the village life in Java. This new floating subjectivity (which peasants only recognized through words such as pindah ["moving"] or rantau ["commute"] but never "migrate") could be seen as the peasants' own modality of survival, but such strategy is connected to the state's technique of population control via occupational mobility. "Peasants on the move," to use Li Tana's phrase,[42] keep flexibility and variety in people's livelihood and as a result, as Hill points out, "rural people are in many areas less than committed to agriculture having added significant off-farm and non-farm employment to their domestic economies."[43] In the city, as I will discuss in the following section, they are often demonized as "vagrants" (*gelandangan*) for the practices of their "circulatory migration" (and to keep costs low) demand no commitment to establishing a "home" in the city. This peasants' tactic of survival has therefore constituted a floating world, but one that is inseparable from the state's modality of governance.

The diversity and mobility of the peasant world is certainly not new; one could trace patterns of such movement within the history of Southeast Asia.[44] The "new wave" of such diverse mobility in present times, however, lies in its "new non-farm activities, sustained or created by the contemporary process of development, which are underpinning diversification."[45] This new type of diversification has taken place largely since the 1970s[46] and, in the case of Indonesia, is inseparable from the state's politics of modernization and discourses of stability and security. Ali Moertopo understood that dislocation of peasants from their places to become a floating mass via rural diversification and mobility would allow them to be part of the experience of modernity and modernization. Participation in this process was central to aid in the de-politicization of the peasants in the rural areas and the organization of their production and wage levels. He claimed that, "this process of modernization will naturally involve conflicts, as new norms come into conflict with traditional norms. Consequently, modernization requires planned social and cultural change. . . . As 'planned change,' modernization must clearly determine the direction which will be taken."[47]

Central to this "planned social and cultural change" was the creation of periurban areas as the industrial zones for the containment of the otherwise scattered floating mass. The creation of the periurban areas as exceptional spaces designated for national development in which peasants could find accommodation as off-farm "productive laborers" was not only a plan for sociocultural change in the village. Instead, it was connected to the politics of the city. The state and the city authorities were just too willing to let rural-urban migrants locate themselves in periurban regions. They wanted to alter the sociopolitical ground of the peasantry by detaching the peasants from their village, but they did not want them to end up in the city.

To understand the political significance of the periurban, we need to first turn to the city, for the urban, like its rural counterpart, also plays a role in the governing of the "peasants." In the city, too, the floating mass of the urban population has been left either unorganized, or they have become members of the tightly control state-sponsored social (but never political) organizations. They, too, are ideally to be absorbed into the periurban areas away from the center, which fears the return of populist politics and, in any case, as a foreign consultant hired by the government points out, "the leadership simply doesn't want rustic looking people pushing bikes around in their capital city."[48]

THE URBAN

Peasants in the City

The floating mass strategy of cutting the rural population adrift from organized political activity and the politics of "clean environment" (*bersih lingkungan*) has immediate consequences for the city.[49] In her study of the labor market in the urban construction sector, Kartini Sjahrir points out that the "stabilization and rehabilitation" program has pushed many villagers to leave the countryside for the city, where they are able to find new jobs and hope to disappear into the general urban population without being interrogated and harassed.[50] For villagers, escape to the city was thus considered favorable.

The cleaning up of the village in the era of "stabilization and rehabilitation" had a spatial implication as it generated significant flow of migration to the urban center, especially the capital city, which, by then, had become the focus of national development. Ali Sadikin, the new governor of Jakarta at the time, recalled in his memoir that the waves of migration from the village had already entered the city even though urban development had not yet "taken off."[51] During the era of "stabilization and rehabilitation," Sadikin also witnessed many "vagrants" (*gelandangan*) in the city.[52] In the governor's words, "so visible were vagrants in many parts of the city. The numbers increased almost on the daily basis. And this posed a problem for me. . . . In short, vagrants in the capital city have become a serious problem. Their numbers are high."[53] Most of the vagrants, the governor believed, were not home grown, but were from different parts of rural Java. Vagrancy in Indonesian political tradition, for both the left and the right, connotes instability and indecisiveness, qualities that could lead to destruction.[54] For the governor, with the mandate from the state to help prevent social unrest and political disturbance, vagrants were not only a nuisance for the view of the city but were also potentially threatening to the public order.

Ali Sadikin witnessed the impact of labor migration from the countryside in the aftermath of 1965. Many villagers escaped to the city with the hope of getting new jobs without harassment from the state's mission of "clean environment." However, as a floating mass in the city, they became subjected to the play of power and knowledge from the municipality. Instead of recognizing the *gelandangan* as "circular migrants," Ali Sadikin considered them "illiterate and unskilled cheap laborers from the countryside, trishaw drivers, construction workers, vendors, the homeless, beggars, and prostitutes."[55] Thus, he viewed them as deviant "others" in need of a space, which would take them away from the visibility of "clean" Jakarta (the heart of the nation's modernity). The circular migrants, as pointed out earlier, just could not afford settling a family permanently in the city.[56] They would prefer moving alone and along by sleeping under bridges or in their "trishaw" (*becak*) or putting up temporary accommodation in squats or staying in a *pondok* (a hut-like lodging place, especially one made of cheap and impermanent materials) all of which the governor considered as unacceptable for a city that was trying hard to become a modern metropolis.[57]

At the beginning of his tenure, Sadikin called on the central government for help, and two measures were carried out in the early 1970s. The first was the effort of making Jakarta a closed city, and second, through the enforcement of the state, the deportation of migrants to outer islands under a national program known as *transmigrasi*. Several scholars and activists have written about the deportation and relocation of less desirable people from the city and the politics of *transmigrasi* to the outer islands.[58] It is sufficient to emphasize here that these programs of sending villagers away are related to the violent discourses of "clean environment" and the "floating mass." Furthermore, these measures point to the problematic relations between the city and the countryside and perhaps more importantly, the importance of finding a spatial solution for a productive governing of the floating mass, especially in the context of the realization on the part of the policymakers that "*Urbanisasi* [meaning rural migration to the city] never stops as it cannot be stopped."[59] And, perhaps, following the logic of the floating mass it should never be stopped for the (circular) migrants are seen as valuable resources to be exploited for national development.

It eventually became clear to Sadikin that the method of closed city and *transmigrasi* were insufficient, impractical, and counterproductive. The question is more on how to control and in some ways make use of the labor power embedded in the floating mass for the advantage of the city and the nation. For instance, many migrants from villages were young men, and it was soon discovered that they would be a great labor pool for the construction industry necessary for capital city building.[60] Consistent with the concept of floating mass, the government left these migrant laborers unregulated to prevent unionization and put them in the hands of "patron-client" informal networks of construction workers in the city, which continued to fuel and supply labor to and from rural areas.[61] They were allowed to occupy unused land close to where they worked and many continued to stay there more permanently but there was no base for them to organize.

The millions of "village" (*kampung*) folks in the city thus found themselves living in shantytowns with no organized political life. They remained without any protection from the state and had to enact practices of self-help and mutual helping out, which constituted the informal sector. Their presence was and is tolerated because the city needs their labor, but their settlements are considered illegal and subject to eviction at any time, especially when investments have become available for "national development." In some ways, one could understand the formation of "informality," the term used for and by the urban poor, as actually a form of governance in which survival intersects with the deorganization of the urban floating mass. As peasants have become important nonfarm labor forces in the city, a new kind of space was called on to resolve the problem of *urbanisasi*.

THE PERIURBAN

Guarding the City on the Fringe: The Rise of the Periurban

In 1967, a year after Suharto came to power, the government issued a master plan of Jakarta (1965–1985). The plan indicates that the city will expand outward concentrically 15 kilometers from the National Monument, the "center" of the city. The governor of Jakarta, Ali Sadikin, was given the authority to interpret the plan, and he was quick to realize that the plan was part of the stabilization and rehabilitation program. The governor was also delighted that the concentric development plan of Jakarta was essentially a means to manage population growth, for it included, for the first time, the areas of BOTABEK (an acronym for Bogor, Tangerang, and Bekasi, each representing the extended area of Jakarta to the south, west, and east respectively). The governor recalled that "in its development, the area of JABOTABEK [an acronym for Jakarta, Bogor, Tangerang, and Bekasi] consists of 'urban area,' 'rural area' and the 'transitional area' each with its specificity."[62]

For Sadikin, the notion of *transisi* is more than just referring to a transitory space in the process of becoming a city. Instead, the transitional area is designated to be more of an exceptional space, which would serve as a "countermagnet" for migrants to Jakarta. The governor was interested in the concept of the extended space insofar as it could resolve the population problems he had been facing in Jakarta. In his mind, the creation of periurban zones would protect Jakarta from the influx of less desirable migrants and "push population from Jakarta outwards to the development zone (*wilayah pengembangan*)."[63] Furthermore, the extended space would give clarity to the issue of territory, boundary, and authority. His memoir recorded his obsession with boundaries and the difficulty of arriving at an agreement with the governor of West Java. He emphasized the importance of dealing with the private sector without diminishing the authority of the city hall. The concept of JABOTABEK thus offered the opportunity for the governor to fulfill his wish to retain the authority of Jakarta to the city hall while allowing the private sectors to advance their own entrepreneurial spirit away from the controlled center.[64] Once developed by private developers, the periurban would alleviate population and security problems in the city. The city authorities did not have to suffer from the headache of planning. They did not have to deal with issues of service provision and not even transport, because it should be arranged privately by the capital to move the labor to work. We thus heard about the "success" story often told in the 1990s of the Mitsubishi Colt pickup, which was associated with the efficiency of transportation provided by the multinational (including Japanese) corporations at the periurban for their workers and staffs.[65]

The experiment with the concept of "extended space for development" (*wilayah pengembangan*) first took place in the coastal areas of North Jakarta (better known as the backyard of the city) rather than the BOTABEK areas. In 1973, the first export processing zones (EPZs) in Indonesia were formed in North Jakarta in an area of 10.5 hectares adjacent to the Tanjung Priok harbor facilities. Defined as an area of land "lying outside the normal customs of jurisdiction," the area offered "substantial incentives (in order) to attract foreign firms into the zones."[66] In detail, the zone included the following special treatment:

> combination of duty-free import of manufactured intermediate goods and raw materials, company income tax holidays, subsidized provision of factory space and/or utilities, streamlined bureaucratic and administrative procedures to avoid costly "red tape," exemptions from industrial regulations applying outside the zones, guarantees on the absence of strikes and guaranteed repatriation of profits.[67]

Under the control of (but not necessarily owned by) a state company, PT Bonded Warehouses Indonesia (BWI), the EPZ in North Jakarta was a pilot project for many more new zones to come. This export processing zone, an invention of the postwar geopolitical economic space for the operation of multinational corporations, opens the subsequent periurban areas of Jakarta as an economic space of exception.[68] These World Bank–prompted free trade export processing zones have since become the prime locations for the operation of international industrial capitalism; not surprisingly, the exploitation of the low-wage floating mass population becomes an added bonus for these capitalists, thereby showing the many forms of indirect stress and everyday exploitation of the "freedom" to work and stay in and around Jakarta.

This strategy of containing the floating mass by ways of zoning was officially carried out in 1976 under the Presidential Instruction No. 13.[69] Clusters of industrial zones in the surrounding inland areas of Jakarta were created to absorb both the capital and the floating labor mass. Consistent with the idea of protecting the capital city by deflecting migration to the periurban areas, over a thousand industries in the city were relocated in 1975 to the outskirts of Jakarta. They were expected to become part of the newly established Jakarta Industrial Estate of Pulo Gadung, which, by 1977, had already absorbed some 13,000 workers and expected to be soon absorbing 150,000 workers.[70] By the mid-1980s (pushed by the liberalized economy of Repelita V), investment by the private sector in industries increased sharply, which drove up the growth rate of the surrounding areas of Jakarta such as Tangerang and Bekasi.[71] The deregulation immediately resulted in the absorption of about 18 percent of the country's labor force while contributing some 25 percent to the overall GDP.[72] The workers were part of the mobilization that Diane Wolf described as "ten large-scale modern factories, driven by Western machinery and technology [commanding] in the middle of the agricultural land of two villages [in Java] that still have neither running water nor electricity."[73] In these factories, the floating mass was turned into a productive force and, as Diane Wolf has shown in her *Factory Daughters*, this included young, unmarried village women who left the rural areas, some against the wishes of their parents, to find nonfarm-related occupations. "Because of these industries," Hasan Poerbo, then a researcher at the Institute of Technology Bandung, indicates, "you have tens, hundreds of thousands of people actually moving around. And many of the people employed by these industries are young, unmarried women."[74] Women thus are absorbed into the "formal" sector because "their labor is cheaper and women are more industrious when it comes to working with small parts needed for the manufacturing of electronics, garments and shoes," while "men are employed in the informal sector."[75] Yet, as Soetjipto Wirosardjono points out, "only because of the informal sector, workers can be paid such a low salary."[76]

By the 1980s, the metropolitan press reported that the extended space has become the destination of migrants from rural areas and outer regions.[77] A series of Presidential Instructions has made possible the development of the periurban areas and further the *desakota* region of Java, all of which have immediate impact on the flow of population.[78] Ida Ayu Indira Dharmapatni and Tommy Firman indicate that, "besides receiving migrants from Jakarta city, BOTABEK has been increasingly targeted as the destination of migrants from all over Indonesia, mainly from Java. Migrants have chosen BOTABEK instead of Jakarta because of its lower living costs, employment opportunities resulting from the spillover of industrial growth from Jakarta, and its high accessibility to Jakarta via a well-developed transportation system."[79] A series of decrees and permits was issued to domestic and foreign private enterprises to develop the periurban areas as the space for the floating mass to "live in calm, to work and construct."[80] Hundreds of licenses were issued in the early 1990s to both domestic and foreign trade company representatives, especially those from the industrialized countries of Asia such as Japan, Hong Kong, Taiwan, Singapore, and South Korea; these countries have turned the periurban areas of Jakarta into "the largest concentration of both foreign and domestic investment in Indonesia."[81] This contour of investment represents just the instance of regional restructuring of economic space in which Indonesia provides cheap labor power for the low-end subcontracting network of industrial production in Asia. With the periurban designated as a zone for the restructuring of economic and social life, domestic developers, often with ties to the ruling elites, mobilized their capital to build a series of new towns for the growing members of the middle class.

The consequence is clear, as Dharmapatni and Firman indicate, that "in Bekasi alone, for example, if we assume a person-land ratio of four persons per hectare, the 3,000 hectares of industrial estate development will have to displace 12,000 farmers. If this assumption is valid for the whole of BOTABEK, then the 6,500 hectares planned for industrial development will have to displace about 26,000 farmers."[82] We may never know exactly the responses of the peasants to this draconian displacement, but under the doctrine of the floating mass, they would have most likely disappeared into the general work force of the factories in support of the national "development effort." Such displacement also indicates to us that although the periurban areas of BOTABEK have their own histories, under Suharto's politics of space, they were in "no-man's land" in which the juridical and the political intersected for the governance of the floating mass. As far as the city of Jakarta is concerned, the result was unambiguous, for as Dharmapatni and Firman point out, "permanent movement from West Java (including Botabek) and other parts of Indonesia into Jakarta city declined during 1975–1990 and was accompanied by a reverse movement of permanent migrants from Jakarta city to Botabek area."[83] We do not know how the establishment of the periurban might have contributed to the decrease in the number of *gepeng* (*gelandangan and pengemis*—"vagrants and beggars") in the city of Jakarta, but Soetjipto Wirosardjono reported that "in the census of October 1990 only 24,000 people were counted as *gelandangan* while they used to number more than 100,000."[84]

The political economy of space and the control of population are, therefore, interconnected, and they are central to the "stabilization and rehabilitation" of Indonesia under the New Order of Suharto. The exodus of villagers from the rural areas has finally prompted the government to create a space for containing them. The periurban areas of JABOTABEK offer just such a space "to exploit incarceral modes of labor control."[85] Not surprisingly, this extended space was never left alone. Instead, the administration of the periurban areas around Jakarta was initially staffed by personnel working for the Department of Internal Affairs, a major apparatus of political control responsible for the "development of village society."[86]

The Periurban as the Space of Exception

Anne-Marie Willis, after surveying a number of uses of the term periurban by various scholars, summarizes the association underpinning the notion of periurban:

> Over-reading, then, the periurban seems to be characterized by flux: rapid changes in land-use, built forms, economic activities; mismatches between administrative structures and territory; influxes of new populations; conflicts between new and existing landholders; and visually, somewhere that seems disjunctive, that jars with longstanding preconceptions of the distinctiveness of places, as either fundamentally rural or urban. Linked to this is that the periurban is also nearly always associated with the naming of problems, whether these be issues of urban governance, exploitation of labor, lack of planning and infrastructure, degradation of natural resources and biodiversity or threats to urban food security through loss of agricultural land. This would suggest that change in these territories is undirected, random, opportunistic. The periurban could be considered as a naming of ever-changing spaces of opportunism.[87]

What we learn from this characterization of the periurban is that it is a space filled with both potentials and problems where lack of planning and governance could mean excessive control and vice versa. In this sense, the lack of governance is a form of governance. Periurban may be better understood as a "space of exception" which, to appropriate Giorgio Agamben, is set "in an ambiguous, uncertain, borderline fringe, at the intersection of the legal and the political."[88] As with the case of the periurban of Jakarta, the region was made possible and thus governable and productive by the construction of the category of floating mass. The periurban, with all its problems, informality, and opportunities outlined by Willis, is, in fact, a space with *political* calculation and a mode of governing population through violence of category. In this sense, the periurban can be defined as the establishment, by means of the space of exception, to appropriate Agamben again, "of a legal civil war that allows for the physical elimination not only of political adversaries but of entire categories of citizens who for some reason cannot be integrated into the political system."[89]

As a space of exception, the periurban has its own form of governance, one that is often considered exceptional. It is exceptional because the borderline fringe keeps alive the possibilities for new enterprises and for the state to exploit its resources in the project of constructing new subjects. For instance, in cooperation with the Ministry of Home Affairs, the extended space of Jakarta (especially in the extended areas to the south and the west) was made available for private investors to invest in and develop into a series of organized, and thus secured, new towns for residences.[90] Based on the principle of "large public-private partnership in urban land development and management,"[91] this new space at the fringe is expected to absorb some of the burden of population growth in Jakarta. For instance, the first major consortium, Bumi Serpong Damai (BSD), which consists of ten real estate companies, represented just this attempt "to establish a self-contained New Town" for a new life.[92] The new town is managed by private developers and not by the city hall of Jakarta. However, it would be misleading to say that the residential and industrial zones have developed outside the state policies. Instead, while government has refrained from getting involved in the management of new town, it exerts benefit from the politics of space, which is to turn the fringe into a territory supportive of "national development."[93]

On the edge of Jakarta, occupying an exceptional space, the periurban allows the private sector and the local government to benefit from overriding land use planning, permits, and regulation. For instance, in the course of the 1990s, when large-scale constructions of profitable new towns were booming, the government regulation on land in the areas had changed several times for the convenience of developers and to attract further investments. The effect was a series of land conversions, as Dharmapatni and Firman point out, such that "pressures on prime agricultural land in other places such as Teluk Naga, Tangerang, have continued, as a consortium of seven private developers is presently applying for 4,500 ha to be developed as a 'modern tourism city.'"[94] Situated at the uncertain intersection between the legal and the political, there are ample opportunities for different informal enterprises to grow. One among others is the proliferation of informal fees and "brokers" (*calo*), including "thugs" (*preman*), in the system of land acquisition and building construction for development.[95] The extended space is characterized by lack of ambiguity and looseness, a condition that allows possibilities for informal enterprises to grow. It seems advantageous for the space of the periurban to maintain such a degree of ambiguity, and thus endless possibility for the informal exploitation of the resources of the area. In the end, the ultimate agent is not the state but the assemblage of loosely affiliated social political forces and actors capable of preparing "development programs" for themselves.

Finally, as a space of exception for the exercise of displacement, one might also raise the question of resistance and what the space has meant for the displaced, as did Maruli Tobing and Emmanuel Subangun in 1980. These two well-known journalists asked precisely this question in a metropolitan press:

> When all the efforts of the poor, year after year, decade after decade, have brought no prospect of real change into their experience, we may ask: why do these hungry,

> debt-ridden people not protest? Isn't protest against injustice a continual, central element in the *wayang* (traditional shadow-puppet) stories and in all other kinds of popular myths? . . . Then why, in the concrete reality that has surrounded millions of poor peasants for decades, as the village has been incorporated into the open economy and extreme poverty is now juxtaposed with excessive life-styles—why do the peasants not protest?[96]

Depending on how we interpret differentiation within the seemingly monolithic notion of "the peasant," it seems that Tobing and Subangun were nonetheless disturbed by the absence of resistance. One could look for "resistances of everyday life" and the subtle expression of the "weapons of the weak,"[97] but the periurban has been sustained (for over three decades) not merely by force and isolation but also by opportunity and mobility in which the exploited, too, are contributing to the operation of power. The decline of the peasantry in the periurban and indeed beyond is due in large measure to the regime intolerance of any political organization in the village, the military coercion and self-policing of the victims,[98] but it is also due to the mobile opportunities opened up by the spatial ambiguity of the periurban.

For instance, on the side of the "soft power," the new town (with its conception of an American suburban house) could never be as exclusive and self-contained as it has been promoted. For the operation of their daily lives, the residents of the new town continue to rely on housemaids, vendors, security guards, drivers, and workers from outside the "gated community." The new towns provide opportunities for rural family members to work as off-farm workers. They promote the integration of rural and periurban labor markets and help to alleviate poverty in the village, but at the same time, they contribute to the decline of labor in the agricultural sector. Meanwhile, the imposition of the new town raises land prices, and even with the draconian method of land acquisition, agricultural landowners are inclined to benefit from selling their property to developers. Dharmapatni and Firman point out that "uncontrolled conversion of prime agricultural land has been exacerbated by the reluctance of farmers to retain their land as land prices increase,"[99] for they, too, are eager participants of the wheel of fortune opened up by the space of exception. The massive conversion from agricultural land to development sites was marked by power relations, in which agricultural households basically gave up their lands with unfair compensation. However, such "submission" was encouraged in part by the decline of agriculture where, for farmers in the areas, selling their land became much more profitable than cultivating the fields for paddy.

Many farmers' lands are continuously being sold, often in an unjust marketplace, but many of these displaced individuals have found options of relatively higher wages in the low-wage regime of the industrial and housing construction sectors developed in their region. In some ways, the systematic decline of the wages in the farming sectors is due to the state policy of integrating rural and urban labor markets. Studying the relation between economic development and poverty reduction in Indonesia, Rick Barichello indicates that over the past two decades (starting from the mid-1980s), "there have not been large budget allocations to the agricultural sector" and "little has been done to enhance productivity of the agricultural crops and commodities."[100] And yet, why do the peasants not protest in the midst of declining rural livelihoods? The reason may well be that, as Barichello and others have pointed out, the income growth and poverty reduction in rural areas are being taken care of by nonfarm income and the integration of rural-urban labor markets. In accomplishing this task, the periurban has played a historical role.

The world of the peasantry has been transformed via the formation of the periurban areas. Such spatial formation, I argue, needs to be understood as a paradigm of governance with a mission to temporarily and permanently solve problems that are at once demographic, economic, and political.

EPILOGUE

The Last Circularity? Back to the City and Return to the Village

Max Lane, in his *Unfinished Nation: Indonesia Before and After Suharto*, indicates that mass action politics (banned since 1965), such as street protest mobilizations, factory strikes, and land occupations, have been revived since the late 1980s.[101] However, it is still fair to say that since the establishment of the JABOTABEK in the mid-1970s (after the Malari protest event) and up to the collapse of the Suharto regime, no serious political unrest took place in the capital city and its periurban areas even though social, economical, and environmental crises have become clearly visible in the city. It may sound "spatially deterministic" to claim that the relative peace and order in both the city and the countryside under the authoritarian state were due to the production of the periurban. Nevertheless, we could say that the rural-urban linkages and the exceptional space of the periurban have served to turn the floating mass into a self-policing and self-benefiting "productive" population throughout much of the Suharto era.

The power of space remains an issue to be speculated on and research is still needed to examine the ways in which the periurban was, in fact, received and used daily by the multitude. What we do know is that the "Asian crisis," which has substantially scaled down factories and housing construction in the BOTABEK area, has unleashed a mass amount of unemployed workers back to the streets of the capital city. Many of the floating mass, having lost their jobs in the periurban factories and construction sectors, decided to take up occupations associated with the informal sector in the city.[102] In such time of crisis, many ignored the government offer of 70 percent discounts on economic fare train tickets for traveling across Java back to their villages (perhaps back into agricultural work).[103] The reality bites thus are vividly expressed in the post-Suharto *reformasi* era as portrayed in a metropolitan press in the year 2000:

> The presence of vendors (*kaki lima*) in the capital city is not surprising. However, today their presences have been extremely ignited (*marak*). They do not just display their merchandises on pushcarts or under plastic or canvas tents. Instead they set up their places with permanent stalls, which they also use as their dwellings.[104]

The vendors have registered their presence in the city as part of the post-Suharto urban "social movements" claiming for the rights to survive in the city. Unlike the past, today they do not seem to be afraid of the authority, as a vendor points out, "for today's condition is different from that before the *reformasi*. Today's traders are more daring compared with the past. If they (the security personnel) dismiss us, we will react against them."[105] These forces from below contributed to what Sutiyoso, the post-Suharto governor of Jakarta, described as "the multidimensional crisis," which has contributed to what the governor thought to be "the change in people's behavior," and with fewer job opportunities have caused "difficulties in upholding security and order."[106] The governor, (appointed during Suharto's regime of order), found it unbelievable that "during my first term as governor between 1997 and 2002, 4,538 demonstrations were staged by Jakartans against me . . . from small-scale rallies to ones that led to anarchy.[107] The responses that eventually came, however, were equally harsh. An activist indicates that massive evictions took place in the course of five years in post-Suharto Jakarta, leaving 78,000 urban poor homeless, and at least 65,000 street vendors lost their jobs.[108]

By way of conclusion, it may be useful to acknowledge that these "social movements" claiming "rights to the city" after the fall of Suharto are largely taking place in the center of the city and not so much in the outskirts of the periurban areas. One could only reflect or speculate on the historical roles of the city as the arena of conflicts, but for sure, the periurban is equipped with neither memory nor institutional capacity to organize in part because of the effect of the floating mass.[109] This is a phenomenon that indicates to us the profound connection between space and politics. It also points to the connection between the floating mass, the capital city, and the periurban "space of exception" that the political regime has created.

Finally, are the politics of space and the creation of the periurban as the space of exception described above correct not only for Jakarta or other megacities in Indonesia but also for other megaurban regions of Southeast Asia, which have often been understood as undergoing processes of periurbanization? This is a question that I don't yet have the capacity to answer but I think some basic geopolitical conditions shared by different cities in this post-WWII region may provide some reflections for future research. One might, for instance, suggest the following ideas.

The first was Washington's Cold War largesse in the region, which initiated massive intervention from the Americans and their allies to prevent communist insurrection.[110] In this effort, the largely agricultural societies of Southeast Asia would need to be managed through capitalistically authoritarian anti-communist regimes by ways of controlling the political life of the countryside and the governing of its peasants through the concept of floating mass. Perhaps one needs to look at the security-based development "aid" and its urban-rural planning apparatus made available by Washington in the postwar era to see how it was connected to the spatial organization of the periurban region.

The second condition, related to the first, was the peculiar "subcontracting" discourse led by Japan in its attempt to create an economic zone, which, by the 1970s, had dominated Southeast Asia. The huge inflows of Japanese capital (which generated the first massive demonstration, called the Malari event, in Jakarta in 1974) and later capital from South Korea and Taiwan have made possible the growth of industrial zones at the periurban areas of major capitalist countries in Southeast Asia. The cooperation between Japan and the United States has created not only a particular economic regime for Southeast Asia but also a particular space in which the organization of labor and population was at stake.

These geopolitical forces have produced the periurbanization of capitalist countries in Southeast Asia. But the concretization of this possibility, even after the Cold War has disappeared, owed much to, in Terry McGee's words, "the particular role of the state as a central institutional element in the process of social change."[111] This essay has shown just how important the particular role of the state has been in leading the process of (peri)urbanization to "the end of the peasantry."

Where are the peasants to be located in the post–Cold War era and, more specially, after the collapse of the authoritarian regime of Suharto?[112] The new era that followed has its own markers: in another power, in the legacies of imperialism and postcolonialism, in the institutions of neoliberalism. Here, too, there are witnesses and voices that continue to weigh heavily and importantly to ask what obligations the present bears for the past, which seems to carry over to the future. For instance, Achmad Ya'kub, a member of the post-Suharto Indonesian Federation of Peasant Unions (*Federasi Serikat Petani Indonesia*, FSPI) reports that (although the peasants he described did not come from just periurban areas),

> On May 17, 2006, the streets of Jakarta filled with thousands of peasants. More than ten thousand men, women and children from the remote villages of Java flocked to the city centre with their banners, songs and the sound of the drums to one of the largest protests for agrarian reform since the end of the New Order in 1998. They were joined by workers, students, youth groups, urban poor, and other civil society representatives.
>
> The Indonesian Federation of Peasant Unions (FSPI) and La Campesina initiated this mass mobilisation to protest against two major events in Jakarta critical to the direction of agrarian policy nationally and regionally. Firstly, the Food and Agriculture Organisation (FAO) which in its 28th Regional Conference for Asia and the Pacific in Jakarta declared faith in trade liberalisation to alleviate poverty "in line with the spirit of the WTO Doha Development Agenda." . . . Secondly, farmers in Indonesia are alarmed by the current move by the National Land Body (an institution directly under the presidency of the republic) to implement the World Bank's concept of "market led land reform" which focuses on the liberalisation of the land market (through land titling) and not on land distribution. . . .
>
> Protestors left from the Istiqlal mosque early morning and walked to the Presidential Palace. There, the president sent an official delegation (the minister of Agriculture, the chief of the National Land Body, the cabinet secretary and its spokesperson) to meet the farmers' leaders. The official delegation told the protestors that they had "the same heart and mind" as the farmers, but that "even if power was in their hands, they could not use it alone." The peasants replied that if no concrete step was taken towards genuine agrarian reform, they would organize more mass actions and land occupations in the future.
>
> The protesters then marched to a central circle (*Bundaran Hotel Indonesia*) to spread out information about agrarian reform among the public passing by. . . . The march then went to the Parliament building where representatives from vari-

ous parties addressed the farmers. From the top of a truck, they promised them to implement land reform, but farmers had heard it before. They shouted at the parliamentarians: "Don't promise it, do it!" They also shouted: "Come to our village, and see for yourself how we live!"

After an exhausting day of protest under the sun, some 7500 peasants which had come to Jakarta in 120 buses spent the night in the city and left at dawn to return to their villages. That same day, some protestors from Ciamis (West Java) occupied 300 hectares of land belonging to a teak plantation. A sign that agrarian reform in Indonesia cannot wait anymore.[113]

NOTES

1. An earlier version of this paper was first presented as part of the workshop, "The End of the Peasant? Global Capitalism and the Future of Agrarian Society," organized by Arif Dirlik and Alexander Woodside for the Peter Wall Summer Institute for Research, University of British Columbia, 2009. This version was presented at the Asian Research Institute (ARI) Seminar Series, National University of Singapore, June 1, 2010. Thanks to participants of the seminars for their helpful comments.

2. This kind of debate in some ways is influenced by the urban bias thesis. For this theory see, among others, Michael L. Lipton, *Why Poor People Stay Poor: Urban Bias in World Development* (London: Temple Smith, 1977).

3. Terry McGee, "Presidential Address: Eurocentrism in Geography—The Case of Asian Urbanization," *The Canadian Geographer* 35, no. 4 (1991): 341. McGee indicates that "what I mean by urbanization is the process of the growth of urban places within the administrative boundaries defined by nations as urban as well as at the margins of cities. The advancement of this process of urban spread into the densely crowded rural hinterlands created a *desakota* region. Desakota thus is one spatial and conceptual part of the urban phenomenon" (personal communication, May 15, 2009). Efforts to explore the characteristics of Asian urban geography have been made earlier by Dutch and other European scholars in the pre-WWII era. For a recent attempt, see Paul Kratoska, Remco Raben, and N. H. Schulte, eds., *Locating Southeast Asia: Geographies of Knowledge and Politics of Space* (Singapore: Singapore University Press, 2005).

4. Terry McGee, "The Emergence of *Desakota* Regions in Asia," in *The Extended Metropolis: Settlement Transition in Asia*, ed. Norton Ginsburg, Bruce Koppel, and Terry McGee (Honolulu: University of Hawaii Press, 1991): 7.

5. Phillip Kelly, "Everyday Urbanization: The Social Dynamics of Development on Manila's Extended Metropolitan Region," *International Journal of Urban and Regional Research* 23 (1999): 283–303.

6. Mike Davis, "Planet of Slums: Urban Involution and the Informal Proletariat," *New Left Review* (March–April 2004): 8.

7. Jonathan Rigg, "Rural-urban Interactions, Agriculture and Wealth: A Southeast Asian Perspective," *Progress in Human Geography* 22, no. 4 (1998): 515.

8. Gregory Eliyu Guldin, *What's a Peasant to Do? Village Becoming Town in Southern China* (Boulder, CO: Westview Press, 2001).

9. For an examination of the cultural ideological and economic forces driving the development of the periurban areas of Jakarta, see Tommy Firman, "The Emergence of Extended Metropolitan Regions in Indonesia: Jabotabek and Bandung Metropolitan Area," *Review*

of Urban and Regional Developmental Studies 7 (1995): 167–188; Tommy Firman, "The Restructuring of Jakarta Metropolitan Area: A 'Global City' in Asia," *Cities* 15, no. 4 (1998): 229–243; Michael Leaf, "The Suburbanization of Jakarta: A Concurrence of Economic and Ideology," *Third World Planning Review* 16, no. 4 (1994): 341–356; Michael Leaf, "Building the Road for the BMW: Culture, Vision, and the Extended Metropolitan Region of Jakarta," *Environment and Planning A*, no. 28 (1996): 1617–1635.

10. To understand the political history of an urban formation is to respond to the call for "geography of engagement." See McGee, "Presidential Address: Eurocentrism in Geography," 241.

11. The labor demand of the wet-rice agricultural system is not only large but also fluctuates by the on- and off-seasons. The off-season has prompted farmers to take up various non-agricultural occupations. Historically, farmers in Indonesia thus have multiple occupations.

12. In addition to these, there are categories that one could find in the politics of urban Indonesia such as *massa* (mass) and *rakyat* (people). See James Siegel, *A New Criminal Type in Jakarta: Counter-Revolution Today* (Durham: Duke University Press, 1998).

13. Kenneth Watts, "Tanggerang: A Case Study in Planning Policy for a Small Town within a Tropical Metropolitan Region," *Planning Outlook* 5, no. 4 (1962): 5.

14. Pramoedya Ananta Toer wrote in 1955, "Before I came to Jakarta, I thought as you do. I dreamed that I would do great things, that I would be equal in mind and body to the opportunities I would find. Perhaps you will be luckier than I was. The wind blows through the provinces whispering that one cannot be fully Indonesian until one has seen Jakarta." Pramoedya Ananta Toer, "Letter to a Friend from the Country," in *From Surabaya to Armageddon*, ed. and trans. H. Aveling (Singapore: Heinemann Books, 1955).

15. J. M. van der Kroef, *Indonesia in the Modern World*, vol. I (Bandung: Masa Baru, 1954): 157.

16. Watts, "Tanggerang," 5.

17. Ibid., 19.

18. For a development of Jakarta's planned deconcentration after Kenneth Watts, see Christopher Silver, *Planning the Megacity: Jakarta in the Twentieth Century*. (London: Routledge, 2008): 111–124; see also Lambert Giebels, "JABOTABEK: An Indonesian-Dutch Concept on Metropolitan Planning of the Jakarta Region," in *The Indonesian City: Studies in Urban Development and Planning*, ed. Peter Nas (Dirdrecht: Foris Publication, 1986): 101–115. Dirdrecht: Foris Publication, 1986: 101-115.

19. Most analysis estimates the number of people slaughtered to be between 500,000 and 2 million. In addition, over 10,000 were detained for more than ten years. The killings and arrests mostly took place in the rural areas. See Robert Cribb, *The Indonesian Killings of 1965–1966: Studies from Java and Bali* (Melbourne: Monarch University, 1990). For a recent account about the event, see John Roosa, *Pretext for Mass Murder: The September 30th Movement and Suharto's Coup d'etat in Indonesia* (Madison: University of Wisconsin Press, 2006).

20. D. N. Aidit (1957), "Indonesia's Class Structure," in *Indonesian Political Thinking 1945–1965*, ed. Herbert Feith and Lance Castles (Ithaca, NY: Cornell University Press, 1970): 254. The communist party leader, D. N. Aidit, who must have picked up the sophisticated view of the peasantry from Marx, Lenin, and Mao Tse-Tung, had a nuanced definition of the peasants, which in some ways, helped determine the target of violence. "What we mean when we use the term 'peasants' is mainly the poor and middle peasants that make up the majority of the inhabitants of the villages. In leading the people's struggle in the countryside, the Party must always strive to be able to draw in and mobilize 90 per cent of the village inhabitants and must firmly base itself on the poor peasants and the peasant laborers as well as to make an alliance with the middle peasants." Ibid., 254–255.

21. In 1950, soon after the transfer of sovereignty, Indonesian and Dutch experts were appointed by the Ministry of Public Works and Energy, and the team produced a proposal under the name of *Jakarta Raya* (the Greater Jakarta), which according to Giebels, "had much in common with the later JABOTABEK." See Lambert J. Giebels, "JABOTABEK: An Indonesian-Dutch Concept on Metropolitan Planning of the Jakarta-Region" in *The Indonesian City*, edited by Peter J. Nas (Dirdrecht: Foris Publication, 1986): 102.

22. His mission was to ensure that Jakarta would eventually become a metropolitan region, which would ultimately get rid of the negative image of Jakarta, the big village. See Ali Sadikin, "The Big Village Harus Jadi Metropolitan [The big village must become a metropolis]" in *Bang Ali: Demi Jakarta, 1966–1977* [Bang Ali: For Jakarta, 1966–1977], written by Ramadhan K. H. (Jakarta: Pustaka Sinar Harapan, 1995): 436–445.

23. See Ernst Utrecht, "Political Mobilizations of Peasants in Indonesia," *Journal of Contemporary Asia* 6, no. 3 (1976): 284.

24. Gary Hansen, *Rural Local Government and Agricultural Development in Java, Indonesia*, The Rural Development Committee Report, Center for International Studies (Ithaca, NY: Cornell University, 1974): 35.

25. Ben White, "Organization of peasants and rural poor in Indonesia, past and present," in *Ontwikkeling van Onderop: Zelforganisatie in de Derde Wereld*, ed. J. P. de Groot (Amsterdam: VU Uitgeverij, 1993): 98.

26. Gary Hansen, *Rural Local Government and Agricultural Development in Java, Indonesia.*

27. Salim Rashid and M. G. Quibria, "Is land reform passé? With special reference to Asian agriculture," in *Critical Issues in Asian Development: Theories, Experiences and Policies*, ed. M. G. Quibria (Hong Kong: Oxford University Press, 1997): 145. For a review of the agricultural debate during the eras of Sukarno and after including a critical assessment of Clifford Geertz's work on agricultural involution, see Ben White, "Java and Social Theory: Agrarian Debates, Past and Present," in *The Java that Never Was: Academic Theories and Political Practices*, ed. Hans Antlov and Jorgen Hellman (Munster: LIT Verlag, 2005): 157–185. For an assessment of the agrarian issues on the eve of the New Order, see Ina Slamet, *Views and Strategies of the Indonesian Peasant Movement on the Eve of Its Annihilation in 1965–1966* (The Hague: Institute of Social Studies, 1988). See also, Soekarno (1957), "Marhaen and Proletariat," in *Indonesian Political Thinking 1945–1965*, ed. Herbert Feith and Lance Castles (Ithaca: Cornell University Press, 1970): 154–160; D. N. Aidit, *Kaum Tani Mengganjang Setan-Setan Desa: Laporan Singkat Tentang Hasil Riset Mengenai Keadaan Kaum Tani dan Gerakan Tani Djawa Barat* [Peasants fighting against rural demons: A short report from research on the conditions of peasants and their movements in West Java] (Jakarta: Yayasan Pembaruan, 1964): 35.

28. Ernst Utrecht, "Political Mobilisations of Peasants in Indonesia," 284.

29. Gillian Hart, Andrew Turton, and Ben White, *Agrarian Transformations: Local Processes and the State in Southeast Asia* (Berkeley: University of California Press, 1989).

30. Gary Hansen reported that "in summary, while the Green Revolution has demonstrated its capacity to increase productivity, there is less convincing evidence concerning the flow of rural benefits to the producers." Gary Hansen, *Rural Local Government and Agricultural Development in Java, Indonesia*, 57.

31. Suharto, "Plans for Development," *Bulletin for Indonesian Economic Studies* 11 (1968): 101–102.

32. For an analysis of agrarian change as an issue of class formation and the exercise of class power during the era of the Green Revolution, see Jonathan Pincus, *Class Power and Agrarian Change: Land and Labour in Rural West Java* (London: Macmillan Press, 1996).

33. Ben White, "Organization of peasants and rural poor in Indonesia," 92.

34. Ben White, "Java and Social Theory: Agrarian Debates, Past and Present," 176–177.

35. As cited in Ian Chalmers and Vedi Hadiz, eds., *The Politics of Economic Development in Indonesia: Contending Perspectives* (London: Routledge, 1997): 73.

36. Max Lane, *Unfinished Nation: Indonesia Before and After Suharto* (London: Verso, 2008): 2.

37. Max Lane, *Unfinished Nation: Indonesia Before and After Suharto*, ibid., 45.

38. Ina E. Slamet, *Cultural Strategies for Survival: The Plight of the Javanese* (Rotterdam: The Comparative Asian Studies Programme, 1982): 38.

39. Ali Moertopo (1972), "The Acceleration and Modernisation of the 25 Years' Development," reprinted under "Ali Moertopo: The Floating Mass," in *Indonesian Politics and Society: A Reader*, ed. David Bourchier and Vedi Hadiz (London: Routledge, 2003): 47–48.

40. See the editorial comment in *Kompas* on the concept of the floating mass published on 25 December 1971. Reprinted in David Bourchier and Vedi Hadiz (eds.), *Indonesian Politics and Society: A Reader*, ibid., 70. Kompas at least was critical to the concept and asked, "If, for instance, the interests of the majority of the people in the villages are damaged by some individual in authority, to whom shall they turn for political protection?" Ibid.

41. Koentjaraningrat, "Population mobility in villages around Jakarta," *Bulletin of Indonesian Economic Studies* 11, no. 2 (1979): 112–113.

42. Li Tana, *Peasants on the Move: Rural-Urban Migration in the Hanoi Region* (Singapore: Institute of Southeast Asian Studies, 1996). Graeme Hugo recognized peasants' mobility as "circular migration" in his PhD dissertation. G. J. Hugo, "Population Mobility in West Java, Indonesia." Department of Demography, Australian National University, 1975.

43. R. D. Hill, "Stasis and Change in Forty Years of Southeast Asian Agriculture," *Singapore Journal of Tropical Geography* 19, no. 1 (1998): 1–25.

44. The existence of nonagricultural secondary economic activities in rural areas is an ancient phenomenon that seems to be widespread in Southeast Asia. See Anthony Reid, *Southeast Asia in the Age of Commerce* (New Haven: Yale University Press, 1988).

45. Jonathan Rigg, "Evolving Rural-Urban Relations and Livelihoods," in *Southeast Asia Transformed: A Geography of Change*, ed. Chia Lin Sien (Singapore: Institute of Southeast Asian Studies, 2003): 235.

46. Jonathan Rigg points out that "what village studies since the 1980s almost invariably show is a dramatic diversification in people's livelihoods away from agriculture and into assorted non-farm activities." Jonathan Rigg, "Evolving Rural-Urban Relations and Livelihoods," ibid., 234.

47. As cited in Ian Chalmers and Vedi Hadiz (eds.), *The Politics of Economic Development in Indonesia*, 77.

48. As cited in Michael Specter, "Letter from Jakarta," *Far Eastern Economic Review* (March 8, 1984).

49. The *bersih lingkungan* was a program to the nation of communism. It was institutionalized in 1980 but had started in 1966.

50. Kartini Sjahrir, *Pasar Tenaga Kerja Indonesia: Kasus Sektor Konstruksi* [The labor market in Indonesia: The case of construction sector] (Jakarta: Grafiti Press in association with the Center for Policy and Implementation Studies, 1995): 49.

51. See Ali Sadikin, *Bang Ali: Demi Jakarta 1966–1977*: 271. It is a common practice for Indonesian dignitaries to "write" memoirs at the end of his or her tenure in the government to be remembered as patriots who have served the nation. The publisher made a special comment about the memoir of Ali Sadikin. At the half-page preface, the publisher pointed out that "Ali Sadikin who worked as the Governor of Jakarta from 1966 to 1977 has tried to build Jakarta which at the beginning of his term did not look like a modern capital city. The still

unstable political environment (*gejolak politik*) [after the failed attempt of the 30th September Communist movement] has contributed to the problems in the city." Ali Sadikin, *Bang Ali: Demi Jakarta 1966–1977*, 7.

52. Ali Sadikin did not define *gelandangan* for us, but Soetjipto Wirosardjono, Deputy Chairman of the Central Bureau of Statistics in the 1980s and 1990s, at least tried to identify *gelandangan* as

> new comers who have recently moved from rural areas to the city for employment and have not succeeded. Because they are poorly educated and have few contacts they start by becoming a scavenger. If the leader of scavengers has a house they will live there; if they cannot stay with him for some reason they will find themselves in the homeless status. They are socially ashamed to go back to the rural areas so they adapt to the situation [in the city]. They normally don't have any relatives in the city, or other people to fall back on. Although they are eligible to stay in the rehabilitation centers organized by the Ministry of Social Affairs, they often choose to stay outside. There are a lot of regulations in the rehabilitation centers. For example, as a homeless you can still find some income as a scavenger or as a beggar, which you can spend as you wish. So at least, outside the rehabilitation centers, they still possess a certain amount of freedom, which is very important for them. Soetjipto Wirosardjono, "The Informal Sector: Victims of a Double Standard," *Prisma* 51 (1991): 67.

53. Ali Sadikin, *Bang Ali*, 148–149.

54. Vagrants didn't even find a place in Sukarno's most inclusive category of "Marhaen," which referred to all kinds of the destitute people (of Indonesia). See also D. N. Aidit's (1957) position toward vagrants in "Indonesia's Class Structure," in *Indonesian Political Thinking 1945–1965*, ed. Feith and Castles, 256–257.

55. Ali Sadikin, *Gita Jaya: Catatan H. Ali Sadikin, Gubernur Kepala Daerah Khusus Ibukota Jakarta, 1966–1977* [Gita Jaya: Notes from Ali Sadikin, the Governor of Jakarta, 1966–1977] (Jakarta: Pemda Khusus Ibu Kota Jakarta, 1977): 160.

56. Graeme Hugo points out that "circular migration allows highly valued social benefits of village residence to be essentially maintained." Graeme Hugo, "Circular Migration," *Bulletin of Indonesian Economic Studies* 13, no. 3 (November 1977): 62.

57. For a discussion of *pondok*, see Lea Jellinek, "The Pondok of Jakarta," *Bulletin of Indonesian Economic Studies* 13, no. 3 (November 1977): 67–71. I discussed the political attempt of Jakarta to become a metropolis in Abidin Kusno, *Behind the Postcolonial: Architecture, Urban Space and Political Cultures in Indonesia* (London: Routledge, 2000): 97–119.

58. For *transmigrasi* see J. M. Hardjono, *Transmigration in Indonesia* (Kuala Lumpur: Oxford University Press, 1977); and M. Otten, *Transmigrasi: Indonesian Resettlement Policy, 1965–1985*, International Work Group for Indigenous Affairs, Document 57 (Copenhagen: IWGIA Publication, 1986).

59. Ali Sadikin, *Bang Ali: Demi Jakarta*: 177. Governor Ali Sadikin used *urbanisasi* to refer to population growth.

60. Construction industries were prosperous in the 1970s due to the oil boom. See Kartini Sjahrir, *Pasar Tenaga Kerja Indonesia: Kasus Sektor Konstruksi*, 53.

61. See Kartini Sjahrir, ibid., 49.

62. Ali Sadikin, *Bang Ali*, 366.

63. See Ali Sadikin, *Gita Jaya*, and also Edi Sedyawati, et al., *Sejarah Kota Jakarta, 1950–1980* [History of Jakarta, 1850–1980] (Jakarta: Departemen Pendidikan dan Kebudayaan, 1986/87): 85.

64. Sadikin, *Bang Ali*, op. cit., 386.

65. I would like to thank Terry McGee for the story of the Mitsubishi Colt.

66. See Peter G. Warr, "The Jakarta Export Processing Zone: Benefits and Costs," *Bulletin of Indonesian Economic Studies* XIX, no. 3 (December 1983): 28.

67. Warr, "The Jakarta Export Processing Zone," 28–29.

68. Peter Warr indicates that "the nominal ownership of firms operating in the zone differs radically from that seen in EPZs elsewhere in Asia. Of the 18 firms occupying the zone by 1982, three were nominally Indonesian-owned, three were joint ventures between Indonesians and foreign Chinese or Indians, one was Indian and the remaining eleven were owned by Hong Kong, Singapore or Taiwan interests" (Warr, "The Jakarta Export Processing Zone," 30). Warr notes that these firms are also indirectly owned by North American and European firms.

69. See Lambert J. Giebels, "JABOTABEK," op. cit.; also Sadikin, *Gita Jaya*, op. cit., 223.

70. See Edi Sedyawati et al., *Sejarah Kota Jakarta 1950–1980* (Jakarta: Departemen Pendidikan dan Kebudayaan, 1986/1987): 34.

71. Soetjipto Wirosardjono, Deputy Chairman of the Central Bureau of Statistics, pointed out in 1991 that the agglomeration of urban centers in the surrounding area of Jakarta was purely the power of the market economy. Soetjipto Wirosardjono, "The Informal Sector: Victims of a Double Standard," *Prisma* 51 (1991): 61.

72. Soetjipto Wirosardjono, ibid., 61.

73. Diane Wolff, *Factory Daughters: Gender, Household Dynamics, and Rural Industrialization in Java* (Berkeley: University of California Press, 1989): 109.

74. Hasan Poerbo, "A Glimpse of Tragedy and a Question of Morality," *Prisma* 51 (1991): 76.

75. Hasan Poerbo, ibid., 77.

76. Soetjipto Wirosardjono, "The Informal Sector," 62.

77. See Her Suganda, "Fenomena Kota Baru Sekitar Botabek," *Kompas* 10 (September 1995): 9.

78. For instance, Presidential Instruction No. 53 of 1989 has made possible some 36,800 hectares for the development of a *desakota* industrial zone along the corridor of Purwakarta-Serang with possibility for further expansion. See Her Suganda, "Fenomena Kota Baru Sekitar Botabek," *Kompas* 10 (September 1995): 9.

79. See Ida Ayu Indira Dharmapatni and Tommy Firman, "Problems and Challenges of Mega-Urban Regions in Indonesia: The Case of Jabotabek and the Bandung Metropolitan Area," in *The Mega-Urban Regions of Southeast Asia*, ed. T. G. McGee and Ira M. Robinson (Vancouver: UBC Press, 1996): 308.

80. In 1989, through the Presidential Decree No. 53, the state reorganized Bekasi (the periurban to the east of Jakarta) into clusters of industrial zones along the toll road to Purwakarta (on the way to Bandung).

81. See Tommy Firman, "The Restructuring of Jakarta Metropolitan Area," *Cities* 15, no. 4 (1998): 237.

82. Ida Ayu Indira Dharmapatni and Tommy Firman, "Problems and Challenges of Mega-Urban Regions in Indonesia," 308.

83. Ida Ayu Indira Dharmapatni and Tommy Firman, ibid., 307.

84. Soetjipto Wirosardjono, "The Informal Sector," 67.

85. Ong Aihwa, *Neoliberalism as Exception* (Durham: Duke University of Press, 2006): 21.

86. For a description of the role of the Department of Internal Affairs in the governance of urban politics and economy, see Ali Sadikin, *Bang Ali*, op. cit., 83–87; see also Ben White, "Organization of Peasants," 100.

87. Anne-Marie Willis, "From Peri-urban to Unknown Territory," *Changing City Structures* 14 (2005): 3. Available: http://www.griffith.edu.au/__data/assets/pdf_file/0020/81209/city-structures-14-willis.pdf.

88. Giorgio Agamben, *State of Exception*, trans. Kevin Attel (Chicago: University of Chicago Press, 2005): 1 (citing Alessandro Fontana).

89. Giorgio Agamben, *State of Exception*, ibid., 2.

90. The periurban gave rise to Real Estate Indonesia (REI), an association of corporate housing developers that was approved by Governor Sadikin in 1975.

91. See Jo Santoso, "The Bumi Serpong Damai New Town – A Large Public-Private Partnership in Urban Land Development and Management," *Trialog* 32 (1992): 36.

92. Jo Santoso, one of the senior planners for the new town described the rationale behind the construction of BSD: "One of the most important results of modernization process is the increasing number of the urban population specially the genesis of the middle and low-income classes. These groups of people are basically looking for a new living environment, which conforms more to their new life styles. From the cultural aspects the birth of BSD, the new city project can be seen as an attempt by this new 'middle class' of realizing their 'dream' to create a new living environment that is able to accommodate their prerequisites for a higher standard of life." See Jo Santoso, "The Bumi Serpong Damai New Town" ibid: 36.

93. For a discussion of the relations between the construction of the new town and the formation of "middle class" in the context of the New Order's politics of nation building in Jakarta, see Abidin Kusno, *Behind the Postcolonial.*

94. Ida Ayu Indira Dharmapatni and Tommy Firman, "Problems and Challenges of Mega-Urban Regions in Indonesia," 305.

95. See Tommy Firman, "New Town Development in Jakarta Metropolitan Region: A Perspective of Spatial Segregation," *Habitat International* 28, no. 3 (2004): 349–368; Michael Leaf, "Building the Road for the BMW."

96. As translated by and cited in Ben White, "Organization of peasants and rural poor in Indonesia," 97. At the time of the 1997–1998 political and financial crises, groups of unemployed workers in the periurban area of Jakarta occupied "golf courses." Some inscribed "this is people's land" with their hoes, and others began to grow vegetables. See "Ratusan petani tanami lapangan golf Cimacan" [Hundreds of peasants plant golf course at Cimacan] *Kompas online* (June 15, 1998).

97. James Scott, "Everyday Forms of Resistance," in *Everyday Forms of Peasant Resistance in Southeast Asia*, ed. James Scott and Ben Kerkvliet (London: Frank Cass, 1986), 5–35; James Scott, *Weapons of the Weak: Everyday Forms of Peasant Resistance* (New Haven: Yale University Press, 1985); and Ong Aihwa, *Spirits of Resistance and Capitalists Discipline: Factory Women in Malaysia* (Albany, NY: State University of New York Press, 1987).

98. Ben White, "Organization of peasants and rural poor in Indonesia," 97.

99. Ida Ayu Indira Dharmapatni and Tommy Firman, "Problems and Challenges of Mega-Urban Regions in Indonesia," 305.

100. Rick Barichello, "Economic Development and Poverty Reductions in East Asia: The Impact of OECD Agricultural Policies," paper for seminar on "The Impact and Coherence of OECD Country Policies on Asian Developing Economies," Paris, 10–11 June, 2004 (in possession of the author).

101. For a history of Indonesian mass politics, see Max Lane, *Unfinished Nation: Indonesia Before and After Suharto* (London: Verso, 2008).

102. For a discussion of the social environment of Jakarta in the immediate post-Suharto era, see Abidin Kusno, "Whither Nationalist Urbanism? Public Life in Governor Sutiyoso's Jakarta," *Urban Studies* 41, no. 12 (2004): 2377–2394.

103. M. Cohen, "Easing Labour's Pain," *Far Eastern Economic Review* 29 (January 1998): 17.

104. "Jakarta mirip kota kaki lima" [Jakarta is like a city of vendors], *Kompas* (June 12, 2000): 29.

105. "Belum efektif, penanganan pedagang kaki lima" [Not yet efficient, the management of vendors], *Suara Pembaharuan* (August 12, 1999): 16.

106. *Jakarta Post,* "Sutiyoso blames public for his failure," 19 July 2002: 2.

107. *Jakarta Post,* "Sutiyoso: most maligned governor?" 11 November 2002: 8.

108. Sri Maryanti, "*Upaya Warga Meraih Kota* [Attempts by citizens to have their rights to the city]," in *Mendengarkan Kota,* [Listening to the city] (Jakarta: Institute for Ecosoc Rights, 2007): 175.

109. One of the political memories of the area that the state has incorporated into its narrative of "sacrifice for the nation" is the fight in 1945–1949 in Jakarta, Karawang, and Bekasi for the nation's independence against the returning Dutch. The event inspired poet Chairil Anwar to write "*Antara Karawang—Bekasi* [Between Karawang and Bekasi]," and Promoedya Ananta Toer (1951) to produce a novel: *Di Tepi Kali Bekasi* [At the riverside of Bekasi].

110. For an assessment of the rise and the fall of Southeast Asian developmentist regime in relation to the Cold War, see Benedict Anderson, "From Miracle to Crash," *London Review of Books* 16 (April 1998): 3–7.

111. Terry McGee, "Presidential Address: Eurocentrism in Geography—The Case of Asian Urbanization," *The Canadian Geographer* 35, no. 4 (1991): 341.

112. For a detailed study of Indonesian peasants in the post-Suharto era, see Anton Lucas and Carol Warren, "The State, the People, and Their Mediators: The Struggle over Agrarian Law Reform in Post-New Order Indonesia," *Indonesia* 76 (October 2003): 87–126.

113. Achmad Ya'kub, "Peasants march for agrarian reform in Jakarta: 'Don't promise it, do it!'" June 29, 2006. Available: http://www.landaction.org/display.php?article=428.

CHAPTER 12

Land Occupations and Land Reform in Zimbabwe

TOWARD THE NATIONAL DEMOCRATIC REVOLUTION[1]

SAM MOYO AND PARIS YEROS

INTRODUCTION

The land occupation movement in Zimbabwe has obtained the first major land reform since the end of the Cold War. It has also been the most important challenge to the neocolonial state in Africa under structural adjustment, and if judged by its effectiveness in acquiring land, it has also been the most notable of rural movements in the world today.[2]

Yet it has proved an intellectual challenge and a matter of political ambivalence. On the one hand, the land reform process has presented genuine intellectual challenges, raising fundamental analytical questions regarding peripheral capitalism, the state, and nationalism. On the other hand, neither academia nor "progressive" political forces have risen to the task. Most have readily denounced the land reform process as "destructive" of the state, its nationalism as "authoritarian" or "exhausted" (i.e., belonging to a previous era); others have gone the other way, celebrating the land reform as the culmination of "black empowerment" or "economic indigenisation."

The polarization of the debate has less to do with the peculiarities of Zimbabwe and more to do with the state of academia in the 1990s. This has been marked by a diversion into rarefied debates over "identity politics," nationally and internationally, and a generalized embourgeoisement of nationalist intellectuals. Certainly, twenty years ago, radical land reform in Zimbabwe would have received a different response.

While the event would have presented considerable analytical difficulties even then, progressive intellectuals would have proceeded to debate the relevant issues rigorously, and these would have concerned the nature of the neocolonial state, intercapitalist conflict, peasant-worker relations, the class struggles within the land occupation movement, and the direction of the national democratic revolution.

Why such a change in just twenty years? Is it that neocolonialism is no longer relevant? Did structural adjustment deliver national democracy? Or is it that the national form of sovereignty itself has been superseded by neoliberal globalization? Nothing, of course, could be further from the truth. The answer lies precisely in the cooptation of both academia and "oppositional" politics, to the point where imperialism has become mystified, national self-determination demoted, the state obscured, and the agrarian question abandoned.[3] Such intellectual reversals have had real political effects, perhaps most clearly in relation to Zimbabwe, whose radical nationalism and land reform have proved unpalatable to the "civic" and "post" nationalisms of domestic and international social forces.

THE POLITICAL ECONOMY OF NEOCOLONIALISM

The political economy of Zimbabwe is comparable to that of other African, Latin American, and Asian states that have remained in a disarticulated pattern of accumulation with unresolved agrarian questions. This persisting underdevelopment is part and parcel of the neocolonial situation, that is, the failure of juridically independent states to complete the national democratic revolution. This remains the case despite complete transitions to capitalism in the twentieth century.

The case of Zimbabwe, and Southern Africa more generally, consists in a subtype of neocolonialism, deriving from the white-settler colonial experience. One crucial aspect of white-settler colonial capitalism was that, periodically, it manifested strong contradictions between introverted and extroverted capitalist accumulation strategies. This was especially the case in Zimbabwe upon the emergence of an industrial bourgeoisie in the course of the two World Wars. In this sense, the historical experience of Zimbabwe (together with South Africa) can be understood as comparable to semiperipheral Latin American countries. A second aspect of white-settler capitalism, however, was that, in the organization of the labor process, white capital exercised both "direct" and "indirect" power over the indigenous black population. This contrasts with recent interpretations regarding the primacy of "indirect" rule in Africa,[4] and it also contrasts with Latin American experiences, where the postslavery *latifundio-minifundio* system did not institutionalize racial segregation. These two aspects of white-settler capitalism have given a particular shape to neocolonialism in Zimbabwe, notably in its dynamics of class, race, and nation.

The White-Settler Colonial State

The political economy of colonial Zimbabwe began to exhibit its peculiar tendencies early in the twentieth century, as the initial speculative incursion by mining capital gave way to the establishment of a white agrarian bourgeoisie with a partial interest in the home market. The ensuing years were marked by an intensifying intercapitalist conflict between white agrarian capital, on the one hand, and mining capital and London-based finance on the other.[5] This culminated in 1923 in the establishment of white "self-government" in the colony of Southern Rhodesia, by which the white agrarian bourgeoisie both established its political leadership and struck a compromise with extroverted capitals.

Also established under the leadership of white agrarian capital, however, was the institutionalization of racial segregation. In itself, this was a profound contradiction to whatever designs white agrarian capital may have had for the development of the home market—for the vision of the "home market" held by white agrarian capital would thereafter be confined to the white settler element and would only partly be challenged in due course by the emergence of a white industrial bourgeoisie. This white supremacist framework was to leave an indelible mark on the development of capitalism in the white-settler colonial state. From an early stage, white agrarian capital demonstrated that, while it was "more than comprador," it was "less than national";[6] and over time, while intercapitalist conflict would challenge the foundations of racial segregation, it would never do so to the point of becoming properly "national," that is, of producing an alliance between white industrial capital and popular nationalist forces for the concerted development of the home market.

The seeds of black capitalism were also sown from the early days of the white-settler colonial state. In the interwar years, the state allowed for the creation of a small black agrarian capitalist class outside the communal areas—in the Native Purchase Areas—as a means of cultivating a bourgeois alliance across the racial divide. But this project remained insignificant, as the white-settler colonial state refused to support black capital for its expansion and, indeed, competition with white agrarian capital. Beyond Purchase Area farmers, a small black bourgeoisie also developed within the communal areas, together with the development of commodity production, but this, too, was to be prohibited from dynamic development.

The labor process in colonial Zimbabwe came to be characterized by an enduring contradiction between proletarianization and a politically engineered functional dualism, by which petty-commodity production in the communal areas, and especially unwaged female labor, would subsidize the social reproduction of male labor power on mines and farms. This contradiction would produce neither a settled industrial proletariat nor a viable peasantry, but a workforce in motion, straddling communal lands, white farms, mines, and industrial workplaces. This was the semiproletariat, the aggregate of peasant-worker households, differentiated by gender, and torn between ethno-linguistic particularities and a developing sense of nationhood.[7] Under such conditions, trade union organization was an onerous struggle. The obstacles inherent in semiproletarianization—migration, rural-urban duality, poverty, ethnic and gender cleavages—were compounded by state repression and, in the postwar period, by the onset of divisive tactics by international trade unionism.[8] Nonetheless, early after World War II, trade unionism in the white-settler colonial state did make advances, even to the point of mobilizing successful countrywide strikes in 1945 and 1947.

The mode of rule in colonial Zimbabwe combined direct and indirect forms, for indirect rule in itself was far from self-contained or sufficient to organize the labor process. The segregationist project of white agrarian capital proceeded actively after 1923, in the combined form of territorial segregation, notably by the Land Apportionment Act (1930), and even more crucially, *legal* segregation. As the institutional lynchpin of African-style functional dualism, this consisted in the transfer of judicial authority within communal areas to chiefs, under the Native Affairs Act (1927) and the Native Law and Courts Act (1937), while its social lynchpin was the binding of women to the land by kinship relations, adjudicated by chiefs.[9] Beyond this "indirect rule," white agrarian capital continued to exercise direct power over the vast tracts of "European" land that it appropriated; and there it reproduced relations of personal dependence vis-à-vis black tenants and labor.[10] For its own part, mining capital would perfect the "compound system," by which labor would be bound to the mining compounds by means of a variety of economic and extra-economic instruments.[11] The power of the central state would also be used to undermine African agriculture systematically, taxing it and manipulating it, most notably by the Maize Control Acts (1931, 1934), for the purpose of subsidizing white agrarian capital and reinforcing its economic-structural supremacy, while agrarian, mining, and later industrial capitals as a whole would resort systematically to the deployment of the security forces of the state to suppress trade union organization—notably by the Industrial Conciliation Act (1937, 1937) and the Sedition Act (1936)—as well as, in due course, nationalist mobilization.

World War II and its aftermath brought about a restructuring of the economy, in two important ways. First, industrial capital embarked on a spectacular growth path, expanding output fivefold between 1939 and 1948—in such industries as food-processing, construction, textiles, and clothing[12]—and maturing politically to pose a new challenge to functional dualism. Second, agrarian capital redirected its accumulation strategy resolutely to the external market, by the conversion of its farmland from maize to tobacco.[13] Thereafter, intercapitalist competition would produce a closer alliance between mining and agrarian capital against the industrial bourgeoisie.

Between the late 1940s and the late 1950s, a new compromise was struck among white capitals to further broaden the home market, by two means: first, by the Native Land Husbandry Act (1951), whose intention was to reorganize the communal areas along capitalist lines and to create a settled urban proletariat, and second, by the enlarging of the sphere of influence of white-settler capital beyond Southern Rhodesia to colonial Malawi and Zambia (Nyasaland and Northern Rhodesia) by means of the establishment of the Central African Federation. This process was accompanied by limited reforms in labor relations, as well as in the electoral system, the latter intending to co-opt a black petty-bourgeoisie within the framework and ideology of racial "partnership."

The reforms and the partnership did not succeed or survive. By the late 1950s, the perennial constraints of disarticulated accumulation were imposing themselves on the Federation, and thrusting its balance of payments into crisis; by 1958, class balances and capitalist alliances were entering a new period of reconfiguration. On the one hand, black trade union organization was continuing to advance, now resonating with the popular anticolonial nationalism spreading across the continent. On the other hand, a black bourgeoisie had not emerged in time under the wing of white capital to defend a neocolonial solution. Instead, the white-settler colonial state became polarized between a cross-class African nationalism, led by the black petty-bourgeoisie, and a cross-class white supremacism, led by white agrarian capital.[14] In the following years, nationalist organization was suppressed and driven underground, de-colonization was aborted, unilateral independence declared (UDI) in 1965, and, ultimately, the transition to neocolonialism postponed. With the collapse of the Federation in 1963, Zambia and Malawi would make their neocolonial transitions on their own.

Under UDI, the white-settler colonial state went from boom to bust. It experienced rapid industrial development, as all capitals, including industrial capital, closed ranks under a highly interventionist capitalist state, to be steered into an introverted white-supremacist survival project. This would be facilitated by United Nations–sponsored international sanctions that were permeable by design, de facto allowing for the financing of Rhodesia by Western banks, the importation of oil, military aid, and direct investment by transnational capital—the latter expanding its capital stock by 37 percent in 1966–1976.[15] Until 1974, "sanctions" and state dirigisme would drive an annual average industrial growth rate of 9 percent. However, by the mid-1970s, the white-settler economy was once again overheating, as its unresolved internal and external constraints were reimposing themselves. The state never broadened the home market beyond the settler element, even as it turned inward; instead, it reinforced functional dualism in its segregationist form and relied on the super-exploitation of black labor for rapid capital accumulation. The crisis would be compounded politically and economically by the reorganization of the nationalist movement in two parties, Zimbabwe African National Union (ZANU) and Zimbabwe African People's Union (ZAPU), and the launch of armed struggle in the countryside, with the support of China and the Soviet Union, respectively.

The remaining years of colonial occupation were riveted by guerilla warfare in a Cold War context. By the late 1970s, British and American foreign policies were becoming intensely preoccupied with the possibility of radical outcomes in Southern Africa, henceforth focusing their energies on a negotiated transition to neocolonialism. In 1979, after years of guerilla warfare, and under a Patriotic Front (PF) coalition, the liberation movement would sign up to the neocolonial transition at Lancaster House in London.

From Liberation to Liberalization

The independence of Zimbabwe was celebrated on April 18, 1980, and at long last, Zimbabwe would embark on a nation-building project of its own. But in the new state, the national democratic revolution would remain a matter of social struggle. The "post-white-settler colonial state" was a particular variety of the neocolonial state, for formal power had not been ceded to a black petty-bourgeoisie alone; instead, the aspiring black bourgeoisie would share power with the established white-settler capital.[16] Ideologically, this political dispensation was cast in the form of "reconciliation," an echo of postwar "partnership," consisting effectively in a reconciliation *not* "between the races" but "with capital."[17] Economically, industrial and mining interests remained wholly owned by local white and foreign capital, under monopoly conditions.

For its own part, the white agrarian bourgeoisie, approximately 6,000 white farmers, differentiated in terms of land sizes and quality[18] holding 15.5 million hectares (45 percent of the agricultural land), most of which land was located in better agroecological areas, where the colonial state had concentrated national public investments in agriculture, dams, and other rural infrastructures. A small-scale commercial farming sector comprised 8,500 black farmers on 1.4 million hectares. These farmers held long leaseholds and had the option of buying more land located in drier regions. About 700,000 black families held 16.4 million hectares (formerly called Tribal Trust Lands) located mainly in agroecologically marginal areas and held land under a customary tenure system. From 1978, the state expanded the black townships for the black poor (although this did not adequately meet the needs of thousands of families for homesteads) and opened up the LSCF land markets and urban real estate to blacks. A few middle class and black elites joined the white minority in these land markets.

In all, the white minority, at below 3 percent of the population, commanded nearly two-thirds of national income, while the black majority, at 97 percent, took the remaining one-third. Constitutionally, the Lancaster House agreement established the "willing-buyer, willing-seller" principle as the basis of land transfers, with an expiration date of 1990, and it reserved 20 percent of parliamentary seats for the white community of 3 percent, with an expiration date of 1987.

The Zimbabwean economy at this time was the second most industrialized in sub-Saharan Africa, following South Africa. Zimbabwe inherited the UDI agroindustrial complex, characterized by significant articulation between the sectors (almost half of agricultural output was feeding domestic industry), and diversified production of 7,000 commodities, ranging from food and clothing, to fertilizers and chemicals, to metal products, electrical machinery, and equipment, even to locally assembled automobiles; manufacturing accounted for 25 percent of GDP and earned 40 percent of foreign exchange.[19] Yet, the economy remained fundamentally in a disarticulated pattern of accumulation, and the home market a luxury market, effectively restricted to less than 15 percent of Zimbabwe's seven million people. Moreover, agriculture remained the most important sector, accounting for 40 percent of GDP and employing 70 percent of the population.[20]

Nation-building was rightly cast as a matter of endogenizing the economy, that is, deepening sectoral and social articulation. Yet, under the new political dispensation, facilitated not least by the ongoing organizational weakness of the semiproletariat (to which we will soon turn), the national plan invoked the reformist United Nations language of the 1970s, labeled "Growth with Equity" in the case of Zimbabwe, by which redistribution would be subordinated to the growth/stagnation of industry. In turn, the latter would be seen as the leading developmental sector, not as auxiliary to the technical development of agriculture.

Intercapitalist conflict in the neocolonial state began to manifest new tendencies and alliances. The conventional conflict between introverted and extroverted capitals was compounded by new sources of conflict, namely, between the aspiring black bourgeoisie and white capital, but also *within* the black petty-bourgeoisie itself. Racial conflict was to produce a particular scenario, marked by deep resentment *and* instrumentalization of race by both whites and blacks—the latter to extract concessions, the former to "window dress" monopoly capitalism with black managers. Meanwhile, the intrablack petty-bourgeois conflicts intensified rapidly and tragically. The black petty-bourgeoisie—effectively shut out of the white private sector—was to redirect its accumulation strategies through the state, and moreover resort to the instrumentalization of ethnicity. This would culminate in a violent crackdown by the state in the southern provinces of Matabeleland, from 1983 to 1987, pitting the ruling ZANU-PF party against dissident former PF-ZAPU guerillas. As was astutely observed at the time, under neocolonialism "ethnic diversity becomes employed not to enrich the cultural heritage of the nation but to advance the class interests of groups or segments. The racial divisions are utilized not to entrench national unity but to consolidate class domination and exploitation."[21]

Yet, of most immediate concern to imperial power was the more conventional conflict between introverted and extroverted accumulation strategies. This concern synergized with the distrust of black majority rule generally, and of the ruling party specifically, which continued to profess Marxism-Leninism, despite its Growth and Equity program. In this sense, the Lancaster House constitutional provisions would not be sufficient to quell Anglo-American fears of African nationalism. The imperial task hereafter would be to ensure that extroverted capital would prevail in national politics, and this meant focusing political energy and finance on the cooptation of industrial capital, as represented by the Congress of Zimbabwe Industries (CZI); the other sectors, mining, commerce, and agriculture, were already inclining back to an extroverted alliance with transnational capital, given that the white supremacist state had been defeated.

The imperialist campaign was led by the World Bank and the IMF: the former focusing on industry specifically, by establishing an "export-revolving fund" for the sector in 1985, the latter focusing on gaining leverage over the government by means of debt. At independence, Zimbabwe was seen as "underborrowed," with a debt-service ratio of only 10 percent, which would soon change. Zimbabwe reentered a balance of payment crisis as early as 1982, and this was quickly seized upon.[22] "Within a year of joining [the IMF] from an 'underborrowed' position, Zimbabwe was drawing on a stand-by agreement and was, therefore, in the position of being dictated to in its economic policies."[23] The debt-service ratio soon ballooned to 32 percent. But this was not yet the launch of structural adjustment, only its postponement, as government opted instead for "self-imposed" austerity, in the form of cutbacks in rural development, including land acquisition and resettlement.

A limited amount of land reform took place in the 1980s under the market mechanism. In all, government resettled 58,000 on 3 million hectares of land, reducing the white commercial farming sector to 11 million hectares, 29 percent of agricultural land. As we will see, this was far short of the targeted 162,000 families for resettlement, while the land acquired was largely of low agroecological value.[24] Under the Lancaster House constitutional constraints, more emphasis was placed on rural development in the peasant sector—on research, extension services, roads, and marketing depots—with a budget increase of 37 percent annually in 1980–1985, plus heavy spending on education and health.[25] These would be complemented by rising producer prices in the same period for the main commodities (maize, wheat, beef), such that by 1985, peasants were producing 45 percent of marketed output (up from 8 percent in 1980), although differentiated in terms of agroecological region and class.[26] But in the second half of the 1980s, under economic austerity and industrial stagnation, rural spending would enter a process of reversal. At the same time, the division of labor in agriculture would also shift, with peasants specializing in maize and cotton, and large-scale farmers on the high foreign-exchange earners, tobacco and coffee, as well as maize and cotton. One important political result was that large-scale farmers once again became more clearly extroverted and with an interest to dismantle—that is, liberalize—the price support systems that were being used by the state to transfer income, through infrastructural development, back to the peasant sector.[27]

Industry remained in a state of overcapacity, and by the late 1980s was being co-opted into export markets. Indeed, by 1988, all capitals across sectors had realigned behind a common policy stance of extroversion, specifically the liberalization program promoted by the World Bank. Importantly, this realignment was matched by the ongoing embourgeoisement of the black elite, whose accumulation strategies were still operating on the fringes of monopoly capitalism—in petty commerce, real estate, and the hospitality industry—and with the assistance of the state—a process known as "corruption." It was also in an advanced stage of "compradorization," as a small but powerful group established itself within the white-dominated financial circuit.[28] After 1987, with the end of the Matabeleland violence via the Unity Agreement, and consequently the absorption of PF-ZAPU into the ranks of ZANU-PF, nationalist elites would finally set aside their ethnicized divisions and clear the way for a joint strategy of accumulation.[29] In the following year, discussion would begin for the foundation of the Indigenous Business Development Centre (IBDC), a black business lobby aiming at a better deal against white capital (CZI), and it would soon turn its lobbying energy on "affirmative action" in the course of liberalization. Importantly, the whole process of embourgeoisement, compradorization, and national unification was accompanied by a new political project to establish, by constitutional amendment, a "one-party state," that is, a dictatorship of the bourgeoisie stripped of democratic formalities. As we will see, this would ultimately be defeated, by popular mobilization led by the Zimbabwe Congress of Trade Unions (ZCTU).

If in the rest of the periphery structural adjustment was being imposed by means of the balance of payments crisis,[30] in Zimbabwe, it occurred by cooptation of its domestic capitals. Although Zimbabwe was pursuing austerity policies, it was not yet in a payments crisis.[31] The change of economic direction was further enabled by political transformation in the global arena, specifically the collapse of the Soviet Union, which translated locally into a collapse of legitimacy for statist economic policy. Thus, events moved rapidly: in 1989, a liberal Investment Code was implemented; in 1990, the foreign exchange allocation system was replaced by an Open General Import License; and, finally, in 1990, the Economic Structural Adjustment Programme was launched; this involved the standardized recipe of cuts in public spending, currency devaluation, and the liberalization of prices, interest rates, and trade, followed by deregulation of the capital account and labor relations.

The liberalization program was implemented fully over the next few years, and led to the standard stagflationary effects. By 1992, the trade deficit had ballooned, inflation had tripled to 42 percent, and monetary authorities were implementing "sado-monetarism."[32] The economic results were as follows. Between 1991 and 1995, deindustrialization would set in, with a new round of downsizing and bankruptcies, involving the closure of one-fourth of the clothing sector. Utilization of industrial capacity was further reduced to 65 percent, while by 1998, the contribution of manufacturing to GDP had fallen to 17 percent, down by one-fourth.[33] By 1993, real wages had fallen by two-thirds; by 1995, job losses in both public and private sectors amounted to 45,000, while the share of wages in the national income had dropped from 64 percent to 40 percent, as against the increase in the profit share from 37 percent to 60 percent.[34]

Agricultural policy underwent similar reversals. Marketing boards were commercialized or privatized, extension services, subsidies, and credits reduced, all of which synergized adversely with currency devaluation, to the effect of raising the cost of production for petty-commodity producers and hence eroding farm incomes.[35] The focus of ESAP agricultural policy was the promotion of traditional exports (tobacco, cotton, beef, etc.), plus "nontraditional" export activities (specifically ostrich husbandry, horticulture, and wildlife management), the latter peddled as Zimbabwe's "comparative advantage" and tailored exclusively to large-scale farmers, who rapidly expanded operations to the new activities. By mid-decade, about one-third of commercial farmers had taken up horticulture and ecotourism, and to lesser extent ostrich husbandry, while only 10 percent of smallholders had become involved in these nontraditional land uses.[36]

Finally, land policy entered a period of ambiguity and new contradiction. On the one hand, the Lancaster House constitutional safeguards for market-based land transfers expired in 1990; on the other hand, the liberation movement had, by this time, been co-opted into structural adjustment, a macroeconomic policy framework that would submerge the land reform agenda. The contradictory result would be a series of constitutional amendments (1990, 1993) and a new Land Acquisition Act (1992) that thereafter would enable the state to designate and acquire land compulsorily; but such legislation retained the principles of legal recourse for landowners and compensation, and importantly, it would not renounce the "willing-buyer, willing-seller" method. For the next several years, the two methods (state and market) would coexist constitutionally, and the constitutional framework for compulsory acquisition would effectively remain dormant. In 1992–1997, about 800,000 hectares were acquired, the bulk of which in less fertile regions.[37]

Structural adjustment had a devastating effect on Zimbabwe, economically and politically. The second-most-industrialized country in Africa entered rapid deindustrialization, while the postindependence social gains in the fields of health and education began to be reversed.[38] The burden of adjustment was carried by the peasant-worker household, and particularly women, whose productive and reproductive labor was, by necessity, intensified. To make matters worse, ESAP would synergize with the onset of the HIV/AIDS pandemic. Thus, deteriorating physical capacity, loss of employment, erosion of real wages, declining farm incomes—all would put pressure on the semiproletarianized peasantry and force it deeper into marginal economic activities, illegality, and social conflict. Politically, the meaning of national liberation, and the land question specifically, would be transformed by aspiring black capital into a project of "indigenisation," in effect "a racial substitution formula for the development of capitalist farming."[39] In the 1990s, the IBDC and other lobbies would demand that government "set aside" land for "indigenisation," but generally to little effect, as the economy was in a downward spiral. By this time, black agrarian capital amounted to only about 350 farmers who had purchased land, plus 400 farmers leasing 400,000 hectares of land.[40] Henceforth, intercapitalist conflict would be not one of introversion/extroversion but more clearly racial. And nationalism would be animated by more pronounced class contradictions, but also, as it would soon emerge, by the possibility of a cross-class nationalist alliance on land.

Civilizing Society

Intercapitalist conflict is one natural driving force of capitalist society; another is class struggle. Interpreting class struggle is a challenge of a different magnitude, given its diverse manifestations, from its "hidden" forms to the more overt and organized, and across its fractures of gender, generation, and ethnicity. The challenge is greater in semiproletarianized societies, where the labor process aggregates capitalist and ostensibly noncapitalist forms and where politics are split between town and country. An even greater challenge is to understand class within the wider context of imperialism and its nationalist antithesis—that is, to link class struggle to the principle of national self-determination. In Africa, analysis of class and nation historically has been among the most insightful,[41] although over the years such analysis has been overtaken by observers who have either tended to see nationalism uncritically, or not to see it at all. Upon Zimbabwe's independence, the study of nationalism set off on a new course of critical engagement, especially among Zimbabwean intellectuals. This produced robust debate, focusing on elite politics,[42] urban and organized working class politics,[43] and rural and low-profile working class politics.[44]

In the 1990s, the study of nationalism dovetailed with liberalization and the new preoccupation with "civil society." A landmark in the African debate was the publication of Mahmood Mamdani's *Citizen and Subject* (1996), which successfully brought back the agrarian question to the civil society debate. Pathbreaking as this would be, it nonetheless fell short of robust political economic analysis: it reduced the agrarian question (classically understood as a transition to modern statehood) to a mere question of local government, and it confined the national question (the fulfillment of national self-determination against imperialism) to the realm of peasant-state relations. By consequence, a whole series of crucial issues were left aside, including the organization of the labor process as a whole (the labor question) and intercapitalist conflict (whether introverted/extroverted or racial); or they were obscured, most notably by the removal of the state and civil society from their specific *neocolonial* context. Our analysis of the case of Zimbabwe serves as a counterpoint.

It is well acknowledged that the liberation struggle in Zimbabwe was a mass popular uprising with far-reaching international implications. It is also well acknowledged, however, that the movement never attained a clear class understanding of itself or an articulate socialist project.[45] Its petty-bourgeois leadership, acting as the fulcrum between imperialism and the semiproletariat, was never tilted decisively in favor of the latter, which in turn remained organizationally and ideologically dependent: trade unionism in the urban areas was chronically fragmented and subsumed during the war under the competing nationalist parties, while rural mobilization was undertaken directly by the parties themselves. In turn, the primary social base of the liberation struggle was located in the countryside, where the war was fought, and included mainly peasant-workers but also the rural petty-bourgeoisie, while its ideological structure was anticolonial, with a strong emphasis on land and its repossession. This ideological structure of Zimbabwean nationalism and its rural base were to continue to exercise power of judgment over the fate of national liberation, especially in the course of its embourgeoisement.

Upon independence, Zimbabwe was riveted by an outburst of wildcat strikes in the urban areas (200 strikes in 1980 alone) and widespread land occupations in the countryside, in what was described as a "crisis of expectations."[46] These were compounded, as we have seen, by an elite split in Matabeleland. In the event, the civilization of society to the requirements of neocolonialism was swift, as the ruling party moved to "put a reign on its mass base."[47] The tactics pursued consisted, first, in the splitting of the semiproletariat organizationally between town and country; second, in the corporatization of political expression through ruling party channels; and third, in the use of the Rhodesian state apparatus to suppress dissent, most violently in Matabeleland. Yet, neocolonialism also exhibited its schizophrenia by proceeding to deliver a number of social goods, especially in rural development, and including land reform. In fact, neocolonialism would never rest at ease against the semiproletarianized masses, whose land occupation tactics, outside civil society, would compel the government from early on to implement an "accelerated resettlement programme" involving lands abandoned by white farmers during the war.

It is often posited that civil society in Zimbabwe was subordinated to the "state." But this is to fall into the liberal trap of dichotomizing state and civil society. First, the state is the institutional expression of the *capital-labour* relation[48]: not only is the state inseparable from society, it is also active in its "civilisation" to the requirements of capital. Second, the state is the *local* institutional expression of capitalist society, within a larger capitalist society that transcends the state and that operates through a states-system. Three implications follow: (a) while the resulting world order is formally "anarchical," "multilateral," and founded on the principle of national sovereignty, it remains imperialist in substance, in violation of national sovereignty; (b) the sources of "civilisation" to capital are "state," "supra-state," and "trans-state," to include inter alia international finance, covert and overt military operations, donor agencies, and international trade unionism; and (c) most crucially, breaking with the state is not a sufficient condition for autonomous self-expression; breaking with the civility of *capital* is the requirement, and this task is a much more demanding one. In the case of Zimbabwe, such "incivility" has been present throughout the postindependence period, but has generally been fragmentary, low profile, loosely organized, and inarticulate. How this "uncivil society" obtained radical land reform *through the state* and *against imperialism* is a question that challenges the prevailing wisdom.

The civilization of society in Zimbabwe was led by the neocolonial state and assisted by international agencies, always through tensions and contradictions. In labor relations, the state proceeded to corporatize trade unionism, by separating public- and private-sector workers institutionally, under the Public Service Association (PSA) and the ZCTU, respectively, imposing a client leadership, and intervening in wage determinations. In the case of the ZCTU, its inauguration in 1981 was sponsored by the ICFTU and the United States–led AALC (the AFL-CIO's regional body), in a message clearly targeted at international capital. Real wages remained virtually unchanged for the next five years, while in the agricultural and domestic sectors, they remained below the poverty datum line.[49] Over these years, the ZCTU remained under the wing of the state, while also receiving funding from both the ICFTU and the Soviet-led WFTU.

But by the mid-1980s, the national labor center would begin to assert its independence from the state and embark on a collision course with capital. Between 1984 and 1988, the center purged corruption within its ranks, elected an independent leadership, implemented an internal recruitment and democratization campaign, and entered a new era of adversarial labor relations. The latter included not only concerted demands for collective bargaining but also national mobilization against the "one-party" state and, ultimately, against structural adjustment. But the shortcomings of the labor center were also clear: it still lacked strong links to the shop floor, remained financially weak and dependent, and was confined to the formally employed workers, largely in urban areas; the labor center had no organizational links to rural areas, except on commercial farms where workers remained weakly organized and in semiservile conditions.

These shortcomings were the Achilles' heel of the labor center, which were to bring about its "re-civilisation." While in the first half of the 1990s it led a defiant campaign against liberalization, by mid-decade, it was seen moderating its stance, technicalizing its development language, and calling for "social dialogue." This transformation was due to the combination of state repression to which it was subjected *and* the wholesale adoption of the labor center by the ICFTU and other donor agencies in the wake of the Soviet collapse. By the late 1990s, the ZCTU was dependent for two-thirds of its income on foreign sources. By this time also, it had abandoned the task of establishing organizational links with the unemployed and the communal areas, and instead was challenging the ruling party on the grounds of "good governance," the language of late-twentieth-century ultra-imperialism. This was also to become the ideological structure of the new party to which the ZCTU would give birth, the Movement for Democratic Change (MDC), to challenge ZANU(PF) in the millennium elections.[50]

In the rural areas, the process of civilization was no less tense and contradictory. On the one hand, the ruling party proceeded to implement "accelerated" land reform under pressure from mass land occupations; as has been observed, "land redistribution was a key demand of the government's most populous constituency and, at least initially, people had access to powerful patrons and the space to act outside state structures."[51] Moreover, government established modern political structures to replace chiefdom, in the form of village, ward, district, and provincial development committees; and it amalgamated the previously segregated European and African areas into Rural District Councils (RDCs). On the other hand, government would soon proceed to *re*subordinate local government to central government and to the requirements of neocolonialism. "In theory, government had established democratic, secular, and non-racist channels of popular participation in planning and policy-making from village to provincial level"; in practice, these structures were marginalized and regarded by central government "primarily as policy implementing, not formulating, agencies"; in due course, even chiefdom was resurrected, even to regain control of courts and thus to reinforce patriarchal order.[52] Besides local government, the ruling party succeeded in corporatizing farming interests, with the exception of the white Commercial Farmers' Union (CFU). The strategy here would be to merge all farmers into one union, and thereby to dilute class and racial cleavages; the result in 1991 was the merger only of black small-scale commercial farmers and communal area farmers into the Zimbabwe Farmers' Union (ZFU), under the control of bourgeois farming interests, while the CFU would remain independent.[53]

By the 1990s, both urban and rural organizations, whether or not under the wing of the state, had been well-civilized to the requirements of neocolonialism; this would also give rise to a gaping political vacuum; and this would be compounded by the ESAP-induced economic decline. By the late 1990s, no civic organization could claim to have a class project to unify the semiproletariat; none had organizational links to the countryside outside commercial farming, and none could claim financial independence—even the formally democratic ZCTU. Whatever advocacy for the land question existed among civic organizations, it was ambiguous, rhetorical, and submerged in "good governance" and liberal "human rights" language. By 1999, the collectivity of Zimbabwe's civil society—the largely urban-based and/or bourgeois/petty-bourgeois civic organizations, including labor, churches, and NGOs—would proceed to unify itself into a National Working Peoples' Convention to discuss and ultimately found a new political party, the MDC.

Yet, the land cause had never been abandoned by the semiproletariat itself. Throughout the independence period, the landless and landshort continued to pursue land occupations.[54] These were generally low profile and diffuse but, in aggregate, presented a grave threat to the legitimacy of the ruling party. As an internal memorandum in the Ministry of Local Government noted as early as 1988,

> it is needless to emphasise that, bearing in mind the century-long Land Question, the severity and centrality of the squatting problem has its own inertia. That is, squatting generates itself as a pressing priority on the agenda before our national leadership. At the moment, there are about 100 squatter concentrations of proportions enough to merit urgent attention and these concentrations comprise thousands of persons who have already tasted battle with the authorities.

Land occupations were to intensify over the decade of structural adjustment. And whatever action would thereafter be taken on land, this would happen outside the civic network.

LAND OCCUPATIONS AND LAND REFORM

Land occupations were the driving force of land reform throughout the independence period, despite the official land acquisition model. The latter remained committed to the market principle, at first in accordance with the Lancaster House constitutional provisions, and then with the terms of the structural adjustment program. Nonetheless, with the expiry of the Lancaster House provisions, the government began to redefine the official model by enacting legislation in 1992 that would enable compulsory acquisition, but without, in effect, implementing such acquisition or replacing the market method. The three models—popular, market, and state—would interact dynamically over the decade of structural adjustment.[55]

The land reform process may be usefully divided into three periods: 1980–1992, characterized by the relatively secure predominance of the market method; 1992–1999, characterized by the beginning of an official challenge to the market method and leading to a real threat of compulsory acquisition in 1997, in the context of deepening social and political crisis; and 2000–2002, the period in which the market method was resolutely abandoned and replaced by radical, compulsory acquisition.

The Interaction of Land Reform Models, 1980–1997

The first period can be further subdivided into two, 1980–1985 and 1985–1992: in the first, political emphasis was placed on engaging actively with the market and delivering land to the peasantry, while in the second, land redistribution tapered off, alongside the deteriorating fiscal status of the state and the embourgeoisement of the liberation movement. As such, the first subperiod was also the one in which the ruling party sought to appease its main constituency, and the second was the one in which the social base of the ruling party would shift to the aspiring black bourgeoisie and in which a rift would emerge between the ruling party and the countryside.

Yet, the land occupation tactic was not relinquished from one period to the next, it was only modified in form. The early independence years were characterized by "low profile, high intensity occupations,"[56] which received sympathetic support and even encouragement from political leaders at the local level of the ruling party, mainly in Manicaland province. And in these years, the pace of land acquisition and redistribution through the market was relatively rapid, totaling approximately 2,200,000 hectares, at 430,000 hectares per year. This included land that had been abandoned by white landowners in the liberated zones of the war and, hence, was more easily acquirable. In Matabeleland, the land occupations and the land reform process itself would fall victim to the ZANU-ZAPU power struggle and the security crackdown by the state; only after the Unity Accords in 1987 did the political climate in Matabeleland begin to tolerate land reclamations, but even then to little effect, as the land posture of the state was already under transformation.

From 1985 to 1992, the countrywide pace of acquisition diminished dramatically to 75,000 hectares per year and to a total of about 450,000 hectares. This deceleration was accompanied by a reversal of the political response to land occupations at the local level, including the Mashonaland provinces, as well as by a transformation of land occupations to what we may term "normal low intensity."[57] Significantly, from 1985 onward, the state resorted to the establishment of a "squatter control" apparatus at the local level, through Squatter Control Committees accountable to the Ministry of Local Government, for the purpose of monitoring illegal self-provisioning of land and carrying out mass evictions.[58] This meant, in effect, that, on the one hand, the semiproletariat lost whatever informal influence it may have once had over national land policy, but on the other hand, the state itself would not succeed, even through squatter control, to stem the process of land self-provisioning. Thus, a political stalemate in the battle over land would set in and form the background of structural adjustment.

Over the period of 1980–1992, market-driven land reform proved its inability to deliver on Zimbabwe's land question. The process not only was slow and incremental but also delivered land of low agroecological value and imposed onerous fiscal demands on an already financially constrained state. As has been noted elsewhere,[59] only a small proportion of the land acquired (19 percent) was of prime agroecological value, the rest in the less fertile regions. By the mid-1980s, the state realized that it was facing diminishing returns on its resources devoted to land acquisition. This was the case despite the fact that the United Kingdom, as the former colonial power, provided financing for land reform on a matching-grant basis. On the whole, Britain contributed US$44 million to land reform, an amount grossly inadequate to the resolution of Zimbabwe's land question. The slow and mistargeted nature of the land reform process would become, from the mid-1980s onward, a source of bitter diplomatic conflict between the governments of Zimbabwe and the United Kingdom.[60] This was compounded by the gradual emergence of black large-scale commercial farmers, who had also benefited from the market method.

This conflict intensified on the expiry of the Lancaster House provisions for "willing-buyer, willing-seller" land transfers and the enactment of constitutional provisions for compulsory acquisition. In 1990, despite the launch of structural adjustment, the government signaled a change of direction on land policy, and in 1992, it proceeded with a new Land Acquisition Act, legalizing compulsory acquisition with provisions for compensation and legal recourse, and without displacing the market principle. Thereafter, the market method would continue to prevail in the political process, as structural adjustment submerged the land question resolutely, but the two methods (state and market) would enter a period of open competition. Importantly, compulsory acquisition was the favored principle not only of the semiproletariat, but more immediately, of the aspiring black capitalist class. In fact, black capital in the 1990s would enhance its presence in the large-scale commercial farming sector, such that by the end of the market-based reform period, about 800 black commercial farmers had emerged, either through land purchases or leases on approximately 10 percent of large-scale commercial farmland. But in all, the pace of land reform remained slow. In 1992–1997, about 790,000 hectares of land were acquired, at a pace of 158,000 hectares per year; this involved the resettlement of 600 peasant families displaced by the construction of the Osborne Dam.

The combination of structural adjustment and "indigenisation" of the land question had as its corollary the intensification of low-profile land occupations. As private and public sector jobs were shed, real wages reduced, and farm incomes undermined, the demand for land and its natural resources increased among the semiproletarian households, in both rural and urban areas.[61] Thus, several new squatting trends emerged in the 1990s. In one trend, squatting spread from large-scale commercial farming areas to other land tenure regimes, to such an extent that the bulk of officially recognized squatters were now in communal areas (33 percent), plus resettlement areas (12 percent), urban areas (10 percent), and state lands (31 percent), and only a minority (14 percent) on commercial farms.[62] In another trend, land sales and rental markets deepened *within* communal and resettlement areas. Title to such land is legally vested in the state and administered "customarily" by traditional authorities in the first instance. But in the 1990s, communal land was increasingly commoditized by payment of fees or political obligation to local MPs, ruling party members, chiefs, headmen, and spirit mediums. In turn, land conflicts among "villagers" and "squatters" also intensified.

These new squatting trends rendered "squatter control" ever less effective, though the apparatus continued to be applied with vigilance. In 1992, the squatter control policy was reconstituted within the Ministry of Local Government to establish a hierarchy of national, provincial, and district squatter control committees and to grant "the land authority or owner" the legal power to evict. In effect, this meant that the national land problem would be "parochialised" on communal land and "privatised" on commercial farms. And on this basis, mass evictions were repeatedly implemented under structural adjustment, in some cases involving hundreds of squatter families at a time, in a manner reminiscent of the methods of the white-settler colonial state.[63]

Nationalism and Land Reform Reradicalized, 1997–2002

By the end of the first structural adjustment program in 1996, national politics had come to a boil, and the legitimacy of the ruling party as the "guardian" of the nation was under severe challenge. Strike action would spread from private to public sector workers, whose union (the Public Servants Association) would even become affiliated with the ZCTU, in open defiance of the government's divide-and-rule tactics. In 1997, strikes would grip several industries, including construction, commercial, hotel and catering, clothing, cement and lime, railways, urban councils, and postal and telecommunications. In all, the year saw more than 230 strikes in 16 sectors. Most notably, farm workers downed tools for the first time, in what appeared to be a wildcat strike, in protest over poor working conditions and wages, which stood at less than one-sixth of the poverty datum line.

But the ruling party was not only being challenged from the outside. It was also entering a new period of internal polarization, marked by the open return of war veterans to national politics, through the National War Veterans Liberation Association. Precipitated by a financial scandal and collapse of the state-sponsored War Veterans Compensation Fund, the war veterans demanded that the state compensate them from the national budget. While this appeared to be a "self-serving" demand—in both media and academic analysis—it was indicative of a class split within the ruling party, between the elites at the forefront of "indigenisation," on the one hand, and the lower echelons, on the other, which had never been accommodated by the postindependence state and many of whom were indeed living in poverty. Moreover, the demands resonated with a reradicalized nationalism and discontent with the fate of national liberation. The government succumbed to their demands and disbursed a large compensation package, which had not been foreseen in the national budget. Moreover, the government would turn its sights back to the land question and designate 1,470 white commercial farms for compulsory acquisition, promising 20 percent to the war veterans. These moves, in turn, sent the economy into a downward spiral, led by a crash in the Zimbabwe dollar by 74 percent, in one day (November 14). These moves, too, appeared as "self-serving"—in this case on the part of President Mugabe—but in fact, the war veteran challenge was of a different magnitude, for the war vets were also firmly embedded in the state apparatus and, indeed, were in charge of security, including the President's office.

Thereafter, events in Zimbabwe began to move in a markedly different direction. The second structural adjustment program (ZIMPREST) was abandoned, balance-of-payments support from the IMF was suspended, and the economy continued on a rapid decline. But this was not yet the time of radical land reform and structural change, for the white farms listed by the government were not acquired. Instead, the threat of compulsory acquisition would galvanize the land question nationally, and even internationally, giving rise to a new round of negotiations with foreign donors, including the World Bank and the British government. In 1998, a Donors' Conference was held in Harare, where a tense agreement was reached to proceed with both compulsory and market acquisition, as well as other complementary approaches. Importantly, on the eve of the conference, a wave of high-profile land occupations swept through the country for the first time since the early years of independence. This was loosely organized at the local level, by dissident ruling party politicians, traditional leaders, displaced workers, and the war veterans association, further demonstrating the class cleavages within the ruling party.[64] This wave of land occupations was intermittently condoned and used by the government as an instrument against the donors, but it was clear that government was not firmly in control. Before long, the government would resort to the use of force to control the occupiers, together with promises to accelerate land reform. The peasants, in turn, agreed to "wait."

Between 1998 and 2000, no progress was made on the land question, despite the conference agreements. Instead, national politics continued to boil ever more fervently, especially with the launch of the MDC and the euphoria over the prospect of defeating the ruling party at the millennium elections. Indeed, by 2000, the ruling party was in its most severe crisis of legitimacy since independence. And at this time, the balance of class forces within the ruling party was tipped in favor of radical nationalist solutions. In February 2000, mass land occupations, led by war veterans, began in the southern province of Masvingo and spread to every province, such that at the height of the land occupations in June about 800 farms had been occupied, and government was implementing compulsory land acquisition and mass redistribution. By the end of 2002, "fast-track" land reform had compulsorily acquired some 10 million hectares of land—approximately 90 percent of white commercial farmland—and redistributed most of it to 127,000 peasant households and 8,000 middle capitalist farmers (to be discussed). In the course of this rebellion, national elections were manipulated and civil society subjected to violence, resulting in over 100 politically related deaths in 2000–2002. Violence would also lead to deaths on the farms (including six white farmers and eleven farm workers) and would also involve cases of rape and torture.

As national politics boiled over, international politics also entered a period of renewed conflict, including an international propaganda war, a financial boycott, and regional instability. The private national press and international media networks, led by the British, denounced the land reforms as "land grabs" and the ruling party as a "corrupt and brutal dictatorship," even likening President Mugabe to Milosevic.

The MDC and the ZCTU joined the imperial repertoire, demanding "free and fair multiparty elections" and joining in an alliance with white commercial farmers against the land reform. Foreign donors and their funds fled the country to begin a long international boycott, except for "humanitarian" purposes. And regional states and civil societies themselves were forced to choose sides, with the former cautiously backing the land reform, and the latter generally condemning it. For its own part, the new Landless Peoples' Movement of South Africa entered the realm of civil society and was immediately confronted with the contradiction of forming civil alliances and supporting a radical nationalist strategy on land; in the event, members of the LPM defended the occupations, but the LPM did not issue an official position.

There is certainly much to criticize in Zimbabwe's land reform process. But this would be impossible without identifying its class structure and dynamics, its weaknesses, and its failures, but also its successes and, indeed, its fundamentally progressive nature.

The Structure of the Land Occupation Movement

The land occupations unfolded in a complex way, driven by local and regional peculiarities, but they shared a common social base, that of the rural-based semiproletariat, across gender and ethno-regional cleavages. The strengths of the land occupation movement are to be found precisely in this social base, and, moreover, in its militant commitment to land repossession—a commitment that no other civic organization had ever been willing to make. Over time, this social base expanded to include urban poor and petty-bourgeois elements, who were also co-opted into the fast-track redistribution program. This would strengthen the movement, especially by bridging the organizational divide among the rural and urban poor, while the petty-bourgeois overture would not threaten, as yet, the overall class content of the movement. The movement was also strengthened in its momentum by the endorsement of the process by the black capitalist lobby and, ultimately, by the stitching together, through the war veterans association, of a tense but resolute cross-class nationalist alliance on land. In this case, too, the black capitalist lobby would not yet threaten the working-class content of the movement. In all, this cross-class nationalist alliance would stand opposed to the cross-class "post-national" (or "civic national") alliance of civil society, including the MDC, trade unions, NGOs, and white farmers.

The land occupation movement was organized and led by the war veterans association. This was also a profound source of strength, combining militancy on the land question with an organizational structure permeating state and society. The war veterans activated their organizational roots as much in rural districts, through the local branches of the association, as in all levels of the state apparatus, including local and central government, the police, the military, the Central Intelligence Organisation, the state media (print, TV, and radio), and the ruling party. This pervasive weblike structure would contain the unique potential to mobilize both the rural areas and the state apparatus behind the land cause.

The state bureaucrats would, however, seek to develop hegemony over the land occupations and even own the land revolution. And this would occur through the control of the ideological content of media representations of the "Third *Chimurenga*"

("Uprising"); insistence on the use of a state right, legislatively defined (i.e., through amendments to the constitution and the Land Acquisition Act), to expropriate the occupied lands and the larger areas required by an expanding movement; and by its custody of land reform policy as defined in the fast-track program documents and of oversight of implementation at both central and provincial levels. This way, the land occupation movement gradually became "programmatised."

In this context, the war veterans association would also become a source of weakness for the movement, for several discernable reasons. First, the war veterans association emerged as a single-issue movement, focusing exclusively on the immediate question of land repossession and not on longer-term political economic questions, particularly the post-fast-track phase. Relatedly, the war veterans association would not seek to establish self-sustaining, democratic peasant-worker organizational structures, with a view to prepare for longer-term class-based political education and ideological struggle. Third, while its nationalism was itself organic and indispensable, its class content was not clearly articulated. The movement sustained a militant anticolonial nationalism, focused organizationally and ideologically on land repossession, and as effective as this would prove for land repossession, the class direction of the movement would remain threatened by the direction of class conflict within the war veterans association itself and the ruling party.

The principle tactic of the movement was the land occupation. This tactic built on the previous sporadic and scattered land occupations, specifically those that unfolded during the 1998 Donors' Conference. The new and much larger wave of land occupations began in February 2000, following a preelections referendum on constitutional reform in which the proposal of the ruling party was defeated, thereby signaling the end game for the liberation movement. Land occupations began in Masvingo but spread to the Matabeleland and Mashonaland provinces, at a slower pace in the former and a faster pace in the latter, which would, in turn, become the epicenter.[65] Land occupations focused on white farms but also sporadically on farms owned by black capitalists and the political elite. In the beginning, land occupations focused on underutilized land, but this, too, would change to include productive land, especially land that fit other criteria, such as multiple ownership, foreign ownership, and contiguity to communal areas. Land occupations also expanded to periurban areas, upon the entry of urban poor and petty-bourgeois elements. In a few cases, leadership to the land occupations was not provided by war veterans but individual MPs and traditional leaders, who, in turn, sought to "formalise" their occupations by appealing to war veterans. There were also instances of antagonism between the local initiatives and the higher echelons of the war veterans' command structure, which would cause friction within the movement. And violence occurred on an estimated 300 farms, depending on the response of the farmers as well as relations with farm workers.

Farm workers, in some cases, supported and joined the land occupations, while in many other cases, they resisted the land occupations, and violence and evictions were used against them. This would prove another weakness of the land occupation movement: its rapid emergence, without a preexisting process of political education and mobilization on the farms, would pit the landless workers against the farm workers, in a climate of distrust, in which the latter would be perceived as having been mobilized by landowners to vote against the government's constitutional proposals. On the one hand, the farm workers had never been mobilized by their trade union representatives toward land repossession; instead, representatives had always focused on reformist workers' issues (wages and conditions of employment). On the other hand, war veterans had an ambiguous, even arrogant, posture toward farm workers, viewing them as incapable of nationalist political consciousness. In a tense conjuncture, farm workers were faced with the choice of either defending their jobs and employers or joining the land occupations and staking their hopes on accessing land either through the war veterans directly or through family links in the communal areas. A minority of farm workers of non-Zimbabwean origin were in a particularly precarious situation, and so were women farm workers, the majority of whom were employed casually on the farms and had weak access of their own to the land application process in the rural areas. Farm workers thus found themselves in a confounding antagonism in which their erstwhile employers and exploiters—the landowners—were defending them, and vice versa, in opposition to land redistribution. And this contradiction would not be resolved by initiative of the war veterans, who did not see it fit to win over the farm workers by providing them access to land, beyond 5 percent of the 150,000 displaced workers (to be discussed).

Finally, the strategy of seeking land reform through the ruling party and the state was also both a strength and a weakness of the land occupation movement. On the one hand, the ruling party proceeded rapidly with constitutional reforms to expedite compulsory land acquisition procedures, modifying existing provisions for compensation by limiting it only to improvements on the land and explicitly relegating any other responsibility for compensation to the British government. These were complemented by presidential decrees, under the Presidential Powers Act, to amend the Land Acquisition Act (2000) several times so as to postpone compensation and remove legal recourse and other procedural impediments to land acquisition. Thereafter, the ruling party passed the Rural Land Occupiers (Protection from Eviction) Act (2001), by which the landless would be afforded legal protection from eviction. These legislative changes were conducted through repeated confrontation with the High and Supreme Courts responsible for the protection of private property. In the countryside, the security apparatus of the state (police, military, and CIO) would intervene to provide logistical support to the land occupation movement, as well as protection against possible militarization on the part of the landowners and other violence outside its control. Finally, the state also entered the propaganda war vociferously through the state media, even to the point of threatening the existence of private media (followed, in late 2003, by the shutting down of the leading private daily newspaper, the *Daily News*).

On the other hand, the fundamentally bourgeois structure of the bureaucracy would not be dissolved. That is, the leadership of the land occupation movement remained unable, even unwilling, to wrest control of the ruling party and state from the black elite. On the contrary, the black elite employed the state apparatus to retain its power and prepare the ground for its reassertion in national politics. And here, the basic tactic was the same as that employed throughout the colonial and neocolonial periods, that is, the splitting of the semiproletariat organizationally between town and country. Besides facilitating and protecting the land occupation movement, the leadership of the ruling party used the state apparatus to drive a forceful wedge between organized urban workers and their rural counterparts, by repressing urban working class demonstrations, persecuting trade union leaders, and disorganizing trade union structures. The immediate objective of this instrumentalization of violence would be twofold: the safeguarding of the land reform process against reactionary trade unionism and the securing of the parliamentary (June 2000) and presidential (March 2002) elections against the "post-nationalist" alliance. This practice would survive both fast-track and the elections, to the point of undermining systematically any source of working class organization outside elite ruling-party control, in both town and country.

In this contradictory process, the class balances within the nationalist alliance would also begin to shift against the semiproletariat. The black elite exercised its bureaucratic power not only to make room for the urban petty-bourgeoisie on 22,896 small/middle capitalist farms (by 2010) but also for itself, appropriating 150,000 hectares (0.5 percent of the acquired land) for the benefit of an estimated 178 elites. It also steered the land reform process away from several key agroindustrial estates of private (individual and corporate) and state ownership and, in all, ensured that lands redistributed to the semiproletariat would be largely confined to those of relatively lower agroecological potential and limited access to irrigation infrastructure. The urban working class was further segmented by the offer to over 10,000 families of small (3–20 hectares) plots in the periurban zones and the initiation of land for housing among the homeless and others who pursued this new entitlement on the basis of urban land occupations. Moreover, with the end of fast-track land redistribution and the withering away of the land occupation movement under the single-issue leadership of the war veterans association, there would remain a minimum of an organized structure among the peasantry to exercise influence over the post-redistribution phase of agrarian reform.

We may conclude that the strategy of pursuing land reform through the ruling party and the state did not go far enough *within* the ruling party and the state to safeguard the peasant-worker character of the movement or to prepare the semiproletariat organizationally against the reassertion of the black bourgeoisie, especially in the post-fast-track phase. Despite this, however, we must also conclude that the land occupation movement succeeded in compelling the expropriation of over 90 percent of commercial farmland, broadening substantially the structure of the home market, removing the racialized structure of class struggle, and laying the necessary foundations for the next phase of the national democratic revolution.

THE NATIONAL DEMOCRATIC REVOLUTION AT A CROSSROADS

The academic debate over the land reform has largely failed to identify the class dynamics of the process, pitting two camps against each other, the "civic/post-nationalists" and the "indigenisationists," both including liberals and self-professed Marxists, but all reproducing the categories of bourgeois social science. The former camp has proceeded to denounce the land reform merely as an "assault on the state," without a class analysis of the neocolonial state specifically, or civil society, or the land occupation movement and its nationalism,[66] while the latter camp has defended the land reform but obscured the class struggles within the liberation movement and celebrated fast-track as the culmination of "black empowerment," in line with the accumulation priorities of the indigenization lobby.

Neither of these two positions can properly serve the next phase of the national democratic revolution. This remains at a crucial juncture and requires ongoing critical analysis. The immediate result of the land reform is clear and urgent, marked by worsening poverty and the inability to supply food to the population. On the one hand, imperialism continues to exercise its financial power deliberately to isolate Zimbabwe and smother the process of agrarian reform, such that the currency has hyperinflated to 500 percent, agricultural production has been severely impeded from recovery—and compounded by two years of drought—and the urban and rural population has been relegated to a state of "humanitarian aid." For its own part, the state has not yet devised a coherent plan for reconstruction and development, given that it cannot cajole private capitals into a national plan of introverted accumulation. This situation lingers on by the absence of working class unity across town and country (indeed undermined by the fall in food production) and is compounded by the ongoing repression of civil society and the emerging dominance of the black bourgeoisie in the policy-making process, against the interests of peasants and workers. The danger is the full reversal into a process of recompradorization and recolonization under a dictatorship of the bourgeoisie, and ultimately the failure to fulfill the developmental potential of the new agrarian structure.

The New Agrarian Structure

A full analysis of the new agrarian structure is not possible here.[67] In what follows, we provide a condensed overview. Our data derives from various sources such as the Presidential Land Review Committee (PLRC), which reported, in July 2003, Government of Zimbabwe A2 Land Audit of 2006 and other data from the Ministry of Lands and Rural Resettlement.[68] The PLRC was appointed by the President, and the land audits were in response to continuing pressure from within the ruling party to establish the facts on the ground, including the status of farm workers and the misappropriation of land by elites. Table 12.1 provides the land acquisition and redistribution figures for the fast-track land reform from 2000 to 2010; the table is organized in terms of Zimbabwe's land tenure regimes. Table 12.2 combines these figures with preexisting or remaining landholding patterns to provide the holistic picture of the agrarian structure today; this table is reorganized to capture, as much as possible, the emerging *class* structure, which is not well-grasped by reference to tenure type and farm size per se.

Repeasantization has been the dominant phenomenon under fast-track land reform: the new petty-commodity-producing establishments account for 86.3 percent of total new farming establishments, thus far on 56.8 percent of the land acquired. The large majority of the beneficiaries had their origin directly in the communal areas. This process has combined with a renewed "merchant path" of urban professionals, petty-bourgeois, and bureaucrats, amounting to 22,896 small, middle, and large farm-

Table 12.1 Fast-track land reform (2000–2010): Land allocation pattern

	Settlers (households/farmers)		*Farm Area Targeted*	
Land Tenure	*Number*	*% Total*	*Hectares*	*% Total*
A1* (peasant)	145,775	86.3	5,759,153	56.8
A2† (capitalist)	22,896	13.6	3,509,437	34.6
Remaining white LSCF‡	198	0.1	117,409	1.2
Total land allocated (as of June 2010)			9,385,999	92.5
Land unallocated (as of June 2010)			757,578	7.5
Total	**168,869**	**100.0**	**10,143,578**	**100.0**

Source: Calculated from various sources by Moyo, 2011.

**A1 tenure (permissory)*: Consists of use rights to a family plot plus common grazing land; family plots are inheritable but nonmarketable

†*A2 tenure (leasehold)*: Consists of leasehold title with a proposed option to buy

‡*LSCF (large-scale commercial farming) tenure*: Consists of individual freehold title

ers, on 34.6 percent of the acquired land. Urbanites have also entered the A1 model, such that we may estimate that urban beneficiaries make up approximately 20 percent of the total. The land reform process has also proceeded to downsize and retain (as opposed to fully expropriate) 198 white large-scale commercial farms. We note also that, as of June 2010, a small amount of land (7.5 percent) had not yet been allocated and remains subject to the political process.

Further analysis of the figures[69] shows that war veterans received less land than originally targeted and that women and farm workers were more severely prejudiced. War veterans received less than the 20 percent threshold set by government after the initial listing of farms in 1997. Tentative estimates suggest that a possible maximum of 25,000 war veterans, former detainees, and *mujibhas* (youth collaborators in the liberation struggle) received 10 percent of total land, the majority on A1 tenure and at a national average below 50 hectares per war veteran.

The patterns of the land redistribution in terms of women's access to land plots in both A1 and A2 areas suggest a new dynamic in the gender relations in land access and tenure. Indeed, more women have been offered land in their individual right under the fast-track program than in the past; such women landholders do not seem to predominantly come from the "vulnerable" groups, such as widows and divorcees, as obtains in communal and older resettlement areas. A larger proportion of women (about 18 percent) now own land in their own right,[70] compared to the 4 percent of white women who owned LSCF lands[71] and the 5 percent of black women who owned land in previous resettlement and communal lands. Other studies suggest that women "beneficiaries in their own right" range between 10 percent and 28 percent of the total.[72] Thus, women received titles of their own at a low national average rate of 16 percent; the false assumption here has been that heads of household are typically men, while women in need of land are married or otherwise access land through various family links.

The case of farm workers has presented analytical and empirical difficulties, given their dual "identity" as migrant workers (national and foreign) and communal area farmers. Prior to the fast track, the large-scale commercial farming sector (LSCF) employed 350,000 workers, of which 75 percent were of communal-area origin. If we were to add official fast-track figures of declared "farmworkers" and fieldwork estimates of farm workers applying for land as "landless peasants" via communal areas, it is probable that about 10 percent of the land beneficiaries were former farm workers, who were allocated A1 or A2 plots as farm workers qua farm workers, a few as "land occupiers" alongside war veterans,[73] while others gained access to land as members of communal area structures.[74] These data also mean, as recent studies have shown,[75] that a large number of farm workers were stranded. Of the original total of 350,000, half of them were part-time/casual workers (largely consisting of women), the other half being permanent workers (mainly men). Of the permanent workers, over 50 percent (85,000) retained employment positions, largely in the agroindustrial estates (specializing in sugar, coffee, tea, and forest plantations) that were not expropriated, while the other half generally lost employment, with some providing labor to new farmers. Of the part-time and casual workers, approximately 80,000 continue to provide labor on the remaining LSCF farms. The general estimate is that about 90,000 farm workers were completely stranded, with women being most severely affected; the stranded workers have either remained on their residential plots on the farms, relocated to the communal areas, or formed new "informal settlements" under desperate conditions. This struggle for land between former farm workers and beneficiaries, due to the related policy deficiency and local contestations, is a potential threat to the tenure security of A2 beneficiaries.[76] A related result is that employment conditions on new farms have deteriorated, with piecework and casualization on the rise.

The external financial punishments imposed on the Zimbabwean economy, combined with internal policy incoherence and ongoing repression, will continue to aggravate the living and working conditions of the urban and rural proletariat and semiproletariat. Persisting landlessness, unemployment, casual employment, poor working conditions and incomes, low peasant farm incomes, and food shortages will all remain pressing economic and political issues for the foreseeable future. Meanwhile, the new peasantry on A1 farms will itself maintain the dual semiproletarian income strategy of petty-commodity production and wage labor, especially as differentiation proceeds apace.

In Table 12.2, we seek to estimate the emerging agrarian class structure. This task is, by nature, imprecise, and more so in the absence of new census data and household surveys. But the task remains essential, and its objective is to capture the differential capabilities (and vulnerabilities) of capitalists in the accumulation process. The basic

Table 12.2 Emerging agrarian class structure

		Households/Farms		Farm Area		
Class	*Land Tenure*	*Number*	*% Total*	*Hectares*	*% Total*	*Ave. (ha)*
Proletariat in transition (employed, casuals, unemployed)	Resident on farms Relocated to CAs Stranded	(350,000)	n.a.	n.a.		
Peasantry (semiproletariat, small capital)	CAs and A1	1,321,000	97.6	25,826,000	76.8	20
Small/middle capital	Old SSCF	8,500	0.6	1,400,000	4.2	165
	New A2	22,679	1.7	3,000,000	8.9	133.9
	Subtotal	**31,179**	**2.3**	**4,400,000**	**13.1**	**142**
Large capital	Large A2	217	0.02	508,991	1.5	2,345
	Black LSCF	956	0.07	530,631	1.6	555
	White LSCF	198	0.01	117,409	0.3	593
	Subtotal	**1,371**	**0.1**	**1,157,031**	**3.4**	**844**
Corporate capital	Corporate	20	0.001	806,414	2.3	40,320
	Parastatal	106	0.01	295,545	0.9	2,788
	Church/institutions	113	0.01	145,700	0.4	1,289
	Conservancies	8	0.001	247,364	0.7	30,875
	Subtotal	**247**	**0.03**	**1,495,023**	**4.4**	**6,051**
Land in transition	Unallocated			757,578	2.3	
	Total	**1,353,977**	**100.0**	**33,635,632**	**100.0**	

Source: Calculated from various sources by Moyo, 2011.

Peasants: Land sizes range from 1 to 30 ha, depending on natural region, with family arable land ranging from 0.2 to 5.0 ha, plus common grazing land. Communal land and A1 are of the same tenure type; the former refers to preexisting lands, the latter to resettlement lands.

Small and middle capitalists: Comprise "old" farmers from the colonial period and "new" black farmers, including those with postindependence allocations on "small-scale commercial farms" (SSCF) and the fast-track beneficiaries. "Small capitalist" farms range between 30 and 100 ha, depending on natural region, while "middle capitalist" farms range between 40 and 150 ha, again depending on natural region.

Large capitalists: Farms range between 150 and 400 ha in NR I/II to 1,500 ha in NR IV.

Corporate farms: Range from 1,000 to 1,500 ha, but few are near the lower hectarage mark.

criterion is land size, which is then adjusted to account for tenure type, agroecological potential, and technical capacity. Tenure type becomes particularly significant in accounting for the disadvantages of communal and A1 tenure in the mobilization of resources. Agroecology varies in Zimbabwe between five Natural Regions (NR I-V), from the more fertile lands of relatively lesser hectarage per farm and intensive cropping, to the less fertile lands of larger farm sizes and extensive cropping (small grains) and livestock/wildlife management. The level and type of technology thus also differs across the natural regions.

Land reform had, by 2010, led to deep structural changes, through reconfiguring Zimbabwe's landholding structure in terms of land sizes in relation to the agroecological potential of the landholdings (see Table 12.2) and the social character, including race, gender, and other demographic features,[77] and through creating diverse farming societies.[78] The preexisting landholding patterns represented a skewed agrarian structure, dominated by a "*race-class* structure," analytically based on large-scale capitalist farms and estates. The main four classes of farmers were retained but their numbers changed substantially. The numbers of peasants and small- to medium-scale farmers increased, while reducing the number of large-scale farms and estates. The scale of state farmlands increased slightly. A broadly based agrarian capitalist class, built on former and new farming "elites," has emerged, with a small segment of large-scale capitalist farmers and estates persisting, including both black and white farmers. Their landholdings have been substantially downsized to an average of 844 hectares, compared to the average of 2,000 hectares previously held by large-scale landowners, while over 75 percent of the new capitalist farmers have plots below 100 hectares, and these vary across agroecological regions. In area terms, however, the A2 and other larger-scale classes of farmers obtained a relatively higher proportion of the land area compared to their numbers. Altogether, about 20 percent of Zimbabwe's entire agricultural land (including the communal areas and unacquired agricultural estates) is now held by small-, middle-, and large-scale farmers, while 70 percent is held by peasants, and 10 percent by large farms and estates compared to the pre-1980 situation.

The sustainability of the new agrarian structure has been questioned by some who allege the existence of widespread land disputes among the land beneficiaries, quite apart from the white land owner litigations. Research, however, shows that fewer than 20 percent of the A1 settlers report that they experience tenure insecurity, that their farming is limited by the current form of land tenure, or that they experience land conflicts.[79]

The "peasant" category refers to petty-commodity production on communal and A1 resettlement land; this now accounts for 97.6 percent of total farms, on 78.6 percent of total land. There is class differentiation within this category, which is not captured here, and which is driven inter alia by agroecological variation, off-farm incomes, and local political power. Whether under adverse or positive economic conditions, this differentiation is expected to continue, as is the operation of informal land markets under the aegis of traditional authority. It is notable that the institution of chiefdom has not been challenged in the process of mobilization for land reform.

While "small capitalists" historically comprise below 10 percent of the peasantry in communal areas and they employ substantial nonfamily labor from other peasants and the remaining landless there, we have not segmented them into the category due to insufficient data. We may only note here that they would be of great political significance, as they are likely to return to dominate the Zimbabwe Farmers' Union, together with the small capitalists on A2 land. What we have also done tentatively is merge the "small capitalist" category with that of "middle capitalists," as there is much overlap across the natural regions. Generally, small capitalists range from 30 to 100 hectares, and middle capitalists from 40 to 150 hectares, and they employ substantially more hired labor than is provided by their own family. The important point to note is that there is likely to be ongoing reconfiguration of these two categories, as the two compete. Notably, middle capitalists have great advantage in the land bidding and accumulation process, by virtue of their better access to other means of production (credit and technology), to contacts and information, and to the policy-making process itself.

"Large capitalist" farms range from 150 to 1,500 hectares, depending on natural region, and enjoy even better access to economic and political resources. At present, middle and large capitalists are in political alliance under the banner of "indigenisation," seeking to appropriate the remaining land and also to tailor the agricultural policy framework to their needs. Their vision is of a differentiated agricultural sector, in which middle/large capitalists specialize in the production of high-value commodities for export (tobacco and hybrid beef) and peasants in the production of grains for domestic consumption. The contradictions between small and middle/large farmers and between internal/external orientation will thus accentuate as they bid over public and private resources (infrastructure, water, and credit) and policy instruments (interest rates policy and foreign exchange allocations). It is important, finally, to note that a significant process of reorganization of capital is underway across the economic sectors, by which the emerging agrarian bourgeoisie is joining forces, economically and politically, with the nascent indigenous bourgeoisie in transport and retail, and most importantly with finance, which has seen the emergence of a dozen new indigenous institutions. Together, they recognize the significance of agricultural production and distribution to their own reproduction.

Importantly, the entire range of these capitalist farmers pays wages, whether or not these are above the regulated minimum rates, which are well below the current poverty datum line.[80] Such labor is procured from the retained and retrenched former LSCF workers, unemployed relatives from communal area households, and growing numbers of unemployed urban workers. There was a high variability in the wages and benefits paid to farm workers by new farmers, with some paying more than the official wages while others pay less. Wage levels seem to be better where high-value commodities (e.g., tobacco) and mechanization are established, as these require skilled operators.[81] Some new farmers do not provide employment contracts, and the provision of social services to workers by employers has greatly diminished. It is reported that, in some newly resettled areas, arbitrary firing of workers, lack of protective clothing, lack of leave days, and lack of consideration for special needs of female workers prevail.[82]

The emerging picture, therefore, is of a significantly broadened home market, including a larger peasantry and a larger black capitalist class. Further research would need to examine three interrelated processes: agroindustrial reorganization and consolidation of the black capitalist class; differentiation within the peasantry, including the trajectories of rich (small capitalist) and poor (semiproletarians) peasants; and the labor process that underpins both of the above and that will continue to be characterized by functional dualism. This process will become more entrenched, the more that black capital, together with its downsized white counterpart, succeeds in reentrenching a disarticulated pattern of accumulation.

The New Challenges

In the best of strategies, national development should prioritize agricultural reconstruction with an emphasis on the development of the home market, that is, sectorally and socially articulated.[83] Agriculture indeed carries the heaviest of burdens, including production for domestic food consumption (food security and self-sufficiency), production for domestic industrial consumption, and production for the earning of foreign exchange. Industrial development should be seen as auxiliary to the technological upgrading of agriculture and to the production of consumer goods, while finance should be firmly subordinated to the long-term investment requirements of introverted agroindustrial development. Such a strategy would require careful control of imports and currency allocations, and importantly, repudiation of debt, as well as deconcentration of mining rights and guarding against the institution of land property rights that can promote the reconcentration of land and agrarian capital against the accumulation and social reproduction of small farmers and rural workers.

The fate of such a strategy, however, will remain subject to the correlation of political forces, between the proletariat/semiproletariat and capital, and between national self-determination and imperialism. In this sense, the national democratic revolution is at a critical juncture. The organizational task remains the reconstitution of the working class across the rural-urban divide, independently of the state and capital, and at an arm's length of the "civility" of international trade unionism; while the political objective remains to compel the state to commit to the development of the home market, against the comprador aspirations of the new agrarian bourgeoisie and the aspirant middle classes at the forefront of neoliberal economic policies founded on narrow liberal democratic reforms.

The reinstatement of civil and political liberties is central to this process, but it also presents the challenge of overcoming the (reactionary) civilizing forces that will be unleashed. As the comprador bourgeoisie consolidates itself across political party lines, it will seek to enlist the state to its own accumulation strategy and employ its repressive and cooptation tactics towards the splitting of the semiproletariat across the rural-urban divide and the corporatization of political expression. The further expansion of traditional authority to the resettlement areas will itself be central to this process. Resisting the repressive tendencies of both central and local government and advocating the entrenchment of a redistributive framework of national resource allocation should remain the priority for advancing the national democratic revolution.

The emerging labor process, grounded in the formal and informal, rural and urban sectors, is most inauspicious. It requires a long-term, systematic commitment on the part of trade unions to extricate itself from current alliances with capital and sink new roots on the new farms and rural areas more broadly and to confront the new black employers and traditional authority. In this regard, the new labor process will also present a new ideological space to be conquered, namely, the reassertion of a new class-based nationalism against the racialized, bourgeois nationalism of the "indigenisation" lobby, and against neoliberal democracy politics. Indeed, with the removal of the hegemony of the white agrarian bourgeoisie, the anticolonial claims of the black bourgeoisie will become tenuous and implausible, as class assumes importance, while the specter of ethno-nationalism remains a threat. The added challenge to new working class organization will be to create commensurate space for women peasants and workers, to make itself relevant to their specific demands, and provide for the ascendance of women to leadership positions within its ranks. As distant as this struggle may appear at present, it is an essential requirement in confronting the strategies of the agrarian and wider bourgeoisie and traditional authority.

On the international front, working class organization must confront the Eurocentrism of international trade unionism and the antiglobalization movement. The agrarian question is far from resolved in Zimbabwe, despite radical land reform. Introverted accumulation requires the articulation of a new development vision, which not only condemns neoliberalism but formulates clearly an economic framework for sustainable accumulation in the periphery as a whole, as well as a political strategy for its realization. Only then will the principle of national self-determination begin to be wrested from its imperial grip.

NOTES

1. The original version of this chapter was published in *Reclaiming the Land: The Resurgence of Rural Movements in Africa, Asia, and Latin America*, ed. Sam Moyo and Paris Yeros (London: Zed Books, 2005).

2. We wish to thank Henry Bernstein for comments on an earlier draft. Errors of fact and interpretation remain our own.

3. For two of the starkest examples, see Amanda Hammar, Brian Raftopoulos, and Stig Jensen, (eds), *Zimbabwe's Unfinished Business: Rethinking Land, State and Nation in the Context of Crisis* (Harare: Weaver Press, 2003); Patrick Bond and Masimba Manyanya, *Zimbabwe's Plunge: Exhausted Nationalism, Neoliberalism and the Search for Social Justice* (Scottsville, London, and Harare: University of Natal Press, The Merlin Press, and Weaver Press, respectively, 2002).

4. Mahmood Mamdani, *Citizen and Subject: Contemporary Africa and the Legacy of Late Colonialism* (Princeton, NJ: Princeton University Press, 1996).

5. Giovanni Arrighi, "The Political Economy of Rhodesia," in *Essays in the Political Economy of Africa*, ed. Giovanni Arrighi and John S. Saul (New York and London: Monthly Review Press, 1973).

6. Ian Phimister, *An Economic and Social History of Zimbabwe, 1890–1948* (London and New York: Longman, 1988), 180.

7. Paris Yeros, "The Political Economy of Civilisation: Peasant-workers in Zimbabwe and the Neo-colonial World," PhD diss., University of London, 2002.

8. Brian Raftopoulos, "Labour Internationalism and Problems of Autonomy and Democratisation in the Trade Union Movement in Southern Rhodesia," mimeo, 1996.

9. Elizabeth Schmidt, "Negotiated Spaces and Contested Terrain: Men, Women, and the Law in Colonial Zimbabwe, 1890–1939," *Journal of Southern African Studies* 16, no. 4 (1990): 622–648.

10. Robin Palmer, *Land and Racial Domination in Rhodesia* (London, Ibadan, Nairobi, Lusaka: Heinemann, 1977).

11. Charles Van Onselen, *Chibaro: African Mine Labour in Southern Rhodesia, 1900–1933* (Johannesburg: Ravan Press, 1976).

12. Ian Phimister, "From Preference Towards Protection: Manufacturing in Southern Rhodesia, 1940–1965," in *Zimbabwe: A History of Manufacturing, 1890–1995*, ed. A. S. Mlambo, E. S. Pangeti, and I. Phimister (Harare: University of Zimbabwe Publications, 2000), 32–33.

13. Giovanni Arrighi, "The Political Economy of Rhodesia," 350–358.

14. Ibid.

15. D. G. Clarke, *Foreign Companies and International Investment in Zimbabwe* (London and Gwelo: Catholic Institute for International Relations and Mambo Press, 1980).

16. Ibbo Mandaza, "The Political Economy of Transition," in *Zimbabwe: The Political Economy of Transition, 1980–1986*, edited by Ibbo Mandaza (Dakar: CODESRIA, 1986); Ibbo Mandaza, "The State and Politics in a Post-White Settler Colonial Situation," in *Zimbabwe: The Political Economy of Transition, 1980–1986*, edited by Ibbo Mandaza (Dakar: CODESRIA, 1986).

17. Arnold Sibanda, "The Political Situation," in *Zimbabwe's Prospects: Issues of Race, Class, State and Capital in Southern Africa*, edited by Colin Stoneman (London and Basingstoke: Macmillan Publishers, 1988).

18. Sam Moyo, "Three decades of agrarian reform in Zimbabwe," *Journal of Peasant Studies* 38, no. 3 (2011): 493–531; Sam Moyo, "ESAP, Land Policy, and Land Markets," mimeo, 1998.

19. A. S. Mlambo, "Manufacturing in Zimbabwe, 1980–90," in *Zimbabwe: A History of Manufacturing, 1890–1995*, ed. A. S. Mlambo, E. S. Pangeti, and I. Phimister (Harare: University of Zimbabwe Publications, 2000), 80.

20. Colin Stoneman and Lionel Cliffe, *Zimbabwe: Politics, Economics and Society* (London and New York: Pinter Publishers, 1989), 43.

21. Arnold Sibanda, "The Political Situation," 266–267.

22. Theresa Chimombe, "Foreign Capital," in *Zimbabwe: The Political Economy of Transition, 1980–1986*, edited by Ibbo Mandaza (Dakar: CODESRIA, 1986); Colin Stoneman, "The World Bank and the IMF in Zimbabwe," in *Structural Adjustment in Africa*, edited by Bonnie K. Campbell and John Loxley (Basingstoke: Macmillan Press, 1989); Patrick Bond, *Uneven Zimbabwe: A Study of Finance, Development, and Underdevelopment* (Trenton, NJ and Asmara: Africa World Press, 1998).

23. Colin Stoneman, "The World Bank and the IMF in Zimbabwe," 41.

24. Sam Moyo, *The Land Question in Zimbabwe* (Harare: SAPES Books, 1995).

25. Michael Bratton, "The Comrades and the Countryside: The Politics of Agricultural Policy in Zimbabwe," *World Politics* 39, no. 2 (1987): 174–202.

26. Lionel Cliffe, "Zimbabwe's Agricultural 'Success' and Food Security," *Review of African Political Economy* 43 (1988): 4–25.

27. Tor Skålnes, *The Politics of Economic Reform in Zimbabwe* (Basingstoke: Macmillan Press, 1995).

28. Patrick Bond, *Uneven Zimbabwe: A Study of Finance, Development, and Underdevelopment.*

29. Brian Raftopoulos, "Beyond the House of Hunger: Democratic Struggle in Zimbabwe," Part I, *Review of African Political Economy* 54 (1992): 59–74; Brian Raftopoulos, "Beyond the House of Hunger: Democratic Struggle in Zimbabwe," Part II, *Review of African Political Economy* 55 (1992): 57–66.

30. Peter Gowan, *The Global Gamble* (London and New York: Verso, 1999); Stephen Haggard and Sylvia Maxfield, "The Political Economy of Financial Liberalization in the Developing World," in *Internationalization and Domestic Politics,* edited by Robert O. Keohane and Helen V. Milner (Cambridge: Cambridge University Press, 1996).

31. Patrick Bond, *Uneven Zimbabwe: A Study of Finance, Development, and Underdevelopment.*

32. Ibid.

33. ZCTU, *Beyond ESAP: Framework for a Long-term Development Strategy in Zimbabwe Beyond the Economic Structural Adjustment Programme* (Harare: Zimbabwe Congress for Trade Unions [ZCTU], 1996); UNDP/UNCTAD, *Zimbabwe: Globalization, Liberalization and Sustainable Human Development,* Country Assessment Report, first draft, mimeo, 2000; UNDP/UNCTAD, *Zimbabwe: Globalization, Liberalization and Sustainable Human Development,* Country Assessment Report, first draft, mimeo, 2000.

34. ZCTU, *Beyond ESAP: Framework for a Long-term Development Strategy in Zimbabwe Beyond the Economic Structural Adjustment Programme* (Harare: Zimbabwe Congress for Trade Unions [ZCTU], 1996); Godfrey Kanyenze, "Labour Markets and Employment During ESAP," mimeo, 1996.

35. ZCTU, *Beyond ESAP: Framework for a Long-term Development Strategy in Zimbabwe Beyond the Economic Structural Adjustment Programme* (Harare: Zimbabwe Congress for Trade Unions [ZCTU], 1996); UNDP/UNCTAD, *Zimbabwe: Globalization, Liberalization and Sustainable Human Development,* Country Assessment Report, first draft, mimeo, 2000.

36. Sam Moyo, *Land Reform under Structural Adjustment in Zimbabwe: Land Use Change in the Mashonaland Provinces* (Uppsala: Nordiska Africainstitutet, 2000).

37. Government of Zimbabwe, Ministry of Lands and Agriculture, "National Land Policy Framework Paper," November 1999; Sam Moyo, *The Land Question in Zimbabwe.*

38. UNDP, Poverty Reduction Forum, and IDS, *Zimbabwe Human Development Report 1998* (Harare: UNDP, PRF, and IDS, 1998).

39. Sam Moyo, *The Land Question in Zimbabwe,* 7.

40. Sam Moyo, "The Interaction of Market and Compulsory Land Acquisition Processes with Social Action in Zimbabwe's Land Reform," public lecture, Millennium Lecture Series, London School of Economics, 2 May 2001.

41. Amilcar Cabral, *Unity and Struggle* (New York: Monthly Review Press, 1979); Frantz Fanon, *The Wretched of the Earth* (London: Penguin Books, 2001).

42. Ibbo Mandaza, "The State and Politics in a Post-White Settler Colonial Situation."

43. Brian Raftopoulos, "Beyond the House of Hunger: Democratic Struggle in Zimbabwe," Parts I and II; Brian Raftopoulos and Tsuneo Yoshikuni, eds., *Sites of Struggle: Essays in Zimbabwe's Urban History* (Harare: Weaver Press, 1999).

44. Sam Moyo, Land and Democracy in Zimbabwe, Monograph Series (Harare: SAPES Books, 1999); Sam Moyo, *The Land Question in Zimbabwe*; Sam Moyo, *Land Reform under Structural Adjustment in Zimbabwe: Land Use Change in the Mashonaland Provinces*; Sam Moyo, "The Land Occupation Movement and Democratisation in Zimbabwe: Contradictions of Neoliberalism," *Millennium: Journal of International Studies* 30, no. 2 (2001): 311–330.

45. Ibbo Mandaza, "The State and Politics in a Post-White Settler Colonial Situation."

46. Lloyd Sachikonye, "State, Capital and Trade Unions," in *Zimbabwe: The Political Economy of Transition, 1980–1986*, edited by Ibbo Mandaza (Dakar: CODESRIA, 1986); Brian Wood, "Trade-Union Organisation and the Working Class," in *Zimbabwe's Prospects: Issues of Race, Class, State and Capital in Southern Africa*, edited by Colin Stoneman (London and Basingstoke: Macmillan Publishers, 1988).

47. Ibbo Mandaza, "The State and Politics in a Post-White Settler Colonial Situation."

48. Karl Marx, "Critique of Hegel's Doctrine of the State," in *Early Writings*, with an introduction by Lucio Colletti (Harmondsworth: Penguin Books, 1975).

49. Wood, "Trade-Union Organisation and the Working Class."

50. Paris Yeros, "Zimbabwe and the Dilemmas of the Left," *Historical Materialism* 10, no. 2 (2002): 3–15; Paris Yeros, "The Political Economy of Civilisation: Peasant-workers in Zimbabwe and the Neo-colonial World."

51. Jocelyn Alexander, "The State, Agrarian Policy and Rural Politics in Zimbabwe: Case Studies of Insiza and Chimanimani Districts, 1940–1990," PhD diss., Oxford University, 1993, 185.

52. Ibid., 168–173.

53. Michael Bratton, "Micro-Democracy? The Merger of Farmer Unions in Zimbabwe," *African Studies Review* 37, no. 1 (1994): 9–37.

54. Sam Moyo, *Land Reform under Structural Adjustment in Zimbabwe: Land Use Change in the Mashonaland Provinces*; Paris Yeros, "The Political Economy of Civilisation: Peasant-workers in Zimbabwe and the Neo-colonial World."

55. Sam Moyo, "The Interaction of Market and Compulsory Land Acquisition Processes with Social Action in Zimbabwe's Land Reform," in *Pan-Africanism and Integration in Africa*, edited by Ibbo Mandaza and Dani Nabudere (Harare: SAPES Books, 2003).

56. Sam Moyo, "The Interaction of Market and Compulsory Land Acquisition Processes with Social Action in Zimbabwe's Land Reform," public lecture, *Millennium* Lecture Series, London School of Economics, 2 May 2001.

57. Sam Moyo, "Peasant Organisations and Rural Civil Society in Africa: An Introduction," in *Peasant Organisations and Democratisation in Africa*, ed. S. Moyo and B. Romdhane (Dakar: Codesria Book Series, 2002), 1–26.

58. Jocelyn Alexander, "The State, Agrarian Policy and Rural Politics in Zimbabwe: Case Studies of Insiza and Chimanimani Districts, 1940–1990" (D.Phil., Oxford University 1993); Sam Moyo, *Land Reform under Structural Adjustment in Zimbabwe: Land Use Change in the Mashonaland Provinces*; Paris Yeros, "The Political Economy of Civilisation: Peasant-workers in Zimbabwe and the Neo-colonial World."

59. Sam Moyo, "Peasant Organisations and Rural Civil Society in Africa: An Introduction," 1–26.

60. Prosper Matondi and Sam Moyo, "Experiences with Market Based Land Reform in Zimbabwe," in *The Negative Impacts of World Bank Market Based Land Reform*, edited by Flávia Barros, Sérgio Sauer, and Stephen Schwartzman (Brasilia: Rede Brasil, 2003).

61. Sam Moyo, *Land Reform under Structural Adjustment in Zimbabwe: Land Use Change in the Mashonaland Provinces.*

62. Sam Moyo, "ESAP, Land Policy, and Land Markets," mimeo, 1998.

63. Paris Yeros, "The Political Economy of Civilisation: Peasant-workers in Zimbabwe and the Neo-colonial World."

64. Sam Moyo, "The Land Occupation Movement and Democratisation in Zimbabwe: Contradictions of Neoliberalism."

65. Jocelyn Alexander and JoAnn McGregor, "Elections, Land and the Politics of Opposition in Matabeleland, Zimbabwe," mimeo, 2000; Sam Moyo, "The Land Occupa-

tion Movement and Democratisation in Zimbabwe: Contradictions of Neoliberalism," 311–330.

66. Amanda Hammar, Brian Raftopoulos, and Stig Jensen, eds., *Zimbabwe's Unfinished Business: Rethinking Land, State and Nation in the Context of Crisis* (Harare: Weaver Press, 2003); Patrick Bond and Masimba Manyanya, *Zimbabwe's Plunge: Exhausted Nationalism, Neoliberalism and the Search for Social Justice.*

67. Sam Moyo, "Three decades of agrarian reform in Zimbabwe."

68. Ministry of Lands and Rural Resettlement (MLRR), "Land Audit Framework," September 2009.

69. Sam Moyo, "Three decades of agrarian reform in Zimbabwe."

70. Buka Report, "A preliminary audit report of Land Reform Programme." Unpublished report, Government of Zimbabwe, 2002; Presidential Land Review Committee Report (PLRC), *Report of the Presidential Land Review Committee under the Chairmanship of Dr. Charles M. B. Utete, Volumes I and II: Main Report to His Excellency the President of the Republic of Zimbabwe* (Harare: Government Printers, August 2003).

71. Sam Moyo, "ESAP, Land Policy, and Land Markets," mimeo, 1998.

72. Sam Moyo, Walter Chambati, Tendai Murisa, Dumisani Siziba, Charity Dangwa, Kingstone Mujeyi, and Ndabezinhle Nyoni, *Fast Track Land Reform Baseline Survey in Zimbabwe: Trends and Tendencies, 2005/06* (Harare: African Institute for Agrarian Studies, 2009).

73. Wilbert Sadomba, "War Veterans in Zimbabwe: Complexities of a Liberation Movement in an African Post-Colonial Settler Society," PhD diss., Wageningin University, Netherlands, 2008.

74. Walter Chambati, *Emergent Agrarian Labour Relations in New Resettlement Areas, Zvimba District* (Harare: AIAS Monograph Series, 2009).

75. Walter Chambati and Godfrey Magaramombe, "The Abandoned Question: Farm Workers," in *Contested Terrain: Land Reform and Civil Society in Contemporary Zimbabwe*, ed. Sam Moyo, Kirk Helliker, and Tendai Murisa (Pietermaritzburg: S&S Publishers, 2008); Walter Chambati, *Emergent Agrarian Labour Relations in New Resettlement Areas, Zvimba District* (Harare: AIAS Monograph Series, 2009); Walter Chambati and Sam Moyo, *Land Reform and the Political Economy of Agricultural Labour*, mimeo (Harare: African Institute for Agrarian Studies, 2003); Lloyd Sachikonye, "The Situation of Commercial Farmers after Land Reform in Zimbabwe," report prepared for the Farm Community Trust of Zimbabwe, 2003.

76. Sam Moyo, "Three decades of agrarian reform in Zimbabwe."

77. Ibid.

78. Sam Moyo, Kirk Helliker, and Tendai Murisa, eds., *Contested Terrain: Land Reform and Civil Society in Contemporary Zimbabwe* (Pietermaritzburg: S&S Publishers, 2008); Wilbert Sadomba, "War Veterans in Zimbabwe: Complexities of a Liberation Movement in an African Post-Colonial Settler Society," PhD Thesis, Wageningin University, Netherlands, 2008; Tendai Murisa, "Emerging Forms of Social Organisation and Agency in the Newly Resettled Areas of Zimbabwe: The Cases of Goromonzi and Zvimba Districts," PhD diss., Rhodes University, 2010; Ian Scoones, Nelson Marongwe, Blasio Mavedzenge, Felix Murimbarimba, Jacob Mahenehene, and Chrispen Sukume, *Zimbabwe's Land Reform: Myths and Realities* (Harare: Weaver Press, 2010).

79. Sam Moyo, Walter Chambati, Tendai Murisa, Dumisani Siziba, Charity Dangwa, Kingstone Mujeyi, and Ndabezinhle Nyoni, *Fast Track Land Reform Baseline Survey in Zimbabwe: Trends and Tendencies, 2005/06.*

80. Godfrey Kanyenze, "Giving Voice to the Unprotected Workers in the Informal Economy in Africa: The Case of Zimbabwe," in *Restart: Our Path to Social Justice—The MDC's*

Economic Programme for Reconstruction Stabilisation Recovery and Transformation (Harare: Movement for Democratic Change [MDC], 2004).

81. Walter Chambati, *Emergent Agrarian Labour Relations in New Resettlement Areas, Zvimba District* (Harare: AIAS Monograph Series, 2009); Sam Moyo, "Three decades of agrarian reform in Zimbabwe."

82. Parliament of Zimbabwe, "Second Report of the Portfolio Committee on Public Service, Labour and Social Welfare on the Plight of Farm Workers and Newly Resettled Farmers," 2003.

83. Samir Amin, *The Future of Maoism*, trans. Norman Finkelstein (New York: Monthly Review Press, 1981).

Chapter 13

Polycultures of the Mind

The "End" of the Peasant and the Birth of Agroecology

Alejandro Rojas

INTRODUCTION

This discussion examines the contributions that peasant agriculture and agroecology have made to food security and food sustainability in Latin America and draws from these experiences lessons for long-term sustainability and environmental education that is centered on food. Food is an essential terrain for environmental and sustainability education, because it represents the pinnacle of the presently unbalanced relationship between humankind and nature. During a time of food peak and unprecedented vulnerability of the food system, we are examining here the impending extinction of a social group that has provided food in a sustainable manner since the beginning of the Neolithic Revolution, some 10,000 years ago. In Latin America, despite the drastic and negative effects of neoliberal policies, about 17 million peasant production units occupy close to 60.5 million hectares, or 34.5 percent of the total cultivated land with average farm sizes of about 1.8 hectares, and produce 51 percent of the maize, 77 percent of the beans, and 61 percent of the potatoes for domestic consumption.[1]

The evidence concerning the productivity of small-scale, polycultural agriculture is very persuasive and has increasingly been gaining recognition through the work of agroecologists, cultural ecologists, and cultural and ecological anthropologists, as it calls attention and demands recognition for the historical contributions made to sustainable agriculture and food, by the historically devalued and underappreciated reserves of knowledge held by peasant farmers.

The advent of industrial agriculture in Latin America since the beginning of the Green Revolution has experienced ideal conditions for rapid expansion under the hegemony of the neoliberal model of development, of which agrifood corporations have been the main proponents.[2] The most vocal proponents of this agricultural model have continued to acquire access to the best remaining lands on the continent and to expand fossil-intensive, heavily irrigated monocultural agricultural systems orientated toward export-based production for international and deregulated markets. We are in the process of witnessing the possible demise of the peasantry, which despite its high heterogeneity and structural, geographical, cultural, historical, and ecological differences, has represented a way of life, an approach toward working with the land and a wealth of knowledge that has consistently been identified with the key ecological principles and processes most needed by the agricultural and food production and cultivation models of the future: stable, diverse, and locally based food production with minimal adverse impact on the environment, low emission of greenhouse gases (GHG) shorter food mileages, and full reintegration of "waste" into the productive cycle.

This list of positive attributes associated with this approach to agriculture, which at one time was primarily proposed almost exclusively by NGOs, peasant movements, and environmentalists, has now gained an unprecedented level of attention and support from mainstream entities. This new level of recognition and validation is due, in part, to the position taken by the climate change scientific community,[3] which considers among the key responses to climate change the necessity of shortening the food chain, by reducing food mileage and completing as much as possible the productive cycle in agriculture by reintegrating its end products into the process. Although the debate on what is the best approach toward agricultural production continues unabated and radically different paradigms continue to collide,[4] the intensity of the current food crisis (now called "food peak") has recognized several profound changes, which must be taken into consideration. Peak food is actually related to four other intertwined crises: peak farmable land, peak water, peak oil, and global warming.

Our intent is not to idealize or in any way romanticize the lives of peasants, which due to structural constraints resulting from the developmental strategies imposed throughout the continent, in most cases are marginal and stricken with poverty and hardships that most peasants themselves do not desire their children to have to endure. Once again, we are faced with the reality that the peasantry is a diverse and heterogeneous group, and we should approach any vast sweeping generalizations about this moving target with serious and healthy doses of skepticism. However, despite all the variations,[5] agroecologists have identified many peasant communities practicing ecologically sound forms of agricultural living for centuries, while mainstream agricultural science and technology and the structural forces that drive them continually make industrial agriculture one of the most environmentally offensive industries in the world. What is it that these peasants know? And how do they know what they know?

This discussion will begin by placing the question of whether or not we are facing the "end of the peasant" in the broader context of the current vulnerabilities of the global food system and the possible threats that exist against the ability to attain food security and to create sustainable food systems. This section also provides a very brief examination of the position of peasants in society and the role of peasant agriculture in Latin America.

The second section examines encounters between science and local peasant knowledge, and the emergence in Latin America of the science of agroecology. This body of knowledge is based on the legacy of peasant agriculture that articulates both a mode of inquiry and a possible vision of sustainable agriculture and food systems for the future in this era of environmental crisis. This section also points out the relationship between current peasant movements in Latin America and the ecological agenda.

The third section discusses some of the lessons drawn from peasant agriculture and agroecology that can be integrated into the sustainability education required to develop workable adaptation strategies to the intertwined effects of global warming and globalization. What are the peasants' collective experiences that have lead them to understand the ecological processes that have been obscured by modern education? How did they acquire this knowledge? What are the original sources of this knowledge, which has been passed on one generation to the next? These are the educational implications of the "polycultures of the mind" that inhabit the peasant mindset, as opposed to the "monoculture of the mind" that is harbored and demonstrated by industrial agricultural planners.

THE PROBLEM

Although the question that immediately concerns us is that of the possible future of the peasantry ("The End of the Peasant?"), my focus here is on retrieving elements of the cultural legacy of peasants to aid in our current objective to attain food sustainability and develop sustainability education. This approach toward the problem suggests from inception that regardless of what the demographic future of the peasants will look like, there are elements of their cultural heritage that may transcend them into the future.

In this regard, the discussion should be read as a new chapter in the rich tradition of popular adult education in Latin America as initiated by Paulo Freire, who constructed his Pedagogy of the Oppressed through his observations of the learning experiences of Latin American peasants and of their strategies to attain food security, often under conditions of severe resource scarcity and minimal land bases. Freire is internationally recognized as the founder of a dynamic movement in adult education, which has branched out all over the world to become a well-established and respected scholarly tradition.[6]

Food is the ultimate and most recognizable mediator in the relationship between humans and the natural environment and, therefore, an essential field to explore in our efforts to increase environmental awareness through sustainability education. However, the connection between humans and our food sources has become strained and fractured by the industrial food system. The consequence of this disconnect is the physical and psychological distancing of people from the sources of the food we eat and therefore from the environment in which we thrive.

Thus, food comes from "everywhere and nowhere,"[7] travels thousands of miles before reaching the consumer's plate, and impacts ecosystems throughout the entire production cycle to the disposal of end products. Most consumers do not know (and in many instances do not care) who produces their food or under what conditions it is produced. However, this situation is beginning to change, with the global prominence of a broad array of food-related movements, the growing convergence of the goals of food security and ecological sustainability, and the increasing international presence of the peasant movements. The question of public education and public debate as it concerns the ecological, social and economic, and health impacts of food have moved to the front and center of world attention.

The peasant farmer, the historical provider of food agriculture, has come to represent a form of direct connection between humans and the land, only comparable to the profound belonging of the gatherers and hunters to the ecosystem that sustains them. I propose that, in the midst of the multitude of debates concerning the definition and conceptualization of the peasant, it is safe to stress that compared to urban dwellers, peasants live closer to the "natural" (non-human-built) environment, although it is a given that agriculture is a distinctly human creation. It is the direct connection with the sources of our food in nature that allows us to identify the peasant as an "other" from which we can learn a great deal. Thus, our interest is to learn from peasant communities and the variety of ways in which they have—by necessity—been addressing environmental insecurities and the vulnerability of food systems and what learning processes have led them to be the earliest practitioners of sustainable agriculture.

Food security is best defined as the condition made possible by a food system that delivers food that is affordable, available, accessible, appropriate, safe, and sustainable for all. The general goal of our studies has been to develop a better understanding of the impact of large forces (e.g., climate change; loss of biodiversity; depletion of natural resources; changes in forms of production, distribution, consumption, and disposal of end products; and environmental and social impacts of food) on the global food system. This globalized food system is characterized by a continued growth in food production and by a trend toward specialization by comparative advantages for liberalized trade. These trends, however, have not alleviated widespread malnutrition, nor have they reduced severe and environmental impacts on the food system. In fact, these trends (supported by a particular mentality and approach toward the environment) have increased the adverse impacts of the food production system, placing agriculture among the most environmentally disruptive of industries.

The global food system has failed to provide sufficient food for everyone. Approximately 4 billion out of the 6 billion human beings on the planet suffer from malnutrition, with roughly 2 billion underfed, of which some 800 million suffer from chronic hunger. Yet, at the same time, 2 billion are overfed.[8] Nutrition and food experts are alarmed by the continued contradictory growth of both chronic hunger and obesity, with both forms of malnutrition affecting all age groups.[9] At the same time, the impact and demands of our globalized food system on energy, water, and the environment in general, and on traditional food systems and labor, are increasingly unsustainable, raising serious concerns about its viability.

Global climate change is affecting every single factor in the production of food from water and soil to biodiversity and will dictate many key food production decisions of the future.[10] Increased temperatures and severe fluctuations (drought, flooding, storms, etc.) bring stress on essential ecosystems and affect entire regional food systems. Even the most self-reliant food systems can become vulnerable if its links with others become weak, thus making emergency and crisis intervention more difficult. As is now becoming increasingly recognized, agriculture is the most thirsty industry on the planet, consuming 72 percent of all global freshwater at a time when the United Nations says 80 percent of our water supplies are being overexploited.[11] The science of agroecology and working with peasant farmers offer some answers, responding to the diagnosis of the situation eloquently summarized by M. Altieri, a professor at the University of California, Berkeley and the president of the Latin American Society of Agroecology:

> This crisis which threatens the livelihoods of millions more than the already 800 million hungry people throughout the world, is the direct result of the dominating industrial farming model, that not only is dangerously dependent on fossil fuels but that has also become the largest source of human impact on the biosphere. In fact, there are now so many pressures on dwindling arable ecosystems that farming is overwhelming nature's capacity to meet humankind's food, fiber and energy needs. The tragedy is that agriculture depends on the very ecological services (water cycles, pollinators, fertile soil formation, benevolent local weather, etc.) that intensive farming continually degrades or pushes beyond their limits.[12]

In the face of these threats, it is ironic that the practice of peasant agriculture that represents the application of the key principles and processes advocated by the climate change scientific community to adopt are under threat by the expansion of the system of production that is behind anthropogenic environmental and climate change.

PEASANTS AND PEASANT AGRICULTURE IN LATIN AMERICA

There is a wide consensus in the scholarship on Latin American peasants not only in acknowledging significant regional and national variations in the historical development of the peasantry but also in the identification of key shared traits through the different historical moments of its rather dramatic history.

It is not possible within the confines of this discussion to do justice to the richness of the literature and the complexity of the debates among historians, anthropologists, rural sociologists, and development scholars. Suffice it to say that the relationships between peasants and the sources of our food have been historically determined and, to this day, keep the peasants, despite immense variations, in various forms of direct connection with the sources of our food in nature. In Latin America, as a result of colonial conquest and domination, large estates took shape and began the era of the haciendas, or *latifundios*, which, despite many changes in the pattern of development, have survived through the epoch of industrialization for import substitution (1930s to the end of the 1970s), a period when the governments of the region embarked on various ambitious efforts to create processes of industrialization with strong support and involvement of the state. Two major agrarian formations dominate the rural landscape of the continent since colonial conquest: the hacienda, or *latifundios*, and the *minifundios*.

These two formations, the hacienda and the minifundio, remained key factors in Latin American agriculture until the demise of the hacienda through the processes of Agrarian Reform, which came as a concession to the emergence of massive peasant movements at the end of the 1960s and 1970s (with the exception of Mexico in the 1920s and Bolivia in the 1950s), while the minifundios continue to exist in various forms to this day. In the 1960s the latifundios comprised approximately 5 percent of farm units but nonetheless owned about five-fifths of the land. Minifundios comprised four-fifths of the farm units but had only 5 percent of the land.[13] The composition of the peasantry that worked in these units was complex and varied, ranging from agricultural workers who owned small holdings (the minifundistas) to those who had limited land access through a tenancy (sharecroppers, share-tenants, or labor-service tenants) to those who were landless.

In 1969, an estimated quarter of the total active agricultural work force consisted of landless peasant waged workers (proletarians), and three-quarters had access to land. Of the latter, two-thirds were independent peasant farmers ("external peasantries") and a third were tenants. Slightly over half of the independent peasant farmers were minifundistas (semiproletarians) and the remainder were formed by larger or richer peasant farmers whose household members did not need to seek outside employment.[14] With respect to employment, half of the agricultural labor force worked on peasant plots, mainly as unpaid domestic workers. Larger estates employed less than one-fifth of the total agricultural labor force but accounted for 90 percent of the total hired labor force.[15]

The study conducted by S. Barraclough for the United Nations Research Institute for Social Development revealed important findings about the productivity of labor and the use of land in latifundios and minifundios. Although the average production per agricultural worker was five to ten times higher on latifundios than on minifundios, production per hectare of agricultural land was roughly three to five times higher on minifundios. Overall, this structure was inefficient and socially unjust, and the widespread perception that it was so made agrarian reform one of the key demands of the social and political climate of agitation and unrest of the 1960s and 1970s in Latin America.

Besides the particular case of Mexico, where the early agrarian reform began in the 1920s in most countries throughout the region, agrarian reform remained limited in scope, in terms of land expropriated and peasant beneficiaries. Despite an explicit commitment to agrarian reform and peasant farming (with the exception of Cuba), governments were either too weak to implement a substantial agrarian reform or had the underlying intention of promoting capitalist farming.[16]

Nevertheless, the mass mobilizations for agrarian reform and the rise of rural trade unions, cooperatives, and other associations served to integrate the peasantry into the national economy, society, and political system, and many peasants themselves, upon receiving a land title, felt for the first time that they were first-class citizens.[17] Agrarian reform led to the demise of the oligarchy and created ideal conditions for the full commercialization of agriculture.

According to Lopez-Cordovez,[18] the peasant economy, by the end of the 1980s, accounted for almost two-thirds of the total agricultural labor force, the remaining third being employed by private capitalist farms. In addition, peasant agriculture supplied two-fifths of production for the domestic market and a third of the production for export.

In the era of neoliberal model dominance, Latin American peasants have experienced a land squeeze and an employment squeeze. De Janvry[19] reports that these processes mainly affect the small peasantry (minifundistas) who comprise about two-thirds of peasant farm households. Their average farm size fell from 2.1 hectares in 1950 to 1.9 hectares in 1980.

Kay[20] concluded in 2000 that the process of semiproletarianization is the dominant tendency currently unfolding among the Latin American peasantry. An increasing proportion of total peasant household income originates from wages. Income from own-farm activities often accounts for under half of the total. The small peasantry (minifundistas), who comprised two-thirds of all peasant households, are best characterized as semiproletarian, as approximately two-fifths of their household income is derived from off-farm sources, principally from seasonal agricultural wage employment on commercial farms and estates

Peasants' access to off-farm sources of income, generally seasonal wage labor, enables them to keep their small land base, keeping them in touch with the land, thus allowing them to avoid fully becoming waged laborers. This arrangement tends to favor rural capitalists, as it eliminates small peasants as competitors in agricultural production and makes them available for employment as cheap labor. Semiproletarianization is the only option open to those peasants who wish to retain access to land for reasons of security and survival, or because they cannot find alternative long-term employment, in either the rural or urban sector.[21]

However, neoliberalism would soon face significant opposition by peasants. Indeed, the peasant rebellion in Chiapas, Mexico in 1994 has come to symbolize the new character of rurally based social movements in Latin America.[22] In fact, the Chiapas uprising seems to mark a turning point and the beginning of a decade in Latin America where the effects of neoliberalism have led to a new wave of center-left and left-wing governments. It is still too early to assess the impact on the peasantry as a result of the presence of new center-left and left-wing governments in Chile, Uruguay, Peru, Brazil, Argentina, Nicaragua, Venezuela, Ecuador, and Bolivia, but many observers are skeptical about the real capacity, political will, or power of these governments to enact real transformations of the neoliberal model, although the cases of Venezuela, Bolivia, and Ecuador present some important and notable differences compared to the more left-center positions of the others.[23]

As we have seen, scholarly accounts of the demographic significance and the structure of rural labor present a complex picture of the situation of Latin American peasantry, one that makes it difficult to make firm generalizations. *However, what remains a well-established fact is the continued critical role of peasant farmers in providing staple food throughout the continent.* Despite the increased use of the world's agricultural lands to grow agroexport crops, biofuels, and soya beans as food for cattle, peasant farmers continue to provide most of the staple crops that sustain the world's population. The situation in Latin America confirms the role of peasant farmers as key providers of food security.

PEASANT KNOWLEDGE AND THE EMERGENCE IN LATIN AMERICA OF AGROECOLOGY: THE PEASANT AS PRACTITIONER OF ECOLOGICAL PROCESSES

A widespread organizing principle essential to the peasant approach to agriculture is the maintenance of a livelihood dependent on a *set of strategies based on the reproduction of the diversity of life*, while facing structural constraints that confine them to a small land base. Comparatively speaking, a small plot of land of a few hectares set aside for peasant agriculture is likely to contain more varieties of life than thousands of hectares dedicated to monocultural production. The peasant works with this life diversity, and the aim of this production system is to work with what is naturally in place in the ecosystem were one dwells. Certainly, the ways in which the things in place are named, how they are viewed, and what is ultimately done with them has very little in common with the narratives of science.

If we travel through the countryside in Latin America, we will still find that the average peasant family (of four to six) dwells in a 1- to 2-hectare land base. We will find (with some variations) (a) a relatively humble house built with local materials (adobe, grass, branches, or local wood) and (b) a polycultural plot containing several combinations of plants that are known to complementarily and symbiotically coexist. Typically, across the Andes, this usually consists of a combination of beans, squash, corn, potatoes, and legumes, often articulated in some form of integration between producers at different altitudes in the Andes and through networks linking various communities into a regional system, linked together by a common cultural pattern of economic linkages and shared rituals.[24] If peasant families are based in areas where fruit trees grow in abundance, there will always be fruit trees for household consumption, and (c) the plot will be "rented" from the larger landowner, either lent in exchange for work in the larger property or sharing products and some kind of arrangement with the absentee owner, alongside a variety of other arrangements, including surviving cooperatives from the times of the agrarian reform and individual and family-owned peasant farms. Also, (d) there will be several domestic animals, with the most common combination being chickens, ducks, one or two pigs (or depending on the altitude, one or two llamas), a cow or a goat, plus many dogs and cats. Finally, (e) the plot will be filled with bees, birds, and butterflies, and the soil will be rich in organic matter and minerals and be massively inhabited by worms, the most eloquent indicator of the health of the soil.

The peasant farm will be a place booming with life, including the kind that is uncomfortable and inconvenient for humans and smaller animals, such as mosquitoes, flies, snakes, wild animals, and sometimes poisonous insects. Although almost impossible to define with a single definition that encompasses all, there will be a small land-base, worked by the peasant farmer and family and a surrounding community with whom the peasant will tend to be in a relatively close-knit network of mutual support, while never being entirely free of conflict.

Agroecologists have a variety of names with which they refer to this picture, the most common one being an agroecosystem characterized by a rich biodiversity, where the productive cycle is characterized by close loops, where the energy of the sun is processed by a panoply of plants, where nutrients cycle through the system in relationships of mutuality, symbiosis, and competition. The peasant uses all three to enhance desirable traits of the system (i.e., nitrogen-fixing properties of legumes) and to control pests and discourage predators. Animals are always integrated with all the other functions of the farm in food provision, manure production for fertilizer, and nutrient cycling. These are communities involved in important relations based on reciprocity and mutual aid, thus endowed with social capital.

To survive, these "traditional" farmers require a profound and detailed practical knowledge of their local ecosystems. They are rooted in their physical locations, which equip them with a type of knowledge that is involved and participatory, rather than detached and remote. It is also subjective and value laden, because it overtly appreciates personal experiences and beliefs as resources for knowledge, rather than as obstacles. It is centered on the interests of the local community and its aim is to produce food for the local communities, with the goals of sufficiency and long-term stability, rather than fast production for foreign or remote markets with strictly quick, short-term profit in mind.

Traditional peasant ecological knowledge is also experimental and is always based on shared experiences of what has been shown and proven over the course of generations. However, the experiments conducted by peasant farmers are experiments in situ (they take place in their natural context), not in vitro (in an artificial context), as is typically the case in standardized scientific experiments. The latter approach aims to purposefully and systematically control the environment to identify the cause of the single effect under investigation. The former remains by necessity more open-ended and evolves through trial and error, often involving several simultaneous effects. By comparing Western scientific knowledge with local, experiential knowledge, we can realize that the requirements of these types of knowledge tend to be very different. Science was born and has evolved mainly from the interest of finding universals, that is, the ability to make generalizations about phenomena. So scientific research looks for regularities and uniformities of phenomena that can be replicated under controlled conditions, and such findings have been among the greatest contributions of Western science. Traditional knowledge, on the other hand, tends to be site specific and grounded in place; it seeks singularities and does not claim validity beyond the place where it evolved in local ecosystems. Thus, both systems of knowledge illuminate different aspects of reality and have their own demands, merits, and weaknesses, depending on the aspect of reality they intend to illuminate. The key question is this: is integration/translation between these different forms of knowledge possible and desirable? As we shall see, the agroecological answer is yes.

POLYCULTURES AND MONOCULTURES OF THE MIND

In a celebrated essay on the value and efficacy of peasant knowledge written several years ago, Vandana Shiva articulated the concept of the "monocultures of the mind."[25] In my view, this concept possesses the merit of explaining with a powerful metaphor how the design of rural landscapes reflected a state of mind (and a state of being, I may add) and provided a mirror that feeds back in the human mind. The image summarized the grand illusion of the industrial era: that the land could be completely redesigned to fulfill its grand promise to provide for all the needs and wants of the human as the conqueror of the natural world.

The hope was that scientific and technological ingenuity could remove all constraints and limits and that there would come a day when humans would live in a world where material goods would flow in such abundance that the realm of necessity would give way to the realm of freedom. This ideal, a child of the industrial revolution, was shared right, center, and left by all sectors of the ideological spectrum. Happiness and freedom were equated with unlimited access to possessions. The assembly line, with its straight lines, would make the world predictable, calculable, controllable, and fully quantifiable. The controversial question was just how to distribute and share the bounty. Revolutions and counterrevolutions were fought about it, but those provided the consensus of the times: happiness was a question of abundance, not of sufficiency, stability, security, or meaning, because all that would be obtained *by homus economicus* endless ingenuity.

Shiva's monoculture of the mind speaks of the north's particular cultural project and its underlying dominant mode of investigating and shaping reality, a mode of understanding and meaning which led to the system of monoculture in agriculture and food production. This mode of understanding and designing served to displace the ecologically sounder indigenous peasant's age-old experiences of truly sustainable food cultivation, forest management, and animal husbandry. This increasingly accelerating process of technological innovation for control has produced large amounts of material goods and particular types of food that ended up threatening both the collective health of the people and that of the ecosystems that sustained them.

We do not need to revisit here the impressive body of evidence that has demonstrated the manner by which the monoculture has failed in all fundamental respects.[26] The purpose here is rather to reflect on what it has done to us educationally, as a representation of the unity of mind and nature, that is to say, the ecology of the mind of which G. Bateson wrote and that others have expanded on to speak of ecologies of the heart, meaning the relationships between humans and nature.[27]

Shiva also writes and speaks about the disappearance of local knowledge, made to disappear first by simply not seeing it and negating its very existence. While negating the existence of the others (systems of knowledge and meaning grounded in place), the dominant, expansionist model would present itself as universally valid (as "human nature"), in a state of denial or just blinded to the fact that it was also a local system, socially based on a "particular culture, class and gender. It is not universal in any epistemological sense. It is merely the globalized version of a very local and parochial tradition. Emerging from a dominating and colonizing culture, modern knowledge systems are themselves colonizing."[28] And, if local knowledge appears through this globalizing vision, "it is made to disappear by denying it the status of a systematic knowledge, and assigning it the adjectives 'primitive' and 'unscientific.' Correspondingly, the Western system is assumed to be uniquely 'scientific' and universal."[29] However, in Shiva's account, this has less to do with knowledge and more to do with power. The knowledge system that claims universal validity does so as the result of an expanding sociocultural system. "Positivism, verificationism, falsificationism were all based on the assumption that unlike traditional locally-based views of the world, which are socially constructed, modern scientific knowledge was thought to be determined without social mediation."[30]

The appeal of the metaphor of the monoculture of the mind strongly resonates in my view in that it explains how a system of knowledge that proclaims its ultimate superiority (monoculture) lacks the mechanisms of internal control that alternative explanations of reality can provide (like the suppression by chemical fertilizers and pesticides of the diversity of living organisms prevents those organisms from performing ecological services needed for the stability of the system). I like to equate this with the experiences of an observer inside a dark forest armed with a powerful, highly focused flashlight that confuses the whole of reality with the narrow bit illuminated by the beam of light. The more focused the view, the narrower the vision it provides, and the darker becomes its own background, to the point that the fragment of the world that can be seen becomes the only totality, the world as a whole.

Paradoxically, in the eloquence of her own criticism of the hegemonic discourse that she describes, Shiva makes one important error: In her narrative, she becomes oblivious to the fact that scientific discourse is not monolithic, nor has it ever been. Although the basic traits of her argumentation are appealing and fundamentally appropriate, what is missing and marginalized in her own narrative are all the streams of thought that have critiqued Western science from within, starting with but not limited to the claims of superiority of positivism, materialism, and mechanicism.[31] Ironically, a significant component of her own critique of the dominant paradigm of Western science is provided by arguments, ideas, and insights that have their own origins not only in the traditions of local knowledge of peasant and indigenous communities from around the world but also from Western scholarship. However, in our view, the greatest merit of her work, like that of many Western scholars, resides in the value and significance she assigns to knowledge grounded in place.

Thus, what follows from Shiva's discussion are the insights that can be derived from systems of knowledge that anywhere (and everywhere) have led to (even partially) sustainable livelihoods. In the end, hers is an argument that highlights the inseparability of cultural diversity and biological diversity. What may generate alternatives capable of guiding us to move out of the crisis of this civilization, again, in my interpretation of her work, are the myriads of flashlights, the diversity of local knowledge bases, which, when combined, give us one essential insight: the understanding that by attempting to replicate the complexity, diversity, and resilience of the natural world we can find the path toward cultural adaptation to the fundamental challenges faced by humanity today.

I have interpreted the mind and nature unit, which Bateson speaks of in his argument for ecology of the mind, as a challenge to create learning experiences and settings that cultivate what I call "polycultures of the mind"—that is, knowledge that attempts to mimic and to assimilate the complexity and uncertainty of life, accompanied by a learning process, which inspires the opening of the collective mind, through viable and feasible learning outcomes.

THE PEASANT AS A BEARER OF POLYCULTURES OF THE MIND

The picture that emerges from the examination of this story of the peasant farmer as ecological discoverer has now become a familiar one for agroecologists and ecological anthropologists. We know now that these "rooted people," as ecological anthropologists call them,[32] who identify themselves with the fabric of life that surrounds them is an ongoing theme of narratives describing the lives of indigenous peasants. Many anthropologists and pioneers of environmental thought understood this long ago. The same themes appear repeatedly almost everywhere: the land and its creatures, perceived as beautiful, mysterious, and, often, as all-too-powerful, and thus, to be treated with respect, reverence, and often fear.

The land, understood as a living and powerful being, is inhabited also by a community that is formed by a plethora of living beings of which humans are just one part, while at the same time, the land has continuities in the human body; the conviction that all living beings are relatives and the extent to which life is to be realized and reproduced depends on the recognition and reverence of this "family" of relationships. Finally, the principle of generalized reciprocity (*hoy por mi, mananaporti*) and the required balance of the relationships among humans, other living creatures, and the land as a whole permeate all aspects of daily life. Therefore, for everything that is taken away from the land, something must be returned. Within this universe, the loss of species breaches the balance of the world. Life is sacred, but in a manner that is incomprehensible to people that oppose all forms of animal killing: People hunt, learn to kill animals, and learn what to do with their bowels and their blood. They raise them, feed them, care for them, and then kill them for food without grand tribulations. Their animals have a life, too.

THE CONVERGENCE OF PEASANT KNOWLEDGE, ANTHROPOLOGY, AND ECOLOGY IN AGROECOLOGY

One of the most insidious effects of the paradigm of progress and development has been the ethnocentric contempt and neglect for the traditional, locally-rooted-in-place ecological knowledge. Peasants (as native people, pastoralists, fishermen, and gatherers and hunters) have deep knowledge of their natural environments and of the constraints and possibilities presented by the ecosystems, as well as the environmental effects of their productive practices.

Interestingly enough, it was the eloquence of empirical realities of massive ecological disruption some thirty years ago that led to a noticeable and stimulating process of ongoing reappraisal of the ecological knowledge of local traditional peasant and indigenous communities.[33] This reappraisal pointed to the remarkable environmental wisdom displayed by "rooted-in-nature communities" in taking care of their commons. The idea that peasant farmers were the main ones responsible for the environmental degradation of their land was soon discredited, as it was understood that whenever they overused their land it was due mostly to overpopulation pressures or their displacement by industries, agriculturalists, and governments to the worst lands in hillsides or those with very little access to water.

AGROECOLOGY

For our purposes, of particular interest are the developments achieved by agroecology, a scientific field that has resulted from the integration of agronomic studies, ecology, ethnographic research reporting on traditional knowledge, the findings of studies on rural development, and environmental thought.[34] Agroecology attempts to re-create, amplify, and scale-up—using many of the tools of Western science—what peasants have been practicing for a long time. Thus, agroecology becomes a sort of cultural translation that validates traditional knowledge and explicitly attempts to learn from it. The translation-validation occurs when the findings are presented in the discourse and with many of the methods of Western science and can eventually be listened to and understood by communities that otherwise would continue to ignore and neglect traditional ecological wisdom of the peasants.

Agroecologists have been documenting how systems of modern agriculture are the product of a structural evolution, which displaced stable ecological interactions, imposing in Latin America (and elsewhere) in its place productive forms requiring intense external inputs. While high-cost external inputs in industrial agriculture can increase yields, traditional agroecosystems can achieve the same if not better results, at less cost with far less environmental disruption. The diversity of local adaptations happens, though, within a wide range of similarities. Local communities involved in traditional farming place their accent on the varieties of crops that are planted and harvested for local consumption or local exchange; they use a full range of environments differing in characteristics such as soil, temperature and altitudes, the recycling of organic waste materials, the successful pest suppression through the use of biological interdependencies of animals and plants, and finally, the use of local resources plus human and animal energy for minimal input of technologies.[35]

These discoveries remained relatively marginal for decades. However, the combined effect of the empirical demonstration of the anthropogenic causes of global warming by the climate change scientific community through the work of the Intergovernmental Panel on Climate Change (IPCC) and the current food crisis has lent new credibility, urgency, and actuality to agroecological solutions. Moreover, new evidence indicates that agroecosystems designed along agroecological principles not only provide feasible directions for the transition toward an ecologically sustainable agriculture but are productive and efficient in food production. In a landmark study conducted for the International Development Research Centre of Canada (IDRC), leading agroecologist Jules Pretty from the University of Essex, reviewed 286 agroecological projects in 57 countries and concluded that the evidence tends to demonstrate that most preindustrial and modernized farming systems, using agroecological approaches, can make rapid transitions to both sustainable and productive farming.[36]

The projects reviewed showed that projects managed with agroecological techniques increased their yields by 64 percent, while increasing soil fertility and accumulation of organic matter, increasing water on carbon dioxide retention, recovering native seeds, and drastically reducing agrotoxics usage. At the same time, there were significant increases in social capital: stronger social organizations at the local level, new rules and norms for collective management of natural resources, and growing connections to external policy institutions. The studies also showed improvements in human capital: increased capacity to experiment and solve local problems, improvements in the status of women, improved sanitary conditions, better health and nutrition, and reversed migration and more local employment. Pretty's study concludes that these improvements, more often than not, take place despite the absence of enabling policies. Despite the fact that some agroecological technologies and social processes for local scale adoption of more sustainable agricultural practices are increasingly well tested and established, the social and institutional conditions for spread are less well understood, but in several contexts, have rapidly spread during the 1990s–2000s decade. However, it is the political conditions for the emergence of supportive policies that have not been established, with only a few examples of real progress.[37]

In a summary of recent data, Altieri[38] shows evidence emerging from dozens of studies that conclusively state that new approaches and technologies spearheaded by farmers, local governments, and NGOs around the world are already making a sufficient contribution to food security at the household, national, and regional levels. A variety of agroecological and participatory approaches in many countries show very positive outcomes even under adverse conditions. Potentials include raising cereal yields from 50 to 200 percent, increasing stability of production through diversification and soil/water management, improving diets and income with appropriate support and spread of these approaches, and contributing to national food security and to exports. Most importantly, the agroecological process requires participation and enhancement of the farmer's ecological literacy about their farms and resources, laying the foundation for empowerment and continuous innovation by rural communities. A recent systematization of findings from the literature by *The Ecologist*[39] leads to similar conclusions.

Thus, the knowledge of peasant farmers illustrates in practice key ecological principles for a (socially and ecologically, if not always economically) sustainable agriculture. They survive under conditions of scarcity of financial resources and live frugally without destroying their environment (although there are many who have), more often than not, with an extremely small land base.

One of the most visible responses to the limitations of the system of globalized industrial agriculture has been provided in Latin America by the horizontal networks linking peasants through organizations and movements like Via Campesina.[40] The peasant economy and its network have been able to overcome significant obstacles, such as the predominance of a neoliberal economy, the concentration of economic power and resources, the continued commodification of nature and labor and its reduction to tradable comparative advantages, the shortcomings of food governance, and the continued support of Latin American government to the model of development open to free markets.

It was the systematic study of traditional peasant agriculture that led, some thirty years ago, to the emergence of agroecology. What we witness now is a reverse cultural process that shows how the science of agroecology provides the intellectual tools that amplify the peasants' legacy, traditionally conveyed through local narratives that were difficult to scale up. Agroecology is assisting the peasant movements from around the world to realize that, despite the myriad of variations of approaches used by peasant agriculture, some ecological processes and principles can be generalized. Thus, key principles systematized by agreocology are as follows:

I. the integration of biological and ecological processes such as nutrient cycling, nitrogen fixation, soil regeneration, allelopathy, competition, predation and parasitism into food production;
II. minimizing the use of those non-renewable inputs that cause harm to the environment or to the health of farmers and consumers;
III. making productive use of the knowledge and skills of farmers, so improving their self-reliance and substituting human capital for costly external inputs;
IV. making productive use of people's collective capacities to work together to solve common agricultural and natural resource problems, such as for pest, watershed, irrigation, forest and credit management.[41]

The implementation of these principles demonstrates efficient production of healthy food, clean water, habitats for wildlife, carbon sequestration, flood protection, groundwater recharge, landscape amenity, and a new type of environmentally responsible agro-eco-tourism.[42] These principles and the vast array of techniques (site specific and grounded in place) employed to implement them are the subject of thousands of peasant encounters animated by NGOs and by the rapidly developing local, regional, and international networks of the peasant movement and gaining increasingly the attention of research funding agencies like IDRC in Canada and equivalents in other countries. These, in turn, have made possible the rapid development of networks animated by a new generation of researchers and professionals who conduct their work within the frameworks of agroecology and ecological economics, working side by side with rural communities.

In Latin America, the strongest expression of this scholarship is provided by the recent formation of the Latin American Society of Agroecology (SOCLA, in Spanish), which celebrated its first congress in August 2007, in Medellin, Colombia. SOCLA is spreading rapidly with chapters in more than twenty countries; current preparations for a Latin American Graduate Program in Agroecology to be based in Colombia; increasing organizational networks with universities, NGOs, and the international peasant movements; and an impressive body of scholarly and popular education publications.[43]

Those activities have, in turn, made visible newly emergent ecological economic activities, which are opening new channels of circulation linking small-scale ecologically sound rural producers to green consumers in the First World. Not only do these new channels open up markets for peasant farmers but they bring the concerns of urban environmentalism back to the rural producers, who can now retrieve the best of their own traditions, previously marginalized and suffocated by the hegemony of industrial agriculture and the pressures imposed by the corporate world. Needless to say, the painfully emerging new green economy is struggling for every inch with the relentless expansion of the industrial agricultural project epitomized by the penetration of genetically engineered soya monocultures and biofuels.[44]

The strategic significance of the growing convergence between the demands of the peasant movement and the green platform was anticipated several decades ago by various agroecologists and social scientists in Latin America. It was perceived that the articulation of the ecological platforms would create new conditions to bring together the historically separated struggles for the property of the land (territorial struggles) on the one hand and, on the other, the struggles for the control of productive processes, that is, for economic and political self-reliance. It is the articulation of the social and economic demands of the peasants with the ecological question that renders new weight to the peasant indigenous cosmovision.[45] Thus, the traditional indigenous peasant view of nature based on an organicistic view, depicting it as a living, sentient being, is retrieved to provide a cultural foundation for the ecologically sound appropriation of natural resources.[46]

Equally important, the peasant movements' advocacy for egalitarian principles and for generalized reciprocity tends to provide appropriate controls to avoid overexploitation of natural resources and to facilitate the establishment of collective mechanisms of control and correction in the management of natural resources. Thus, as pointed out by Toledo, if every fraction of deforestation results in a new contribution to global warming, the struggle conducted by a microscopic rural community to arrest it is a battle on behalf of humanity and life as a whole. When a localized movement of resistance like that becomes a part of a worldwide effort to protect biodiversity and bring with it the potential attention, support and solidarity of a vast array of international actors follow, strengthening, in turn, the movement's reach. Following the Zapatista rebellion in Chiapas, the impressive new political presence of the peasant movements in Latin America can be explained to a very significant extent by this encounter between the traditional peasant platforms of struggle and their new environmentalism.

Founded in 1993, the Via Campesina International Peasant Movement is perhaps the best example of this new situation:

> We are an autonomous, pluralist and multicultural movement, independent of any political, economic, or other type of affiliation. Our members are from 56 countries throughout Asia, Africa, Europe, and the Americas. . . . The principal objective of La Via Campesina is to develop solidarity and unity among small farmer organizations in order to promote gender parity and social justice in fair economic relations; the preservation of land, water, seeds and other natural resources; food sovereignty; sustainable agricultural production based on small and medium-sized producers.[47]

It is beyond the scope of this discussion to analyze the different stages of development of the peasant movement. However, in the section that follows, we present a number of ideas about possible educational lessons that can be extracted, both from the learning experience of the peasant and from the actual collective manifestations of their aspirations.

POLYCULTURES OF THE MIND AND EDUCATION

What kind of learning experiences are behind the planting and cultivating of polycultures of the mind and networking to share its fruits? I propose that the most important one is the direct exposure to biodiversity and to the horizontal, decentralized, pluralistic, and nonhierarchical networks of support and mutual aid that have characterized the informal networks of peasants.

The peasant cannot avoid being engaged and deeply involved in assessing his or her landscape—the quality of the water, soil, and seeds; the interaction between birds and insect pollinators; crops with plants and organisms that provide biological controls; the food chain linking plants, animals, and humans; the recycling of manure; the seasonality of it all. Every observation makes the participation of the human mind and body, hands, hearts, and heads inevitable and that, in turn, has transformative learning for sustainability effects.[48] It epitomizes what we have called elsewhere, "Learning with Life Education." Sounds, smells, colors, landscape, weather, animals' signs, and birds' migratory patterns are permanently, intentionally or not, by necessity in the peasant gaze.

The approach is fully experiential, and there is a constant critical appraisal of ideas through the conversation between peasants that is ecologically highly sophisticated. It is a conversation about the practicality of ways of seeing and ways of doing: what works in practice, and what does not? They watch their geography every day, see mountains and plains, rivers or dry landscapes; have picked all fruits from the trees since they started walking; chewed all plants; gathered the eggs from the chicken nests, learned to kill a hen, to hunt rabbits, to kill a lamb and (in many places) even to drink blood, watering the soil with it to feed ceremonially the land. People feel cold and heat; they sweat and shiver. Seasons are felt; diets change seasonally; duties change seasonally; sleeping patterns change with comings and goings of the light of the sun. Mind, heart, and body are in constant mobilization through demanding physical, emotional, and intellectual activity. The power and presence of nature reminds daily that it must be treated with respect, reverence, and fear. There is, of course, nothing easy or rosy about all that: it requires huge physical and mental effort. The peasant must make hundreds of decisions, based on endless, detailed observations, which are all connected by the needs of the entire biological community of the farm.

In comparison, urban culture is almost purely human made. The context of the learning process is a straight line, square shape (we learn surrounded by square rooms, in square buildings, with square tables, square floors, square-blocks, square screens in square auditoriums with immobile chairs arranged in rows facing the scenario for the solo lecturer). The quest for predictability, calculability, and control are all over the place, despite discourses on freedom, creativity, and critical thinking. That is, the hidden curriculum (a critical component of the ecology of knowledge) becomes the medium and process that shapes the message. It is a miracle that so much human creativity still unfolds in a situation so removed from the symphony of the natural world. The design of a peasant agroecosystem is almost the contrary: it is wavy, diverse in species and shapes. The presence of the complexity of life is the dominant theme. Unlike the city and its classroom, the "classroom" of the peasant is filled with other kinds of classmates in addition to humans. The diversity and complexity of urban life is immense, but it is entirely intra-human. The complexity of the peasant life is inter-species.

WHAT KIND OF CLASSROOM MAKES POSSIBLE THE DEVELOPMENT OF THE POLYCULTURES OF THE MIND?

We argue that the polycultures of the peasant mind provide clues to pursue of the kind of education needed to support the cultural transformation that a society experiencing a sustainability crisis must undergo. As already pointed out, we are not interested in romanticizing the life of the peasants, who suffer from marginality and must work so hard and face discrimination, poverty, migration, and constant encroachment of their way of life and that of their communities. Rather, the point is to suggest that their intellect is no better or worse than that of the urban dweller. *What is of particular interest is simply the way their ecological sensitivity takes shape.* Neither are we seeing the peasantry as the historical subject who will "liberate humanity from its chains" or the new privileged subject of a history in the making. They are just like all of us and, in addition, still have too little power and too little political clout in the governments of the region, although they have formed a social movement of extraordinary vitality that represents a very important cultural resistance against the impacts of globalization that tend to displace them by taking away their land base.

The important clue for us is the peasants' impressive ecological sophistication and the capacity to sustain with only local inputs and with a very small land base an agriculture that feeds millions of Latin Americans with very little negative environmental impact (unless forced in to the worst conditions, that is). And more often than not, these peasants have very little schooling; many of them are illiterate and do not even know how to use computers. Another key learning for the sustainability education classroom is the actual experience of the peasants in securing food through local food systems and through local systems of exchange. Corporate domination, trade agreements, and government policies do not permit the expansion of this practice, but despite their marginality, the record of its contribution to food sovereignty security is impressive.

THE GRAND CLASSROOM

The grand classroom is the classroom where life (not just human life) unfolds. Children love living creatures, and the more and the earlier they are exposed to them, the more they learn about them, the more they care, the more they will defend them. Forests, beaches, and the sky are the grand classrooms where the connections of all forms of life are present. Students, just like peasant farmers, will learn more and better about ecological processes and about sustainable practices if they are directly exposed to it *in addition* to being exposed to it only conceptually or virtually.

"Directly exposed to it" may admit a range of experiences. Community-based action research and community service learning are one way of being directly exposed, of being there. Restoring an urban landscape to biodiversity, planting a community garden, working with real people in their places, their problems, experiences, memories, and hopes and dreams deliver knowledge of incomparable depth. If I have a memory about something and I am invited to share it with others; if I have a dream about something and I am invited to share it, then my encounter with expert knowledge will allow me to see critically that, although it will provide me with a wealth of systematized knowledge, it will never be reality as it is, facts without the mediation of experience and emotion. The irony is that if *good knowledge is adaptive knowledge*, humble practitioners of the mirrors of polycultures of the mind have done better than the practitioners of the monocultures of the mind and have not threatened biological communities and life with excessive demands.

We must learn also from the peasant movements and the kind of networks and knowledge they have generated. In the face of marginalization, they have created forms of cooperation, mutual support, and mutual aid that have translated into the creation of knowledge: seeds banks, for example, and the horizontal exchange of experiences. Learning with life—these schools have usually no campuses other than someone's field. Networking has the quality of creating knowledge that is related to others as opposed to atomized, purely individualistic, and competitive knowledge produced for power and prestige.

TOWARD AN ECOLOGY OF THE INTEGRATION OF KNOWLEDGE

I have recently reported elsewhere on our attempts at University of British Columbia's Faculty of Land and Food Systems to implement a new pedagogy based on the principles of a community of learners,[49] an approach that draws significant elements from the tradition of popular adult education in Latin America but that also modifies it substantially to reflect the challenges of the era of climate change and environmental and food insecurity and vulnerability. Questioning the efficacy of conventional modes of delivery of curriculum on sustainable agriculture, we have experimented during the last ten years with an approach guided by an "ecology of the integration of knowledge." The most important aspect of that educational process is its community-based, highly participatory process that takes the students out of the classroom and links them with other communities, within and without the university. Our students are working, within our courses, with the food providers on campus to transform the food system of this university, which feeds 50,000 bodies every day, into a more sustainable food system, one with shorter food miles and a lighter ecological footprint.[50] This is a central subject matter in a stream of required courses.

We also have an organic farm that is probing agroecological methods, many similar to those used by peasant farmers. The farm had been abandoned twelve years ago, and it was the mobilization of our students supported by a handful of faculty members and staff that have so far rescued it from commercial housing. It is a working park, run by our students. It is a living laboratory of the interface between the urban space and agriculture. It is providing some local menus for our food providers and, through its farmers market, has become the knot of an important network of local farmers. It is the only working farm left within the limits of the City of Vancouver. Our incipient agroecology program and several other courses are learning to use it as a grand classroom that complements in various degrees the intramural learning, which has also been deeply transformed.[51]

CONCLUSION

The question of the possible end of the peasant in Latin America remains clouded with question marks. Despite a relative decline in numbers and in area covered by peasant agriculture, the contribution of peasant farmers to feed the Latin American population remains critical. Moreover, the new articulation of the peasant movements with the ecological concerns of our times makes the peasant a potent political and cultural actor that has entered with unprecedented vigor in the debate about what is to be done to overcome the severe vulnerabilities of the food system at the global, regional, national, and local levels. Emerging from the encounter of the cultural legacy of peasant agriculturalists and from the ecological critique of our civilization, agroecology is providing increasingly appropriate answers to the challenges and urgencies of creating a sustainable agriculture and sustainable food systems.

The learning processes of the peasant, the polycultures of their minds, systematized and amplified by agroecology, provide many lessons of great significance for scholars interested in sustainability education, and the elements for an understanding of a new ecology of knowledge. The peasant and his or her world, neglected and regarded often with some contempt by urban intellectual elites, have ended up teaching us more than we ever expected, about living in a lighter way on this planet. In an era where the future of humanity has become uncertain, and at a time when we finally seem to be acknowledging that we are in trouble, this peasant legacy may end up providing us with important clues about where to go. The direction will certainly not be to go back to a past that cannot be recreated, even if it were desirable. But the lessons learned and the emergence of the new green economy accompanied by a new green culture, vision, and political will, may open up a new future for the peasant and for the entire human society.

NOTES

1. M. Altieri, "Mobilizing to take back our food systems in the post-peak oil era," *Berkeley Daily Planet* (Weekend Edition), April 18–21, 2008: 1. Available: http://www.berkeleydailyplanet.com/pdfs/04-18-08.pdf.

2. W. Pengue, *Agricultura industrial y transnacionalizacion en America Latina. La transgenesis de un continente?* CEPAMA, Universidad de Buenos Aires. SerieTextos Basicospara la Formacion Ambiental (Buenos Aires: PNUMA, 2007).

3. IPCC, P. Smith, D. Z. Martino, D. G. Cai, H. Janzen, P. Kumar, B. McCarl, S. Ogle, F. O'Mara, C. Rice, B. Scholes, and O. Sirotenko, "Agriculture," in *Climate Change 2007: Mitigation. Contribution of Working Group III to the Fourth Assessment Report of the Intergovernmental Panel on Climate Change*, ed. B. Metz, O. R. Davidson, P. R. Bosch, R. Dave, L. A. Meyer (Cambridge: Cambridge University Press, 2007).

4. T. Lang and M. Heasman, *Food Wars: The Global Battle for Mouths, Minds and Markets* (London: Earthscan, 2004).

5. D. K. C. Bryceson and J. Moij, *Disappearing Peasantries? Rural Labor in Africa, Asia and Latin America* (London: Intermediate Technology Publications, 2000).

6. P. Freire, *Education for Critical Consciousness* (New York: Continuum, 1973); P. Freire and A. M. Araujo-Freire, *Pedagogy of Hope: Reliving Pedagogy of the Oppressed,* trans. Robert R. Barr (New York: Continuum, 2004).

7. J. Kloppenburg Jr., J. Hendrickson, and G. W. Stevenson, "Coming to the foodshed," in *Rooted in the Land,* ed. W. Vitrek and W. Jackson (New Haven: Yale University Press, 1996).

8. M. Nestle, *Food Politics: How the Food Industry Influences Nutrition and Health* (Berkeley: University of California Press, 2002); FAO, *Global Forum on Food Security and Nutrition* (2008). http://km.fao.org/fsn/.

9. T. Lang and M. Heasman, *Food Wars*; Y. Wang, "Cross-national comparison of childhood obesity: the epidemic and the relationship between obesity and socioeconomic status," *International Journal of Epidemiology* 30 (2001): 1129–1136, available: http://www.citeulike.org/article/1341663; M. Beydoun and Y. Wang, "Effect of socio-economic status on fruit and vegetable consumption and diet quality among US adults: Is it modified by nutrition knowledge and beliefs?" *Preventive Medicine* (July 4, 2007), [e-pub ahead of print].

10. IPCC et al., "Agriculture"; T. Lang, and M. Heasman, *Food Wars.*

11. *The Ecologist online*, "10 reasons why organic can feed the world—Can organic farming feed the world? Ed Hamer and Mark Anslow say yes, but we must farm and eat differently." January 3, 2008. Available: http://www.theecologist.org/

12. M. Altieri, *Agroecology: The Science of Sustainable Agriculture* (Boulder, CO: Westview Press, 1995), 1.

13. S. Barraclough, *Agrarian Structure in Latin America* (Lexington, MA: Heath Lexington, 1973); D. Bryceson, C. Kay, and J. Mooij, eds., *Disappearing Peasantries? Rural Labor in Africa, Asia and Latin America* (London: Intermediate Technology Publications, 2000), 16.

14. Ibid.

15. Ibid., 22.

16. C. Kay, "Latin American Agrarian Transformation: Peasantization and Proletarianization," in *Disappearing Peasantries? Rural Labor in Africa, Asia and Latin America,* ed. D. Bryceson, C. Kay, and J. Mooij (London: Intermediate Technology Publications, 2000), 128–129; A. De Janvry, *The Agrarian Question and Reformism in Latin America* (Baltimore: Johns Hopkins University Press, 1981); W. C. Thiesenhusen, *Broken Promises: Agrarian Reform and the Latin American Campesino* (Boulder, CO: Westview Press, 1995).

17. C. Kay, "Latin American Agrarian Transformation: Peasantization and Proletarianization."

18. L. Lopez-Cordovez, "Trends and recent changes in the Latin American food and agricultural situation," *CEPAL Review* 16 (1982), 7–41.

19. A. De Janvry, *The Agrarian Question and Reformism in Latin America*, 74.

20. C. Kay, "Latin American Agrarian Transformation: Peasantization and Proletarianization."

21. Ibid., 3–34.

22. N. Harvey, *The Chiapas Rebellion: The Struggle for Land and Democracy* (Durham, NC: Duke University Press, 1998).

23. A. Mattos, "Exploring Hugo Chavez's New Left Wing Movement in Latin America," paper presented at the annual meeting of the MPSA Annual National Conference, Palmer House Hotel, Hilton, Chicago, IL, April 03, 2008, available: http://www.allacademic.com/meta/p267602_index.html; J. Petras, "'Centre-Left' Regimes in Latin America," *Countercurrents* (2006), available: http://www.countercurrents.org/; F. Panizza, "Unarmed Utopia Revisited: The Resurgence of Left-of-Centre Politics in Latin America," *Political Studies* 53, no. 4 (December 2005), 716–734; J. Castaneda, "Latin America's Left Turn," *Foreign Affairs* (May–June 2006).

24. T. Brass, "Latin American Peasants: New Paradigms for Old?" *Journal of Peasant Studies* 29, no. 3–4 (2002): 1–40; J. Murra, "Andean Societies," *Annual Reviews of Anthropology* 13 (1984): 119–141; J. Murra, "Current Research and Prospects in Andean Ethnohistory," *Latin American Research Review* 5, no. 1 (Spring 1970), 3–36; J. Bastien, *The Mountain of the Condor* (New York: West Publishing, 1985); B. Orlove, "The History of the Andes: A Brief Overview," *Mountain Research and Development* 5, no. 1 (1985): 45–60; C. Classen, "Cosmology: Equilibrium and Exchange," in *Inca Cosmology and the Human Body* (Salt Lake City: University of Utah Press, 1993), 11–25.

25. V. Shiva, *Monocultures of the Mind* (London: Zed Books, 1993), 9–59.

26. D. Pimentel and S. Pimentel, *Food, Energy and Society* (Boca Raton: CRC Press, 2008); W. Pengue, *Agricultura industrial y transnacionalizacion en America Latina*; M. Altieri, "Small farms as a planetary ecological asset: Five key reasons why we should support the revitalization of small farms in the Global South," *Food First* (May 9, 2008), available: http://www.foodfirst.org/en/node/2115; S. Gliessman, *Agroecology: The Ecology of Sustainable Food Systems*, 2nd ed. (CRC Press Online, 2006); J. Pretty, *Regenerating Agriculture* (Washington, DC: Henry Press, 1995).

27. G. Bateson, *Steps to Ecology of the Mind* (Chicago: Chicago University Press, 2000); E. N. Anderson, *Ecologies of the Heart: Emotion, Belief and Environment* (New York: Oxford University Press, 1996); S. DeSouza and S. Boaventura, "Beyond Abyssal Thinking: From Global Lines to Ecologies of Knowledge," *Review* (2007).

28. V. Shiva, *Monocultures of the Mind*, 9.

29. Ibid.

30. Ibid., 11.

31. A. N. Whitehead, *Science and the Modern World*, Lowel Lectures (New York: The Macmillan Company, 1925); G. Bateson, *Mind and Nature: A Necessary Unit* (New York: Bantam Books, 1980); L. Mumford, *The Pentagon of Power: The Myth of the Machine* (New York: Harcourt Brace, 1967); F. Fernandez-Amesto, *Truth* (London: Black Swan, 1998).

32. J. P. Orrego, *On Rooted and Uprooted Peoples* (Toronto: Faculty of Environmental Studies, York University, 1985); J. Bastien, *The Mountain of the Condor*.

33. M. Altieri, "*Porqueestudiar la agriculturatradicional?*" *Agroecologia y Desarrollo* 1, no. 1 (March 1, 1991): 16–24; M. Altieri and S. Hecht, eds., *Agroecology and Small Farm Development* (Berkeley: University of California Press, 1990); S. Hecht, "The evolution of agroecological thought," *Agroecologia y Desarrollo* 1, 2–16 (March 1, 1991); M. Johnson, ed., *LORE: Capturing Traditional Environmental Knowledge* (Ottawa: IDRC, 1992); P. Knudston and D. Suzuki, *Wisdom of the Elders* (Toronto: Stoddards, 1992); F. Cassidy, "Indigenous Peoples and Sustainable Development," *Redirections* (Victoria: Centre for Sustainable Development, University of Victoria, 1994); D. Posey, "Intellectual Property Rights: What is the position of ethnobiology?" *Journal of Ethnobiology* 10, no. 1 (1990): 93–99.

34. S. Hecht, "The evolution of agroecological thought"; J. Pretty, "Agroecological Approaches to Agricultural Development," (RIMISP-Latin American Centre for Rural Development and IDRC, 2006), available: http://siteresources.worldbank.org/INTWDR2008/Resources/2795087-1191427986785/PrettyJ_AgroecologicalApproachesToAgriDevt%5B1%5D.pdf; M. Altieri, *Agroecology: The Science of Sustainable Agriculture*; S. Gliessman, *Agroecology*; V. Toledo, "*Utopia y Naturaleza: El Nuevo movimientoecologico de los campesinos e indigenas de America Latina*," *Nueva Sociedad* 122 (November–December 1992), 72–85.

35. M. Altieri, *Agroecology: The Science of Sustainable Agriculture.*

36. J. Pretty, "Agroecological Approaches to Agricultural Development," 2.

37. Ibid., 3–4.

38. Ibid., 2; "Mobilizing to take back our food systems in the post-peak oil era"; "Small farms as a planetary ecological asset: Five key reasons why we should support the revitalization of small farms in the Global South."

39. *The Ecologist online*, "10 reasons why organic can feed the world—Can organic farming feed the world? Ed Hamer and Mark Anslow say yes, but we must farm and eat differently."

40. Via Campesina, Via Campesina International Peasant Movement, http://via campesina.org/main_en/index.php.

41. J. Pretty, "Agroecological Approaches to Agricultural Development," 3.

42. Ibid.

43. Sociedad Latinoamericana de Agroecologia (SOCLA), http://www.agroeco.org socla/.

44. W. Pengue, *Agricultura industrial y transnacionalizacion en America Latina. La transgenesis de un continente?*

45. V. Toledo, "*Utopia y Naturaleza: El Nuevo movimientoecologico de los campesinos e indigenas de America Latina.*"

46. A. Rojas, "Sustainable Development or Development of Ecological and Social Sustainability?" (Spanish), in *Environment in Development* [Medioambiente en Desarrollo], ed. R. Katz and G. Favero (Santiago: Centro de Estudios Publicos CEP, 1993), 61–103; V. Toledo, "*Utopia y Naturaleza: El Nuevo movimientoecologico de los campesinos e indigenas de America Latina.*"

47. Via Campesina, Via Campesina International Peasant Movement.

48. L. Sipos, "Non-traditional pedagogies in advanced education: engaging head, hands and heart for environmental and educational benefit," paper submitted to the NATO Sponsored Advanced Research Workshop, Rethinking Higher Education to Meet the New Challenges of Environmental Security Karkiv, May 21–25, 2008.

49. A. Rojas, "Towards integration of knowledge through sustainability education and its contribution to environmental security," in *Addressing Global Environmental Security Through Innovative Educational Curricula*, ed. Susan Allen (New York: Springer-Verlag, 2009), 131–135.

50. A. Rojas, "Towards integration of knowledge through sustainability education and its contribution to environmental security"; A. Rojas, L. Richer, and J. Wagner, "The University of British Columbia Food System," *EcoHealth* 4 (2007): 86–94; L. Richer and A. Rojas, The University of British Columbia Food System Project 2008, http://www.landfood.ubc.ca/research/faculty_webpages/rojas.htm.

51. UBC Farm 2008, http://www.landfood.ubc.ca/ubcfarm.

Chapter 14

Community Capacity and Challenges of Ecuadorian Agrarian Farmer Organizations for Generating Alternatives to Pesticide Use

A Case Study

Fabio Cabarcas[1]

The development of modern crop varieties from the 1950s and 1960s, known as the Green Revolution, has also been accompanied by an increased use and development of pesticides and artificial fertilizers. This is exemplified by the fact that the world trade in pesticides grew roughly by a factor of fourteen worldwide from 1972 to 2002. This worldwide phenomenon has also been experienced by countries in Latin America, including Ecuador.[2] In general economic terms, the Green Revolution may have led to a reduction of prices and an increase in total production yields, but its gains in terms of profit margins by farmers are less clear.[3] Despite this, farmers have needed to use pesticides to maintain their competitiveness in the market. However, regardless of the possible economic benefits, pesticide-related dangers are of particular concern for public health and environmental action. In effect, the intensification of crops and the use of fertilizers and pesticides have contributed to the disruption of biotic loops and biodiversity with serious environmental consequences.[4] In terms of human health, pesticide use accounts for millions of poisonings and thousands of deaths a year in the world.

This requires urgent change toward safer alternatives such as pesticide-free pest management (integrated pest management) and a more rational use of existent technologies.[5,6]

The need for safer agricultural practices[7] runs parallel to a global crisis in small farming.[8] In recent decades, the political agenda promoted by the Washington Consensus, which entails, among other things, an export-driven model for agriculture, the liberation of domestic markets for imports, and the decrease in direct support from state institutions, has particularly affected small farmers in developing countries.[9] However, according to M. Altieri, small farmers are fundamental for several reasons. First, with just 34.5 percent of the total crop area in Latin America, small farmers produce 51 percent of the maize, 77 percent of the beans, and 61 percent of the potatoes for domestic use. Furthermore, they use more polycultures than large farms, which is important for biodiversity. Polycultures can also have more yields if all the products are accounted for.[10] In Latin America, the marginalization suffered by small farmers in recent decades has led to the rise of different types of farmer movements that clamor for better production conditions, including a more environmentally friendly agriculture.[11]

Given the difficulties faced by small farmers and the visibility that their movement in Latin America has reached at national and international levels, what are the chances of small-farmer organizations for facilitating the adoption of a safer agriculture? Moreover, some organizations, such the World Bank, in its recent World Development Report 2008, *Agriculture for Development*, suggest that strengthening farmers' civil society is one of the fundamental strategies for overcoming the limitations of the Green Revolution.[12] Does civil society, particularly farmer organizations, have the capacity to transform production in their communities for better environmental results as stated by the World Development Report 2008? In this paper, I am going to provide possible answers to these questions by focusing on the case of small farming in the southern ranges of Ecuador. I will focus on identifying elements in the field of agriculture in Ecuador that may make it difficult for small-farmer organizations to lead a possible transition from the Green Revolution to a safer production. Following Bourdieu, a "field" is a system of relationships constituted by social agents related to the production and promotion of a particular product. A field is constituted by two elements: the existence of a common capital and the struggle for its appropriation by different social actors.[13] In a given *field*, different actors compete for the acquisition of determinate forms of accumulated capital.[14] Any field is codetermined by a broader social structure that shapes its organization, even though its internal dynamics are partially autonomous. A field can change over time.[15]

In the case of this work, the Ecuadorian rural setting linked to agriculture is understood as a field.[16] Small-farmer organizations are one of many social actors competing for access to the forms of capital that allow them to survive. I am going to focus on the characteristics as may be experienced by these organizations. Framing the field in which small-farmer organizations struggle, I will discuss some of the determinants related to agricultural production in Ecuador that may weaken their capacity for achieving an environmentally friendly and sustainable agriculture. This paper uses data from a case study in two communities of small farmers in the province of Cañar in southern Ecuador (communities A and B), including mixed research techniques mostly collected from April 2007 to May 2008. For this essay, I will use material from ethnographic techniques applying participant observation and in-depth interviews, and a household survey aiming to identify organizational and socio-demographic elements among other aspects.[17] Furthermore, documents and relevant information, such as hospital discharge records and irrigation databases, were reviewed.[18]

I will argue that if the policy priorities promoted by the Washington Consensus persist, small farmers have little chance to make the transition to safer technologies. If continued, this political agenda, focused on prioritization of exportations, liberation of domestic markets for imports, and decrease in direct support from state institutions, will increase small farmers' long-term disadvantages in access to resources in the field of agriculture. The Washington Consensus policies that predominated in Ecuador since the late 1980s did not generate the long-term inequities faced by small farmers. However, I agree with authors who suggest that the policies contributed to making inequalities worse.[19] Furthermore, without policy changes, the approach to civil society by the World Bank does not offer feasible alternatives for small farmers in Ecuador to undertake a transformation toward new forms of agriculture. I am by no means suggesting that the burden of health and environmental problems of pesticides lies on the shoulders of small farmers. On the contrary, while small farming may offer important alternatives for overcoming the limitations of the Green Revolution as stated before, large-scale farming is associated with great health and environmental problems. However, if the emphasis on small-farmer organizations is not accompanied by a profound change in the field of agriculture by means of strategies such as public policies providing more support, small farming has little chance, not only to make the transition toward new forms of production but also to survive. Agriculture will be the sole domain of large producers who have better access to the forms of capital in the field.

FRAMING THE FIELD OF RURAL DEVELOPMENT IN ECUADOR

Land Reforms and Land Distribution in Ecuador

In the twentieth century Ecuador had three major land reforms, in 1964, 1973, and 1994. The reforms of 1964 and 1973 were part of a group of similar reforms in other Latin American countries, such as Chile, Peru, and Colombia, aiming to transform precapitalist forms of rural production.[20] The two initial reforms helped to dismantle precapitalist forms of production and large landholdings such as the hacienda[21] by (1) establishing a ceiling of hectares by farm; (2) promoting colonization of new lands, mainly in the Amazon, and distribution of fallow lands; (3) providing some alternatives for credit and technical assistance to farmers, including the creation of the Ecuadorian Institute of Land Reform for providing assistance.[22] In addition, a 1994 land reform was executed in the framework of structural adjustment policies and the Washington Consensus.[23] This policy proceeded in an agenda of reinforced market-led strategies such as the freedom to divide and trade communal lands, limitation of state expropriation, and requirement of payment for accessing new land.[24, 25]

Despite some gains for some sectors of farmers, the reforms did not help to significantly change the country's indicators of land concentration.[26] Inequity is still a structural part of land distribution in Ecuador. Similar to other Latin American countries, Ecuador's land distribution is very unequal.[27] The evolution of Land GINI went from 0.86 in 1954 to 0.85 in 1974.[28] There seems to be a small improvement with the 0.80 Land GINI for 2000.[29] However, 60.4 percent of the agricultural land is controlled by the 6.4 percent of units that have more than 50 hectares. On the other hand, the 63.5 percent of units with less than 5 hectares only owns 6.3 percent of the agriculturally productive area. In the province of Cañar, the 2 percent of units with 50 hectares or more controls 53.5 percent of the land, leaving the 77.8 percent of units with less than 5 hectares with just 19.6 percent of the land.[30, 31]

The agrarian reform perpetuated a problem of smallholdings in the Andes. In general, the relative area of smallholdings with less than 5 hectares in the rural ranges in Ecuador has changed little over time. However, the absolute number of productive units with less than 5 hectares has increased.[32] Moreover, small farming is highly concentrated in the Andean ranges, including the province of Cañar. The 87.4 percent of productive units with less than 1 hectare and 72.8 percent of units with between 1 and less than 5 hectares are located in the ranges.[33] Despite the small improvement in the Land GINI described above, some forces threaten to worsen the problem of smallholdings. For instance, the 1994 reform freed communal lands, allowing their fragmentation. In addition to land markets, inheritance practices that divide the land in equal parts among all the children has contributed to increase the number of smallholdings.[34] Small farmers in Ecuador are mostly smallholders.

The fact that small farmers in the Ecuadorian Andes are mostly smallholders represents a challenge for farmer organizations trying to develop environmentally friendly production. In fact, productive units with less than 5 hectares have poor chances of having economic viability in Ecuador.[35] This striking reduced probability, taking into account that they are 63.5 percent of Ecuadorian productive units as already stated, suggests more demanding transaction costs and technical assistance are needed for developing these farms. Moreover, training for proper use of pesticides or development of alternative pest management requires standardization of practices and training, which is more difficult with small and heterogeneous units. For instance, organic farming started worldwide with an important role of small farmers who sought improvement in their situation. However, international standardization and bureaucratic barriers are deterring small producers from it.[36] Complex certification processes and the need for accessing research and knowledge have become a burden particularly for small farmers in developing countries.[37] In addition, as small producers can afford very little economic risk, they require important levels of support over the initial years for achieving suitable organic production.[38] Farmer organizations alone will have little chance to coordinate the efforts deemed necessary for building environmentally friendly and economically viable alternatives for small farmers.

Summarizing, the agricultural field in Ecuador is marked by long-term inequities in land distribution, leaving in a marginal position a majority of small farmers and smallholders in the Ecuadorian ranges. Washington Consensus policies did little to improve small farmers' disadvantages. Small farms, which are very important for generating employment, face important limitations to survive and adapt their productive system to the challenges imposed. This makes it more difficult to replace the technology brought on by the Green Revolution.

Market for Rural Products in Ecuador

The Ecuadorian domestic market has been fundamental for the survival of small farmers. As shown in Figure 14.1, internal markets are supplied by small farmers, whereas export-oriented production is dominated by larger productive units. This two-modal system also reflects differences in the type of product and region. Bananas and flowers, the main export-oriented agricultural products, account for 38.9 percent and 18.2 percent, respectively, of the net agricultural production in Ecuador. On the other hand, products such as rice, sugarcane, corn, and potatoes, which are destined mainly to the internal market, account for 36.3 percent of the total production. Traditionally, while most of the export products have been located in the coastal region, the ranges have been mostly focused on the internal market.[39] In recent decades, Washington Consensus policies favoring export-oriented agriculture have been adverse for the domestic market used by the small-farmer based agriculture of the ranges. In this section, I will focus on domestic markets, as they are more important for small farmers. I am going to argue that Washington Consensus policies in Ecuador are deleterious for small farmers and for any attempt by their organizations to promote environmentally friendly practices.

Figure 14.1 Relative contribution of different-size productive units to net agricultural production according to their final market, Ecuador 2000

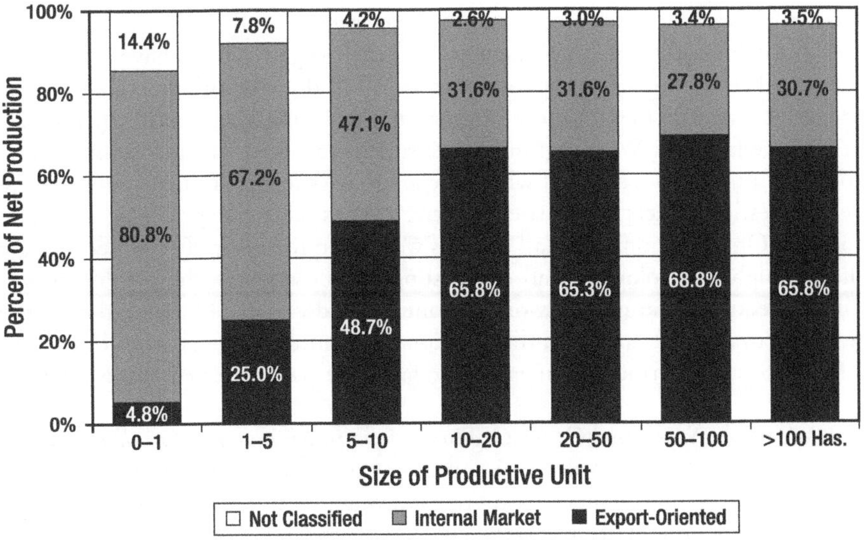

Source: By Fabio Cabarcas, according to data of the 2000 National Agriculture and Livestock Census as shown by Leon et al. 2003: INEC-SIICA, SIISE.

The Washington Consensus policies that started in Ecuador in the 1980s left the small farmers in poor competitive conditions vis-à-vis long-term inefficiencies of the market.[40] While the initial reforms to liberalize the Ecuadorian economy took place from 1988 to 1992, the core of the reforms happened from 1992 to 1996 during the government of Duran Ballen.[41, 42] As in other Latin American countries, the Ecuadorian state support in terms of subsidies, direct services, and technical assistance was essentially dismantled without building adequate assistance to support small producers and farmer organizations to build capacity to deal with the inefficiencies. The result was that the competitive conditions of small producers deteriorated.[43] In addition, free trade agreements and the reduction of import taxes in Ecuador introduced products at a lower production cost, reducing even more the profit margins by small producers. The relative cost of crops and livestock as a percentage of total imports in Ecuador increased from 2.5 percent in 1980 to 4.7 percent in 1995.[44] This increase is indicative of higher volumes of food imports that compete in traditional markets. Furthermore, chains of supermarkets in Ecuador have almost doubled their number from 1998 to 2004.[45] The volume of supply required and the technical specifications that supermarkets ask for represent a challenge for small farmers. As a result, small farmers' access to internal markets has decreased.

In addition to the difficulties that markets present for small farmers, they provide very limited incentive for pesticide-free or organic production. Worldwide, despite the rapid growth of markets for organic products, mainly in developed countries, their size remains rather small. For instance, in the year 2000, the share of organic foods in the markets of the United States, Japan, and Europe was barely close to 1 percent. The market with the highest percentage of organic products was Denmark, with just close to 3 percent of the total food trade.[46] Moreover, in developing countries, internal demand for products such as organic bananas is very small.[47]

In such conditions, small farmers and their organizations have little chance to access markets without the proper assistance. While domestic markets are fundamental for small farmers in Ecuador, the internal market's long-term inefficiencies are worsened by the fact that Washington Consensus policies have favored competition from products from abroad, some of which are artificially low cost due to subsidies. Moreover, domestic markets offer little incentive for pesticide-free or ecologically oriented products. Organizations of small farmers would require not only marketing expertise but also high technological and credit support to overcome these challenges. They will also require an ample network of contacts and clients. Thus, market challenges are added to the difficulties in distribution of resources such as land to make it very difficult for small-farmer organizations to facilitate viable alternatives to pesticide use.

The Role of the State and Other Organizations in Supporting Small Farmers

L. North and J. Cameron describe the extent to which, from the mid-1980s, there was a worldwide shift to allocate programs through Non-Governmental Organization (NGO) led programs. This shift was heightened in the mid-1990s. Institutional reform, decentralization, and promoting social capital were part of the Washington Consensus policies.[48] This process was accompanied by a reduction in state-level investment. M. Chiriboga describes the extent to which the adjustment policies for rural Ecuador have involved (1) the reduction in investment on public services and infrastructure; (2) the dismantling of sector-specific policies and the organizations in charge of carrying them out; and (3) the emergence of groups and organizations that provide project-based assistance.[49] This process may have been deleterious for the capacity of organizations to face the challenges of a changing rural scenario. However, the social situation for small farmers remains problematic. Several factors may contribute to this. First, while some indigenous and farmer organizations have gained some capabilities, their capacity is not enough for replacing the need for effective state-led initiatives and policies. Second, the increased number of local organizations has meant an inefficient use of resources. External actors and sectors also compete for the same resources. In this section, I will focus on the above-mentioned factors to discuss the extent to which Washington Consensus policies may affect the farmers' organization local-level capacity.

The support by the Ecuadorian state for development of agriculture, and particularly small farmers, has never been strong. In effect, some important development initiatives in the rural areas were led by NGOs, showing the weakness of state intervention. For instance, in the 1960s and early 1970s, Andean Mission, an NGO linked to some sectors of the church, helped to trigger the creation of infrastructure such as roads and schools in the rural areas. In addition, it provided technical assistance that introduced the technological package of the Green Revolution.[50] Other actors such as agrochemical distributors also helped to provide technical support to consolidate the use of pesticides.[51]

Regardless of the inefficiencies of the policies, the reduction of this already small role by the state left a vacuum that could not be filled by a myriad of lower scale programs led by small organizations. With a fiscal crisis in the early eighties, there was a diminution in the direct presence of the state followed by a proliferation of organizations and NGOs harnessing funds from international agencies through small programs targeted for special interest groups. However, Figure 14.2 shows the extent to which the relative weight of NGOs and other organizations for providing credit for farmers of any productive unit size is small. Also small, the relative weight of both the National Development Bank and the private banks is highly skewed toward the producers of higher unit size. To access credit, small farmers have little support. They are left with the assistance of financial cooperatives, usually small in size, and moneylenders, who usually offer high interest rates. It is important to highlight the larger importance that family loans have for small farmers. In another important illustration shown in Figure 14.3, the role of NGOs providing technical assistance to small farmers, despite being relatively important for farmers with 5 or fewer hectares, is not enough for overcoming the gap of technical assistance between small farmers and large landholders. Again, the role of state institutions such as the Ministry of Agriculture is relatively small and heavily skewed to providing technical assistance to farmers in the largest productive units. Small farmers have little support to overcome the difficulties of a disadvantaged position in Ecuadorian agriculture. Without proper credit or technical assistance, they have little chance to engage in a process of environmentally friendly, sustainable, and healthy agriculture.

The withdrawal of an already weak state also left different types of small organizations without resources such as technical assistance and financial and institutional

Figure 14.2 Ratio of farmers receiving different types of credit by 1,000 productive units according to unit size, Ecuador 2000

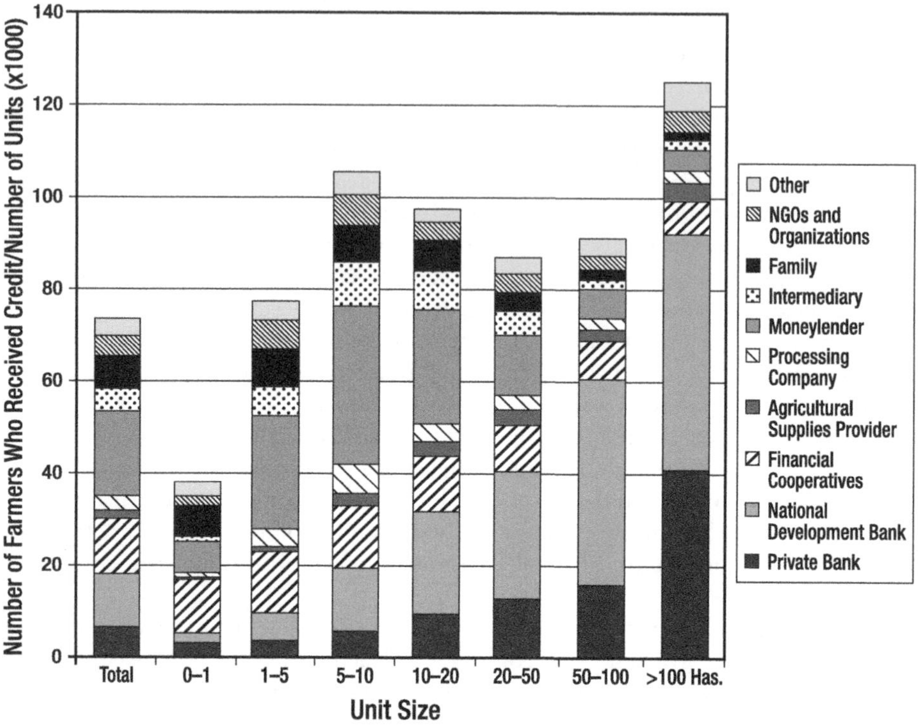

Index calculated by F. Cabarcas according to data from INEC-SICA (2000), *III Censo Nacional Agropecuario* [III national census of agriculture and livestock production], Quito, Ecuador.

support. As an example, A. Bebbington et al. warn about the fact that traditional organizations may be fragile. Discussing the case of the Zhuar Federation in the Ecuadorian Amazon, the authors point out that the rise of the indigenous organizations had brought political and economic power. However, the federation had failed to adopt strategies for self-financing, and instead depended on external funding. In addition, the organizations also lacked adequate internal control and accountability mechanisms, allowing leaders to push their own agendas. These internal problems were exacerbated by national political and economic problems such as the macroeconomic public policy for the Amazonian region.[52] In another case, D. Bates identifies the combined effect of the disappearance of state subsidies and environmental degradation in worsening the agricultural crisis and favoring the migration of the labor force.[53]

In addition to the void left by the state, the increasing number of organizations has caused a fragmentation of approaches and lack of coordination, generating competition among different groups. Basically, the need for accessing limited resources that are distributed in market-like conditions generates competition. This competition is favored by the fact that a high number of organizations tend to concentrate in some areas, while some communities have a lower organizational density. In effect, in the Ecuadorian ranges, as more NGOs are working in a determinate area, more indigenous organiza-

Figure 14.3 Ratio of farmers receiving technical assistance by every 1,000 productive units according to unit size, Ecuador 2000

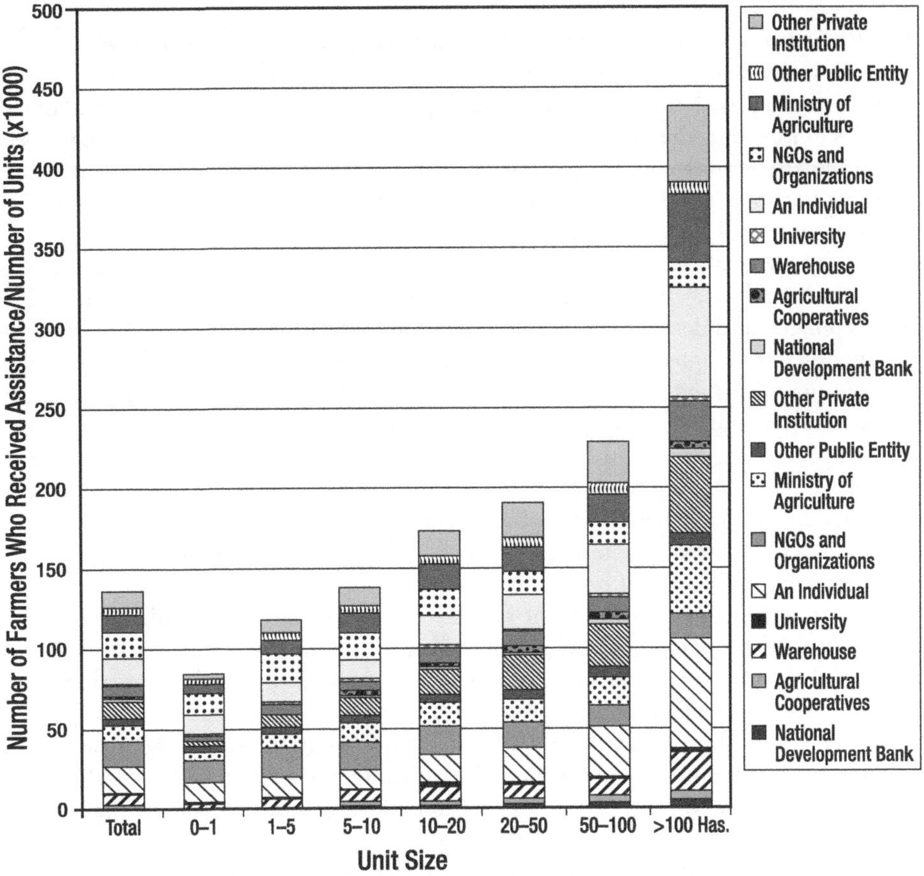

Index calculated by F. Cabarcas according to data from INEC-SICA (2000), *III Censo Nacional Agropecuario* [III national census of agriculture and livestock production], Quito, Ecuador.

tions are located in the same area. This higher density of organizations is triggered by the requirements of development agencies. In effect, NGOs usually have to promote local organizations for accessing funding, generating exaggerated density in some particular regions of interest by the donors. The diversity of organizations grouped in this complex structure lends itself to multiple sources of conflict and rivalry among different groups.[54] The multiplicity of micro-projects could also contribute to masking important structural inequities and thereby promote the Washington Consensus agenda.[55]

To sum up, small farmers have traditionally had little support for developing sustainable production with reduced use of pesticides. Even technical assistance, required for training in appropriate use of pesticides, is reduced for small farmers. Even though some organizations may have gained space in generating alternatives for small farmers, their scope is not enough for replacing the void left by a state system that is not only small but also skewed in favor of larger producers. Furthermore, the need to compete for resources and in different settings generates overlap and potential conflicts among well-intended organizations.

Small Farmers and the Emergence of the Indigenous Movement in Ecuador

Taking into account that small farming in Ecuador is highly concentrated in the ranges, which is the area with the highest indigenous population, it is logical that in the last two decades in Ecuador, the demands in protection of small farmers in Ecuador have been raised mostly by indigenous organizations. In the 1990s, the Ecuadorian Indigenous movement gained worldwide attention due to several uprisings that partially contributed to the instability of several governments in the following years.[56] These events have been described by several authors as indicative of the indigenous movement strength, at least at the national level.[57] The movement has been clearly opposed to Washington Consensus policies and demands better conditions for agrarian production while rejecting international trade agreements.[58] However, indigenous groups have also had important ethnic demands. In effect, they have been characterized as primarily focusing on class and ethnic demands.[59] In this section, I am going to briefly describe the emergence of the indigenous movement in Ecuador as a very important defender of small farmers' interest. I am also going to discuss the extent to which identity politics,[60] despite its importance, may have helped to further divide the initiatives.

Currently, the indigenous movement in Ecuador consists of various levels of organization: A diversity of organizations that group local traditional structures and new community ones constitutes the first level. A second level of organizations groups several of the first-level organizations in a determinate area of influence. A third level is made up of provincial-level organizations that group the second-level organizations. Provincial level organizations are grouped in three confederations that correspond to the three geographic regions in Ecuador. In 1986, a national-level organization was constituted, the Confederation of Ecuadorian Indigenous Nations (CONAIE). This structure has allowed for a capacity of national-level political advocacy that did not exist before.[61]

In the case of indigenous organizations, the political process of approval of the land reform in 1994 is illustrative of both their strengthened capacity and their weakness. In effect, in the 1960s and 1970s, some indigenous uprisings helped to promote the land reform that they favored. However, the reform was mostly promoted from the top down. The indigenous uprising happened with little national coordination in some specific areas where local elites were opposed to the initiative of the government. By contrast, the indigenous organizations in the 1990s were in one of their most influential periods in Ecuadorian history. For instance, unified in a National Indigenous Confederation (CONAIE), they led the formation of an Agrarian Coordinating Association (Coordinadora Agraria) with other sectors. In addition, they organized demonstrations in the early 1990s that made their organization probably the most important social movement in the country. They had the capacity to shock the country with their mass actions. Furthermore, they presented an alternative bill to congress to promote more rights for small farmers.[62] However, despite all their coordination and effort, the fact that the indigenous organization could not stop the law is also indicative of its limitations, even though they had gained so much ground since the first land reforms.

In addition, the emergence of agricultural policies based on ethnicity help to further divide the efforts by groups that otherwise may have had similar interests. On one hand, the creation of new projects and settings for defending the rights of indigenous peoples has constituted an asset for ethnic groups that have always been marginalized in Ecuador. For instance, the creation in 1998 of the Project for the Development of the Indigenous Population and People of African Descent of Ecuador (PRODEPINE) with participation by the state, international development agencies, and the communities, has brought some benefits such as rural development projects and land claims for indigenous communities.[63] On the other hand, despite the beneficial gains for particular groups, the emergence of rural funding linked to identity has blurred the collaborative efforts for common problems such as agrarian reform and access to markets, which also affects mixed-race farmers. In effect, even though the agrarian reform is still part of the discourse of indigenous leaders, the political visibility of issues affecting different ethnicities, such as the need for land reform, is blurred by channeling the demands divided by ethnic groups.[64] Furthermore, the institutionalization of ethnic demands by the state and international agencies may have generated a cooptation of the discourse, limiting its political efficacy by excluding social and economic inequities from the agenda.[65]

Rural policies based on ethnicity may also help to concentrate efforts on the wrong targets. In a study exploring the geographical correlation between poverty and development projects, V. Breton showed that there is some correlation between development projects by NGOs and poverty. However, some of the poorest rural areas do not have the density of projects that they should. However, some relatively wealthy regions such as indigenous Otavalo in the north receive much attention. In effect, the correlation between development projects and poverty seems to be less important than the correlation between development projects and predominantly indigenous areas. Despite the fact that indigenous inhabitants are in statistical terms the poorest of the country, they are not alone, particularly in areas such as the southern Andes where some mixed-race farmers also face the burden of inequalities. Being indigenous is the most important factor in Ecuador to be the target of development projects by NGOs.[66]

To summarize, this phenomenon of ethnic policies for political and economic gain is one of the fundamental elements integrating the field of community organizations involved in reduction of pesticide exposure in the communities of the case study. It plays a role together with the challenges faced by small farmers' agricultural production in the midst of Washington Consensus market changes. In addition, structural problems such as smallholdings and inequities linked to the agrarian reforms have made it increasingly difficult for small farmers to build alternatives for agricultural development. On the other hand, the advance of fragmented programs and projects led by NGOs and small organizations does not compensate for the lack of a more supportive policy and technical assistance by the government. Problems regarding the capacity of organizations and small farmers are not resolved by the structural adjustment policies. Meanwhile, Washington Consensus policies have contributed to make them worse.[67]

WHAT IS HAPPENING IN CAÑAR? A CASE STUDY

Communities A and B are indigenous communities located between 3,000 and 3,400 meters above sea level in Cañar province in the southern ranges in Ecuador. A's population is close to 2,300 inhabitants, while B's is close to 600, with an average of 4.4 members per household for both communities. According to the survey, more than 70 percent of households in both communities reported income lower than US$300 monthly. Together, the two adjacent communities are perceived as the organizational nucleus for farmer and indigenous organizations whose influence goes beyond their geographic boundaries. Table 14.1 includes details on the most important organizations located

Table 14.1 Farmer organizations in communities A and B and percentage of household leaders with perception of little trust in their capacity for improving the welfare of their communities

Organization (number)	*Details*	*Trust Perception**
Second-level organization	This organization groups fifteen communities and four land cooperatives. Its activities include conflict resolution, planning and coordination of agricultural activities, technical assistance and training, and micro-credits. However, its more important role is to control the irrigation system that covers fourteen communities in the area. It also has a demonstration farm for activities such as integrated pest management.	14.04%A 12.86%B
Farmer association and credit cooperative	Originated as an agricultural development initiative linked with seed production, it has a solid financial institution for farmers. In addition, it contains a grain processing and trade program. It also has a demonstration farm for activities such as integrated pest management.	14.04%A 11.43%B
Association of indigenous agronomists	Professional association of agronomists dedicated to planning, development, and technical assistance on development projects for agricultural and livestock production. It has a market located in the urban centre, which provides support for the commerce of some farmer products. It has built some small irrigation subsystems for some communities. It also has a demonstration farm for activities such as integrated pest management.	7.02%A 4.29%B
Trade organization	Recently created, it groups close to sixty farmers with the goal of eliminating intermediaries and trading their products directly at the urban centre. One of its main objectives is to position themselves as organic producers.	NA

continues

Table 14.1 Continued

Organization (number)	*Details*	*Trust Perception**
Women's	A community-level women's organization that generates association several projects for women's welfare, including some development projects and projects for entrepreneurship.	2.63%A 1.43%B
Community assemblies (2)	Community-level organizations for planning and conflict resolution in a geographical area. Conflict resolution.	43.86%A 14.29%B
Land cooperatives (2): Community A and B	Originated with land reform, they distributed land when this was available. According to land distribution, they group the farmers and help to plan and coordinate projects such as irrigation and rural development.	29.95%A 10.00%B
Other Relevant Institutions		
Bilingual institute of technical education	Part of the bilingual education system controlled by Ecuadorian First Nations, this is a training institute for future teachers in their schools. It contains basic training in agronomy as part of its program.	NA
Technical college	Catholic high school with technical training at a bachelor level in agronomy.	NA

*Percentage of household leaders who trust that this organization can help to improve the community's welfare; NA = not available. Source: Author's survey and field notes.

in the two communities. Based on institutional capacity and coverage, the first three organizations are the most important. This high density of organizations is connected to a network of cooperation that supports their action.[68]

Similar to other Andean communities, farmers in the two community sectors studied have resorted to the extensive use of pesticides to protect their crops. The use of pesticides, which is generally poorly handled in terms of human and environmental protection, has helped to reduce crop damage and assure quality for a more competitive market. According to the survey, more than 95 percent of the households had at least one person who used pesticides on a regular basis. A great majority of them did not use gloves or protective equipment when applying pesticides. Moreover, some of the pesticides used in the community are of high toxicity, as in the case of Carbofuran, which is banned by the Environmental Protection Agency in the United States.[69]

This pesticide use occurs despite the high density of farmer organizations and their explicit involvement for years in activities and programs to reduce pesticide-related problems. In effect, social organizations have attempted to reduce the human and environmental risk from pesticides on several occasions but without significant results. For instance, in association with some NGOs and government institutions, farmer organizations in the past have offered courses on proper pesticide management. In addition, some attempts for promoting clean production (products that do not rely on the use of pesticides or fertilizers) have failed.[70] For instance, some years ago, the second-level organization tried to coordinate a trade chain in Quito for pesticide-free quinoa, a traditional Andean cereal. Despite their best efforts, the harvested product was rejected because (1) the cleaning and packaging post-harvest process was inadequate, and (2) the product did not have the homogeneity required by the quality standards (data from interviews). In general, the organization leaders are very active and committed to their vision of environmental and healthy productive alternatives for their communities.

The fact that the organizations in the area face some of the challenges for agricultural production described above may explain the reason why their activities have not yielded better results. For instance, most of their products are traded locally by intermediaries, who target local markets that are in crisis due to imports and demand changes. Basically, the farmers' main products in the communities are potatoes, corn, and beans, none of which are important export products for Ecuador. At the provincial level, most of the sales are through intermediaries (50.5 percent), while direct sales are just 16.6 percent. Sales to food processing or exporters are just 2.5 percent.[71] My interviews with intermediaries show that prices of traditional products are continuously pushed down because of imports from countries such as Colombia and Peru.

The difficulties offered by the market are worsened by the fact that the area has a problem concerning smallholdings. This reduces crop productivity and makes coordinating activities more difficult for farmer organizations. In the fifteen communities belonging to the second-level organization, 63 percent of the families have farms of 5 hectares or fewer.[72] The average area of land is decreasing at a very quick pace. According to my analysis of the database for their irrigation system, from 1997 to 2007, the average of productive affiliated units reduced from 0.43 hectares to 0.35 hectares. As discussed above, two factors contribute to making smallholdings a problem for organizations. First, smallholdings may require bigger investment by the organizations to cover transaction costs and to provide proper technical assistance. Small-farmer organizations may not have this capacity. The second element is that coordination for sustainable projects is more difficult. If the land is owned by smallholders, it is more onerous to coordinate a common strategy.

Adding to the problems offered by smallholdings, the phasing out of some of the state programs for technical assistance in the late 1980s and early 1990s has left a void that is still to be filled by the organizations. By contrast, during the same period, most of the organizations consolidated by taking some of the spaces left by the state and other organizations. For instance, the credit cooperative took advantage of the state's reduced alternatives for rural financial assistance. Nevertheless, this process has not filled the gap of assistance left by the suspension of state programs. For instance, when the National Autonomous Institute for Agricultural Research (INIAP) left, and the local personnel of the National Ministry of Agriculture and Stockbreeding saw its personnel reduced from close to ten technicians to just two, the programs of rural schools, a tool for teaching alternative pest management, stopped. Thus, while some organizations may have been strengthened in the previous twenty years, their real capacity is far from the type needed for reducing pesticide-related problems in the area.

In addition to not replacing the need for state programs, the relative strengthening of farmer organizations faces scarcity of resources. They have limited amounts of different types of resources necessary for establishing comprehensive programs. For instance, funding of development projects is temporary and scarce, while their own small businesses still lack the strength to support agriculture programs. Community organizations' main leadership positions are either voluntary or poorly paid (due in part to scarce financial resources), making it difficult to retain their best human capital. This shortfall has caused, for example, many of the available agronomists to emigrate. In another illustration, the organization in charge of the irrigation system has recently laid off its technical coordinator. Concomitantly, it has increased the irrigation fees several times to balance its budget. Furthermore, the scarcity of resources has led to increased competition at different levels among the organizations, favoring fragmentation and inefficient use of resources, which sometimes occurs despite the best efforts for coordination. Together, these elements have forced the community organizations to struggle to face the needs of the community. In fact, Table 14.1 shows that most household leaders in the survey have little trust in the capacity of their farmer organizations to improve the quality of life in their communities.

As trust in farmers' community organizations declines, family strategies, such as migration and multiple employments, seem to be the most important alternatives sought for maintaining the household economy. According to the survey, an average of at least one family member lives outside the community. This would explain the reason why, although most of the families still consider agriculture an important source of income, remittances and other sources are also gaining importance. Figure 14.4 shows the number of households with at least some contribution from different sources of income, showing an important position for migration. It also shows a process of increased reliance on employment. For the region, the wages calculated for a farmer are lower than the wages of a construction worker. Only a handful of crops can generate enough income to compete with wages from other activities. However, the demand for the most profitable type of products is limited, forcing peasants to resort to wage income instead of farm income.[73]

L. Martinez, in a previous study of the area, showed the extent to which agriculture had declined in favor of other activities in which migration occupied a principal position. This study, which included twelve communities in the area, showed the extent to which migration was precipitated immediately after the process of dollarization, indicating its impact on farmers' income. However, the study also indicated that migrants, usually males, were not the poorest. Families close to urban centers and with higher levels of income had a higher probability of migrating. The process has resulted in the transformation of the traditional networks and structures in the communities and new forms of identity.[74] This process, confirmed by my field experience, is accompanied by a struggle for redefining forms of cultural capital in the community such as the employment of urban patterns of prestige. For instance, an increasing percentage of families (especially the families of migrants) prefer to pay fines instead of being part of the collective activities organized by the communities.

Migration and the need for other occupations are core determinants for pesticide use. Increasingly, due to the possibilities of other sources of income, farmers use agriculture for food security. In a study in the area, B. Jokisch describes the extent to which migration has not led to agricultural abandonment because semisubsistence agriculture remains important.[75] Basically, they farm for self-consumption, while taking care of other occupations such as construction jobs. Contrary to what would be expected, this fact worsens the use of pesticides and their related problems. In fact,

Figure 14.4 Percentage of households with at least some income from specific sources in communities A and B, 2007

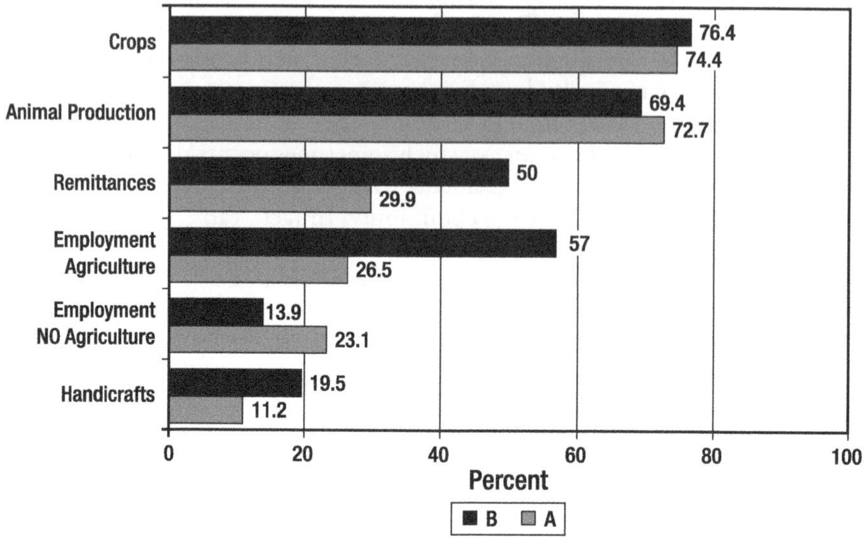

Source: Household survey.

while maintaining the agricultural use of the land, the lack of human resources is one of the phenomena most closely related to the intense use of pesticides. Due to migration of young men, mostly elders and women (in their free time) take care of the crops and other multiple occupations. The integrated pest management and some rational pesticide use alternatives require a more intensive use of workforce. This means that a farmer with little time would prefer to apply pesticides three or five times every four months instead of having to do frequent visits to the crop.

The problem of human resources in the communities and the use of pesticides may have other undesired results. Two major unexpected health problems emerged in the field trip. First, accidental pesticide poisoning by an annual average of seven children younger than eleven years old was found in hospital discharge records from 1998 to 2006. Second, there is a marked increase in the adult rate of suicide by pesticides in the same period. According to the interviews, the rate of suicides may be related to family divisions, the economic crisis, and the easy access to pesticides. On the other hand, a plausible hypothesis for the cases in children is that traditional forms of child care are threatened by the fact that adults have migrated or are very busy with multiple obligations.

In summary, in the context of Washington Consensus policies, the scarcity of resources available in a community's supporting networks has forced different organizations to compete in enhancing and maintaining their networks. Resources already available in the community are not used efficiently because community organizations are forced to compete with each other. Moreover, as trust in farmers' community organizations declines, family strategies such as emigration and multiple employments in the urban centers seem to be the most important alternatives sought for maintaining the household economy. However, migration and multiple employments may also produce unexpected effects, such as accidental pesticide poisoning in children, depression, and further environmental destruction.

CONCLUSION

What are the chances of small-farmer organizations for facilitating the adoption of a safer agriculture? Given the long-term inequalities in access to resources such as land, markets, technical assistance, and credit, their possibilities are very slim. Moreover, I agree with authors who suggest that, despite the fact that Washington Consensus policies did not create problems for rural Ecuador, they contributed to making them worse.[76] For instance, they have contributed to weakening the markets to which small farmers had access while reducing state support. However, the weak position of small farmers in the field of agriculture has persisted for long time and across different development approaches in Ecuador. As competitors in the field of Ecuadorian agriculture, small farmers and their organizations will have little chance to survive if the Washington Consensus policies persist. Compared, for instance, to large producers and capital-intensive agriculture such as floriculture, small-farmer organizations have little control of the forms of capital that would allow them to transform agriculture into a safer practice. Indeed, they have little chance to survive over time.

Despite these difficulties, in the Andes, there are some examples of successful productive experiences by small farmers. Some of them have even been doing well in adopting safer production. However, I agree with authors who suggest that these examples have been possible due to particular circumstances that have allowed them access to networks and resources. By drawing on this support, they have been able to reach new markets with new products. Unfortunately, the experiences can only be explained by local circumstances and cannot be generalized as a rule.[77] Small farmers need appropriate technologies, strong institutional support, and high market demand.[78] As pointed out by several authors, the general dynamic of the field in agriculture offers challenges that are difficult to overcome by small farmers who are compelled to look for other strategies such as becoming labor workers or emigrants.[79]

Faced with the challenges for agricultural production, small farmers have resorted to family strategies such as emigration and multiple employments in the urban centers. However, migration as an alternative offers further challenges to rural production and farmer organizations. The important role of migration is indicative of fundamental changes in the field of agriculture in Ecuador and the region. In Latin America, the changes of the field of agriculture have been described by some authors as a new rurality. New rurality has been characterized as the adoption of multiple forms of employment by farmers, closer connections between urban and rural centers, the emergence of new types of employment, and the emergence of new actors such as NGOs in the scenario of rural development.[80]

Despite the changes in the new rurality, according to the elements identified in this document, there is little indication that the long-term difficulties faced by small farmers and their organizations may be overcome in the persistence of Washington Consensus policies. This is indicative of the shortfall of the role of farmer organizations suggested by the World Bank to promote alternatives to the Green Revolution and to reduce poverty. If rural development policies are designed using the same rationale defended in Ecuador in the past several decades, there is little chance for building sustainable and clean alternatives for small farmers. Despite acknowledging the need for more state support, the World Development Report emphasizes a role that is coherent with the policies adopted in Ecuador in recent decades. The suggested role of the state consists of correcting market failures, regulating the private sector, and promoting partnerships for favoring small farmers. Furthermore, while arguing in favor of much-needed credit and technical assistance for small farmers, it also promotes market-led policies that have affected them. For instance, the report promotes liberation of markets for agricultural products and market-led land reforms.[81]

The experience of marginalization of small farmers in Ecuador, which has transcended different decades and development models, is suggestive of the need for a profound change in the conditions of the structure of the field of agriculture to give small farmers a real chance of surviving with safer production. In effect, for small farmers to have a chance to adopt sustainable and safer forms of agriculture production, the structure of the field needs to be actively changed. This means the need for a different type of land distribution, access to markets, and efficient state support for small farmers. It is not enough to call for more state involvement, because the credit and technical assistance offered by the Ecuadorian state is biased in favor of big producers. The effort needs to be accompanied by public policies that favor the development of safer development alternatives for small farmers so that a new field with favorable conditions for small farmers is determined. However, the involvement of the state and other support agents such as NGOs and universities need to clearly address the structural inequities in the field of agriculture if viable alternatives are really intended for small farmers. If the conditions of the field are not changed, there is a serious risk of threatening agricultural production of small farmers as a whole. There is an ethical dilemma in asking small-farmer communities to take up the burden of problems generated in a field that go beyond their scope of reach. Their organizations will have problems building alternatives if they are not appropriately supported.

Contrary to favoring democratic alternatives and a profound change in the field of agriculture, the emphasis on the role of small-farmer organizations can delay important and required changes for reaching a safer production worldwide. Despite having specific circumstances, the crisis of the peasantry is a worldwide problem. In effect, the deruralization of the world is described by Wallerstein as one of the main causes of the limits in growth in global capitalism. Basically, farmers, and particularly poor farmers, have contributed to maintain a pool of cheap labor for capital expansion. This means that, worldwide, farmers have had a structural disadvantage in negotiating better remuneration for their work. This confirms a weak position in accessing resources. For the same reason, they do not have the capability of assuming the burden of promoting safer forms of production. In contrast, large producers and capitalists, which have a more powerful position for accessing resources, are at the core responsible for the world environmental degradation, but they also have a limit because of their need for profit and the limits of growth of capital. According to Wallerstein, it would be very expensive to have them pay the real price of their use of natural resources in the current world system. The only real solution is to change the current dynamic of endless accumulation of capital. Otherwise, any reformist strategy for reaching cleaner levels of production is very limited. However, one of the possible strategies to delay real changes in the world system and maintain their positions is to place the burden of the changes on the shoulders of the politically weakest. For instance, the rich countries of the north stress the need for environmental protection in the poor countries of the south.[82] In agriculture, stressing the importance of farmer organizations in reaching safer practices without transforming the conditions of the field has a similar effect. It does not transform the structural conditions that generate their disadvantage, while it moves the responsibility away from key actors in the field.

The emergence in Latin America of social movements that have defended the rights of small farmers offers an important political alternative to highlight. In effect, similar to the indigenous movements in Ecuador, in other countries such as Brazil, peasant movements have raised the need from everything from changes in the field of agriculture to the political agenda. This has been denominated by some authors as the Via Campesina ("The Peasant's Way").[83] E. Wallerstein has highlighted the importance of this type of struggle in promoting a more equitable world system in an era of crisis.[84] I agree. These struggles have a transcendental political importance that can promote favorable changes in the field of agriculture. In countries such as Ecuador and Bolivia, for instance, indigenous peasants have engaged in constitutional changes that aim for better conditions for small farmers. The period covered in this article does not allow for discussion of the effects of these changes. However, the challenges that they need to overcome are paramount.

NOTES

1. I am grateful for the support of the Environmental Health Program at the International Development Research Centre and the Canadian Institutes for Health Research through their PhD scholarship program. I would also like to acknowledge the contribution by Rafael Alulema, an indigenous leader whose partnership as a master's student in Ecuador has made it possible to collaborate for data collection and development of a bigger research project. In addition, my supervisors Dr. J. Spiegel and A. Yassi have provided the niche and proper guidance for developing this work.

2. See A. Gaybor, C. Nieto, and R. Velasteguí, *TLC y plaguicidas: impactos en los mercados y la agricultura ecuatoriana* (Quito: Sistema de Investigación sobre la Problemática Agraria en el Ecuador, Punto y Línea, 2006), 57–66. In the Ecuadorian case, this increased use of pesticides is determined by several factors: (1) an expanding agriculture frontier, (2) the increased use of monocrops contributes, because these have more intensity in the use of pesticides than the combined crops. Also, the short cycle crops use more pesticide (affecting mainly small farmers). Finally, (3) there is a trend to use higher concentrations of pesticides by hectare to reduce the resistance to the ingredients and to obtain better pest control.

3. R. E. Evenson and D. Gollin, "Assessing the Impact of the Green Revolution, 1960 to 2000," *Science* 300, no. 5620 (2003): 758–762.

4. P. A. Matson, W. J. Parton, A. G. Power, and M. J. Swift, "Agricultural Intensification and Ecosystem Properties," *Science* 277, no. 5325 (1997): 504–509.

5. Ibid.; Tilman, David, Joseph Fargione, Brian Wolff, Carla D'Antonio, Andrew Dobson, Robert Howarth, David Schindler, William H. Schlesinger, Daniel Simberloff, and Deborah Swackhamer, 2001, "Forecasting agriculturally driven global environmental change," *Science* 292, no. 5515 (2001): 281–284.

6. Pesticide management or elimination requires actions at several levels. First, the use of personal protective equipment is possible for reduction of deleterious processes. Second, good agricultural practices such as the rotation of crops, early pest surveillance, the use of proper doses of chemicals, and the proper use and storage of equipment and chemicals could be implemented. Third, advocacy and political action are fundamental at the local, national, and international levels so that favorable policies can be adopted. In this context, integrated pest management (IPM) techniques are also an option. Methods used in IPM may include strategies for early detection of diseases, continuous surveillance of crops to assure more specific control, and alternatives to the control of pests. See A. Yassi, T. Kjellstrom, T. de KoK, and T. Guidotti, "Food and Agriculture," in *Basic Environmental Health*, ed. T. Guidotti (New York: Oxford University Press, 2001).

7. "Safe agriculture practices" is used in this text to make reference to production healthier for humans and less contaminating and disruptive to natural environments.

8. Except when otherwise stated, in this paper, "small farming" refers to both smallholdings and small farmers in the strict sense. "Smallholdings" are understood as productive units with 5 or fewer hectares, having little chance for economic viability. Small farmers in strict sense have more than 5 hectares but less than 20, with better chances for maintaining production. This corresponds to what has been described for the Ecuadorian case by Manuel Chiriboga, *Desafíos de la pequeña agricultura familiar, in El desarrollo sostenible en el medio rural*, ed. L. Martinez (Quito: FLACSO-Ecuador, 1997). However, it has also been suggested that farmers with 1 hectare or less should be classified as farmers without land; ibid.

9. M. Mazoyer and L. Roudart, "Development of agricultural inequalities in the world and the crisis of the comparatively disadvantaged peasant farming sector," *Land Reform, Land Settlement and Cooperatives* 1 (1997): 6–17.

10. Miguel A. Altieri, "Small farms as a planetary ecological asset: Five key reasons why we should support the revitalization of small farms in the Global South," Food First/Institute for Food and Development Policy 2008 [cited July 2008], available from http://www.foodfirst.org/en/node/2115; P. Rosset, "The multiple functions and benefits of small farm agriculture in the context of global trade negotiations," *Development* 43 (2000): 77–82.

11. Philip McMichael, "Peasant prospects in the neoliberal age," *New Political Economy* 11, no. 3 (2006): 407–418.

12. World Bank, *World Development Report 2008: Agriculture for Development* (Washington, DC: World Bank, 2008), 188–189.

13. P. Bourdieu, "Structures, habitus, practices," in *The Logic of Practice* (Stanford, CA: Stanford University Press, 1980); P. Bourdieu, "The forms of capital," in *Handbook of Theory and Research in the Sociology of Education*, ed. J. Richardson (Westport, CT: Greenwood Press, 1986).

14. For P. Bourdieu, capital in general is accumulated labor, which can be expressed in objects. When appropriated by groups or individuals, capital can harness social energy for specific objectives. The forms of capital include other kinds of capital different from the economic type, which is the most commonly acknowledged. They include, for instance, social capital, defined as resources embedded in more or less institutionalized networks of mutual acquaintance and recognition and used by groups or individuals according to their interests. Furthermore, cultural capital refers to forms of knowledge, including skills and education,

which may provide benefits to groups or persons according to their positions in society. Habitus, as socially constructed knowledge, is very important for cultural capital. See Bourdieu, "The forms of capital."

15. Ibid.

16. Among other social spaces, the notion of "field" was applied by P. Bourdieu to rural settings linked to agricultural production in Algeria and France; Pierre Bourdieu, *The Bachelors' Ball: The Crisis of Peasant Society in Bearn* (Chicago: University of Chicago Press, 2008). The sociology of P. Bourdieu has also been suggested as appropriate for rural studies in Ecuador in Luciano Martinez, "*La desventura de ser soltero: introducción a la sociología rural de Pierre Bourdieu*," *Iconos* 21 (2005): 81–90.

17. Simple randomized sample of households in two adjacent communities; sample size (prevalence: 5%; error: 95%; IC: 95%): community A, Number of families (N) = 396, Sample size (n) = 120; community B, Number of Families (N) = 136; Sample size = 80.

18. Finally, a participative action research and constant consultation with community leaders is used for the discussion and some intervention initiatives.

19. Carlos Larrea and Liisa L. North, "Ecuador: Adjustment policy impacts on truncated development and democratisation," *Third World Quarterly* 18 (1997): 913–934.

20. See Cristóbal Kay, "Latin America's agrarian reform: lights and shadows," *Land Reform* 2 (1998). According to C. Kay, except for some countries such as Argentina and, to some extent, Brazil, agrarian reforms were adopted in most countries of Latin America. Several reasons may be mentioned as driving forces for the policies of agrarian reform: (1) the governments' fear of left-wing revolutions in the region after the experience of the Cuban revolution—in effect, agrarian reforms were part of the Alliance for Progress initiative by the United States government; (2) the pressures from farmers' uprisings in some regions—conflicts favouring deeper changes arose even in some regions where top-down reforms were implemented; and (3) the attempt by some reformist governments to promote higher yields in agricultural production by strengthening capitalist forms of production.

21. Common to other Latin American countries, the Ecuadorian hacienda was a productive system usually associated with debt peonage on large ranches. In the 1950s, the haciendas were mostly located in the Ecuadorian ranges, owned by mixed-race elites, and mostly populated by indigenous farmers. Further details will be provided below. The *huasipungos* were farmers (and their families) who had the right to cultivate in exchange for labor. Other farmers (not *huasipungos*) who did not live on the hacienda also had the possibility of working for it in exchange for payments in kind, as described in Simon Commander and Peter Peek, "Oil exports, agrarian change and the rural labor process: The Ecuadorian sierra in the 1970s," *World Development* 14, no. 1: 79–96. In addition, the Catholic Church, which was also a landowner, was very important in maintaining a complex structure of authority and reciprocity among landowners and farmers. See Barry J. Lyons, *Remembering the Hacienda: Religion, Authority, and Social Change in Highland Ecuador* (Austin: University of Texas Press, 2006).

22. G. Viteri-Díaz, *Reforma Agraria en el Ecuador* [*Agrarian Reform in Ecuador*], Edumed.net, BIBLIOTECA VIRTUAL de Derecho, Economía y Ciencias Sociales 2007 [cited June 2008], available from www.eumed.net/libros/2007b/298/.

23. Market-led reforms of this type were also carried out in other countries in the world. They were promoted by international institutions as an alternative for improving agricultural production. However, there is evidence to suggest that this policy is prejudicial for small and poor farmers, favoring dominance by large landowners. See Edward Lahiff, Saturnino M. Borras, and Cristobal Kay, "Market-led agrarian reform: Policies, performance and prospects," *Third World Quarterly* 28, no. 8 (2007): 1417–1436; Susana Gauster and S. Ryan Isakson, "Eliminating market distortions, perpetuating rural inequality: an evaluation of market-assisted land reform in Guatemala," *Third World Quarterly* 28, no. 8 (2007): 1519–1536; and

Saturnino M. Borras Jr., Danilo Carranza, and Jennifer C. Franco, "Anti-poverty or Anti-poor? The World Bank's market-led agrarian reform experiment in the Philippines," *Third World Quarterly* 28, no. 8 (2007): 1557–1576.

24. Carlos Nieto, "*El acceso legal a la tierra y el desarrollo de las comunidades indígenas y afroecuatorianas: la experiencia del PRODEPINE en el Ecuador*," in *Land Reform: Economic and Social Department*, FAO.

25. See Nathalia Novillo-Rameix, Virgilio Hernández-Enríquez, and Pablo Dávalos, "*La Ley de desarrollo agrario y el debate en torno a la modernizacion del agro: Propuestas, actores y estrategias*," *Ecuador Debate* 46. According to the authors, different from the reforms in 1964 and 1973, this law had opposition from indigenous organizations and some farmer organizations. First, while the uprisings of the 1960s and 1970s promoted further application of the reforms, the indigenous organizations in 1994 led a coordinated national uprising to oppose the reform, because they perceived it as damaging to the small farmers.

26. With Costa Rica, Honduras, and Uruguay, Ecuador was one of the Latin American countries with the lowest area of land modified by the land reforms. See ECLAC and FAO 1986, as quoted in Cristóbal Kay, "Latin America's agrarian reform: lights and shadows," *Land Reform* 2.

27. Klaus Deininger and Pedro Olinto, "Asset Distribution, Inequality, and Growth," Policy Research Working Paper 2375 (Washington, DC: Development Research Group, Rural Development, World Bank, 2000), 23–24.

28. The Land GINI is an indicator of concentration of the land distribution. It ranges from 0 to 1. A value of 1 is the worst-case scenario in which one person has all the land. The world's land GINI for 1990 was 0.65. Ibid.

29. Mauricio León, César Amores, Santiago Izquierdo, Ruth Lucio, and Juan Ponce, "*Capítulo 10: Concentracion de la tierra*," and "*Capítulo 11: Productividad agrícola y pobreza rural*," in *Informe Social 2003: Desarrollo social y pobreza en el Ecuador, 1990–2001* (Quito: Secretaria del Frente Social, Secretaría Técnica del Frente Social y Unidad de Información y Análisis-SIISE, 2003); Guillermo Otáñez, "Ecuador: Breve analisis de los resultados de las principales variables del Censo Nacional Agropecuario 2000," SICA 2000 [cited Feb. 2008], available from http://www.sica.gov.ec/censo/contenido/estud_an.htm.

30. INEC-SICA, *III Censo nacional agropecuario* [*III National census of agriculture and livestock production*] (Quito, Ecuador: *Servicion de Informacion y Censo Agropecuario—SICA* [Information Service and Census of Agriculture and Livestock Production]; *Ministerio de Agricultura y Ganaderia* [Ministry of Agriculture and Livestock Production], *Instituto Nacional de Estadísticas y Censos de Ecuador—INEC* [Ecuadorian Institutes Livestock Production and Agriculture], 2000).

31. Despite their modest gains in land distribution, the agrarian reforms of 1964 and 1973 favored the rupture of the traditional hierarchies of the hacienda system, especially linked to the indigenous communities. The agrarian reform of 1964 helped to increase the mobility of the farmers, to break the social structures of the hacienda, and to make it easier for the transition to capitalist forms of agriculture. The number of landowners with huasipungos reduced from more than 100,000 in 1950 to close to 2,600 in 1974 (MAG/ORSTON 1978, as quoted by Commander and Peek, *Oil Exports*). The breakdown of the traditional elite of landowners and the Church facilitated the consolidation of some indigenous organizations such as land cooperatives, which were actively promoted by the land reform of 1964. In effect, the period beginning with the first agrarian reform in 1964 was marked by an increasing density and creation of local farmer organizations. See Tanya Korovkin, "Indigenous Peasant Struggles and the Capitalist Modernization of Agriculture: Chimborazo, 1964–1991," *Latin American Perspectives* 24, no. 3 (1997): 25–49.

32. Based on data from National Agriculture Censuses of 1954, 1974, and 2000 as quoted in Guillermo Otáñez, "Ecuador: Breve analisis de los resultados de las principales variables del Censo Nacional Agropecuario 2000." SICA 2000 [cited Feb. 2008], available from http://www.sica.gov.ec/censo/contenido/estud_an.htm.

33. Calculation based on data from INEC-SICA, III Censo.

34. Luciano Martínez, "*El campesino andino y la globalización a fines de siglo (una mirada sobre el caso ecuatoriano),*" *Revista Europea de Estudios Latinoamericanos y del Caribe* 77 (2004): 25–40.

35. Manuel Chiriboga, "Desafíos de la pequeña agricultura familiar," in L. Martinez, ed., *El desarrollo sostenible en el medio rural* (Quito: FLACSO-Ecuador, 1997).

36. Christian Vogl, Lukas Kilcher, and Hanspeter Schmidt, "Are Standards and Regulations of Organic Farming Moving Away from Small Farmers' Knowledge?" *Journal of Sustainable Agriculture* 26, no. 1 (2005): 5–26.

37. Lukas Kilcher, "How Organic Agriculture Contributes to Sustainable Development," in *The World of Organic Agriculture: Statistics and Emerging Trends*, ed. H. Willer and M. Yussefi (Bonn, Germany: International Federation of Organic Agriculture Movements [IFOAM] and the Research Institute of Organic Agriculture [FiBL], 2007), 90.

38. David Crucefix, *Organic Agriculture and Sustainable Rural Livelihoods in Developing Countries* (Bristol, UK: Natural Resources and Ethical Trade Programme [NRI], Natural Resources Institute, Soil Association, 1998).

39. León, *Capitulo 10* and *Capitulo 11, Informe Social.*

40. As in other countries of Latin America during the 1960s and 1970s, customs barriers and taxes blocked the importation of some products that were considered fundamental for development of national industry and food security. See Ricardo Bielschowsky, "*Evolucion de las ideas de la CEPAL* [Evolution of the ideas of the ECLAC]," *Revista de la CEPAL/ ECLAC Bulletin (Special Issue)* (1998): 21–45. However, internal markets were markets that have traditionally been controlled by few people, who force small farmers to reduce prices. The state-led policy subsidized traditional market inefficiencies by assuming some costs and direct trade. However, the state did not help to reduce transport costs, to provide better flow of information, or to strengthen farmer organizations to a point that counterbalanced the traditional monopolies. See Chiriboga, "Desafios."

41. Louis Lefeber, "Agriculture and rural development: a critique of establishmentarian policies in Ecuador," in *Rural Progress, Rural Decay: Neoliberal Adjustment Policies and Local Initiatives*, ed. J. D. Cameron (Bloomfield, CT: Kumarian Press, 2003).

42. The economic crisis starting in 1982 implied one of the reasons for these changes, following a reduction in the oil revenues and an increment in the interest rates of international loans. See J. A. Lucero, "Crisis and contention in Ecuador," *Journal of Democracy* 12, no. 2 (2001); and Jeanne A. K. Hey and Thomas Klak, "From Protectionism Towards Neoliberalism: Ecuador Across Four Administrations (1981–1996)," *Studies in Comparative International Development* 34, no. 3 (1999): 66.

43. Chiriboga, "Desafíos."

44. Banco Central del Ecuador (BCE), *Cuentas nacionales, Varios Años* [*National Economic Statistics. Several Years*] (Quito: Banco Central del Ecuador [Central Bank of Ecuador]).

45. Miguel Zamora, "La rápida expansión de los supermercados en Ecuador y sus efectos en las cadenas agroalimentarias," *Ecuador Debate* 64 (2005).

46. FAO and ITC, *World Markets for Organic Fruit and Vegetables—Opportunities for Developing Countries in the Production and Export of Organic Horticultural Products* (Rome: Food and Agriculture Organization of the United Nations (FAO) and the International Trade Centre (ITC) of the Technical Centre for Agricultural and Rural Cooperation International Trade Centre, 2001).

47. M. Holderness, S. Sharrock, E. Frison, and M. Kairo, *Organic Banana 2000: Towards an Organic Banana Initiative in the Caribbean* (Santo Domingo, Dominican Republic: International workshop on the production and marketing of organic bananas by smallholder farmers, 1999).

48. Despite this emphasis on institutions, the second-generation reform still gave much more importance to the economic policies. See Liisa L. North, "Rural progress or rural decay?" in *Rural Progress, Rural Decay: Neoliberal Adjustment Policies and Local Initiatives*, ed. D. Cameron and Liisa L. North (Bloomfield, CT: Kumarian Press, 2003).

49. Chiriboga, "Desafíos."

50. Victor Breton, *Cooperacion al desarrollo y demandas etnicas en los Andes ecuatorianos. ensayos sobre indigenismo, desarrollo rural y neoindigenismo* (Quito: FLACSO Ecuador, 2001), 39–41.

51. Despite the weakness of the Ecuadorian state, its support helped at some point to develop a field in which not only did some farmer organizations grow but also state policies helped to consolidate development projects. Helped by oil revenues during the 1970s, the state led some infrastructure projects such as road construction, irrigation programs, and technical assistance. For instance, the budget on rural and urban planning and housing was higher than 1 percent of the GDP from 1972 until 1992, when it fell bellow this percentage. See BCE, *Cuentas Nacionales.*

52. Anthony J. Bebbington, Hernan Carrasco, Lourdes Peralbo, Galo Ramon, Jorge Trujillo, and Victor Torres, "Fragile lands, fragile organizations: Indian organizations and the politics of sustainability in Ecuador," *Transactions of the Institute of British Geographers* 18, no. 2 (1993): 179–196.

53. Diane C. Bates, "The Barbecho crisis, la plaga del Banco, and international migration: structural adjustment in Ecuador's southern Amazon," *Latin American Perspectives* 34, no. 3 (2007): 108–122.

54. Breton, *Cooperation al Desarrollo*, 39–50, 125–153.

55. James Petras and Henry Veltmeyer, "Social movements and the state: Political power dynamics in Latin America, *Critical Sociology* 32, no. 1 (2006): 83–104.

56. The indigenous movement has led numerous campaigns and uprisings starting with its first big protest in 1990. The reach of the movement has included, for instance, a people's assembly in 1997, which modified the constitution of the country to recognize ethnic diversity. The uprisings even precipitated the fall of the president Jamil Mahuad in 2000, a process that allowed the indigenous leadership to form part of the transitional government that followed. There was even great support for the candidacy of Gutierrez a few years later, although the effort entailed division after the deception by the government once in power. See Lucero, "Crisis in Ecuador."

57. Luis Macas, Linda Belote, and Jim Belote, "Indigenous destiny in indigenous hands," in *Millennial Ecuador: Critical Essays on Cultural Transformations and Social Dynamics*, ed. N. Whitten (Iowa City: University of Iowa Press, 2003).

58. When, after the first coup in 2000, then-acting President Noboa tried to reassume commitments to the International Monetary Fund, a new movement arose to oppose the policies. See Lucas Kintto, *We Will Not Dance on Our Grandparents' Tombs: Indigenous Uprisings in Ecuador* (London: Catholic Institute for International Relations, 2000).

59. Gerardo Otero and Heidi A. Jugenitz, "Challenging national borders from within: The political-class formation of indigenous peasants in Latin America, *Canadian Review of Sociology & Anthropology* 40, no. 5 (2003).

60. Following the work by Linda Alcoff (2006), I use the expression "identity politics" to acknowledge positive and negative consequences of political practices and policies that resort to identity categories to promote their objectives. Identity is understood as a social construct

that is related to the subjects' experience. It is imposed by the others' perceptions, but it is also self-experienced and reinterpreted. Regardless of the fact that ethnic identity is claimed sometimes to be "visible," it is the subject of social interpretation in a particular social and cultural context.

61. Lucas Kintto, *We Will Not Dance on Our Grandparents' Tombs.*

62. Nathalia Novillo-Rameix, Virgilio Hernández-Enríquez, and Pablo Dávalos, "La Ley de desarrollo agrario y el debate en torno a la modernizacion del agro: Propuestas, actores y estrategias."

63. Carlos Nieto, "*El acceso legal a la tierra y el desarrollo de las comunidades indígenas y afroecuatorianas.*"

64. See Breton, *Cooperación al Desarrollo,* 125–153 and Stalin Herrera, *Percepciones sobre la reforma agraria. Analisis del discurso de dirigentes de organizaciones campesinas e indigenas* (Quito: Sistema de Investigacion sobre la Problematica Agraria en el Ecuador [SIPAE], 2007).

65. José Almeida Vinueza, "The Ecuadorian Indigenous Movement and the Gutiérrez Regime: The Traps of Multiculturalism," *PoLAR: Political and Legal Anthropology Review* 28, no. 1 (2005): 93–111.

66. Breton, *Cooperacion al Desarrollo,* 125–153.

67. Carlos Larrea and Liisa L. North, "Ecuador: adjustment policy impacts on truncated development and democratisation"; Suhas Parandekar, Rob Vos, and Donald Winkler, "Ecuador: Crisis, poverty and social protection," in *Crisis and Dollarization in Ecuador: Stability, Growth and Social Equity,* ed. A. Solinamo (Washington, DC: The World Bank, 2002).

68. The table does not include other organizations, such as external NGOs, that have influence in the communities. The list does not contain other institutions such as city hall and the provincial-level unions of second-level organizations.

69. Nonetheless, the intensity of pesticide use in this community is lower than the one described in other Ecuadorian communities. In the area of study, three to five applications by crop cycle is the average. By contrast, in northern Ecuador, seven to fifteen application cycles by potato crop are described in David Yanggen, Donald C. Cole, Charles Crissman, and Stephen Sherwood, "Pesticide Use in Commercial Potato Production: Reflections on Research and Intervention Efforts Towards Greater Ecosystems Health in Northern Ecuador," *EcoHealth* 1, no. 0 (2004): SU72–SU83.

70. For instance, one of the organizations coordinated an attempt to market clean products such as organic farming some years ago. Once harvested, the products were rejected by tentative buyers in the largest urban center of the country, because they did not measure up to the quality standards that buyers expected (data from interviews).

71. INEC-SICA, *Censo.*

72. Francisco Quinde, "Development project for rural micro-enterprises in the municipality of Cañar [*Programa de desarrollo de las microempresas rurales en el canton Cañar*]," master's thesis on Development of Microcredits Applied to Microenterprises [*Tesis previa a la obtancion del titulo de Magister en Desarrollo de Microfinanzas aplicado a Microempresas*], Facultad de Ciencias Economicas, Universidad de Cuenca, Cañar, Ecuador.

73. Ibid.

74. Luciano Martínez, "*El campesino andino y la globalización a fines de siglo (una mirada sobre el caso ecuatoriano).*"

75. Brad D. Jokisch, "Migration and agricultural change: The case of smallholder agriculture in highland Ecuador," *Human Ecology: An Interdisciplinary Journal* 30, no. 4 (2002): 523.

76. Larrea and North, "Ecuador adjustment."

77. Anthony Bebbington, "Globalized Andes? Livelihoods, Landscapes and Development," *Cultural Geographies* 8, no. 4 (2001): 414–436.

78. Bebbington, *Social Capital and Rural Intensification.*

79. See Garcia, *Sector agrario*; Carvajal, *Emigracion*; North, "Rural progress or rural decay?" and Martínez, "*El campesino andino.*"

80. Victor Breton, "*Los paradigmas de la 'nueva' ruralidad a debate: El proyecto de desarrollo de los pueblos indígenas y negros del Ecuador,*" *European Review of Latin American and Caribbean Studies* 78 (2005): 7–30; Norma Giarracca, ed., *¿Una nueva ruralidad en América Latina?, Colección Grupos de Trabajo de CLACSO* (Buenos Aires: Consejo Latinoamericano de Ciencias Sociales [CLACSO], 2001).

81. World Bank, *World Development.*

82. Immanuel Wallerstein, "Ecology and capitalist costs of production: No exit," in *The End of the World As We Know It: Social Science for the Twenty-first Century*, ed. I. Wallerstein (Minneapolis: University of Minnesota Press, 1997).

83. Philip McMichael, "Peasant prospects in the neoliberal age."

84. Wallerstein, "Ecology and Capitalist Costs of Production."

Part IV

Epilogue

Chapter 15

Drawing Lessons from the 2008 World Food Crisis

Jomo Kwame Sundaram[1]

THE FOOD PRICE SPIKE OF EARLY 2008

Lack of food is rarely the reason people go hungry.[2] Even now, there is enough food in the world, with a bumper harvest this year, but many more people cannot afford to buy the food they need. Even before the recent food price spikes, an estimated billion people were suffering from chronic hunger, while another two billion were experiencing malnutrition, bringing the total number of food-insecure people to around three billion, or almost half the world's population. The recent sharp increases in food prices are likely to drive the number of people vulnerable to food stress even higher, with at least another 100 million likely to be chronically hungry. Even before these price spikes, about 18,000 children died daily on average as a direct or indirect consequence of malnutrition.[3]

The rapid and simultaneous rise in world prices for all basic food crops—corn (maize), wheat, soybeans, and rice—along with other foods like cooking oils is having a devastating effect on poor people all over the world. The effects have been felt around the world by all except the truly wealthy. Almost everybody's standard of living has been reduced as the middle class becomes increasingly careful about its food purchases, the near poor drop into poverty, and the poor suffer even more. With increased hunger and malnutrition, the young, old, infirm, and other vulnerable groups will die prematurely or be harmed in other ways.

It is useful to distinguish between longer-term and more recent developments in trying to understand and address the current global food crisis.

LONGER-TERM PROBLEMS

The major increases in crop yields and food production associated with the Green Revolution from the 1960s to the 1980s—with considerable government and international not-for-profit support—gave way to new policy priorities in the 1980s. By then, the threat of starvation had receded in most of the world, and the effort in wheat, corn, and rice was not extended to other crops, especially those associated with water-stressed agriculture in arid areas of sub-Saharan Africa. Meanwhile, with Europe, the United States, and Japan offering their own farmers large subsidies to encourage production, food became abundant worldwide, and prices fell. For the rich countries, these subsidies and associated protection not only ensured food security but were also a form of social protection for those living in the countryside.

Agricultural experts have, for years, warned of the risks of the flagging efforts to boost food output. "People felt that the world food crisis was solved, that food security was no longer an issue, and it really fell off the agenda," Robert S. Zeigler, the director general of the International Rice Research Institute (IRRI), told the *New York Times*.[4]

As food supply growth slowed,[5] demand on the other hand continued to grow, and not only due to population increase. From 1970 to 1990, food supply grew faster than the population. Between 1960 and 1970, global grain yields grew by 2.6 percent per year on average. From 1990 to 2007, the average annual increase rose by less than half, that is, by 1.2 percent yearly.[6] Thus, after 1990, the trends have been reversed as the food supply growth rate fell below population growth, according to a U.S. Department of Agriculture source cited by the *New York Times*. The numbers from the World Bank's World Development Indicators (WDI) do not support this claim, because food production rose by around 36 percent in 1990–2004 and population grew by only 21 percent.[7] In recent years, the world has been consuming more grain than it has been producing, cutting into reserves and driving up prices. Early in 2008, as stocks declined further, and investors abandoned their previously preferred financial assets, international grain prices rose sharply.

Meanwhile, many developing countries, most notably China with its large population, have experienced unprecedented economic growth. With higher incomes, diets have shifted toward greater meat and dairy consumption, with increased requirements for grain for animal feed. There has been a tendency to blame the food crisis on such increased consumption.[8]

Having neglected food security and the productive sectors of their economies for several decades, many developing countries' governments now also lack the fiscal capacity to increase public spending to increase food production and agricultural productivity. In recent decades, many developing countries have implemented policies recommended or required by the IMF, the World Bank, and even some Western NGOs working in the poor countries of the Third World. This trend has greatly reduced policy space in developing countries, especially fiscal space.

The problem has been exacerbated by the significant drop in official development assistance for agricultural development in developing countries. Aid for agriculture has fallen in real terms by more than half in the quarter century after 1980. The biggest cutbacks have affected grants to agriculture in poor countries from the governments of wealthy countries and in loans from development institutions that these governments control, such as the World Bank. The World Bank cut its lending for agriculture from US$7.7 billion in 1980 to $2 billion in 2004.

The Green Revolution had led to the creation of a global network of research centers focusing on agriculture and food production, primarily in developing countries, with fourteen institutes in Asia, Africa, and Latin America, such as the IRRI in the Philippines and the International Maize and Wheat Improvement Center in Mexico. Known collectively as the Consultative Group on International Agricultural Research (CGIAR), these research centers have experienced significant budget cuts and face further deep cuts. Commercial seed supplier Monsanto spends seven times as much on agricultural research as these fourteen institutes together.[9]

Agricultural research and development has fallen for all crops in all developing countries, while cuts in agricultural research continue. Adjusting for inflation and exchange rates, rich countries cut such grants by about half from 1980 to 2006, from US$6 billion to $2.8 billion yearly, with the United States alone cutting from $2.3 billion to $624 million. The United States is cutting, by as much as three quarters, its $59.5 million annual support for the CGIAR network. All this has adversely affected research on crops and pests, as well as agricultural extension programs to help farmers adopt improved farming methods. Instead of trying to stay ahead of rapidly evolving pests and the changing climate to ensure global food security, support for agricultural research has declined disastrously.

As budgets have been cut, spending on plant-breeding programs—needed to improve crop productivity—has declined. IRRI's budget, which comes from governments, foundations, and development institutions such as the Asian Development Bank, has been halved—after adjusting for inflation—since the early 1990s. As a result, "several dozen important varieties of rice have been lost from the institute's gene bank through poor storage. Promising work on rice varieties that could withstand high temperatures and saltier water—ideal for coping with global warming and the higher sea levels that may follow—had to be abandoned."[10]

Trade Liberalization

The conventional wisdom holds that a free market economy, with minimal government interference, would function more efficiently, and thus become more productive.[11] Hence, governments should stop subsidizing farmers to purchase fertilizers, stop being involved in the marketing, storage, and transportation of food, or provisioning credit, and just leave farmers alone. Following advice to this effect, including from international development agencies, many developing country governments reduced their subsidies for small farmers and consumers, making their lives more difficult.[12]

Rich countries have continued to subsidize and protect their farmers, and their agricultural subsidies and tariffs have undoubtedly undermined food production in developing countries. However, cutting farm subsidies will increase food prices, at least initially, while reducing agricultural tariffs alone will not necessarily lead to an increase in food production in poor countries without complementary support. Some food security advocates have called for rich countries to compensate for the adverse consequences of their own agricultural subsidies and protectionism by providing additional foreign aid to the developing world, targeting production efforts that enhance food security.

Since the 1980s, governments have been pressed to promote exports to earn foreign exchange and import food. Although enhanced agricultural production is desirable, much of the recent emphasis has been on export crop production. While this may help a country's balance of payments, export-oriented agriculture does not ensure sufficient food. Export-oriented agriculture can induce investment in producing higher-priced luxury crops, rather than the lower-priced food crops needed to meet the needs of the domestic population.

Instead of developing their own agriculture, many poor countries have turned to the world market to buy cheap rice and wheat. In 1986, U.S. Agriculture Secretary John Block called the idea of developing countries feeding themselves "an anachronism from a bygone era," saying they should just buy American. Increased food production and lower food prices have undoubtedly contributed to poverty reduction in much of the world, but the consequences are complex. Higher food prices affect different poor people in different ways, with food producers possibly benefiting while all others will be worse off.

Some countries that were *previously self-sufficient in food now import* large quantities of food. Net food imports are now true for most developing countries, including sub-Saharan Africa. Madagascar President Marc Ravalomana noted that, twenty-five years ago, Africa had a surplus of exports in cereals, rice, soybeans, and other food products. "Over the years, we increasingly shifted toward imports of these products."[13] Thus, food security went the way of various other government interventions associated with the earlier period of high growth and rapid development associated with the "Golden Age." But food should not be treated as just another commodity, and governments should develop appropriate policies, infrastructure, and institutions to ensure food security (not to be equated with total self-sufficiency) at the national or regional level.

Following the recent food price hikes, some countries have lowered tariffs to reduce the impact of much higher prices of imported food, but such stopgap efforts have had marginal impacts at best. Others—mainly but not only net food importers—have restricted food exports to insulate their populations from rising international food prices by limiting the option of exporting food for higher prices.[14] Such export restrictions have undoubtedly further limited supply to a relatively small international rice trade, thus contributing to price increases, especially for rice.

The World Bank and the WTO still claim that agricultural trade liberalization offers the medium-term solution to the current food crisis even though eliminating food subsidies will raise food import costs in the short term.[15] Even if completed, the Doha Round does not envisage very significant reduction of agricultural subsidies and tariffs but would further undermine national food security measures while ensuring greater international dependence on relatively few major food exporters associated with the Cairns group. While higher food prices may make food production in developing countries—for domestic markets and for export—more attractive to farmers, this will not necessarily reduce food prices, the root of the current crisis. If food prices decline, the incentive to continue food production may be undermined once again.[16]

In any case, the complete elimination of agricultural tariffs and nontariff trade barriers is certainly not on the agenda in the Doha Round. The reduction of such trade barriers is likely to mainly benefit existing agricultural exporters of the Cairns group, rather than most poor developing countries. Also, it is now increasingly acknowledged—for example, in the "aid for trade" discussion—that new productive capacities and capabilities do not emerge automatically following trade liberalization but need to be supported by appropriate government support measures. Hence, it becomes necessary to ensure a strong domestic supply response with strong public support for domestic productive capacity building.

Other Longer-term Trends

Other medium- and long-term factors have contributed to the current food crisis, including the following:

- The *growing demand for meat* among those newly able to afford it has increased the use of food crops to feed livestock. Total meat supply in the world quadrupled from 71 million tons in 1961 to 284 million tons in 2007.[17] Developed countries have blamed fast-growing developing countries, such as China and India, for the food price increases, emphasizing the grain requirements of increased meat production, though FAO trend data do not support this claim.
- *Over-fishing* is reducing this important animal protein source for many; the consequently higher fish prices thus further burden the poor and the near poor. The problem is acute for both marine and freshwater fishing, and the growth of fish farming has proved to be problematic for ecological as well as nutritional reasons. There is relatively limited progress toward resolving the very complex issues involved.
- Weather has also adversely affected agriculture in many parts of the world. *Climatic changes* associated with accelerated greenhouse gas emissions are believed to have exacerbated water supply problems, speeding up desertification and water stress, and worsening the unpredictability and severity of weather phenomena, for example, the decade-long drought in Australia.
- Forests have long been an important source of food (e.g., forest fruit, ferns, tubers, fauna) for many rural dwellers living close to subsistence.[18] Continued *deforestation* for logging, agricultural land cultivation, and other purposes has also reduced the natural carbon sink potential—thus accelerating climate change—and biodiversity functions they have long contributed to. The international community has failed to develop equitable deterrents to deforestation and incentives for forest conservation.
- Another reason is the *loss of farmland* to other uses. Growing population pressure, urbanization, other nonagricultural uses of land, as well as the attraction of nonfood agricultural production (e.g., for horticulture) have reduced farm

acreage available for food production, while agricultural land is increasingly used to produce commodities other than food, such as biofuels.[19]

- *Soil erosion* is a slow and insidious process, with ominous implications for agricultural productivity in the long term. Most problematically, the inexorable pressures on commercial farmers' short-term interests to maximize net agricultural income threaten soil quality and the efficacy of soil conservation efforts. The quality of top soil, crucial to agriculture, has been declining over the years owing to a variety of reasons related to agricultural and land use practices[20] such as pollution, monocropping, and misuse of fertilizers. *Water supplies*, so essential for agricultural irrigation, are also under threat as underground aquifers and other sources of water supply are being depleted or compromised by such factors.

Finally, fewer and fewer transnational agribusinesses now dominate marketing, production, and inputs.[21] This comes largely at the expense of small farmers and consumers, particularly the poor, who are forced to trade in a less competitive environment in situations of asymmetric power. Transnational corporations that process agricultural commodities, manufacture and sell food as well as agricultural inputs enjoy increasingly *monopolistic and monopsonistic market power*, enjoying attendant rents.[22] In other words, with such industrial concentration, "market competitiveness begins to decline, leading to higher spreads between what consumers pay and producers receive."[23] The four largest agrochemical companies now control 60 percent of world fertilizer supply compared to 47 percent in 1997, while the top four seed supply corporations have a third of the world market, rising from 23 percent over the same decade.[24] Moreover, with less government support, rural credit has often become prohibitively expensive. Although a few agribusinesses have encountered specific problems, most have been profiting exceptionally with the recent price increases.

As such longer-term trends exacerbated over recent decades, the stage was being set for a food emergency.

RECENT DEVELOPMENTS

The acceleration of growth in developing countries in the last half decade has been associated with high primary commodity, especially energy, prices. The boom has mainly involved minerals, particularly oil, rather than agriculture.[25] The prices of the sixty agricultural commodities traded on the world market increased 14 percent in 2006 and 37 percent in 2007.[26] But even among agricultural commodities, world food prices have risen since 2006, especially since early 2008, following the flight of investment from other financial assets to agricultural futures. Nevertheless, recent agricultural price increases have barely reached the average postwar prices in most cases.[27]

Corn prices began their rise in the third quarter of 2006 and soared by some 70 percent within months. Wheat and soybean prices also skyrocketed during this time and are now at record levels. The prices for cooking oils (mainly from soybean and palm oil)—an essential foodstuff in many poor countries—have rocketed up as well. Rice prices have also more than doubled in the year ending in the first quarter of 2008[28] and have almost tripled in recent times. Some of the other reasons for these rising food prices will be mentioned below.

The *increase in oil prices* has affected food prices. Commercial agriculture uses a great deal of oil and natural gas for running machinery, producing chemical fertilizers and pesticides, drying crops, and transportation. In the United States, Europe, and elsewhere, crops are increasingly being grown to produce biofuels. Thus, producing corn for ethanol or soybean and palm oil for biodiesel undermines the use of these crops for food. In 2007, over 20 percent of the entire U.S. corn crop was used to produce bioethanol, although the process does not yield much additional energy over what goes into producing it!

Some biofuels are clearly far more cost-effective and energy-efficient than others, while different biofuel stocks have very different opportunity costs for food agriculture (e.g., sugar has not experienced any significant price increase). Developed countries have provided generous subsidies and other incentives for such increased biofuel production within their boundaries, while developing countries encouraging biofuel production have provided far fewer "market-distorting incentives" to farmers.

According to Brazil's President Lula,[29] sugarcane cultivation only takes up 1 percent of the country's total arable land, with only half of that for ethanol production. He also claimed that ethanol production in Brazil does not encroach on the Amazon where only 21,000 hectares are planted with sugarcane on previously degraded pasture land. India, on the other hand, claims to be developing biofuels using noncereal biomass, crop residues, and cultivating jatropha on degraded land. However, the United States claims that only 2–3 percent of the 43 percent global food price increase forecasted is due to biofuels. Hence, the debate over biofuels in relation to food availability needs to be far more nuanced, differentiated, and specific if we are not to throw the baby out with the bathwater of some undoubtedly poor biofuel policies in recent years, especially in the wealthy economies.

Speculation and hoarding are also contributing to the food price spikes. In addition, more securitization, easier online trading, and other financial market developments in recent years have facilitated greater speculative investments, especially in commodity futures and options markets, including those affecting food.[30] As the U.S. subprime mortgage crisis deepened and spread in early 2008, speculators started investing in food and metals to take advantage of the "commodities super cycle" as the greenback's decline relative to other currencies has induced investment in commodities instead. Falling asset prices in other financial market segments, following the subprime mortgage meltdown in the United States, may be more important for explaining the recent surge in food prices than supply constraints or other factors underlying longer-term gradual upward price trends.

U-TURN IN WASHINGTON?

As is clear from the above, the World Bank has been central to the fate of food security and agriculture over the last three decades, especially by reducing funding for investments in agricultural infrastructure, support institutions, and research as well as by promoting trade liberalization. The mid-2007 publication of the *2008 World Development Report* (WDR) on agriculture for development was therefore remarkable for various reasons. Notably, it was the first *World Development Report*—the World Bank's flagship publication—on the subject after more than a quarter of a century.

This is not the place to try to summarize or criticize the entire report. The report offers a comprehensive review of many aspects of agricultural production and distribution, even addressing previously unaddressed or poorly addressed issues—for the World Bank—such as peasant organizing, political voice, unequal market power, ecological concerns, and gender equity.

Surprisingly, the report lacks historical perspective and does not have much to say about the decline of agricultural production in many developing countries. However, the report does acknowledge policy mistakes, making careful references to the consequences of structural adjustment programs.[31]

Importantly, chapter 4 of the WDR acknowledges that trade liberalization generates winners as well as losers and acknowledges that "the overall effect of trade policy reform on farm incomes of food staple producers in the poorer developing countries is likely to be small."[32] The trade openness discussion focuses on export expansion with little acknowledgement of the problems associated with import growth. With no reference to the 1948 Havana Charter's commitment to trade reform to accelerate growth and create employment, it equates trade reform with trade liberalization and presumes that trade must be liberalized; in this view, governments are expected to compensate the losers, but the report does not specify any mechanisms for international compensation for lost revenue as well as productive and trade capacities and capabilities due to trade liberalization, thus taking a step backward in the aid for trade dialogue.

WDR 2008 acknowledges that transnational corporations dominate a number of agricultural markets, and that "growing agribusiness concentration may reduce efficiency and poverty reduction impacts."[33] It has little to say about corporate power, although it acknowledges asymmetric market power and the differential impacts of policies on different segments and strata of agrarian populations. "Concentration widens the spread between world and domestic prices in commodity markets for wheat, rice, and sugar, which more than doubled from 1974 to 1994. A major reason for the wider spreads is the market power of international trading companies."[34] While apparently sympathetic to peasant organizing and enhanced political voice at the national level, it is silent about the challenges posed by asymmetric and undemocratic economic and political power at the international level.

Agricultural financing has begun to recover recently at the World Bank, perhaps due to the preparation and publication of the 2008 *World Development Report* on agriculture as well as the current food crisis. The Bank has already agreed to double lending for such programs in Africa, and with the ongoing food crisis, it is likely that such institutions will be expected to commit more to supporting a revival of food agriculture.

The June 3–5, 2008, food summit in Rome saw the articulation of many different ostensible solutions to the world food crisis in the short and medium term.[35]

The starkest difference was probably between Food and Agriculture Organization (FAO) Director General Jacques Diouf on the one hand and the alliance of the Washington-based international financial institutions, the World Trade Organization (WTO) and the Organization for Economic Cooperation and Development (OECD), led by World Bank President Bob Zoellick, with the former calling for a renewed commitment to food security as the latter urged agricultural trade liberalization as the solution.

At the Rome meeting, Diouf also criticized the failure of rich country governments following the 1996 World Food Summit despite the preparation of many agricultural plans and programs by many developing countries as well as regional organizations.[36] Consequently, aid for agriculture has fallen in real terms by more than half from US$8 billion in 1980 to $3.4 billion in 2005. He noted the existence of a carbon market worth $64 billion in developed countries, but with no funds to prevent deforestation of an average of 13 million hectares annually. In addition to protective tariffs, $11–12 billion was provided as biofuel subsidies in 2006, diverting 100 million tons of cereal from human consumption to biofuels. According to Diouf, OECD countries provided $372 billion in subsidies for agriculture in 2006; in one country alone, food worth $100 billion was wasted annually; excessive consumption by the world's obese costs $20 billion annually, while the world spent $1.2 trillion on arms purchases in 2002.

The World Bank's Independent Evaluation Group (IEG) has assessed the development effectiveness of Bank assistance in addressing constraints to agricultural development in Africa over the period 1991–2006 in a pilot for a wider assessment of Bank assistance to agriculture worldwide. The study's central finding is that *agriculture has been neglected by both governments and the donor community, including the World Bank.*

The Bank's strategy for agriculture has been gradually subsumed within a broader rural focus, which has diminished agriculture's importance. As much as food agriculture in developing countries is deemed to have limited export potential compared to other cash crops, food crops have generally been especially neglected. Like other advocates of trade liberalization, the commitment to food security has been substituted in favor of the notion of "global food security," with developing countries encouraged to maximize export earnings to pay for food imports and other requirements in a new, ostensibly welfare-maximizing international division of labor.

Both due to and contributing to this, the technical skills needed to support agricultural development adequately have also declined over time. The Bank's limited—and, until recently, declining—support for addressing the constraints on agriculture has not met the diverse needs of a sector requiring coordinated intervention across a range of activities and efforts.

Bank lending has been thinly spread over various agricultural activities—such as research, extension, credit, seeds, and policy reforms in rural space—with little recognition of the synergies among them to effectively contribute to agricultural development. Although there have been areas of comparatively greater success, results have been limited because of weak linkages, for example, of research with extension, and the limited availability of complementary and critical inputs such as fertilizers and water. Hence, the Bank has made little contribution to African agricultural progress in particular as the original Green Revolution's focus on rice, wheat, and corn ignored most African food crops, especially those suited to water-stressed conditions, increasingly prevalent in much of the continent.

APPENDIX: IRRI AND THE BROWN PLANT HOPPER MENACE[37]

IRRI researchers say they know how to create rice varieties resistant to the brown plant hopper menace but that budget cuts have prevented them from doing so. In the 1980s, IRRI employed five entomologists (insect experts), overseeing 200 staff, compared to one entomologist with eight staff in May 2008. Not surprisingly, corridors at IRRI have many empty offices. But even with a sudden reversal of fortunes for agricultural research, it will take time to produce results.

In the case of the brown plant hopper, there will be no quick fix following years of neglect. After all, the insect is not a new problem. In the 1960s, IRRI pioneered ways to help farmers grow two and even three crops annually, instead of one. But with rice plants growing most of the year, the hoppers—which live only on rice plants—have longer to multiply, feed, and cause problems. IRRI responded by testing thousands of varieties of wild rice for natural resistance; it found four types of resistance and bred them into commercial varieties by 1980. But brown plant hoppers soon adapted, and the resistant strains lost their effectiveness in the 1990s. An important insecticide also lost its effectiveness, as the hopper became able to withstand doses up to 100 times those that used to kill it. And as the hopper adapted, IRRI was being undermined.

No fewer than fourteen new types of genetic resistance have been discovered to address the hopper problem. But with the budget cuts, IRRI has not bred these traits into widely used rice varieties. Even if funding materializes immediately, it would take four to seven years to do so. Meanwhile, the hoppers pose a growing threat. In May 2007, China announced it was struggling to control the rapid spread of the hoppers there, which threatened to destroy a fifth of the harvest.

NOTES

1. I am grateful to David O'Connor, Anis Chowdhury, and Rudi von Arnim for their comments and input, but do not implicate any of them.

2. As Josette Sheeran, the head of the United Nations' World Food Program, has said, "There is food on shelves but people are priced out of the market," *The Guardian*, February 26, 2008. *New York Times*, December 2, 2002, headline: "Poor in India Starve as Surplus Wheat Rots." *Wall Street Journal*, June 25, 2004, headline: "Want Amid Plenty, An Indian Paradox: Bumper Harvests and Rising Hunger." For more academic analyses, see B. Guha-Khasnobis, S. S. Acharya, and B. Davis (eds). *Food Insecurity: Vulnerability and Human Rights Failure* (Hammondsworth: Palgrave Macmillan, 2007); B. Guha-Khasnobis, S. S. Acharya, and B.

Davis (eds.) *Food Security: Indicators, Measurement and the Impact of Trade Openness* (Oxford: Oxford University Press, 2007).

3. Associated Press, February 18, 2007. For details, see Report of the Special Rapporteur on the Right to Food, Jean Ziegler, *Implementation of General Assembly Resolution 60/251 of 15 March, entitled, "Human Rights Council,"* A/HRC/4/30, 19 January 2007.

4. The following discussion on the decline of funding for agriculture, especially for research, draws heavily on Keith Bradsher and Andrew Martin, "World's Poor Pay Price as Crop Research Is Cut," *New York Times*, May 18, 2008.

5. Rice yields per acre in Asia have stopped rising; there has been no per-acre increase for at least a decade, while yield increases are not expected in the near future; *Rice Today* (January–March 2008).

6. Bruce Stokes, "Food Is Different," *National Journal*, June 7, 2008.

7. The discrepancy may be due to some treatments of all cereals as food for human consumption, while some cereals are actually used as animal feed and more recently to produce biofuels.

8. *The Economic Times*, "Food crisis: Rice blames it on better diet in India, China," (India) April 29, 2008. This view had been articulated earlier by the Executive Director of the United Nations World Food Programme; see Sheeran, op. cit. According to the World Food Programme country page for India, "nearly 50 percent of the world's hungry live in India, a low-income, food-deficit country." While economic growth has probably increased incomes and food consumption for many, many more seem to be worse off. "The consumption of cereals declined from a peak of 468 grams per capita per day in 1990–91 to 412 grams per capita per day in 2005–2006, indicating a decline of 13 percent during this period. The consumption of pulses declined from 42 grams per capita per day (72 grams in 1956–1957) to 33 grams per capita per day during the same period"; see "Agricultural production and food availability," *Economic Survey of India, 2007–2008* (Ministry of Finance, Government of India, 2008). The average Indian eats about 178 kg of grain annually compared to 1,046 kg by the average American, i.e., almost six times as much. U.S. per capita grain consumption rose from 946 kg per year in 2003 to 1,046 kg in 2007, while Indian per capita grain consumption remained static over the same period; Subodh Varma, "The U.S. eats 5 times more than India per capita," *The Times of India*, May 4, 2008. According to the 2007 Arjun Sengupta Report of the National Commission for Enterprises in the Unorganized Sector, the total number of poor and vulnerable increased from 732 million in 1993–1994 to 836 million in 2004–2005, while 77 percent of India's working population lives on a little over half a U.S. dollar a day. Also see Indulata Prasad and Anuradha Mittal, "The Blame Game: Who Is Behind the World Food Price Crisis?" Policy Brief (Oakland: The Oakland Institute, 2008). http://www.oaklandinstitute.org/pdfs/Blame_Game_Brief.pdf

9. Stokes, "Food Is Different."

10. Keith Bradsher and Andrew Martin, "World's Poor Pay Price as Crop Research Is Cut," *New York Times*, May 18, 2008.

11. A World Bank–commissioned review acknowledged. "In most reforming countries, the private sector did not step in to fill the vacuum when the public sector withdrew"; *New York Times*, October 15, 2007. According to Jeffrey Sachs, "The whole thing was based on the idea that if you take away the government for the poorest of the poor that somehow these markets will solve the problems. . . . But markets can't step in and won't step in when people have nothing. And if you take away help, you leave them to die"; *New York Times*, October 15, 2007.

12. In 2007, Malawi decided to reverse course and reject the policy recommendations received and reintroduced subsidies for fertilizers and seeds. Farmers used more fertilizers,

yields increased, and Malawi's food situation greatly improved; *New York Times*, December 2, 2007.

13. Quoted in Dano Neth, "Diverse Proposals by Political Leaders at 'Food Crisis Summit'," *SUNS—South North Development Monitor* #6489, June 5, 2008.

14. Adil Ali, *India's Export Ban on Foodgrains: A Measure to Ensure Availability of Food for its Poorest Citizens* (Oakland, CA: The Oakland Institute, 2008).

15. Such claims are even disputed by advocates of trade liberalization, e.g., see Jagdish Bhagwati and Arvind Panagariya, "How the Food Crisis Could Solve the Doha Round," *Financial Times*, June 23, 2008.

16. Governments can procure crops from food producers at guaranteed prices or subsidize production and sell at affordable prices. Such food security policies were widespread before structural adjustment programs came in the 1980s. Subsidies and controls are obviously distortions, but the cost of such distortions should be weighed against the benefit of food security and vulnerability to poverty.

17. Fred Magdoff, "The World Food Crisis," *Monthly Review* 60, no. 1 (May 2008): 1–15.

18. Robert Nasi, with David Brown, David Wilkie, Elisabeth Bennett, Caroline Tutin, Gijs van Tol, and Tim Christophersen, *Conservation and Use of Wildlife-Based Resources: The Bushmeat Crisis*, Technical Series no. 33 (Bogor: Secretariat of the Convention on Biological Diversity, Montreal, and Center for International Forestry Research [CIFOR], 2007). http://www.cbd.int/doc/publications/cbd-ts-33-en.pdf

19. Fred Magdoff, "The Political Economy and Ecology of Biofuels," *Monthly Review* 60, no. 3 (July–August 2008).

20. "Soil Under Strain," *Financial Times,* July 17, 2008.

21. Julie Jargon, "Reaping what foreign growers sow: U.S. farmers score big profits selling crops from abroad," *New York Times,* July 15, 2008.

22. See e.g., "Supermarket Giants Crush Central American Farmers," *New York Times*, December 28, 2004.

23. World Bank, op. cit. For example, the share of the coffee retail price paid by U.S. consumers going to coffee-producing countries declined from a third in the early 1990s to about 10 percent in 2002.

24. Stokes, op. cit.

25. Jose Antonio Ocampo and Maria Angela Parra, "This Is a Boom of Mineral, Not Agricultural Prices," *RGE Monitor*, May 6, 2008.

26. *New York Times,* January 19, 2008.

27. Ocampo and Parra, op. cit.

28. "High Rice Cost Creating Fears of Asia Unrest," *New York Times*, March 29, 2008.

29. The rest of this paragraph draws on Dano, op. cit.

30. OECD, *The Relative Impact on World Commodity Prices of Temporal and Longer Term Structural Changes in Agricultural Markets: A Note on the Role of Investment Capital in the US Agricultural Futures Markets and the Possible Effect on Cash Prices* (Trade And Agriculture Directorate, Committee For Agriculture, Group on Cereals, Animal Feeds and Sugar, Group on Meat and Dairy Products, Working Party on Agricultural Policies and Markets [TAD/CA/APM/CFS/MD], March 27–28, 2008), 6; Bart Chilton, "Why the London Loophole Should Be Closed," *Financial Times,* June 23, 2008.

31. World Bank, *World Development Report 2008* (New York: Oxford University Press, 2008), 138.

32. Ibid., 112.

33. Ibid., 135.

34. Ibid., 136.

35. Oxfam, "The Time Is Now: How World Leaders Should Respond to the Food Price Crisis," Briefing Note (Oxford: Oxfam, 2008); Sophie Young and Anuradha Mittal, *Food Price Crisis: A Wake Up Call for Food Sovereignty* (Oakland, CA: The Oakland Institute, 2008). http://www.oaklandinstitute.org/pdfs/Food_Prices_Brief.pdf

36. Dano, op. cit.

37. This appendix draws on Bradsher and Martin, op. cit.

Contributors

Fabio Cabarcas has training in medicine and public health. His research focus has been on better understanding the role of community participation in health promotion programs and interventions to reduce health inequities. He designed, during his master's program, a methodology of evaluation of the World Health Organization–led initiative Healthy Cities in Colombia. This methodology was implemented later in twenty-four municipalities while he was working as a faculty member at the University of Antioquia in Colombia. In Canada, Fabio was a research assistant with an ambitious University of British Columbia–led project for building research capacity in environmental health in Ecuador. The work presented in this volume is part of his PhD dissertation on the challenges for local community organizations in dealing with problems of pesticide exposure in an indigenous community in Ecuador.

Alexander Day is an assistant professor of history at Wayne State University, with a research focus on modern China. He has a PhD in the history of modern east Asia from the University of California, Santa Cruz. His research interests include the history of radicalism and populism, the politics of rural society and the rural-urban relationship, the connection between historical writing and politics, colonialism and anticolonial movements, and transnationalism. He is currently finishing a book that examines contemporary debates on China's emerging rural crisis and its relationship to intellectual politics in the reform era, putting those debates into the historical context of China's changing relationship to global capitalism.

Arif Dirlik lives in Eugene, Oregon, in semiretirement. He most recently (2011) held the Rajni Kothari Chair in Democracy at the Centre for the Study of Developing Societies, Delhi, India. In 1910, he was awarded the first Liang Qichao Memorial Visiting Professorship at Tsinghua University, Beijing. Dirlik taught at Duke University for thirty years as professor of history and anthropology before moving in 2001 to the University of Oregon, where he served as Knight Professor of Social Science, Professor of History and Anthropology, and Director of the Center for Critical Theory and Transnational Studies. From 2007 to 2009, he was Chair Professor of Chinese Studies and Professor by Courtesy of the Departments of History and Cultural Studies at the Chinese University of Hong Kong. His most recent book-length publications include *Culture and History in Postrevolutionary China: The Perspective of Global Modernity (The Liang Qichao Memorial Lectures)* (2011) and *Global Modernity: Modernity in the Age of Global Capitalism* (2006).

Dong Zhenghua is a professor in and the director of the Center for Studies of World Modernization Process, History Department, Peking University, Beijing, China. He received his PhD in 1992 at Peking University, and his main publications include *15 Lectures on World Modernization Process* (2010); *Modernization Process in East Asia* (2009); "The modernization paradigm based on monistic multi-linear theory: a response to some comments," *Frontiers of History in China* 1, no. 2 (June 2006); "On the Modern Transformation of Traditional

Agrarian Systems in Taiwan and South Korea," *Chinese Social Science Quarterly (Hong Kong)* 23 (Autumn 1998).

Abidin Kusno is Associate Professor and Canada Research Chair in Asian Urbanism and Culture at the Institute of Asian Research, University of British Columbia. He wrote *Behind the Postcolonial: Architecture, Urban Space and Political Cultures in Indonesia* (2000) and *The Appearances of Memory: Mnemonic Practices of Architecture and Urban Form in Indonesia* (2010).

Sam Moyo is Executive Director of the African Institute for Agrarian Studies (AIAS) in Harare, Zimbabwe and is the current president of Council for the Development of Social Research in Africa (CODESRIA). He served as the vice president of CODESRIA (1998–2002) and as a member of the executive council (1995–1998). He received his PhD in environmental and rural development issues, with a focus on land reform and agrarian change. His works explore the political economy and dynamics of rural transformations, including the nature of social movements that advocate reforms. His major publications include *African Land Questions, Agrarian Transitions and the State: Contradictions of Neoliberal Land Reforms* (2008); *Land Reform Under Structural Adjustment in Zimbabwe: Land Use in the Mashonaland Provinces* (2000); and *The Land Question in Zimbabwe* (1995).

Utsa Patnaik (of the Centre for Economic Studies and Planning at Jawaharlal Nehru University, India) has researched and written extensively on problems of agrarian transition in the process of industrialization, past and present. Her recent research has focused on two main areas: the measurement of colonial transfers and their roles in metropolitan industrialization, and the past and present impact of globalization on food security and poverty in developing countries. Her publications include *The Republic of Hunger and Other Essays* (Three Essays Collective, second reprint, 2008), *The Agrarian Question in Marx and His Successors Vol.1* (edited; 2007), *Peasant Class Differentiation—A study in method with reference to Haryana* (1987), *The Agrarian Question and the Development of Capitalism in India* (1986), and *Chains of Servitude—Bondage and Slavery in India*, edited with M. Dingwaney (1985).

Pitman B. Potter is a professor of law at University of British Columbia Law Faculty and Hong Kong Bank Chair in Asian Research at UBC's Institute of Asian Research. Dr. Potter's teaching and research focus on People's Republic of China and Taiwan law and policy in the areas of foreign trade and investment, dispute resolution, property law, contracts, business and financial regulation, and human rights. He has published several books, including most recently *Law Policy and Practice on China's Periphery: Selective Adaptation and Institutional Capacity* (2011) and *A Guide to Business Law in Asia*, with Ljiljana Biukovic (2008).

Roxann Prazniak is currently an associate professor of history at the Robert D. Clark Honors College of the University of Oregon. She is the author of *Dialogues Across Civilizations: Sketches in World History from the Chinese and European Experiences* (1998), and *Of Camel Kings and Other Things: Rural Rebels Against Modernity in Late Imperial China* (1999), due to be published in Chinese by the Commercial Press in Beijing in 2011. Dr. Prazniak's more recent work on Eurasian exchanges during the thirteenth century includes an article titled, "Siena on the Silk Roads: Ambrogio Lorenzetti and the Mongol Global Century, 1250–1350," published in the *Journal of World History* 21, no. 1 (2010), and forthcoming in Chinese in *Zhongguo xueshu* (China Scholarship).

Alejandro Rojas is an associate professor at the University of British Columbia with the Faculty of Land and Food Systems, and the coordinator of the graduate program in integrated studies on land and food systems. He is the principal investigator of Think & Eat Green@ School: A Community-University Collaborative Project on Food Security and Institutional Adaptations to Climate Change in Vancouver Schools. He is currently a coinvestigator in a major international collaborative research initiative on institutional adaptations to climate change. He was also the principal investigator in a project on adaptive environmental conflict resolution and conducted research on sustainability, water conflicts, social movements and theory of the state, transcultural psychiatry, and intercultural communications. He is originally from Chile and came to Canada in 1978. He was a student leader and a member of Parliament representing the City of Santiago at the end of the democratic-socialist government of Dr. President Allende.

Leslie Shieh recently completed her PhD at University of British Columbia. Her dissertation, "Shequ Construction: Policy Implementation, Community Building, and Urban Governance in China," examines how the centrally promulgated policy to establish neighborhood units is being implemented locally and what its impacts are for fiscal decentralization, village redevelopment, social service delivery, and housing privatization. Currently, she is carrying out further work on the role of neighborhoods in governance.

Jomo Kwame Sundaram (Jomo K. S.) has been Assistant Secretary-General for Economic Development in the United Nations' Department of Economic and Social Affairs (DESA) since January 2005, and (Honorary) Research Coordinator for the G24 Intergovernmental Group on International Monetary Affairs and Development since December 2006. In 2007, he was awarded the Wassily Leontief Prize for Advancing the Frontiers of Economic Thought. During 2008–2009, he served as a member of the (Stiglitz) Commission of Experts of the President of the United Nations General Assembly on Reforms of the International Monetary and Financial System. Jomo has authored over 35 monographs, edited over 50 books, and translated 12 volumes besides writing many academic papers and articles for the media.

Immanuel Wallerstein is a senior research scholar at Yale University. He is the author of *The Modern World-System* (4 vol.), *European Universalism: The Rhetoric of Power*, and *World-Systems Analysis: An Introduction*. He is the former president of the International Sociological Association (1994–1998).

Shaoguang Wang is a chair professor and chairperson in the Department of Government and Public Administration, the director of Universities Service Centre for China Studies at the Chinese University of Hong Kong, and the chief editor of *The China Review*, an interdisciplinary journal on greater China. He taught at Tijiao High School in Wuhan, China from 1972 to 1977 and at Yale University in the United States from 1990 to 2000.

Wen Tiejun is dean of the School of Agronomics and Rural Development and executive director of the Institute of Advanced Studies for Sustainability at Renmin University in Beijing. He also serves as a member of the State Consultation Committee of Environment Protection, vice chairperson of the China Society of Agricultural Economics, and deputy secretary-general of the China Macroeconomic Research Foundation. He is a renowned expert on social-economic development and rural issues, especially in policy studies on current affairs, macroeconomic, geostrategy, long-term agriculture, and inclusive development. He is the recipient of the State Council Award for outstanding contribution in 1998 and CCTV Annual Top 10 Economic Talent in 2003.

Alexander Woodside has been a professor of Chinese and southeast Asian history at Harvard University and the University of British Columbia. He is currently a research fellow at the Peter Wall Institute of Advanced Study at the latter university. Recently he has written *Lost Modernities: China, Vietnam, Korea and the Hazards of World History* (2006) and cowritten *The Emergence of Modern Southeast Asia: A New History* (2004).

Paris Yeros is an adjunct professor of international relations at the Catholic University of Minas Gerais (PUC Minas), Belo Horizonte, Brasil, and a research associate of the African Institute of Agrarian Studies (AIAS), Harare, Zimbabwe. His main research areas are the agrarian question and the new South-South relations. He is coeditor of *Reclaiming the Land: The Resurgence of Rural Movements in Africa, Asia and Latin America* (2005) and *Reclaiming the Nation: The Return of the National Question in Africa, Asia and Latin America* (2011).